REA

HISTORICAL DICTIONARIES
OF ASIA, OCEANIA, AND THE MIDDLE EAST
Edited by Jon Woronoff

Asia

1. *Vietnam*, by William J. Duiker. 1989. *Out of print. See No. 27.*
2. *Bangladesh*, 2nd ed., by Craig Baxter and Syedur Rahman. 1996. *Out of print. See No. 48.*
3. *Pakistan*, by Shahid Javed Burki. 1991. *Out of print. See No. 33.*
4. *Jordan*, by Peter Gubser. 1991
5. *Afghanistan*, by Ludwig W. Adamec. 1991. *Out of print. See No. 47.*
6. *Laos*, by Martin Stuart-Fox and Mary Kooyman. 1992. *Out of print. See No. 35.*
7. *Singapore*, by K. Mulliner and Lian The-Mulliner. 1991
8. *Israel*, by Bernard Reich. 1992
9. *Indonesia*, by Robert Cribb. 1992. *Out of print. See No. 51.*
10. *Hong Kong and Macau*, by Elfed Vaughan Roberts, Sum Ngai Ling, and Peter Bradshaw. 1992
11. *Korea*, by Andrew C. Nahm. 1993. *Out of print. See No. 52.*
12. *Taiwan*, by John F. Copper. 1993. *Out of print. See No. 34.*
13. *Malaysia*, by Amarjit Kaur. 1993. *Out of print. See No. 36.*
14. *Saudi Arabia*, by J. E. Peterson. 1993. *Out of print. See No. 45.*
15. *Myanmar*, by Jan Becka. 1995
16. *Iran*, by John H. Lorentz. 1995
17. *Yemen*, by Robert D. Burrowes. 1995
18. *Thailand*, by May Kyi Win and Harold Smith. 1995
19. *Mongolia*, by Alan J. K. Sanders. 1996. *Out of print. See No. 42.*
20. *India*, by Surjit Mansingh. 1996
21. *Gulf Arab States*, by Malcolm C. Peck. 1996
22. *Syria*, by David Commins. 1996. *Out of print. See No. 50.*
23. *Palestine*, by Nafez Y. Nazzal and Laila A. Nazzal. 1997
24. *Philippines*, by Artemio R. Guillermo and May Kyi Win. 1997

Oceania

1. *Australia*, by James C. Docherty. 1992. *Out of print. See No. 32.*
2. *Polynesia*, by Robert D. Craig. 1993. *Out of print. See No. 39.*
3. *Guam and Micronesia*, by William Wuerch and Dirk Ballendorf. 1994
4. *Papua New Guinea*, by Ann Turner. 1994. *Out of print. See No. 37.*
5. *New Zealand*, by Keith Jackson and Alan McRobie. 1996

Historical Dictionary of the Republic of Korea

Second Edition

Andrew C. Nahm
James E. Hoare

*Historical Dictionaries of Asia, Oceania,
and the Middle East, No. 52*

The Scarecrow Press, Inc.
Lanham, Maryland • Toronto • Oxford
2004

SCARECROW PRESS, INC.

Published in the United States of America
by Scarecrow Press, Inc.
A wholly owned subsidiary of
The Rowman & Littlefield Publishing Group, Inc.
4501 Forbes Boulevard, Suite 200, Lanham, Maryland 20706
www.scarecrowpress.com

PO Box 317
Oxford
OX2 9RU, UK

British Library Cataloguing in Publication Information Available

Library of Congress Cataloging-in-Publication Data

Nahm, Andrew C.
  Historical dictionary of the Republic of Korea / Andrew C. Nahm, James E.
Hoare.— 2nd ed.
    p. cm. — (Historical dictionaries of Asia, Oceania, and the Middle East ; 52)
  "This second edition has been significantly revised and expanded and includes
more than 400 entries . . . updated" — ECIP data view.
  Includes bibliographical references and index.
  ISBN 0-8108-4949-6 (hardcover : alk. paper)
  1. Korea (South)—History—Dictionaries. 2. Korea—History—Dictionaries. I.
Hoare, James. II. Title. III. Series.
DS904.8.N34 2004
951.95'003—dc22

                                                                        2004001624

For Susan, who has lived with this for a long time,
and to all the Korean people.

Contents

Editor's Foreword

In writing about Korea, one of the handiest words has always been *adversity*. The Republic of Korea was born at the end of the Pacific War, from which it suffered greatly, after a long period of much-resented Japanese colonialism, and earlier centuries of clashes between rival kingdoms and Chinese domination. What became better known as *South Korea* was invaded by North Korea, and almost completely overrun, until the Korean War ended in a stalemate (but not peace), with the constant threat of further attacks. This adversity was one more excuse for paternalistic regimes, some by politicians, others under the military. Another aspect was the need to concentrate efforts to wrest a living from a small, crowded, and poorly endowed territory. Finally, thanks to incredible efforts, South Korea did create a flourishing economy . . . until it faltered during the Asian financial crisis. But, has Korea's luck finally turned? One might think so at present, with democracy in the ascendance, the economy gradually recovering, and, most promising but still uncertain, a possible reconciliation with the estranged brethren to the north.

This change in the situation certainly warrants a new look at a new South Korea. That is the task of the new edition of the *Historical Dictionary of the Republic of Korea*. It extends the introduction and chronology with comments on a happier, if still-difficult, period. The dictionary section adds entries on more political parties and politicians, overshadowing those on the military leaders, whose fate was often instructive. There are more entries on the economy, society, and culture, as well as foreign policy, which underlie and benefit from the improvements. They are also reflected in a broader bibliography. All in all, it shows us how the Koreans have lived with adversity, frequently overcome it, and will hopefully benefit from this lucky streak, which has to be handled with as much or more care and caution.

This second edition builds on a strong first edition, written by Andrew C. Nahm, who sadly passed away in 1996. It updates any necessary material and also expands the coverage in essential directions. The work was undertaken by Dr. J. E. Hoare, who has studied East Asian affairs since 1964 and was with the British Diplomatic Service from 1969 until he retired in 2003. He has served in the British embassies in Seoul from 1981–1985 and Beijing 1988–1991, ending his career with a posting to establish the first British Embassy in P'yongyang. In addition, he has visited both Koreas many times. A graduate of the University of London's School of Oriental and African Studies, Dr. Hoare has published numerous articles and books, including *Korea: An Introduction* (with Susan Pares) and *Embassies in the East*. He has long been a member, and sometimes officer, of such bodies as the British Association for Korean Studies, the Anglo-Korean Society, the Korea Branch of the Royal Asiatic Society, and the Royal Society for Asian Affairs. This was more than ample preparation for a major revision of the historical dictionary on one of Asia's most impressive countries.

Jon Woronoff
Series Editor

PREFACE

This second edition of the *Historical Dictionary of the Republic of Korea* essentially follows the pattern laid down by the late Professor Andrew Nahm in the original 1993 edition. The dictionary proper covers the history of the Republic of Korea (South Korea) since it emerged in 1948. The items included in the book encompass domestic, political and social events, foreign affairs, along with economic and cultural development, together with the men and women who have influenced the multifarious events that make up a country's history. However, the chronology and historical narrative cover the entire history of Korea for the benefit of users of this Dictionary who have little or no knowledge about the history of the Korean people.

The Dictionary is intended as a reference-companion for those who are interested in the history of the Republic of Korea. The selection of topics for a book of this size is difficult: many individuals and incidents have been omitted only with the greatest reluctance.

Biographies of most major political and historical figures are included. Unfortunately, poets, artists, musicians, scientists and businesspersons who have made major changes to the cultural and social life of the people in South Korea are less prominent, mainly because of the lack of space. However this is one area where I have expanded the coverage, and it is hoped that those who are included give an indication of the richness of these fields.

Like Professor Nahm, I have used the best available bibliographies, books, magazines and newspapers, and yearbooks and annuals of various kinds, and have tried to summarize the important historical events that took place up to mid-2003. I have corrected a few minor errors from the first edition, and occasionally rewritten entries in the light of current knowledge. The alphabetical arrangement of the main body of the book is complemented by a chronology, a year-by-year survey of events of major importance in the entire history of Korea, with more items related to South Korea since 1945.

One major change in this edition is the romanization system; this is explained in a separate note.

Professor Nahm expressed the hope that this Dictionary would "provide some help to those wishing to increase their knowledge of Korea in general, its history since 1945 in particular, and also generate further studies in this area." I, in turn, hope that this expanded version will do the same.

I am grateful to Scarecrow Press and the series' editor, Jon Woronoff, for asking me to undertake this update. I am even more grateful for the tolerance both have displayed over the long delay in producing it. Establishing an embassy in P'yongyang proved a more time-consuming task than I had anticipated, and so much planned other work, including the updating of this Dictionary steadily slipped behind. My own family has proved most understanding, as always, and I am equally grateful.

James E. Hoare
London, September 2003

The Korean Writing System and Romanization

Koreans date their own written language from 1446 when King Sejong the Great (r. 1418–1450) created an indigenous alphabet for the Korean language. Until then, Koreans had relied on Chinese characters to write their language, even though the Chinese ideographs were not well suited to writing Korean. Sejong commissioned members of the academy of scholars, called the Hall of Wise Scholars (*Chiphyonjon*), to create a phonetic system that would be more in keeping with Korean grammar. These scholars drew on many sources to create the new script that Sejong adopted. In 1446, he proclaimed it as *Hunmin Chongum*, or the "correct sounds to instruct the people." However, the use of the new script came under attack from orthodox Confucian scholars, who dismissed it as *onmun* (common, or vulgar, letters) and refused to use it. But, it survived, and was widely used by women and writers of popular stories and songs. Only at the end of the 19th century did the use of *Hunmin Chongum* begin to spread among the educated classes. In the Japanese colonial period (1910–1945), its use became patriotic, and it was then that the term *han'gul,* originally "Great Script" but also a pun on "Korean letters," began to be used. *Han'gul* is still the term used in South Korea, where the Korean alphabet is found mixed with Chinese characters. In North Korea, the alphabet, usually called *Chosun muncha* (Korean letters), has entirely replaced Chinese characters. Modern *han'gul* has 10 vowels, 14 consonants, and a number of diphthongs and compound consonants.

In the first edition of this Dictionary, Professor Nahm used the romanization system of the Ministry of Education of the Republic of Korea, introduced in 1984. This system was a modified version of the McCune-Reischauer system, widely used in the United States and Europe since it was devised by two American scholars, and published by the Royal Asiatic Society, Korea Branch, in 1939. The Government of the Republic of Korea decided to abandon the Ministry of Education system in July 2000, when the Ministry of Culture and Tourism introduced a new, Korean-devised method of romanization. This attempted to make romanized Korean more intelligible to non-Korean speakers. However, it has not found universal favor. I have decided that because this work is primarily intended for the nonspecialist to use a modified version of the McCune-Reischauer system, omitting the diacritics but keeping the apostrophe as sign for aspiration; thus the capital of North Korea is P'yongyang, not Pyongyang. Otherwise, consonants are as in English and vowels as in Italian. Like Professor Nahm, however, I have continued to use the romanization preferred by individuals and companies, even though this might not conform to the McCune-Reischauer system. So "Syngman Rhee" is used instead of "Yi Sung-man," and "Hyundai" instead of "Hyondae." For Japanese words, I have used a modified version of the Hepburn system, and for Chinese, *pinyin*.

Abbreviations and Acronyms

ANSP	Agency for National Security Planning (Kukka Anjun Kihoekbu)
ASEAN	Association for Southeast Asian Nations
ASPAC	Asia and Pacific Council
CHAMINT'U	Chauju Minju T'ujaeng (Self-oriented Struggle for Democracy)
CHOKCH'ONG	Chosun Minjok Ch'ongnyondan (Korean National Youth Corps)
CHONDAEHYOP	Chun'guk Taehaksaeng Taep'yo Hyupuihoe (National Council of Representatives of University Students)
CHON'GUK YONHAP	National Alliance for Democracy and Unification
CHON'GYOJO	National Teacher's Union
CHONMINYON	Chun'guk Minjujuui Undong Yonhaphoe (National Coalition for a People's Democratic Movement)
CHONNOHYOP	Chun'guk Nodong Chohap Hyupuihoe (National Council of Labor Unions)
CHON'NONG	Chun'guk Nongmin Chohap Ch'ongyunmaeng (National Federation of Farmers' Unions)
CHONP'YONG	Chosun Nodong Chohap Chun'guk P'yunguihoe (National Council of Korean Labor Unions)
CIC	Counter Intelligence Corps (Dukmudae)
CPD	Council for the Promotion of Democracy (Min jujuui Ch'oksung Hyupuihoe)

CPNR	Committee for the Preparation of National Reconstruction (Kunguk Chunbi Wiwunhoe)
CPV	Chinese People's Volunteers
DJP	Democratic Justice Party (Minju Chung'uidang)
DKP	Democratic Korea Party (Minju Han'gukdang)
DLP	Democratic Liberal Party (Chayu Minjudang)
DMZ	Demilitarized Zone
DP	Democratic Party (Minjudang)
DPP	Democratic People's Party (Minkukdang)
DPRK	Democratic People's Republic of Korea (North Korea)
DRP	Democratic Republican Party (Minju Kong hwadang)
DSP	Democratic Socialist Party
EU	European Union
FIFA	Fédération Internationale de Football Association
FKEA	Federation of Korean Education Associations
GNP	Grand National Party (Hannaradang)
HAN'GUK NORYON	Han'guk Nodong Chohap Ch'ongynmaeng (General Federation of Korean Labor Unions)
HANMINDANG	Han'guk Minjudang (Korean Democratic Party)
IAAF	International Athletic Association Federation
IAEA	International Atomic Energy Authority
ICFTU	International Confederation of Free Trade Unions
IMF	International Monetary Fund
KAIS	Korean Advanced Institute of Science

KAIST	Korea Advanced Institute for Science and Technology
KAL	Korean Airlines
KBS	Korea Broadcasting System
KCFT	Korean Coalition for the Future
KCIA	Korean Central Intelligence Agency (Chungang Chungbobu)
KCP	Korean Communist Party (Chosun Kongsan dang)
KDI	Korean Development Institute
KDP	Korean Democratic Party (Chosun Minjudang)
KEDI	Korean Educational Development Institute
KEDO	Korean (Peninsula) Energy Development Organization
KEPCO	Korean Electric Power Company
KFLTU	Korean Federation of Teachers' Labor Unions
KIST	Korea Institute of Science and Technology
KMA	Korean Military Academy
KNCW	Korean National Council of Women
KNP	Korean Nationalist Party (Han'guk Kung-mindang)
KWDI	Korean Women's Development Institute
KWP	Korean Workers' Party (North Korea)
KOTRA	Korea Trade Promotion Association
LCNS	Legislative Council for National Security (Kukka powi Ippop Hoeui)
LDP	Liberal Democratic Party
LP	Liberal Party (Chayudang)
LWR	Light water reactor
MDL	Military Demarcation Line
MAC	Military Armistice Commission
MBC	Munhwa Broadcasting Corporation
MDP	Millennium Democratic Party (Seochonnyonminjudang, or Minjudang)

MINCH'ONG	Chosun Minju Ch'onguyon Tongmaeng (Alliance of Democratic Korean Youth)
MINCH'UWI	Minjujuüi Ch'ujin Wiwonhoe (Committee for Promotion of Democracy)
MINJON	Chosun Minjujuui Minjok Chonson (Korean National Democratic Front)
MINT'ONGYON	Minjujuui T'ongil Yonmaeng (Joint Masses Movement for Democracy and Unification)
MP	Masses (People's) Party (Minjungdang)
MRC	Military Revolutionary Committee (Kunsa Hyongmyonghoe)
NCNP	National Council for New Politics
NCU	National Conference for Unification (T'ongil Kungmin Hoeui)
NCWO	National Council of Women's Organizations
NDP	New Democratic Party (Shinminjudang)
NDRP	New Democratic Republican Party (Shin Minju Konghwadang)
NDUP	New Democratic United Party (Shin-Minju Yonhaptang)
NIE	National Institute of Education
NIERT	National Institute of Educational Research and Training
NIS	National Intelligence Service (*Kukka chongbowon*)
NKDP	New Korea Democratic Party (Shin Han'guk Minjudang)
NKP	New Korea Party (Saehandang)
NKPH	New Korea Party of Hope (Huimanghui Sinhagukdang)
NNSC	Neutral Nations Supervisory Commission
NONGHYOP	Nong'op Hyoptong Chohap (Association of Agricultural Cooperatives)
NPNPR	Party for New Political Reform (Shin-jongdang)

NPT	Nuclear Non-proliferation Treaty
NTU	National Teacher's Union
PNPR	Party for New Political Reform
PPD	Party for Peace and Democracy (P'yonghwa Minjudang)
PRC	People's Republic of China
RDP	Reunification Democratic Party (T'ongil Minju-dang)
ROK	Republic of Korea (South Korea)
SAM MINT'UWI	Committee for the Three People's Struggles
SCAP	Supreme Commander of the Allied Powers
SCNR	Supreme Council for National Reconstruction (Kukka Chaegon Ch'oego Hoeui)
SCNSM	Special Committee for National Security Measures (Kukka Powi Pisang Taech'aek Wiwonhoe)
SEZ	Special Economic Zone
SKIG	South Korean Interim Government (Nam Chosun Kwado Chongbu)
SKILA	South Korean Interim Legislative Assembly (Nam Chosun Kwado Ippop Uiwon)
SKWP	South Korean Workers' Party (Namchoson Nodongdang)
SNU	Seoul National University
TAEHAN NOCH'ONG	Taehan Tongnip Ch'oksong Nodong Ch'ong-dongmaeng (General Alliance of Laborers for Rapid Realization of Korean Independence)
TEAHAN NORYON	Tachan Nodong Chohap Ch'ongyonmaeng (General Federation of Korean Labor Unions)
TOKCH'OK	Tongnip Ch'oksong Kungmin Hyop'uihoe (National Council for Rapid Realization of Korean Independence)

ULD	United Liberal Democrats (Jayuminju yonmaeng)
UN	United Nations
UNC	United Nations Command
UNCURK	United Nations Commission for Unification and Rehabilitation of Korea
UNKRA	United Nations Korean Reconstruction Agency
UNP	Unification National Party
UNTCOK	United Nations Temporary Commission on Korea
UNP (UPP)	Unification National Party, also known as United People's Party (T'ongil Kungmindang)
USAFIK	United States Armed Forces in Korea
USAMGIK	United States Army Military Government in Korea
USP	Unification Socialist Party
YMCA	Young Men's Christian Association
YPP	Youth Progressive Party (Chongnyon jinbodang)
YUJONGHOE	Yushin Chong'uhoe (Political Fraternal Society for Revitalizing Reform)
YWCA	Young Women's Christian Association

Chronology

Dates prior to 1876 are those of the lunar calendar.

ca. 30,000–2333 B.C. Prehistoric Periods

ca. 30,000 B.C.: Appearance of Paleolithic culture.

ca. 6000 B.C.: Appearance of Neolithic pointed-bottom pottery, flat-bottom pottery, and comb-marked pottery.

ca. 2333–108 B.C. The Old Chosun Period

ca. 2333 B.C.: Traditional date of the founding of the Kingdom of Chosun by Tan'gun.

ca. 1200 B.C.: Beginning of Bronze Age; appearance of black pottery and agricultural tools.

ca. 1122 B.C.: Establishment of Kija Chosun.

ca. 300 B.C.: Beginning of Iron Age.

ca. 194 B.C.: Rise of Wiman Chosun in the north and the three federations of the Han tribes in the south.

108 B.C.: Invasion of Korea by Emperor Wu of the Han dynasty of China.

57 B.C.–668 A.D. The Three Kingdoms Period

57 B.C.: Founding of the state of Saro (later renamed Shilla).

37 B.C.: Emergence of the state of Koguryo in Manchuria.

13 B.C.: Emergence of the state of Paekche in central Korea.

313 A.D.: End of the Chinese Lolang commandery in Korea.

372 A.D.: Official adoption of Buddhism and establishment of a school for Confucian studies in Koguryo.

382 A.D.: Official adoption of Buddhism in Paekche.

427 A.D.: Capital of Koguryo relocated to Wanggomsong (now P'yongyang).

528 A.D.: Official adoption of Buddhism in Shilla.

612: Invasion of the Sui (Chinese) forces; a great military victory for the Koguryo forces.

644–655: Invasions of the T'ang (Chinese) forces.

663: Destruction of Paekche by the combined forces of Shilla and China.

668: Destruction of Koguryo by the combined forces of Shilla and China.

668–918 Unified Korea of Shilla

ca. 670: Invention of the *idu* system of writing (Chinese characters used to give the sound of Korean words).

682: Establishment of a Confucian school.

699: Kingdom of Parhae emerges in Manchuria.

727: Monk Hyecho returns from pilgrimage to China and India.

ca. 750: Printing of Buddhist texts.

751: Reconstruction of Popryu Temple, built in 528; renamed *Pulguk Temple*.

892: Founding of the Later Paekche Kingdom.

901: Founding of the Later Koguryo Kingdom.

918–1392 The Koryo Period

918: Overthrow of Kung'ye; Wang Kon founds Koryo Kingdom.

935: Last Shilla king surrenders to Koryo.

936: Overthrow of the Later Packche: reunification of Korea.

993: Khitan invasion.

998: Adoption of the Chinese civil service examination system.

1011: Wooden block publication of Buddhist *Tripitaka*.

1018: Second Khitan invasion.

1104: Jurchen invasion.

1135–1136: Series of rebellions.

1145: Completion of Kim Pu-sik's *Samguk sagi*.

1170: Chang Chung-bu's Rebellion.

1196: Ch'oe Ch'ung-hon's coup; the establishment of Ch'oe clan dictatorship.

1231: First Mongol invasion.

1232: Flight of the Koryo court to Kanghwa Island; second Mongol invasion.

1234: Casting of movable metal type.

1235: Third Mongol invasion.

1251: Production of new printing blocks; publication of the *Tripitaka Koreana*.

1258: The end of dictatorship of the Ch'oe clan.

1259: Peace with the Mongols; acceptance of Mongol domination.

1270: Return of Koryo court to Kaegyong; Korea's acceptance of Mongol vassalage; *Sambyolch'o* Rebellion.

1273: End of the *Sambyolch'o* Rebellion.

1274: First Mongol–Korean expedition to Japan.

1281: Publication of Ilyon's *Samguk yusa*; second Mongol–Korean expedition to Japan.

1313, 1 April: Population census.

1388: Coup d'état by General Yi Song-gye.

1392: End of the Koryo kingdom.

1392–1910 The Yi Dynasty Period

1394: Hanyang (now Seoul) becomes capital of Korea.

1403: Casting of new metal type.

1420: Founding of the Royal Academy of Scholars.

1432: Publication of *Geography of the Eight Provinces.*

1442: Installation of the first rain gauge.

1446: Promulgation of the new Korean script (*Han'gul*).

1452: Publication of the *Koryosa* (History of Koryo).

1454: Yi Ching-ok's Rebellion.

1467: Yi Si-ae's Rebellion.

1470: Publication of a new code.

1498: First purge of scholars.

1502: Second purge of scholars.

1519: Third purge of scholars.

1545: Fourth purge of scholars.

1562: Lim Ko-jong's Rebellion.

1592, April: Japanese invasion; **July:** construction of ironclad war vessels (turtle boats); Admiral Yi Sun-shin's great naval victory.

1597, January: Second Japanese invasion.

1598, October: Withdrawal of Japanese troops from Korea.

ca. 1610: First Korean contacts with Roman Catholicism.

1624: Yi Kwal's Rebellion.

1627: First Manchu invasion.

1628: Crew of a shipwrecked Dutch vessel rescued off Cheju Island and taken to Seoul.

1636: Second Manchu invasion.

ca. 1650: Beginning of the *Shirhak* movement.

1653, August: Dutch ship, the *Sparrow Hawk*, wrecked off Cheju Island and its crew taken to Seoul.

1654: Korean rifle troops sent against the Russians in Manchuria on behalf of the Manchu.

1712: New Sino–Korean boundary line established.

1728: Yi Rin-jwa's Rebellion.

1784: First Catholic church established in Seoul.

1785: Catholicism banned.

1790: Publication of An Chong-bok's *Outline History of Korea*.

1801: First anti-Catholic persecution.

1812: Hong Kyong-nae's Rebellion.

1831: Establishment of Korean Catholic diocese; arrival of French priests.

1839: Proclamation of anti-Catholic edicts.

1854, April: Arrival of Russian Admiral Putiatin.

1860: Ch'oe Che-u founds the *Tonghak* sect.

1864, 22 January: Beginning of the reign of King Kojong and the regency of the Taewon'gun; execution of Ch'oe Che-u.

1866, February: Beginning of a large-scale anti-Catholic persecution. **August:** Destruction of the American merchant ship, the *General Sherman* at P'yongyang. **September–October:** Attack by French naval forces.

1871, May–July: Attack by United States forces; Korea proclaims policy of isolation.

1873, December: End of the Taewon'gun's regency.

1875, September: Japanese warship *Unyo-kan* incident; Japanese troops land at Pusan.

1876, February: Arrival of six Japanese naval vessels; Kanghwa Treaty with Japan signed 26 February. **April–July:** Korean diplomatic mission to Japan. **26 August:** Supplementary treaty and trade regulations signed with Japan.

1879: Opening of Pusan to Japanese traders.

1880, May: Opening of Wonsan to Japanese. **August–September:** Kim Hong-jip's mission to Japan.

1881, January: Establishment of the Office for the Management of State Affairs.

1882: Publication of William Elliot Griffis's *Corea: The Hermit Nation*. **March:** Beginning of modern military training. **22 May:** Chemulp'o Treaty signed with the United States. **9 June:** Military insurrection; abduction of the Taewon'gun to China by the Chinese. **20 September:** Korean mission to Japan headed by Pak Yong-hyo. **26 December:** Foreign Office established.

1883, 1 January: Chemulp'o renamed Inch'on. **June:** Opening of Inch'on. **September:** Departure of the first Korean mission to the United States headed by Min Yong-ik. **30 October:** *Hansong Sunho*, the first Korean newspaper. **26 November:** Signing of Korean–British and Korean–German Treaties.

1884, 21 June: Korean–Italian Treaty signed. **7 July:** Korean–Russian Treaty signed. **September:** Dr. Horace N. Allen, first Protestant missionary, arrives in Korea. **4 December:** Progressives' (Post Office) coup; Chinese military intervention, and the flight of the Progressives to Japan.

1885, 9 January: Korean–Japanese Agreement. **15 April:** British occupation of Komun Island (Port Hamilton). **18 April:** Sino–Japanese Tianjin (Tientsin) Agreement. **5 October:** Taewon'gun returns from China.

1886, January: *Hansong Chubo* newspaper published; establishment of Ewha school for girls. **4 June:** Franco–Korean Treaty signed.

1887, 27 February: British troops evacuate Komun Island. **October:** Pak Chong-yang arrives in the United States as the first Korean minister.

1888–89: Severe drought in Korea.

1894, March: *Tonghak* uprising begins. **25 July:** Sino–Japanese War begins. **26 July:** Establishment of the Deliberative Council and the beginning of the Kabo Reform. **26 August:** Korea–Japan Mutual Defense Agreement.

1895, 7 January: King Kojong takes an oath before his ancestors' shrine and proclaims a royal charter, *Honghom sipsajo*. **18 January:** Establishment of cabinet system. **17 April:** Treaty of Shimonoseki ends the Sino–Japanese War. **8 October:** Assassination of Queen Min. **30 December:** Hair-Cutting Ordinance.

1896, 1 January: Gregorian calendar adopted; arrival of Dr. Philip Jaisohn (So Chae-p'il) from the United States. **11 February:** Flight of the king and the crown prince to the Russian legation. **7 April:** *The Independent* newspaper published. **14 May:** Waeber–Komura Memorandum. **9 June:** Lobanov–Yamagata Protocol signed. **2 July:** Min–Lobanov Agreement; establishment of the Independence Club. **August:** Division of Korea into 13 provinces. **21 November:** Construction of the Independence Gate.

1897, 20 February: Return of King Kojong from the Russian legation. **12 October:** Empire of Tae Han proclaimed; King Kojong becomes emperor.

1898, 22 February: Death of the Taewon'gun. **20 May:** Opening of Songjin, Kunsan, and Masan to foreign trade. **4 November:** Abolition of the Independence Club and arrest of its leaders.

1899, 4 May: First streetcar operation in Seoul; partial operation of the Seoul–Inch'on railway.

1900, 10 April: Seoul streetlights installed. **12 November:** Opening of the entire Seoul–Inch'on railway.

1901, 23 March: Korean–Belgian Treaty.

1902, 15 July: Korean–Danish Treaty. **23 July:** Korean–Austrian Treaty.

1903: Seoul YMCA and Seoul Medical School founded.

1904, 8 February: Russo–Japanese War. **23 February:** Korean–Japanese Protocol. **22 August:** Korean–Japanese Agreement; *Ilchinhoe* founded.

1905, 21 March: Official adoption of Western weights and measures. **25 May:** Opening of the Seoul–Pusan railway. **June:** New monetary system. **10 August:** *Korean Daily News* published. **5 September:** Portsmouth Treaty; end of the Russo–Japanese War. **17 November:** Japanese–Korean Agreement. **29 November:** Formation of the Corps for the Advancement of Individuals (*Hungsadan*).

1906, 28 January: *Tonghak* sect renamed *Ch'ondo-gyo*. **1 February:** Beginning of Japanese Residency-General; Ito Hirobumi first Resident-General. **April:** Seoul–Shinuiju railway opens. **August:** New public school ordinance.

1907, May: Formation of Yi Wan-yong cabinet. **June:** New cabinet system adopted; Kojong's envoys at The Hague World Peace Conference. **20 July:** Kojong abdicates. **24 July:** New Korean–Japanese Agreement; new press and public security laws. **31 July:** Korean Army disbanded; Righteous Armies begin anti-Japanese guerrilla war. **27 August:** Coronation of Emperor Sunjong. **18 November:** Six-article imperial charter proclaimed.

1908, April: Ordinance concerning girls' schools. **August:** Ordinance concerning private schools.

1909, February–April: New tax laws. **4 March:** Family Registration Law. **5 July:** Sone Arasuke succeeds Ito Hirobumi as Resident-General. **12 July:** Japanese assume judicial administration. **31 July:** Abolition of the Ministry of Defense and the Korean military school. **4 September:** Signing of Sino–Japanese Treaty concerning Chien-tao (Kando); new boundaries established between Korea and Manchuria. **26 October:** Assassination of Ito Hirobumi. **24 November:** Opening of the Bank of Korea (became Central Bank of Chosen in 1910, and was renamed Bank of Chosen on 29 March 1911).

1910, 22 August: Treaty of Annexation signed; end of the Yi dynasty and Korean independence.

1910–1945 Japanese Colonial Period

1910: 1 October: Government-General of Korea established; beginning of land survey.

1911, December: 105 Persons Incident.

1914: Seoul–Wonsan railway opened.

1918: Completion of the land survey.

1919, 22 January: Death of ex-emperor Kojong. **8 February:** Korean students in Tokyo issue Declaration of Independence. **1 March:** Beginning of the Independence Movement. **11 April:** Establishment of the Korean Provisional Government in exile in Shanghai.

1920, 5 March: *Chosun Ilbo* published. **1 April:** *Tong-a Ilbo* published. **21 October:** Victory of the Korean insurgents at Ch'ongsan-ri.

1925, 17 April: Founding of the Korean Communist Party in Seoul.

1926, 25 April: Death of former emperor Sunjong. **10 June:** Independence demonstrations in Seoul.

1927, 15 February: *Shin'ganhoe* and *Kan'uboe* founded.

1929, 30 October: Kwangju student incident. **3 November:** Nationwide anti-Japanese student movement begins.

1931, July: Manbosan (Wanpaoshan) incident in Manchuria; anti-Chinese activities in Korea.

1932, 8 January: Yi Pong-ch'an's attempt to assassinate the Japanese emperor at the Sakurada Gate in Tokyo. **1 March:** Establishment of the Japanese puppet state of Manzhouguo (Manchukuo). **29 April:** Yun Pong-gil's bomb attack at Hungkuo Park in Shanghai.

1937, 7 July: Marco Polo Bridge incident; outbreak of Sino–Japanese War.

1938, 26 February: Enactment of the Special Army Volunteer Ordinance in Korea. **1 October:** Beginning of labor mobilization.

1940, 11 February: Ordinance concerning the adoption of Japanese-style family and given names by the Koreans. **10 August:** Closure of *Tong-a Ilbo*, *Chosun Ilbo*, and other Korean-language newspapers.

1941, 7 December: Japanese attack Pearl Harbor; Pacific War begins.

1942, 8 May: Mobilization of Koreans into the Japanese imperial army. **1 September:** arrest of Korean Linguistic Society leaders.

1943, 20 October: Mobilization of students into the Japanese army. **1 December:** The Allies' Cairo Declaration states that "in due course, Korea shall become free and independent."

1944, 20 January: General mobilization of Korean youth into the Japanese armed forces.

1945, 8 August: Soviet Union declares war on Japan. **11 August:** Soviet Union–U.S. Agreement on division of Korea at 38th parallel in order to take the Japanese surrender; Soviet forces move into Korea. **15–16 August:** Japan accepts Allies' Potsdam ultimatum; end of Pacific War and World War II; liberation of Korea; formation of the Committee for the Preparation of National Reconstruction.

1945–1948 The Allied Occupation Period

1945, 1 September: Nationalist Party formed. **2 September:** Supreme Command of the Allied Powers in the Pacific (SCAP) announces the division of Korea into U.S. and Soviet military operational zones along the 38th parallel line. **6 September:** People's Republic of Korea proclaimed. **7 September:** Landing of United States troops. **9 September:** Japanese governor-general signs surrender document. **11 September:** Establishment of the United States Army Military Government in Korea (USAMGIK). **12 September:** Reestablishment of the Korean Communist Party in Seoul. **16 September:** Formation of the Korean (Han'guk) Democratic Party. **21 October:** Establishment of South Korean national police. **7 November:** Anticommunist uprising by students in Shinuiju in the north. **12 November:** Korean People's Party formed. **28 December:** Announcement of the Moscow Agreement regarding Korea; eruption of antitrusteeship demonstrations. **30 December:** Assassination of right-wing Nationalist Song Chin-u of the Korean (Han'guk) Democratic Party.

1946, 3 January: Nationwide antitrusteeship strikes and demonstrations; fall of the Nationalists in the north and the flight of the Korean

(Chosun) Democratic Party to the south. **19 January:** Democratic People's Front formed. **14 February:** Representative Democratic Council established. **13 March:** Anticommunist student uprising in Hamhung in the north. **30 March:** Communist-inspired labor strikes in Taegu and elsewhere in the south. **October:** Communist-inspired labor uprising and railway workers' strike in Taegu. **7 October:** Coalition Committee for Co-operation between the Rightists and the Leftists formed. **12 November:** Socialist Workers' Party formed. **23 November:** Korean Communist Party renamed the South Korean Workers' Party (merged with the People's and the New People's Party). **12 December:** South Korean Interim Legislative Assembly established.

1947, 18 February: Supreme People's Assembly established in the north; Central People's Committee becomes the central government of North Korea. **24 May:** Formation of the Working People's Party in the south. **3 June:** South Korean Interim Government established in Seoul. **19 July:** Left-wing nationalist Yo Un-Hyong assassinated. **14 November:** United Nations General Assembly adopts Korean resolution; creation of the UN Temporary Commission on Korea (UNTCOK). **2 December:** Right-wing leader Chang Tok-su of the Korean (Han'guk) Democratic Party assassinated.

1948, 3 April: Rebellion begins on Cheju Island. **19–21 April:** Kim Ku, Kim Kyu-shik, and others make a journey to P'yongyang for a joint conference with the North Korean Communists. **10 May:** UN-sponsored general elections in South Korea. **14 May:** North Korea suspends electric power supply to the south. **31 May:** National (Constituent) Assembly of South Korea convenes. **12 July:** South Korea adopts a constitution; election of the president and the vice president.

The Republic of Korea

1948, 15 August: Republic of Korea (ROK) established: inauguration of president Syngman Rhee; end of the U.S. occupation of South Korea. **9 September:** Democratic People's Republic of Korea (North Korea) established. **22 September:** Law Concerning Punishment of Those Who Committed Crimes Against the People (antitraitor law). **2 October:** Military insurrection on Cheju Island. **19–22 October:** Yosu–Sunch'on military insurrection. **2 November:** Military revolt in Taegu. **13 November:** Promulgation of martial law. **30 November:** National Security Law passed. **9 December:** UN recognition of the Republic of Korea.

1949, February: Korean (Han'guk) Democratic Party renamed Democratic Nationalist Party. **18 April:** South Korean Marine Corps activated. **20 May:** Ten National Assemblymen arrested as North Korean spies. **21 June:** Land Reform Law. **26 June:** Right-wing nationalist and head of the Korean Independence Party, Kim Ku, assassinated. **29 June:** U.S. troop withdrawals completed. **12 October:** South Korean Air Force established. **29 October:** South Korean Workers' Party and affiliated groups outlawed.

1950, 30 May: National Assembly elections. **12 June:** Bank of Korea established. **25 June:** North Korean invasion of the south; outbreak of the Korean War. **27 June:** UN Security Council calls on member states to provide assistance to South Korea. **28 June:** Seoul falls; South Korean government retreats to Taejon. **30 June:** President Harry Truman commits U.S. ground forces to Korea. **8 July:** General Douglas MacArthur appointed commander of UN forces in Korea. **20 July:** Fall of Taejon; South Korean government retreats to Taegu. **4 August:** Naktong River (Pusan) perimeter established. **15 August:** South Korean government establishes its wartime capital at Pusan. **15 September:** Amphibious landing of UN troops at Inch'on. **22 September:** U.S. Eighth Army breaks out from the Pusan perimeter. **27 September:** Seoul recaptured by UN forces. **1 October:** Third ROK Division crosses the 38th parallel. **7 October:** U.S. forces cross the 38th parallel; UN General Assembly authorizes the crossing of the 38th parallel; establishment of UN Commission for the Unification and Rehabilitation of Korea (UNCURK). **19 October:** Fall of P'yongyang; Chinese forces ("Chinese People's Volunteers") cross the Yalu River into Korea. **26 October:** South Korean forces reach the Yalu River. **27–31 October:** First Chinese offensive. **25–26 November:** Second Chinese offensive. **5 December:** UN forces abandon P'yongyang. **24 December:** Withdrawal of UN troops from North Korea. **December–January 1951:** Hamp'yong incident. **31 December:** Chinese third offensive, south of the 38th parallel.

1951, 4 January: Fall of Seoul to North Korean and Chinese forces. **1 February:** UN General Assembly condemns the People's Republic of

China as an aggressor. **11 February:** Koch'ang incident. **7 March:** Adoption of new educational system. **15 March:** recapture of Seoul. **3 April:** UN forces at the 38th parallel. **11 April:** General Matthew Ridgway replaces MacArthur as UN commander. **9 May:** Vice president Yi Shi-yong resigns. **15 May:** National Assembly elects Kim Song-su as vice president. **10 July:** Truce negotiations begin at Kaesong behind North Korean/Chinese lines. **23 August:** Truce talks suspended. **25 October:** Truce talks resume at P'anmunjom. **12 November:** Operation Ratkiller begins against suspected guerrilla groups in South Korea. **23 December:** Formation of the Liberal Party.

1952, 18 January: Declaration of the Rhee (Peace) Line. **17 April:** constitutional amendment proposed; premier resigns. **28 April:** General Mark Clark replaces Ridgway as UN commander. **7 May:** Prisoner of war uprising on Koje Island. **25 May:** President Rhee proclaims martial law in the Pusan area. **29 May:** Vice president resigns. **4 July:** First constitutional amendment passed. **5 August:** Reelection of President Rhee by popular vote. **1 October:** Prisoner of war uprising on Cheju Island.

1953, 15 February: Monetary reform replaces the *won* with *hwan* notes, at a rate of 100 to 1. **8 March, 10 May:** Labor laws passed. **20 April:** Sick and wounded prisoners of war released in Operation Little Switch; civilian diplomatic and other detainees released by the North Koreans. **18 June:** President Rhee releases 27,000 Communist prisoners of war. **10 July:** President Rhee refuses to sign armistice agreement but agrees not to disrupt it. **13 July:** Final Chinese offensive in the Kumsong area against South Korean forces. **27 July:** Korean armistice signed at P'anmunjom. **28 July:** First meeting of the Military Armistice Commission (MAC) at Panmunjom. **15 August:** Return of the government to Seoul. **1 October:** U.S.–ROK Mutual Defense Treaty signed.

1954, 20 May: National Assembly elections. **April–June:** Geneva Conference on Korea and Vietnam; it ends in June without finding a solution to the Korean problem. **27 November:** Second constitutional amendment passed.

1955, 18 September: Democratic Party (DP) formed. **8 December:** South Korean UN application vetoed.

1956, 3 March: Korean Stock Exchange established. **20 March:** Republican Party formed. **15 May:** Reelection of President Rhee, election of Chang Myon of the Democratic Party as vice president. **16 June:** Television broadcasting begins. **28 September:** Assassination attempt on Chang Myon. **11 November:** Progressive Party established.

1957, 2 July: Headquarters of the UN Command moves to Seoul from Tokyo. **9 September:** South Korean UN application vetoed.

1958, 1 January: Passage of new election law. **13 January:** Cho Pong-am and other Progressive Party leaders arrested as spies. **February:** New Civil Law promulgated. **16 February:** (South) Korean National Airlines aircraft hijacked to North Korea. **2 May:** National Assembly elections. **8 December:** South Korean UN application vetoed. **26 December:** New National Security Law.

1959, 15 February: Japan–North Korea Red Cross agreement on the repatriation of Koreans from Japan to North Korea. **30 April:** *Kyonghyang Daily News* suspended. **31 July:** Cho Pong-am executed. **14 October:** Repatriation of the first group of Koreans from Japan to North Korea. **26 October:** Formation of the Federation of Labor Unions.

1960, 15 March: Reelection of President Rhee and election of Yi Ki-bung as vice president; beginning of demonstrations for nullification of election results begin; student demonstrations in Masan. **19 April:** Student uprising in Seoul. **24 April:** Resignation of Vice President Chang. **25 April:** Demonstration by college professors and others. **27 April:** Rhee and his cabinet resign. **22 May:** Formation of the Teachers' Labor Union. **29 May:** Rhee exiled to Hawaii. **15 June:** Constitutional amendments replace executive presidential system with a cabinet system. **29 July:** National Assembly elections. **13 August:** Yun Po-son elected president. **15 August:** Second Republic proclaimed. **28 August:** Formation of the Chang Myon cabinet. **23–28 November:** New constitution adopted. **25 November:** Federation of Korean Labor Unions formed.

1961, January: Emergence of the Reform and the Unification Socialist Parties. **February:** New Democratic Party established. **March:** Student demonstrations against the Anti-Communism Law. **May:** Student resolution to hold a conference of students from north and south at Panmunjom. **16 May:** Military coup d'état; fall of the Second Republic. **19 May:** Military Revolutionary Committee established. **20 May:**

Military Revolutionary Committee renamed the Supreme Council for National Reconstruction. **22 May:** Dissolution of all political parties and suspension of the National Assembly. **6 June:** Promulgation of Law Concerning Extraordinary Measures for National Reconstruction. **10 June:** Promulgation of the laws concerning the Supreme Council for National Reconstruction and the Central Intelligence Agency. **3 July:** Promulgation of the Anti-Communist Law. **10 October:** General Federation of Labor Unions established. **11–15 November:** General Park Chung-hee visits Japan and the United States.

1962, 22 March: Promulgation of the Political Activities Purification Law; resignation of President Yun; General Park becomes acting president. **10 June:** Second monetary reform, *hwan* replaced by the *won* at a rate of 10 to 1. **October:** Promulgation of national referendum law. **November:** Revised constitution published. **12 November:** South Korea–Japan agreement (Kim-Ohira Memorandum). **17 December:** National referendum approves new constitution by 78.8 percent. **26 December:** New constitution in force; political party and other laws promulgated.

1963, 1 January: Ban on political activities lifted. **26 February:** Democratic Republican Party formed. **15 May:** Civil Rule Party formed. **18 July:** Democratic Party formed. **1 August:** Nationalist Party (formed 3 September: Liberal Democratic Party (LDP) formed. **15 October:** Park Chung-hee elected president. **26 November:** National Assembly unicameral elections. **17 December:** Inauguration of President Park Chung-hee marks the emergence of the Third Republic.

1964, March–April: Numerous demonstrations against the South Korea–Japan talks on the normalization of relations. **2–3 June:** Violent student demonstrations in Seoul; promulgation of martial law in the Seoul area (to 29 July). **2 August:** New press law passed. **5 October:** Democratic and Nationalist parties merge to form the Democratic Party. **31 October:** South Korea–South Vietnam agreement on the dispatch of South Korean troops to Vietnam. **27 November:** Civil Rule and Liberal Democratic parties merge to form the Civil Rule Party. **6–15 December:** President Park visits West Germany.

1965, 11 May: Civil Rule and Democratic Parties merge to become the Masses (Minjung) Party (MP). **16–17 May:** President Park visits U.S. **22 June:** South Korea–Japan Normalization Treaty signed; ratified by the National Assembly 14 August. **19 July:** Former president Syngman Rhee dies in Hawaii. **13 August:** National Assembly approves the dispatch of combat divisions to South Vietnam. **26 August:** Garrison decree issued in the Seoul area.

1966, February: President Park visits Malaysia, Thailand, and Taiwan. **30 May:** New Korea Party formed. **14 June:** First ministerial meeting of the Asia–Pacific Council in Seoul. **9 July:** U.S.–South Korea Status-of-Forces Agreement signed. **2 November:** U.S. President Lyndon B. Johnson visits South Korea. **December:** Democratic Socialist Party (DSP) formed.

1967, 11 February: New Korea Party and Masses Party unite to form the New Democratic Party (NDP). **22 March:** Populist (Taejung) Party formed. **7 April:** Unification Socialist Party (USP) formed. **27 April:** Liberal Democratic Party (LDP) formed. **3 May:** President Park reelected; inauguration on 8 June. **6 May:** Democratic Party (DP) formed. **3 June:** Election of seventh National Assembly. **8 July:** Korean Central Intelligence Agency announces the East Berlin spy case. **13 December:** All 34 accused in East Berlin spy case convicted by Seoul District Court.

1968, 21 January: North Korean commandoes attempt to storm the presidential mansion in Seoul and assassinate President Park. **23 January:** U.S. intelligence ship, USS *Pueblo*, seized by North Korean naval ships; surviving crew members released on 23 December. **1 April:** Homeland Reserve Forces formed. **30 May:** Kim Jong-p'il, chairman of the Democratic Party resigns from the party and the National Assembly, announcing his retirement from politics. **4 November:** 30-man North Korean commando team infiltrates the east coast. **5 December:** Charter for National Education issued.

1969, 15 May: South Korea's first communications' satellite is built. **June–August:** Mass demonstrations against proposed revision of the constitution. **20 August:** President Park visits U.S. **17 October:** National referendum approves constitutional amendments. **11 December:** South Korean passenger aircraft with 15 passengers is hijacked to the north.

1970, 15 August: President Park declares willingness to open contacts with North Korea if use of force is renounced. **24 December:** Trade Law amended to allow trade with nonhostile communist countries.

1971, 12 March: Following partial U.S. troop withdrawals, South Korean forces take over responsibility for the whole truce line. **27 April:** President Park reelected for third four-year term. **25 May:** National Assembly elections. **6 August:** North Korean Premier Kim Il-sung proposes a summit meeting and contacts between nongovernmental organizations. **20 September:** Opening of talks between the Red Cross societies of the North and the South. **15 October:** Martial law proclaimed in the Seoul area. **6 December:** President Park declares a state of national emergency. **26 December:** Special Measures Law for National Security and Defense.

1972, 11 April: New Community Movement (Saemaul Undong) launched. **4 July:** Signing of the North–South Joint Communiqué and establishment of the North–South Co-ordinating Committee. **29 August:** First round of full North–South Red Cross talks held at P'yongyang to discuss family reunions. **12 October:** First North–South Coordinating Committee meeting held in P'yongyang; formally inaugurated 30 November. **17 October:** President Park imposes martial law throughout the country; some provisions of the constitution suspended; National Assembly dissolved and all political activities banned. **21 November:** Amended (*Yushin*) Constitution approved in a national referendum. **23 December:** President Park elected the first six-year president by the newly formed National Conference for Unification. **27 December:** Inauguration of President Park; beginning of the Fourth Republic. **30 December:** New National Assembly Election Law and the new Political Party Law promulgated.

1973, 27 January: Formation of the Democratic Unification Party. **27 February:** National Assembly elections. **10 March:** Formation of the Yujonghoe, a progovernment group in the National Assembly. **12 March:** North–South political talks in P'yongyang. **23 April:** Announcement of the breakup of a North Korean spying ring. **23 June:** President Park announces that the government will no longer oppose diplomatic relations between third countries and North Korea, and that it is not opposed to simultaneous North–South entry to the UN. **8 August:** Opposition politician Kim Dae-jung is kidnapped from a Tokyo hotel and taken to Seoul. **28 August:** North Korea suspends Red Cross and North–South Co-ordinating Committee meetings in protest of Kim Dae-jung kidnapping. **2 October:** Anti-*Yushin* protests begin. **21 November:** UN agrees by consensus to end

UNCURK. **4 December:** Launch of a movement to collect one million signatures for the revision of the constitution.

1974, 8 January: Presidential Emergency Decrees Numbers 1 and 2 ban all criticism of the constitution. **14 January:** Presidential Emergency Decree Number 3 issued. **3 April:** Presidential Emergency Decree Number 4 issued. **15 August:** Assassination attempt against President Park by a pro-North Korean from Japan; Park escapes but his wife is killed. **23 August:** Cancellation of Presidential Emergency Decrees Numbers 1 and 4. **15 November:** UNC announces the discovery of an infiltration tunnel in the southern half of the demilitarized zone (DMZ).

1975, 12 February: National referendum reaffirms the 1972 *Yushin* Constitution. **26 February:** North and South Korean naval vessels clash in the West Sea. **19 March:** UNC announces the discovery of a second infiltration tunnel in the DMZ. **8 April:** Proclamation of Presidential Emergency Decree Number 7. **13 May:** Lifting of Presidential Emergency Decree Number 7; Presidential Emergency Decree Number 9 issued. **15 September:** 700 pro-North Koreans arrive from Japan on a visit. **19 November:** UN General Assembly passes both pro-North Korean and pro-South Korean resolutions.

1976, 1 March: Declaration of Democratic National Salvation issued by dissident leaders (the Myongdong incident). **22 July:** U.S. Secretary of State Henry Kissinger proposes a conference of North and South Korea, China, and the U.S. to discuss Korea. **18 August:** Two American army officers killed by North Korean troops at P'anmunjom.

1977, 19 January: Operation of the first South Korean atomic power plant begins at Kori. **9 March:** U.S. President Jimmy Carter announces he will withdraw U.S. ground combat troops from South Korea. **October–December:** Intensified student demonstrations for constitutional reform; association of dismissed professors formed and issues Declaration of Democratic Education.

1978, 23 February: Justice Ministry decides to issue visas to nationals of "non-hostile" communist countries and of "left-leaning nonaligned nations" with which Seoul has no diplomatic relations. **21 April:** Soviet Union air force intercepts a Korean Airlines Boeing 707 with 110 passengers and forces it down south of Murmunsk. **30 April:**

Declaration of 12-mile territorial waters. **18 May:** National Conference for Unification (NCU) elections. **12–26 June:** Large student demonstrations in Seoul. **6 July:** Reelection of President Park by the NCU; he is inaugurated on 27 December. **3 September:** South Korean Minister for Health and Social Affairs, Shin Hyon-hwak, becomes the first South Korean cabinet minister to visit the Soviet Union when he attends a World Health Organization conference. **13–14 September:** Violent student demonstrations in Seoul. **27 October:** UNC announces discovery of a third tunnel in the DMZ. **7 November:** U.S.–ROK Combined Forces Command (CFC) established. **12 December:** National Assembly elections.

1979, 30 May: Kim Young-sam elected president of the New Democratic Party. **29 June:** U.S. President Jimmy Carter visits South Korea. **9 August:** Female workers of the Y. H. Trading Co. occupy National Democratic Party headquarters. **8 September:** Student demonstrations in Taegu. **9 September:** Kim Young-sam's party presidency suspended by the government. **4 October:** Kim Young-sam expelled from the National Assembly. **9 October:** Announcement of the arrest of the alleged leaders of the "South Korean People's Liberation Front." **16 October:** Violent student demonstration in Pusan and Masan. **20 October:** Proclamation of garrison law in the Pusan and Masan region. **24 October:** Violent student demonstrations in Taegu. **26 October:** Assassination of President Park. **27 October:** Proclamation of nationwide martial law; Premier Ch'oe Kyu-ha becomes acting president. **6 December:** Election of Ch'oe Kyu-ha as the president by the NCU. **12 December:** General Chun Doo-hwan stages a military coup; arrest of the Martial Law Commander General Chong Sung-hwa; formation of a new cabinet.

1980, April–May: Mass student demonstrations in Seoul, Pusan, and other cities. **21 April:** Coal miners' strike at the Sapuk Mine. **17 May:** Proclamation of martial law and Emergency Decree No. 10 banning all political activities, assemblies and rallies; key political leaders arrested. **18–27 May:** Kwangju Uprising. **31 May:** Special Committee for National Security Measures (SCNSM) formed. **16 August:** Resignation of President Ch'oe. **27 August:** Chun Doo-hwan elected president by the NCU. **1 September:** President Chun inaugurated. **17 September:** Kim Dae-jung given death sentence. **17 October:** Martial law proclaimed.

22 October: Fifth Republic constitution approved; National Assembly dissolved; political parties disbanded. **27 October:** Establishment of the Legislative Council for National Security (LCNS), replacing the National Assembly. **12 November:** 835 former politicians banned from politics for eight years. **10 November:** New Political Party Law promulgated. **14 November:** Drastic plan to reorganize mass media ("massacre of mass media") finalized. **15 November:** Partial lifting of martial law. **1 December:** KBS-TV began color broadcasting. **26 December:** National Security Law adopted; Korean CIA renamed the *Agency for National Security Planning (ANSP)*.

1981, 15 January: Democratic Justice Party (DJP) formed. **17 January:** Democratic Korea Party (DKP) formed. **23 January:** Korean National Party (KNP) formed. **23 January:** Kim Dae-jung's death sentence commuted to life term. **28 January:** President Chun visits U.S. **11 February:** Electoral College elections. **25 February:** Chun Doo-hwan formally elected president. **3 March:** Inauguration of President Chun and the Fifth Republic. **25 March:** National Assembly elections. **25 June:** President Chun embarked on a tour of the ASEAN nations. **30 September:** Seoul beats Nagoya in Japan to host the 1988 Summer Olympics.

1982, 5 January: The 36-year-old midnight-to-4 A.M. curfew lifted. **16 October:** A Chinese MiG fighter plane lands. **23 December:** Kim Dae-jung leaves Korea for U.S. for medical treatment.

1983, 25 February: A North Korean MiG-19 lands and its pilot seeks political asylum. **5 May:** A hijacked Chinese passenger plane lands. **7 August:** A Chinese MiG-21 fighter plane lands. **1 September:** Korean Air flight KE 007 from Anchorage to Seoul shot down by a Soviet fighter plane in Soviet airspace. **8 October:** President Chun embarks on a South Asian tour. **9 October:** Remote-controlled bomb aimed at the assassination of President Chun explodes at the Martyr's Mausoleum in Rangoon, Burma, killing 18 South Korean ministers and advisers. **17 October:** New cabinet.

1984, 25 May: Eight South Koreans visit China for Davis Cup tennis tournament in Kunming, the first to visit China since 1949. **3 May:** Pope John Paul II visits South Korea and canonizes 93 Korean and 10 French martyrs. **30 June–14 November:** Korean Broadcasting System runs family reunion program for those separated during the Korean War. **6–8 September:** President Chun's state visit to Japan. **14 September:** South Korean National Red Cross accepts a North Korean Red Cross offer of flood relief materials. **12–14 November:** Visit by U.S. President Ronald Reagan. **14 November:** Democratic Justice Party HQ occupied by students. **15 November:** First ever inter-Korean economic conference at Panmunjom.

1985, 18 January: New Korea Democratic Party (NKDP) formed. **8 February:** Kim Dae-jung returns from U.S.; largest student demonstration since 1980 in Seoul. **12 February:** National Assembly elections. **23 February:** Roh Tae-woo becomes chairman of the Democratic Justice Party. **6 March:** Lifting of restrictions of the last group on the 1980 political blacklist. **3 April:** Council for the Promotion of Democracy formed, with Kim Dae-jung and Kim Young-sam as cochairmen. **7 April:** Radical student organization, the Three People's Struggle Committee (*Sam mint'uwi*), formed. **22 May:** Students occupy Seoul U.S. Information Service building. **18 July:** Core members of the Three People's Struggle Committee and other radical student groups arrested. **2 August:** Kim Dae-jung and Kim Young-sam named as advisers to the president of the NKDP. **31 December:** Formation of the New Conservative Club by lawmakers defecting from the NKDP.

1986, 6 January: President Chun announces that he has no intention of rewriting the Constitution during his tenure and that the question of changing the presidential election system ought to be debated in 1989. **7 January:** Cabinet reshuffle. **5 April:** President Chun embarks on a four-nation European tour. **29 May:** Rival political parties agree to revise the Constitution, advocating parliamentary government. **26 November:** Government decides to construct a large dam near the 38th parallel in the eastern front in order to neutralize an alleged "water assault" from North Korea.

1987, 11 January: NKDP lawmakers begin sit-in strike at the National Assembly. **19 February:** 270 opposition politicians put under house arrest and headquarters of the NKDP closed. **11 March:** Kim Dae-jung put under house arrest. **4 April:** government realigned 20 business firms. **8 April:** Kim Dae-jung, Kim Young-sam, and many NKDP lawmakers announce intention to form a new party. **13 April:** President Chun forbids debates on constitutional revision; states that his successor will be chosen under the current constitution; widespread antigovernment demonstrations. **21 April:** Hunger strike of Catholic priests and nuns. **1 May:** Kim Young-sam forms the Reunification Democratic Party (RDP) and becomes its president. **26 May:** Major cabinet reshuffle. **1–26 June:** Nationwide antigovernment demonstrations. **10 June:** DJP nominates Roh Tae-woo as its presidential candidate. **24 June:** President Chun agrees to reopen constitutional revision debates. **29 June:** Roh Tae-woo announces democratic reform plan. **1 July:** President Chun accepts Roh's demands. **13 July:** Cabinet reshuffle. **5 August:** Roh Tae-woo elected president of the DJP. **8 August:** Kim Dae-jung joins Reunification Democratic Party. **12 October:** National Assembly passes new constitution. **28 October:** National referendum approves new constitution; Kim Jong-pil reconstitutes the former Democratic Republican Party as the New Democratic Republican Party (NDRP). **12 November:** Kim Dae-jung forms the Party for Peace and Democracy (PPD) and becomes its presidential candidate. **29 November:** Korean Air Lines passenger plane destroyed over Burma by bombs planted by North Korean agents. **16 December:** Roh Tae-woo elected president in first direct presidential election in 16 years.

1988, 8 February: Kim Young-sam resigns as president of the RDP. **25 February:** Roh Tae-woo takes the oath of office as president of the Sixth Republic. **8 March:** National Assembly passes new National Assembly Election Law. **12 March:** Kim Young-sam resumes party presidency. **17 March:** Kim Dae-jung resigned presidency of the PPD. **26 April:** National Assembly elections. **8 May:** Kim Dae-jung resumes PPD presidency. **10 July:** Radical students launch a movement for talks on Korean unification with North Korean students at Panmunjom. **17 September–2 October:** 24th Olympiad held in Seoul. **27 October:** Government lifts ban on works of South Korean writers and artists who either emigrated or were abducted to North Korea. **23 November:** Former president Chun makes formal apology for misdeeds of his relatives and the Fifth Republic on a national television broadcast and begins self-imposed exile with his wife at a remote Buddhist temple. **5 December:** Major cabinet reshuffle.

1989, 21 January: Formation of National Coalition for a People's Democratic Movement (*Chonguk Minjok Minju Undong Yonhap*, or *Chonminyon*) by some 200 dissident groups. **31 January:** 47 former high-ranking officials of the Fifth Republic arrested on charges of irregularities and corruption. **1 February:** Diplomatic relations established with Hungary; first South Korean direct importation of North Korean coal. **13 February:** 15,000 farmers stage a violent antigovernment rally in front of the National Assembly building, clashing with riot police. **14 March:** Minister of Government Administration resigns after issuing a warning against growing leftism. **13 April:** Arrest of Rev. Moon Ik-hwan, who made a secret unauthorized visit to North Korea in March on his return to Seoul. **3 May:** Six police officers killed in a fire set by rioting antigovernment students at Dongeui University in Pusan; U.S. agrees to relocate its military base from Seoul to another location. **12–13 May:** Large peaceful antigovernment student demonstrations in Kwangju in commemoration of the May 1980 Kwangju Uprising. **25 May:** Bills concerning the punishment of firebomb users and the restraining tear-gas use passed by the National Assembly's Internal Affairs Committee. **28 May:** Nationwide teachers union formed in defiance of government ban. **9 June:** President Roh cancels the promised midterm evaluation of his administration; radical student demonstrators call for the resignation of Roh and the withdrawal of U.S. troops. **12–16 June:** Kim Young-sam of the RDP and Ho Dam, chairman of the North Korean Peaceful Unification Committee, meet in Moscow. **19 June:** Cabinet reshuffle; six ministers and director of the ANSP replaced. **21 June:** Female student Lim Su-gyong left Seoul on a secret mission to North Korea, representing National Council of Student Representatives (NCSR). **27 June:** ANSP arrests Suh Kyong-won, former member of the PPD, who made secret visits to North Korea in August 1988, met Kim Il-sung, and received political funds. **29 July:** Chinese delegate to the Korean Armistice Commission and his wife defect to South Korea across the DMZ. **2 August:** ANSP question Kim Dae-jung in connection with the Suh Kyong-won case. **13 August:** Some 5,500 students of 26 colleges hold anti-U.S. demonstrations; 300 students raid U.S. ambassador's residence. **15 August:** Lim Su-gyong and a Roman Catholic priest, Moon Gyu-hyon, who visited North Korea from the U.S. to accompany her, are arrested upon arriving across the DMZ line at Panmunjom. **25 August:** Kim Dae-jung indicted on charge of violation of the National Security Law and the Foreign Exchange Control Law (charges later dropped). **11 September:** President Roh puts forward his new Korean reunification formula at the National Assembly. **4 October:** 44th International Eucharistic Congress opens in Seoul. **7 October:** Pope John Paul II makes second Korea visit. **16 October:** Delegates at North–South Red Cross working-level talks agree to exchange visitors and art tours; President Roh visits U.S. **1 November:** Establishment of diplomatic relations with Poland. **13 November:** 15,000 antigovernment students from 78 colleges clash with riot police. **18 November:** President Roh embarks on a state visit to four European countries. **27 December:** Ministry of Culture and Public Information split into Ministry of Culture and the Office of Public Information; creation of a new Ministry of Environmental Control. **28 December:** Diplomatic relations established with Yugoslavia. **31 December:** Former president Chun testifies at the National Assembly on the wrongdoings of the Fifth Republic; President Roh declares that the issues connected with the Fifth Republic are settled.

1990, 23 January: President Roh announces merger of the DJP with the RDP to form the Democratic Liberal Party (DLP). **9 February:** DLP officially launched. **3 March:** Discovery of fourth North Korean infiltration tunnel. **17 March:** Major cabinet reshuffle. **24 March:** Violent student demonstrations; labor strikes at KBS and Hyundai Heavy Industries. **4 June:** President Roh meets Soviet President Mikhail Gorbachev in San Francisco. **6 June:** Democratic Party formed. **30 September:** South Korea and the Soviet Union establish diplomatic relations. **13 December:** President Roh makes state visit to the Soviet Union. **27 December:** Premier, a vice-minister, and several ministers replaced in a major cabinet reshuffle.

1991, 23 January: 134-man military medical team leaves for Saudi Arabia to join Operation Desert Storm. **30 January:** South Korea opens permanent trade mission in Beijing. **26 March:** First local elections for 30 years for small cities, county, and ward councils. **19–20 April:** President Roh and President Gorbachev hold summit meeting on Cheju Island. **27 April:** 27-member South Korean delegation attends the Inter-Parliamentary Union meeting in P'yongyang. **7 May:** South Korean expedition team reaches the South Pole. **22 May:** Premier Ro Chae-bong resigns. **24 May:** Major cabinet reshuffle. **20 June:** Provincial and Special City assemblies' elections. **22 August:** South Korea and Albania establish diplomatic relations. **17 September:** Two Koreas become full UN members. **1 October:** South Korean army takes over security in the DMZ and the joint security area at Panmunjom. **23–24 October:** Fourth round of talks of premiers of the North and the South in P'yongyang. **8 November:** President Roh calls for a nuclear-free Korean Peninsula in his three-point Declaration. **9 December:** South Korea joins the International Labour Organization. **13 December:** North–South Agreement on Reconciliation, Nonaggression and Exchanges and Cooperation signed. **18 December:** President Roh declares that there is not a single nuclear weapon in South Korea. **31 December:** North–South Joint Declaration on Non-nuclearization of the Korean Peninsula initialled.

1992, 10 January: Unification National Party (UNP) formed. **15 January:** Formation of the New Korea Party (NKP). **7 February:** Unification National Party and the New Korea Party merge to form the Unification National Party (UNP). **24 March:** 14th National Assembly elections. **22 May:** South Korean security forces kill three North Korean infiltrators across the 38th parallel. **10 June:** Director General Hans Blix of the International Atomic Energy Authority voices concerns about a North Korean "radiochemical laboratory" at Yongbyon. **28 July:** North and South Korea agree to open two ports each to trade. **11 August:** South Korea's first satellite, *Uribyol* (Our Star) launched. **24 August:** China and South Korea establish diplomatic relations. **28 August:** Kim Young-sam is elected president of the ruling Democratic Liberal Party; first civilian leader of a ruling party for 31 years. **3 September:** North and South Korea agree to open Seoul and P'yongyang airports to traffic from each country. **27–30 September:** President Roh visits China. **12 October:** Launch of South Korea's first submarine. **2 November:** Britain's Prince Charles and Princess Diana on a four-day visit to South Korea. **19 November:** President Roh and Russian President Boris Yeltsin sign basic relations' treaty. **1 December:** South Korea takes over the ground component command of the ROK–U.S. Combined Forces Command; Combined Marine Forces Command activated. **18 December:** Kim Young-sam becomes 14th president; first elected ruler in 32 years who is not an army general. **19 December:** Kim Daejung announces his retirement from the National Assembly and from politics.

1993, 25 February: Inauguration of Kim Young-sam as president. **12 March:** North Korea announces it will withdraw from the Nuclear Nonproliferation Treaty (NPT). **15 March:** All economic aid to North Korea suspended. **13 May:** 12 December 1979 seizure of power by Gen. Chun

Doo-hwan officially described as "a coup-like" incident. **17 May:** Military training of high school students scrapped after 24 years. **20 May:** South Korea proposes North–South talks to relaunch North–South dialogue. **11 June:** North Korea–U.S. joint statement in New York: neither side will use force against the other; North Korea suspends its NPT withdrawal. **12 June:** President Kim Young-sam says that inter-Korean summit is possible if nuclear issue settled. **10 July:** U.S. President Bill Clinton visits Seoul and says that he supports the immediate reunification of Korea. **4 August:** First official Japanese government admission of the existence of "comfort women" for military prostitution in World War II. **6 August:** EXPO '93 launched at Taejon. **12 August:** "Real-name" financial transactions introduced. **1 November:** UN General Assembly adopts resolution calling on North Korea to accept International Atomic Energy Authority (IAEA) checks. **6 November:** Visit by Japanese Prime Minister Morihiro Hosokawa. **25 November:** South Korea and Taiwan agree to open private representatives' offices in each other's capitals. **22 December:** Visit by UN Secretary General Boutros Boutros-Ghali.

1994, 11 January: South Korean team reaches South Pole. **24 January:** Direct Seoul–Beijing air route agreed. **22 March:** U.S. sends 192 "Patriot" missiles to Korea. **24 March:** President Kim Young-sam visits Japan. **28 March:** President Kim Young-sam visits China. **11 May:** North Korea's deputy ambassador to the UN says that North Korea accepts IAEA suggestion to send an extra inspection team to Yongbyon. **1 June:** President Kim Young-sam visits Russia. **13 June:** Former U.S. president Jimmy Carter visits Seoul on his way to North Korea to discuss the nuclear question. **22 June:** South Korean Prime Minister Lee Yung-duk proposes preliminary North–South talks on a possible summit; offer accepted. **28 June:** North and South Korean officials reach agreement to hold summit meeting in P'yongyang 25–27 July. **8 July:** Death of North Korean leader Kim Il-sung; proposed summit abandoned. **2 September:** North Korea announces that Chinese forces will withdraw from the MAC. **21 October:** U.S.–North Korea "Agreed Framework" on nuclear issues signed in Geneva. **1 December:** Peacetime operational control over all South Korean forces still under U.S. operational command transferred to South Korean armed forces.

1995, 12 January: Daewoo Group delegation in North Korea to conduct investment feasibility study. **16 January:** Samsung Group concludes an agreement with North Korea on building an airport and highways in the Rajin–Sonbong Special Economic Zone (SEZ). **23 January:** Formation of the Korea Peninsula Energy Development Organization (KEDO) to supply light water nuclear reactors to North Korea. **26 January:** Martin Luther King Peace Prize awarded to President Kim Young-sam. **21 February:** Formation of the United Liberal Democrat party led by Kim Jong-p'il, who resigned as chairman of the ruling Democratic Liberal Party. **1 March:** 20 cable television channels open. **2 March:** President Kim Young-sam departs on European tour. **3 March:** Loans from the International Bank for Reconstruction and Development end after 33 years. **17 May:** Government approves Daewoo Corporation plans to invest U.S.$5.12 million in Namp'o Industrial Complex in North Korea, the first ever such approval. **25 June:** South Korean freighter with 2,000 tons of rice leaves for North Korea. **8 July:** South African President Nelson Mandela visits South Korea. **21 July:** South Korea and the U.S. agree that cost of light water reactors for North Korea should be met by a Japan–U.S.–South Korean consortium. **26 July:** President Kim Young-sam visits the U.S. **15 August:** To mark 50th anniversary of liberation, work begins on dismantling the Japanese colonial government's Capitol Building. **5 September:** National Council for New Politics inaugurated, with Kim Dae-jung as president. **14 September:** Government extends South Korean territorial waters from three to twelve miles. **8 November:** South Korea becomes non-permanent member of the UN Security Council; government announces measures to promote economic cooperation with North Korea; South Korean industries allowed to visit North Korea and set up branches. **16 November:** Arrest of former president, Roh Tae-woo, on suspicion of accepting bribes. **2 December:** Seoul District Court special investigation headquarters issues arrest warrant for former president Chun Doo-hwan on charge of leading a military rebellion. **12 December:** KEDO and North Korea agree on supply of light water reactors.

1996, 26 February: European Union decides to contribute $6.25 million to KEDO project. **11 March:** Seoul District Court begins trial of former presidents Chun and Roh for involvement in 1979 coup and 1980 Kwangju massacre. **4 April:** North Korea announces that the Korean People's Army renounces its truce obligations on the maintenance of the Military Demarcation Line and the demilitarized zone. **16 April:** President Kim Young-sam meets U.S. President Bill Clinton on Cheju islands, where they propose four-way talks (North and South Korea, China and the U.S.) on the Korean question. **20 April:** UN Command in Korea asks UN Security Council to take steps so that North Korea does not violate the Armistice Agreement. **31 May:** International Football Federation (FIFA) agrees to award hosting of 2002 Football World Cup jointly to Japan and South Korea. **4 June:** After 35 years, Ministry of Health abolishes penalties for having more than two children. **17 August:** First North–South joint venture opens at North Korean port of Namp'o. **18 September:** North Korean infiltration submarine runs aground near Kangnung on the East Coast. **11 October:** South Korea becomes 29th member of the Organization for Economic Cooperation and Development. **29 December:** North Korean spokesperson expresses "deep regret" over the submarine incident.

1997, 1 February: Government decides to provide 570 billion won emergency aid to prevent Hanbo Steel Corporation from going bankrupt. **10 March:** National Assembly approves new labor laws. **17 April:** Former presidents Chun and Roh sentenced respectively to life and 17 years in prison, plus heavy fines. **20 April:** Senior North Korean party official Hwang Jang-yop and aide Kim Dok-hong defect to South Korea via Beijing. **3 May:** North and South Korean Red Cross Societies agree in Beijing on direct delivery of food aid to North Korea. **17 May:** Arrest of President Kim Young-sam's son, Kim Hyun-chul, on tax evasion and corruption charges. **28 July:** KEDO opens offices in Kumho, North Korea. **19 August:** Ground-breaking for LWR construction at Shinpo-Kumho district in North Korea. **7 November:** Ruling New Korea Party and small opposition Democratic Party agree to merge. **27 November:** International Bank for Reconstruction and Development and the Asian Development Bank agree to participate in international efforts to extend financial support to South Korea. **3 December:** South Korea and the International Monetary Fund (IMF) sign agreement on IMF support for South Korea. **9 December:** Four-party talks involving North Korea, South Korea, the U.S. and China held in Geneva. **10 December:** Operation of five merchant banks suspended. **18 December:** Kim Dae-jung elected president. **22 December:** Special amnesty granted to former presidents Chun and Roh. **23 December:** Won–dollar exchange rate reaches Won 2,000=$1 for first time.

1998, 19 February: Reduction of overseas missions from 145 to 125, to reduce costs. **25 February:** Kim Dae-jung inaugurated as 15th president. **9 April:** Former Seoul National University professor, Ko Yong-bok receives a seven-year sentence for spying for North Korea for 36 years. **25 May:** Lifting of the ceiling on foreign investment on the Korean Stock Exchange. **16 June:** Hyundai founder Chung Ju-yung takes 501 head of cattle to North Korea. **22 June:** North Korean Yugo-class miniature submarine caught in fishing boat's nets off East Coast. **31 July:** Massive flooding in the Mount Chiri National Park leaves 348 dead and missing. **31 August:** North Korea fires a three-stage *Taepodong*-1 rocket, which it claims is to launch a satellite, over Japan. **5 September:** North Korean Supreme People's Assembly appoints deceased former president Kim Il-sung president in perpetuity, while his son Kim Jong-il becomes chairman of the National Defense Commission, which is designated the highest organ of state. **20 October:** Minister of Culture and Tourism announces partial opening of the South Korean market to Japanese films, music, and comic books for the first time since 1948. **18 November:** Beginning of Hyundai-organized tours to the Kumgang (Diamond) Mountains in North Korea.

1999, 15 June: Serious naval clash between North and South Korea in the West Sea. **2 September:** North Korea declares Northern Limit Line invalid and announces a new sea boundary in the West Sea, which is rejected by South Korea. **29 September:** Hyundai group holds a ground-breaking ceremony for a new sports hall in P'yongyang. **15 December:** KEDO and KEPCO sign $4.6 billion contract to build two light water reactors (LWRS) in North Korea. **20 December:** Launch of South Korea's first multipurpose satellite.

2000, 5 January: Italy and North Korea establish diplomatic relations. **9 March:** In Berlin, President Kim Dae-jung proposes talks between North and South on improving the North Korean economy, ending the Cold War on the peninsula, and the separated families issue. **17 March:** North and South Korean officials meet in Beijing to discuss possible North–South summit. **22 March:** North Korea announces "new navigational zones and waterways" in the West Sea. **10 April:** North and South Korea announce a summit meeting in P'yongyang on 12–14 June. **11 April:** Christian Council of Korea holds rally in Seoul demanding the dismantling of statues of the mythical founder of Korea, Tan'gun, erected in primary schools and public parks by the Han Munwha Movement Federation. **29 May:** Japanese Prime Minister

Yoshiro Mori makes one-day visit. **29–31 May:** North Korean leader Kim Jong-il visits China. **29 May–10 June:** P'yongyang State Circus in Seoul. **31 May:** Korean Air pilots form a labor union. **13–15 June:** President Kim Dae-jung visits North Korea. **19 June:** U.S. lifts some sanctions on North Korea. **14 July:** World Bank closes Seoul office established in 1998. **11 August:** South Korean media delegation in North Korea; meets Kim Jong-il. **15 August:** Resumption of North–South family reunion meetings after 15-year gap; North Korea reopens the North–South liaison office at P'anmunjom, closed since 1996. **18 September:** South Korea begins work on reconnecting the North–South railway. **19 September:** Red Cross meeting agrees on further family exchanges, including mail. **25–26 September:** North–South defense ministers meet on Cheju Island for first time ever. **9–10 October:** North Korean defense minister, Jo Myung-rok, visits U.S. **13 October:** President Kim Dae-jung awarded the Nobel Peace Prize. **19–21 October:** Third Asia–Europe meeting in Seoul. **23–25 October:** Madeleine Albright, U.S. secretary of state, visits P'yongyang. **12 December:** Britain and North Korea establish diplomatic relations.

2001, 8 January: Ruling MDP and ULD resume alliance. **31 January:** Tax office announces investigation of leading newspapers. **27 February:** Russian President Vladimir Putin in Seoul. **1 March:** Germany and North Korea establish diplomatic relations. **7 March:** U.S.–ROK summit meeting. **10–11 March:** North–South trade unions meeting at Mount Kumgang. **15 March.** First official letter exchange between separated families since 1945. **21 March:** Death of Chung Ju-yung, founder of the Hyundai Group. **26 March:** U.S.–Japan–South Korean ministerial meeting in Seoul; small Democratic People's Party joins ruling coalition. **2–4 May 2001:** EU delegation in P'yongyang. Kim Jong-il agrees to extend moratorium on missile tests. Delegation also visits Seoul. **14 May:** EU–North Korea diplomatic relations. **6 June:** U.S. announces completed review of policy to North Korea. **13 June:** GNP makes sweeping gains in the local government elections; accidental killing of two girls by U.S. armored personnel carrier leads to demonstrations. **17 August:** Arrest of heads of *Chosun Ilbo*, *Dong-a Ilbo*, and *Kukmin Daily* on fraud and embezzlement charges. **23 August:** ROK repays final U.S.$140 million of emergency loan from IMF. **2 September:** South Korean cabinet resigns after no-confidence vote against minister for unification carried in the National Assembly; ruling party loses control of Assembly. **3–5 September:** Chinese President Jiang Zemin visits North Korea. **13 September:** Groundbreaking ceremony for LWRs at Kumho; North Korea condemns attacks on World Trade Center. **19–20 September:** South Korean forces fire on North Korean forces that cross the MDL at P'anmunjom. **30 September:** South Korea reopens Imjin railway station. **15 October:** Visit by Japanese Prime Minister Junichiro Koizumi; expresses "heartfelt apology" for the Japanese colonial period. **24 October:** Three ROK naval vessels visit China. **25 October:** Opposition GNP wins three by-elections. **24 November:** Launch of National Human Rights Commission. **27 November:** First exchange of fire in DMZ since 1998. **2–12 December:** President Kim Dae-jung visits Britain, Norway, Hungary, and the European Parliament in Strasbourg.

2002, 25 January: Presidential Commission on Anti-Corruption launched. **29 January:** In his State of the Union speech, U.S. President George Bush refers to North Korea as part of an "axis of evil," together with Iraq and Iran. **7 March:** First female graduates of the Korean Military Academy. **7 April:** ROK–Japan Extradition Treaty. **27 April:** Former human rights lawyer Roh Moo-hyun wins MDP presidential nomination. **10–14 May:** Representative Park Geun-kye in North Korea; meets Kim Jong-il. **17 May:** Park Geun-kye launches a new party, the Korea Coalition for the Future (KCFT). **31 May–30 June:** World Cup in Japan and South Korea. **29 June:** North Korea–South Korea naval clash in the West Sea. **13 June:** GNP wins landslide victory in mayor and governor elections. **1 July:** President Kim Dae-jung visits Japan. **17 September:** Japanese Prime Minister Junichiro Koizumi visits North Korea; Kim Jong-il confirms that a number of Japanese were kidnapped by special forces and brought to North Korea and that North Korea has used spy ships against Japan. **29 September–14 October:** 14th Asian Games held in Pusan. **5 October:** After the National Assembly rejects two previous nominations, Kim Suk-soo becomes prime minister. **16 October:** U.S. claims that North Korea has admitted an enriched uranium program, in breach of the Agreed Framework. **26 October:** North Korea publicly denies that it has an enriched uranium program. **5 November:** Chung Mong-joon of Hyundai and the Korean Football Association establishes the political party "National Alliance 21," with himself as its presidential candidate. **14 November:** KEDO suspends heavy fuel oil supplies to North Korea. **15 November:** Sohn

Kee-chung, winner of the 1936 Berlin Olympic Games marathon and a national hero, dies. **19 November:** Representative Park Geun-gye rejoins the GNP. **22 November:** Acquittal of two U.S. servicemen over the deaths of two Korean girls in June sparks off nationwide demonstrations. **25 November:** Following an election run-off, Chung Moon-joon of "National Alliance 21" agrees to support MDP candidate Roh Moo-hyun in the forthcoming presidential election. **13 December:** North Korea announces that it is restarting the Yongbyon nuclear facility, closed under the 1994 Agreed Framework. **19 December:** Roh Moo-hyun of the MDP elected 16th president of the ROK, beating Lee Hoi-chang of the GNP. **26 December:** ROK per capita income reaches U.S.$8,900, compared with $706 in North Korea. **27 December:** Korean Air sends first charter flight to Taiwan since diplomatic relations with the "Republic of China" severed in 1992. **29 December:** North Korea expels IAEA inspectors.

2003, 10 January: North Korea announces its withdrawal from the NPT. **5 February:** A South Korean tourist group going to Mount Kumgang makes the first journey across the DMZ apart from P'anmunjom since the end of the Korean War in 1953. **12 February:** IAEA declares that North Korea is in breach of its agreement with the authority, and refers the issue to the United Nations Security Council. **16 February:** Hyundai Group chairman Chung Moon-han admits that the group paid U.S.$500 million to North Korea for exclusive business rights and that some of this money may have helped to pave the way for the June 2000 summit. **20 February:** North Korean fighter aircraft intrudes into South Korean airspace. **21 February:** A group of government and business leaders cross the DMZ to visit Kaesong. **23 February:** Hahn Hwa-kap resigns as head of the MDP, allowing president-elect Roh Moo-hyun to take over. **24 February:** North Korea fires short-range missile, after warning announcement. **25 February:** Roh Moo-hyun inaugurated as 16th president. **26 February:** Former mayor of Seoul Goh Kun becomes prime minister; National Assembly approves appointment of an independent counsel to investigate the Hyundai Group's links with North Korea. **2 March:** North Korean fighters intercept a U.S. reconnaissance aircraft off the east coast. **10 March:** Unification Church leader Moon Sun-myong announces formation of the Party for God, Peace, Unification and Home. **27 March:** Former Korea University professor and Foreign Minister Han Sung-joo becomes ambassador to the U.S. **2 April:** National Assembly authorizes despatch of non-combatant ROK forces to Iraq. **25 April:** Ko Young-koo, former human rights lawyer, becomes head of the National Intelligence Service. **5 May:** 100 years after King Kojong imported the first car into Korea, Ministry of Construction and Tourism announces that more than 12 million cars are in the ROK. **14 May:** President Roh makes first official visit to the U.S. **10 April:** North Korea's withdrawal from the NPT comes into force. **3 August:** Death of head of Hyundai Asan, Chung Mong-hun. **21 August:** Summer university games open in Taegu, with North Korean participation.

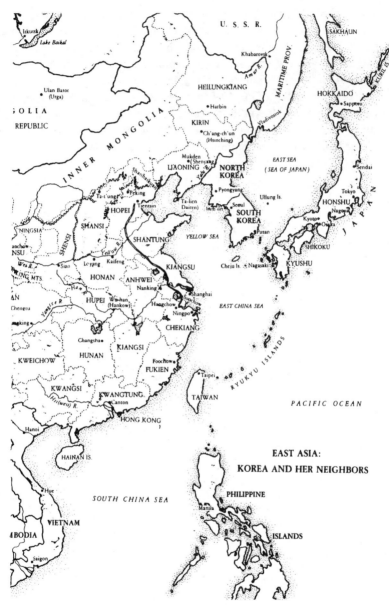

East Asia: Korea and Her Neighbors

CHINA

N. Hamgyŏng

S. Hamgyŏng

N. P'yŏng-an

S. P'yŏng-an

SEA OF JAPAN
(EAST SEA)

Hwanghae

Kangwŏn

Kyŏnggi

Ullŭng Is.

N. Ch'ungch'ŏng

S. Ch'ungch'ŏng

N. Kyŏngsang

YELLOW SEA

N. Chŏlla

S. Kyŏngsang

S. Chŏlla

Kŏmun Is.

Cheju Is.

JAPAN

Korea Before Partition

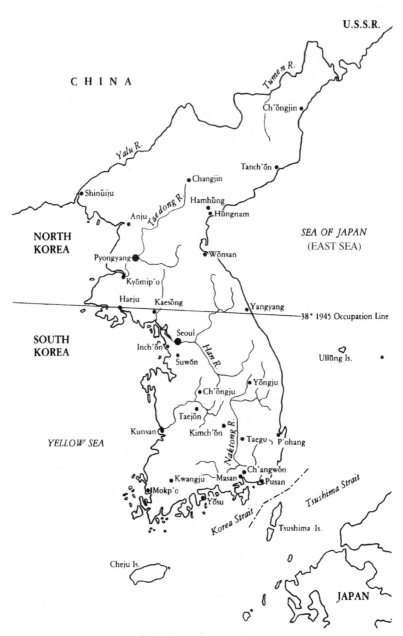

The Partitioned Korea, 1945

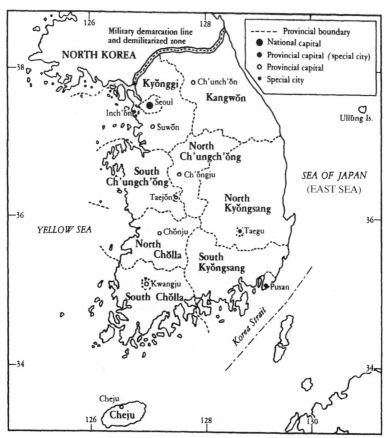

Republic of Korea, Military Demarcation Line and Demilitarized Zone,
Plus Post-1953 Administrative Units

Introduction

The Korean Peninsula lies at the strategic heart of East Asia, between China, Russia, and Japan, and has been influenced in different ways and at different times by all three of them. Faced by such powerful neighbors, the Koreans have had to struggle hard to maintain their political and cultural identity. The result has been to create a fiercely independent people. If they have from time to time been divided, the pressures toward unification have always proved strong.

The most recent division in 1945, following on from some 30 years of harsh Japanese colonial rule and consolidated by a savage war between 1950–1953, has led to the establishment of two very different states on the peninsula. While both retain many of the features of a more traditional Korea, they have also both taken on some of the characteristics of their respective protecting powers. The Democratic People's Republic of Korea (DPRK), or North Korea, modeled itself on Stalin's Soviet Union, while the Republic of Korea (ROK), or South Korea, looked to the Western world, and particularly to the United States. Once North Korea seemed the more successful, with a greater degree of industrialization and higher GNP then the South.

Those days have long since passed, and it is now the Republic of Korea that, despite setbacks, is the more successful of the two, in both economic and political terms. Even the Asian economic crisis of 1997–1998, which hit the ROK badly, has been weathered successfully. That, taken with a steady progress toward democratization, indicates that when the peninsula is eventually reunified, as one day it will be, the new unified Korea will follow the ROK model rather than that of the DPRK.

LAND AND PEOPLE

Physical Features

The Korean Peninsula extends due south from northeast China (traditionally known in the West as *Manchuria*) on the Asian mainland. The peninsula and its associated islands lie between longitudes 124° and 131° east and between latitudes 33° and 43° north. The total area of the peninsula is some 82,242 square miles (221,000 square kilometers) and is about the same as mainland Britain. The peninsula is roughly 688 miles (1,100 kilometers) long and 134 miles (216 kilometers) wide at its narrowest point. The average width is about 170 miles (250 kilometers). It is separated from China by the Yalu and Tumen rivers, and it is surrounded by the East Sea, or Sea of Japan, the Yellow Sea (West Sea), and the Korea Strait. The peninsula has a 640-mile (1,025 kilometer) border with China and a short 9-mile (12 kilometer) one with Russia.

Today, the peninsula is divided into two Korean states along the 150-mile (240 kilometer) military demarcation line laid down in the 1953 Armistice Agreement. The DPRK is slightly the larger of the two, at 46,768 square miles (122,827 square kilometers); the ROK is 38,131 square miles (99,173 square kilometers). The demilitarized zone (DMZ) that separates the two Koreas covers an area of 477 square miles (1,253 square kilometers).

The Western name *Korea* is derived from the Koryo dynasty that ruled Korea from 936 to 1392 A.D. as a unified kingdom. The other name of Korea, Chosun, came from the kingdom that the Yi dynasty established in 1392 and ruled over until 1910. "Chosun" can be translated as "morning freshness," implying the land in the east (relative to China). The popular Western name, "the Land of the Morning Calm," appears to be a misunderstanding of the original Chinese characters. It dates from the 1880s.

The peninsula is mountainous, but the west coast along the Yellow Sea and the southern coast both have low hills with some plains. In the north, the Changbaek Range and its branches cover an extensive area. The highest mountain in the Changbaek Range, which runs along both banks of the Yalu and Tumen rivers, is Mount Paektu (9,000 feet, 2,744 meters), and in the Nangnin Range, the Kaema and the Pujon plateaus constitute the "roof" of North Korea. The T'aebaek Mountain chain, the backbone of the peninsula, runs almost its entire length and parallels the east coast from the eastern fringe of the Kaema Plateau. In this range are found famous mountains such as Mount Kumgang, or Diamond Mountain (5,350 feet, 1,631 meters), Mount Sorak (5,600 feet, 1,703 meters), and Mount T'aebaek (5,100 feet, 1555 meters). Running in a southwesterly direction is a branch of mountains called Sobaek, where the second highest peak in Korea, Mount Chiri (6,250 feet, 1,905 meters), is located.

Whereas the east coast generally has smooth shorelines, the west and southern coasts have extremely irregular ones with numerous bays and inlets. Most of Korea's 3,400 islands are located near the west and southern coasts. Among the major islands are Koje and Wan off the south coast, the Chin Island off the southwestern corner of the peninsula, and the island of Kanghwa near Inch'on on the west coast. Located some 100 miles (160 kilometers) off the southern coast is Cheju, the largest of the Korean islands, created by volcanic activities, which also boasts one of the highest and most majestic mountains, Mount Halla (6,400 feet, 1,951 meters). Finally, in the East Sea are the two Korean islands of Ullung and Tok—the latter, known as Takeshima in Japanese, is also claimed by Japan.

Most major rivers flow westward into the Yellow Sea (West Sea). They are the Yalu (Amnok in Korean), the Ch'ongch'on, and the Taedong rivers in the north, the Imjin, the Han, and the Kum rivers in the south. The exceptions are the Tumen River, which flows into the Sea of Japan, and the Naktong River in the south, which flows southward into the Korea Strait. There are three major plains, one in the northwestern region, one in the west-central region, and one in the southwestern region of the peninsula.

Only about 22 percent of the land is cultivated, while the other 66 percent is mountainous or covered with forests. Most of the arable lands are located in the western and southern regions of South Korea, although a sizeable area of fertile farmlands is located in the western region of North Korea.

Climate

The climate of Korea is more continental than oceanic, and there are four distinct seasons. Spring generally begins in early March, accompanied by warm breezes from the south, and lasts until the end of June with light rainfall at regular intervals. Late June and the month of July are generally the heavy rainy season with July temperatures reaching 77–85° Fahrenheit (26–30° centigrade) in the south. The summer is hot and humid due to southern monsoon winds. Annual precipitation varies from about 24 inches (61 centimeters) in the northeast to more than 60 inches (152 centimeters) in the southern regions.

The autumn is pleasant, starting generally from late September and ending in mid-November with the first frost. Autumn is a period of dry and sunny weather; the Koreans, like the Chinese, refer to it as the time "when skies are high, and horses are fat." The winter begins around mid-December and lasts until February, being extremely cold in the north, where January temperatures can fall to 8°F (−17°C), or even lower in exceptional years. Owing to the influence of the surrounding seas, the winter climate in the south is not as severe. Snowfall is generally light in the lowlands and the southern half of South Korea. The mean January temperature in Seoul is 23°F (−8°C). The extreme southern area of South Korea has only very light snowfall or none at all.

The People

The Koreans are a homogeneous people, speaking the same language, and culturally distinct from their Chinese, Mongol, and Japanese neighbors. In 30,000 B.C., *homo sapiens* inhabited the peninsula, leaving behind numerous Paleolithic culture sites. Later on, around 3,000 B.C., certain tribal units of the Tungusic people, such as the Han, the Kaema or Koma, the Maek, and the Puyo, migrated into the peninsula from the Altai Mountain region via Siberia, Mongolia, and Manchuria, bringing with them Neolithic culture—the Ural-Altaic language and Shamanism—and became the ancestors of the present-day Koreans. Ethnologically, the Koreans belong to the Altaic family of races, which includes the Turkic, Mongolian, and Tungusic peoples. Generally, Koreans are lighter skinned than Chinese or Japanese; some see this as evidence of a Western origin.

Population

The total population of Korea was about 25 million when the country was liberated from Japan and partitioned into military operations zones by the Allies in 1945. The American zone had about 16 million and the Soviet zone a little over 9.5 million people. However, with the steady influx of two million refugees from the north and another two million Koreans who returned from overseas, the population of South Korea had grown to 20 million by 1948. Since then, the population has steadily increased: 24 million in 1965, 35 million in 1975, and 42 million in 1985. In 1990, the total population of South Korea stood at 42.8 million, with a population density of 1,107 per square mile. By mid-1997, the population was estimated to be 45.9 million, and the 2001 census figure was 46.14 million. In December 2002, the United Nations Population Fund quoted a figure of 47.4 million for South Korea.

The average life expectancy was less than 45 years during the Japanese colonial period. In 1945, only 12.5 percent of the total population was over the age of 50. Since liberation, the life expectancy has steadily increased, and in 1995 the life expectancy of men stood at 69.5 and that of women at 77.4 years. At the end of 2002, it was 71.8 for men and 79.1 years for women. The population grew at an annual average rate of 3 percent up until 1960. After that time, the growth rate fell gradually, declining to 0.93 percent by 1985; it has remained about that figure ever since. The average Korean woman had 1.3 children in 2002, compared to 2.5 in 1984, 2.8 in 1980, 4.2 in 1970, and 6.1 in 1960. The disappearance of the traditional large families, and the rapid increase in urbanization in the 20th century, has had a major effect on Korean family life.

On the eve of liberation in 1945, the total urban population was about 3.4 million. It rose steadily during the industrialization of the 1960s and 1970s, and according to the 1985 census, the urban population stood at 26.5 million, representing 65.4 percent of the total population, and the rural population was 14 million, or 34.6 percent of the total. By the mid-1990s, the rural population had fallen further, to some 9.6 million. The urban population has grown at an annual average rate of 5 percent since 1955, while the population in the rural areas has shown a commensurate decrease. The population of Seoul grew from one million in 1948 to 10.7 million by 1990; by 2002 it had fallen back slightly to 10.33 million, though Kyonggi Province, which surrounds the capital, has shown huge growth (see table on p. lxvi).

Seoul's population appears to have stabilized around the 10 million mark, which represents 25 percent of the total South Korean population. The influx of the rural population into Seoul declined after 1970 and has continued to do so ever since, as there was greater population migration into cities other than Seoul due to the rise of new commercial and industrial centers. Among the cities whose population has grown rapidly in recent years are the six other special or metropolitan cities (2002 population figures given in brackets) of Pusan (3.78 million), Taegu (2.53 million), Inch'on (2.5 million), Kwangju (1.3 million), Taejon (1.4 million), and Ulsan (one million), in addition to such industrial centers as Ch'angwon, Masan, and P'ohang.

Provincial populations are as follows:

	1990	2002
Kyonggi	5.6 m.	9.28 m.
South Kyongsang	3.6 m.	3.1 m.
North Kyongsang	2.7 m.	2.8 m
South Cholla	2.1 m.	2.5 m.
North Cholla	2 m.	2.1 m.
South Ch'ungch'ong	1.9 m.	1.9 m.
North Ch'ungch'ong	1.5 m.	1.3 m.
Kangwon	1.6 m.	1.7 .m
Cheju	547,964	507,000

HISTORY

Korean history may be divided into several distinct periods. The first is the period before the rise of the Three Kingdoms: i.e., to about the beginning of the Christian era. The second covers the Three Kingdoms (57 B.C.–936 A.D.), as well as the period during which a unified Korea was ruled by the Shilla dynasty. The third is that of the Koryo dynasty (918–1392). The long fourth period (1392–1910) is the Yi dynasty, lasting until the dawn of the 20th century. The relatively short fifth period (1910–45) saw Korea under Japanese colonial rule, and the sixth, and even shorter, (1945–48) was that of the Allied occupation, at the end of which the two Korean states emerged.

Before the Three Kingdoms

Various groups of Paleolithic people inhabited the Korean Peninsula from about 30,000 B.C., leaving behind many Paleolithic sites throughout the land. From about 3000 B.C., groups of Neolithic people began to migrate into the peninsula. These were the Tungusic tribes who arrived from central Asia via Siberia, Mongolia, Manchuria, and the northwestern Chinese coastal regions. It was these Tungusic people who brought to Korea the Ural-Altaic language, shamanistic religion, and a Neolithic culture. Many dolmens, menhirs, different types of pottery, and a variety of stone tools unearthed in Korea attest to this fact. These new immigrants formed tribal units and built walled towns and pit dwellings.

The traditional legendary history begins in 2333 B.C., when a divinity named Tan'gun (also known as Wanggom) came to earth and became the progenitor of the Korean Race. Tan'gun is said to have formed a "nation," marking the beginning of the Old Chosun period. (Under the brief Chosun Empire, 1895–1910, and again under the First Republic, years were dated from this foundation date, which derives from Chinese records. Thus 1948 was 4281 of the Tan'gun era.) The territory of Old Chosun is said to have included the southern part of Manchuria and the northwestern part of the Korean Peninsula along the Taedong River with its capital at Asadal. Many believe that Asadal was present-day P'yongyang, whose former name was Wanggomsong. Much is made of this version of Korea's early history in North Korea, since it enhances the role of P'yongyang, now the North Korean capital, in the nation. In the mid-1990s, the North Koreans even announced that they had found and excavated Tan'gun's tomb just outside P'yongyang. Although obscurity surrounds Old Chosun and its history, it was said to have been ruled by a new ruler named Kija, a fugitive from China, and his successors from about 1120 B.C. until it was taken over by Wiman in 194 B.C., ushering in the Wiman Chosun period. Wiman too was from China.

Wiman Chosun extended its domination into the northeastern part of the peninsula, establishing the Imdun district there, and into the central region of the peninsula, where it established the Chinbon district. As Wiman Chosun rose, a tribal state named Chin emerged in the southern region of Korea. The state of Chin founded by the refugees from Old Chosun eventually gave way to the rise of the three federations of the Han people, namely Mahan in central Korea, Chinhan in the south eastern region, and Pyonhan in the south central coastal region.

In 190 B.C., Emperor Wu of the Han dynasty of China invaded Korea, and after overthrowing Wiman Chosun in 108 B.C. he established three Chinese commanderies (military colonies), Lolang (Korean name Nangnang), Chenfan (Chinbon), and Lintu'un (Imdun) in the Korean Peninsula, and a commandery named Hsungt'u (Hyont'o) in southern Manchuria along the lower Yalu River region. The Chinese commandery of Lint'un was soon overthrown and was replaced by two Korean states named Okcho and Eastern Ye in the northeastern region.

The Period of the Three Kingdoms

In 37 B.C., a new state, Koguryo, formed by the Yemaek tribes that had emerged in the central region of Manchuria, conquered the state of Puyo, located in the northwestern region of Manchuria. From there, Koguryo extended its territory into the Korean Peninsula with its capital at Kungnaesong (T'ungkuo) on the middle region of the Yalu River. After conquering both Okcho and Eastern Ye during the first century, Koguryo became a recognizable political entity in the third century. In 313, Koguryo first overthrew the Chinese commandery of Lolang, and then a new Chinese commandery of Taifang (Taebang), which was established around 204 A.D. After this, Koguryo moved its capital from Kungnaesong to Wanggomsong (now P'yongyang) in 427, controlling most of the northern half of Korea and the southern part of Manchuria.

As political changes took place in the north, a political metamorphosis also occurred in the southern part of Korea as the state of Saro emerged in the Chinhan area in 57 B.C. and the state of Paekche in the Mahan area in 18 B.C. In the meantime, Pyonhan split into several Kaya states. The state of Saro eventually absorbed other areas of Chinhan, establishing the Kingdom of Shilla in the third century. Paekche did likewise in the Mahan area, becoming an established kingdom in the third century and extending its territory into the southwestern region of Korea. Six Kaya states located in the lower reaches of the Naktong River failed to coalesce into a state, and they were taken over one by one by Shilla in the sixth century. With the rise of Koguryo in the north, Shilla in the southeast, and Paekche in the central region of Korea, the "Three Kingdoms" period in Korean history began. The consolidation of state power also ushered in a long period of warfare between them.

From the end of the sixth and in the early seventh centuries, Koguryo was engaged in frequent warfare not only against Paekche and Shilla, but also against Chinese forces of the Sui and Tang dynasties. Meanwhile, its rulers were also faced with serious internal disunity. Paekche also encountered numerous internal problems. Shilla, however, increased its economic and military strength, thanks to the political and military leadership provided by able bureaucrats and military leaders.

Shilla, in alliance with the Tang forces, destroyed first Paekche in 663 and then Koguryo in 668, thus unifying approximately two-thirds of the Korean Peninsula. When Koguryo fell, its territory in western Manchuria was taken over by China, which established a puppet state named "Lesser Koguryo" in that area. Koguryo's eastern territory in both Manchuria and northeast Korea was invaded by nomads named Khitans and Jurchens. However, a Koguryo general who fled after the fall of Koguryo to eastern Manchuria with a large number of followers established a new kingdom of Chin in 698 (renamed Parhae in 713) whose territory covered the former Koguryo territories in eastern Manchuria and what is now northeastern Korea.

Shilla was able to prevent the reestablishment of Chinese control in the Korean Peninsula, but it encountered growing internal problems, and in 892 a rebel leader established "Later Paekche" in the former Paekche territory in the southwestern region of the Korean Peninsula while another rebel established "Later Koguryo" in 898 in the central region. Once again Korea entered into a brief period of division, known to historians as the "Later Three Kingdoms."

During the earlier Three Kingdoms period, an agricultural economy developed rapidly in the southern region. At the same time, Chinese cultural influence grew in Korea as Buddhism, first introduced in the fourth century, flourished in Paekche and Shilla. As Chinese influence increased, the political system of the Korean kingdoms evolved into a centralized bureaucratic rule under the monarchy, mirroring that of China. This political change also brought about social changes, establishing a new class structure dominated by the aristocracy. While Confucian learning spread, leading to the rise of educational institutions and scholarship, Buddhism also developed rapidly, bringing new art, architecture, crafts, music, dance, and scholarship. Thus, Korea became a cultural satellite of China.

The Koryo Peroid

In 918, Wang Kon, a general of the Kingdom of Later Koguryo, rebelled against his lord and, after overthrowing Later Koguryo, established his own dynasty and a new kingdom named Koryo with its capital at Song'ak (now Kaesong). Soon after the last king of Shilla surrendered to Koryo in 935, Koryo conquered Later Paekche in 936, reunifying Korea, this time without the aid of a foreign power. Gradually, Koryo extended its territory up to the Yalu River region in the west and near Hamhung in the east. After incorporating Cheju Island into the kingdom, Koryo ruled the entire Korean Peninsula except the northeastern region from the early 12th century.

The Koryo dynasty adopted the Chinese model of political structure, including the executive organ called the Secretariat of State Affairs, which had six boards (ministries). It also adopted the Tang code as well as the civil examination system to select qualified civil and military officials into the centralized bureaucracy. With the adoption of a new land system, farmlands were distributed to meritorious persons, and civil and military officials of high rank were given stipend lands, creating a new pattern of absentee landlordism. Meanwhile, a social structure emerged with a new landed gentry class at the top, which was cushioned by a class of petty functionaries in the central and local bureaucracies. The commoner class included the artisans, the merchants, and the peasants (*paekchong*). At the bottom were the low-born (*ch'onmin*), a class that included mostly slaves and domestic servants.

While the Koryo dynasty nurtured Confucian learning and scholarship, establishing many new educational institutions, it nevertheless made Buddhism the state religion and contributed toward the further development of Buddhist culture in Korea. However, it also encouraged a harmonious relationship between Buddhism and the native shamanistic religion. A significant cultural and technical innovation was the production of good quality wooden printing blocks, printing many books, including the 81,137-page *Tripitaka Koreana* (*Koryo Taejanggyong*) in 1251. Among the many history books published were the *History of the Three Kingdoms* (*Samguk sagi*) by Kim Pu-sik and others in 1145 and that of Monk Ilyon entitled *Memorabilia of the Three Kingdoms* (*Samgak yusa*) in 1281. These are the first written accounts of the history of the Korean peoples produced in the peninsula itself.

The Korean Peninsula suffered Khitan invasions in 993 and 1018 and a Jurchen attack in 1104. Meanwhile a power struggle between the civil and military officials in the 12th century led to the rise of the military dictatorship of the Ch'oe clan in the late 12th century. This, together with numerous slave and peasant uprisings, weakened the political structure and brought about the decline of the Koryo dynasty. The most serious threat to the Koryo dynasty occurred in the 13th century when the Mongols invaded Korea several times between 1231 and 1270, making the country a vassal to the Mongol empire. When the Koryo court surrendered to the Mongols, a rebellion of Korean military units called Three Elite Patrols (*Sambyolch'o*) erupted against both the Koryo court and the Mongols. The rebels fled from Kanghwa Island to the island of Chindo, off the southwest tip of the peninsula, but they were again forced to flee to Cheju Island. There they made their last stand in 1273.

The Mongol invasions, and the failure to deal with them, destroyed the legitimacy of the Koryo dynasty. But in the fighting, countless cultural properties such as temples, pagodas, books, and wooden printing blocks were also lost. Much property was destroyed. In what turned out to be the two futile attempts of the Mongols to invade Japan in 1274 and 1281, Korea lost several thousand sailors, soldiers, and skilled craftsmen.

The Yi Dynasty

In 1388, a Koryo general, Yi Song-gye, who subscribed to an anti-Mongol and a pro-Ming (China) policy, carried out a coup, taking control of a government already in disarray. When he met opposition to his reform measures, he overthrew the Koryo dynasty and established his own Yi dynasty (1392–1910). The kingdom was renamed *Chosun*. The capital was moved from Songdo (now Kaesong) to Seoul, to a site chosen because of its central and defensible position. Conquering the northeastern region of Korea, the Yi dynasty brought the entire Korean Peninsula under its control and strengthened its national defense. However, the Yi dynasty maintained Korea's vassal links to China, where the native Ming dynasty had overthrown the Mongol Yuan dynasty in 1368. These links would continue under the Manchu Qing, which overthrew the Ming dynasty in 1644.

The Yi dynasty established an elaborate bureaucracy completely patterned after the Chinese model, introduced many new laws, adopted neo-Confucianism as a state creed, and promoted educational development for Confucian learning. It fully adopted the Chinese civil examination system and reconstructed the social structure of Korea. The

kingdom was divided into eight provinces governed by the central bureaucracy in Seoul through provincial governments. A Privy Council
and State Council headed the central bureaucracy; the latter was the executive branch of the central government. This had six boards (ministries) of Personnel, Rites, Revenue, Punishment, Public Works, and
Military. The Office of the Inspector-General and the Office of the Censors played important roles in controlling the behavior of the monarchy,
the bureaucracy, and the bureaucrats. The top military organ was the
Five Military Commands Headquarters.

The social structure of Yi dynasty Korea was similar to that of the
Koryo period. The upper class was called *yangban*, which included
high-ranking civil and military officials (scholar-gentry known as
sadaebu) and their families. Petty functionaries in the central and local
government were called the "middle people" (*chung'in*); the commoners were called *sangmin* or *sang'in*, a class which included the free
peasants, the artisans, and the merchants in that social order; and at the
bottom was the class of low born (*ch'onmin*) people. As before, the last
group included slaves, domestic servants, and others who were engaged
in unclean or undesirable professions such as butchers, undertakers, and
public entertainers.

With the adoption of Neo-Confucianism as a state creed, the Yi dynasty rejected the Buddhism that had been favored under Koryo. Now
Buddhism was relegated to be the religion of the rural masses. The
monasteries with their monks and nuns were banished from the cities,
to be established in remote mountainous areas. Shamanism, widely
practiced by the people, was allowed some tolerance. Even at court, it
was not unknown for the royal ladies to consult the shamans, whatever
the official line might be. Along with the creation of the Korean alphabet (*Han'gul*) in the middle of the 15th century, the government of the
Yi dynasty brought about a tremendous cultural upsurge. Scholarship
was encouraged, as was the creation of educational institutions from the
primary to university levels for Chinese and Confucian studies. Meanwhile, folk culture also flourished, as new forms of poetry (*sijo*), genre
painting, and popular literature developed rapidly.

However, serious political instability developed. There were several
causes: power struggles between the monarch and the bureaucracy controlled by the Confucian scholar-officials known as *sadaebu*, several
purges of certain scholars carried out by the kings in the late 15th and

early 16th centuries, and factional strife between several politically ambitious groups of scholars. Korea also suffered heavily from the Japanese invasions ("seven-years' war") of the 1592–1598 period and from Manchu invasions in 1627 and 1636. Numerous rebellions and uprisings in the 17th century created serious economic and social problems from which the Korean government found it hard to recover. Two reform-minded monarchs, Yongjo (1724–1776) and Chongjo (1776–1800) adopted reform measures, including tax reform, but they were unable to restore national strength after the disastrous Japanese and Manchu wars, and they could not reestablish political morality and social stability.

This unrest continued into the next century. Popular uprisings occurred in 1811–1812 in the northwest and in 1862 in the southern region. The various reform measures proposed by a new breed of Confucianists known as *Sirhak* ("Practical learning") scholars in the 18th and early 19th centuries fell upon the deaf ears of conservative Neo-Confucian scholars and policy makers.

Korea was thus in a hopeless state when a young boy was put on the throne in 1864 as King Kojong, succeeding an uncle who died without an heir. The boy-king's father was selected to be his regent with the title of *Taewon'gun*. The regent was not only ambitious to strengthen his son's monarchical power but also to recover the prestige and glory of the Yi dynasty. Therefore, he launched various reform measures and made plans to reconstruct palace buildings that had been destroyed by the Japanese during 1592–1598. However, these reform measures antagonized reactionary Confucian scholars and conservative officials, and new taxes and coinage antagonized the commoners. In the end, he was forced to relinquish the regency in 1873, leaving his inept son under the shadow of his wife, Queen Min, and other ladies and their relatives in the court.

From the 1850s onward, Korea, described by some in the West as the "hermit kingdom," was under pressure from the Western powers to open its doors for trade. But it was Japan, itself newly opened by Western pressure in the 1850s, that forced Korea to establish a new relationship by signing a diplomatic and commercial treaty in 1876. The signing of this treaty was followed by the conclusion of diplomatic and commercial treaties between Korea and the United States in 1882 and with other Western powers in the following years. But while the treaties treated Korea as though it was an independent state, there remained ambiguity about the relationship between Korea and China, ambiguity that the Western countries sometimes contributed to, since they regularly consulted China on Korean affairs.

The opening of Korea to the West brought forth a group of nationalist reform advocates who were collectively called *Kaehwadang,* or the "party of the Progressives." The king, who became fond of the Americans, was willing to adopt a new policy and modernize his kingdom. Thus, a new era of national reconstruction began after 1881. However, the growing power struggle between conservative and progressive officials, together with increasing international rivalries among the Western powers in Korea, led to serious political disturbances and social problems. Among these were a military insurrection in 1882, an attempted coup d'etat carried out by the Progressives in 1884, and the Tonghak Uprising, whose adherents were a mixture of a religiously rebellious group and the poverty-stricken and socially mistreated people, including the peasants, in 1893–1894.

The first serious international conflict that developed in Korea was that between China and Japan. China refused to disclaim suzerainty over Korea and recognize it as a completely sovereign and independent nation. The Japanese challenged both Chinese political claims and China's economic position in Korea, leading eventually to the Sino–Japanese War of 1894–1895. After removing Chinese domination over Korea, the Japanese in turn increased their encroachment on the peninsula, leading the Korean government to seek Russian aid.

Korea's growing ties with Russia increased Japan's apprehension for its national security in the face of growing Russian expansionism in Manchuria and Korea. At this juncture, the Independence Club and other reform advocates emerged, preaching self-oriented national regeneration, cultural modernization, and the strengthening of national independence. However, the Korean government was both unwilling and unable to adopt such policies. Russo–Japanese friction increased, culminating in the Russo–Japanese War of 1904–1905. Like the earlier Sino–Japanese War, much of the fighting took place on Korean soil, allowing the Japanese increasingly to establish domination over the peninsula. In 1905 when Japan defeated Russia, Korea became a Japanese protectorate, with a Japanese Residency-General (*Tokanfu*) superimposed on the Korean government. In 1910, after the assassination in 1909 of the Resident-General and Japanese elder statesman, Ito Hirobumi, by a Korean, Japan annexed Korea, ending the rule of the Yi dynasty as well as any hopes for Korean independence

The Japanese Colonial Period

During the Japanese colonial period (1910–1945), Korea was ruled by a central government named the Government-General of Korea (*Chosen Sotokufu*). This was effectively a military bureaucracy normally headed by a Japanese army general on active duty. Despite the Meiji Emperor's Imperial Rescript on Annexation, which promised the extension of the "benevolent rule" of the Japanese emperor to Korea, the Japanese imposed military rule there, referring to Korea as a *gaichi* ("outer land"), and treated it as a colony rather than an integral part of the empire. The Koreans were given no constitutional protection and had no voting rights or voice in politics. The Japanese referred to the Koreans as *senjin*, a derogatory Japanese term for "the people of Chosun." Social integration between the Koreans and the Japanese was nonexistent and intermarriage between them was rare.

In the beginning of their colonial rule, the Japanese made vigorous efforts to suppress and stamp out Korean nationalism. To achieve this end, they closed down all Korean newspaper presses and magazine companies, shut down hundreds of private schools that were allegedly engaged in anti-Japanese activity, outlawed the teaching of Korean history, confiscated all Korean history books, and forbade the publication of nationalistic books and magazines. After this, they proceeded to appropriate farms and forests, forcing hundreds of thousands of Korean farmers into tenancy agreements.

After suffering humiliating Japanese colonial rule for 10 years, in 1919, the Koreans launched independence movements at home and abroad. In February 1919, Korean students in Japan wrote a "Korean Declaration of Independence" and began a campaign calling for an independent Korea. Shortly after, 33 important figures in Korea promulgated another "Declaration of Independence," which led the Koreans of all classes, sexes, and ages to demonstrate their desire for independence in a peaceful manner. The culmination of these developments was the March First Movement (*Samil* or 3–1 movement) in 1919 for national independence. Over two million Koreans were reported to have participated throughout the country in demonstrations against the Japanese.

The Japanese response was fierce. The March First Movement was crushed and its leaders, along with thousands of those who participated in the demonstrations, were imprisoned. Several hundred people were killed, and hundreds of nationalists were forced to flee from their native land. In April 1919, a group of Korean nationalists in Shanghai in China established a "Provisional Government of Korea" with Dr. Syngman Rhee, once a political prisoner under the Yi dynasty, then in the United States, as premier (later president). After that, in cooperation with other nationalists in Korea and elsewhere, they continued to sustain Korea's national liberation movement.

The efforts made by the Korean nationalists at home, including students, were fruitless, but the relentless resistance that the Japanese continued to encounter, together with some degree of international pressure, convinced them that Korea could not be ruled by force and intimidation alone. The harsh rule of the early years was relaxed somewhat after 1920, and Koreans were allowed to establish newspapers and other publications. Some efforts were also made to associate more Koreans with the Government-General, but senior positions at all levels of the bureaucracy continued to be reserved for Japanese. During the colonial period, the modernization of Korea began. It was a process to which Koreans made both voluntary and involuntary contributions, as did various Japanese policies and plans. First of all, the Japanese replaced old laws and administrative and judicial systems with new ones. They also developed the Korean economy so as to strengthen the power of their empire. The result was the appearance of modern financial and commercial institutions, along with a variety of industrial establishments. Although inadequate, education was transformed, as both public and private schools grew in number. Communication and transportation systems were modernized, with the installation of telegraph and telephone networks, construction of more railways and highways, and improvement in harbor facilities.

However, Koreans paid a high price for those changes. Japanese capitalist firms (*zaibatsu*) ruthlessly exploited natural and human resources. The Japanese appropriated rich farmlands and forests, and increasing rice production only helped the Japanese rather than the Koreans as an increasing amount of rice was shipped to Japan. Korean workers' wages were low, working hours were long, and working conditions were poor. If Korea was "thriving," as the Japanese said, it was "thriving" only to enrich Japan. Korean youth lagged far behind the Japanese in regard to educational opportunities. It was Japanese policy not to educate too many Koreans or train Korean scientists and technicians. Indeed, the lack of educational opportunity kept the rate of illiteracy as high as 75 percent even at the end of the Japanese colonial period.

Then, in 1937, the Japanese Government-General in Korea adopted various programs and policies to Japanize the Koreans in order to make them "loyal imperial subjects." To do so, it launched what is called the *Kominka undo* ("Movement for the Conversion of the Koreans to be Imperial Subjects"). Koreans were forced to adopt Japanese-style family and given names, memorize and recite the "Pledge of the Imperial Subjects," and speak only Japanese in public. The teaching of the Korean language was first discouraged, and in 1938 Korean language instruction was abolished altogether. Even the ministers of churches were ordered to deliver their sermons only in Japanese. The Koreans were forced to abandon their traditional white clothes and to become followers of the Japanese Shinto religion. In essence, this was an attempt to wipe out Korea's ethnic identity and nationalist consciousness.

Without giving any political rights and social equality to the Koreans, the Japanese mobilized more than two million workers after 1937 and shipped about half of them to factories and mines in Japan. Tens of thousands of Korean youths as well as college students in Korea and Japan were drafted into the Japanese army and navy during World War II, and several thousand Korean women were forced to go to the war fronts in China and elsewhere as "comfort women" to provide sexual service to Japanese troops. Little wonder then why most Koreans remained anti-Japanese to the bitter end as the savage war between the Allies and Japan was being waged in the Pacific area.

Liberation, Partition, the Allied Occupation, and the Birth of the Republic of Korea

In November 1943, the United States, Great Britain, and China held a conference in the Egyptian capital, Cairo, on the progress of World War II. In a communiqué released on 1 December 1943, they stated that "mindful of the enslavement of the people of Korea" under Japanese colonial rule, the three Allies had resolved "in due course Korea shall become free and independent." The Soviet Union later acceded to this Cairo Agreement.

As agreed at a further allied meeting at Yalta with the United States and Great Britain in February 1945, the Soviet Union declared war on Japan on 8 August 1945. At once, Soviet troops moved into Korea, and within a short time, most of the northern half of Korea was under their occupation. At this juncture, the American government proposed the partition of Korea into two military operational zones along the 38th parallel line—the area south of the line as a United States zone and the northern area as a Soviet zone—in order to prevent the Soviet occupation of the entire Korean Peninsula. The Soviet Union accepted this arrangement, even though it gave the Americans control of Seoul, the capital.

Realizing in early August 1945 that the emperor was ready to capitulate to the Allies, the Japanese Governor-General in Korea became concerned about the safety of the Japanese in Korea. As a result, he made an attempt to establish a transitional government in Korea in the hands of a group of prominent Korean leaders, hoping this would prevent possible anti-Japanese retaliation and allow time to make arrangements for safe repatriation of Japanese subjects. After failing to secure the cooperation of a right-wing nationalist leader, the Japanese turned to Yo Un-hyong, a well-known left-wing nationalist leader, who had formed a secret "Alliance for Korean Independence" in 1944.

When approached by the Japanese, Yo laid down five conditions before the transfer of major governmental functions to his organization in order to preserve law and order, to prevent political chaos, and to establish a Korean government according to the wishes of the people. These conditions were (1) immediate release of all political prisoners; (2) noninterference by the Japanese in his activities for national reconstruction; (3) freedom to organize student and youth corps; (4) freedom to organize labor unions; and (5) guarantee of a three-month supply of food.

Yo's conditions were met on 15 August, the day Japan surrendered to the Allies, accepting the unconditional surrender terms included in the Potsdam Declaration of July 1945. On 16 August, with acceptance of his conditions by the Japanese, Yo organized the "Committee for the Preparation of National Reconstruction" (CPNR), which immediately began to function as a government with its own public security units.

The CPNR organized provincial, district, and local committees to maintain law and order.

Learning on 2 September that the Allies' plan was to partition Korea into two military operational zones, the CPNR called a "National Assembly" of some 1,000 delegates. On 6 September, this body established the "Korean People's Republic" and a cabinet. Dr. Syngman Rhee, still in exile in the United States, was appointed chairman, and Yo Un-hyong was appointed vice-chairman of the Republic. Ho Hon, a prominent leftist, was named premier. Most cabinet ministers appointed were well-known right-wing nationalists.

In the northern half of the peninsula, Soviet forces recognized the legitimacy of the People's Republic. The American occupation authorities, arriving in Korea on 7 September 1945, the day after its formation, did not. After accepting the surrender from the Japanese Governor-General, General John R. Hodge, commander of United States occupation forces in Korea, outlawed the People's Republic and established the United States Army Military Government in Korea (USAMGIK). Meanwhile, exiled political leaders returned to Korea from China and the United States. In the northern half of the peninsula, a contingent of Korean communist troops under Kim Il-sung arrived with the Soviet forces, followed by Korean communist troops from the Yan'an (Yenan) area in China in late December.

In the south, the freedom of assembly, speech, religion, and the press granted by the American military government in the fall of 1945 resulted in the proliferation of political parties of various political and economic orientations and many social and labor organizations of various ideological persuasions, as well as newspapers and magazines. Among the major political parties that emerged in the South were the Korean Democratic Party, the Korean Independence Party, and the National Council for Rapid Realization of Korean Independence, all of which represented the conservative nationalist camp, while the Korean Communist Party and the People's Party represented the leftist camp. In the North, there were similar developments, leading to the rise of a branch of the Korean Communist Party as well as the right-wing nationalists' Korean Democratic Party and *Ch'ong'udang*, a political/ social organization of the religious group Ch'ondo-gyo (formally *Tonghak*). However, in early 1946, the Soviet forces and Korean communists broke up these right-wing organizations.

Although the right-wing groups were more concerned with political matters, the communists were quick to take advantage of a favorable situation for the promotion of socialist and labor movements, and they established subordinate groups of the Korean Communist Party such as the General Council of Labor Unions (*Ch'onp'yong*) in November 1945, the General Federation of Farmers' Unions (*Chon'nong*) in December 1945, the General Alliance of Korean Women (*Chosun Punyo Tonghaeng*), and the Alliance of Korean Youth (*Chosun Minju Ch'ongnyon Tongmaeng*, or *Minch'ong*) in the spring of 1946. All of these leftist organizations in the South were broken up in 1947 when the American military government cracked down on them for their illegal activities. The right-wing organizations in the South belatedly formed labor unions in late 1945. In March 1946, they formed the General Alliance of the Laborers for Rapid Realization of Korean Independence.

From 16–26 December 1945, the foreign ministers of the United States, Great Britain, and the Soviet Union met in Moscow and adopted the Moscow Agreement. This provided for the formation of a U.S.–USSR Joint Commission, consisting of the occupation authorities of the two powers, for the purpose of establishing, in consultation with Korean leaders, an independent nation of Korea and its government. They also agreed to put this Korean government under a five-year trusteeship of the four Allies (the United States, Great Britain, China, and the Soviet Union).

When the news of the Moscow Agreement reached Korea on 29 December 1945, all Koreans, including the communists, opposed the trusteeship plan, and violent antitrusteeship demonstrations swept the country. Then, suddenly, the communists in both zones changed their stand in favor of the plan, polarizing the Korean people; bloody clashes between the Rightists and the Leftists ensued in both zones. In March 1946, in the midst of a chaotic political situation, the U.S.–USSR Joint Commission was formed to carry out the Moscow Agreement. The first session of the Joint Commission was held in Seoul in March–May 1946, but it was unable to achieve its primary objective when the Soviets refused to talk with the right-wing leaders, condemning them as "undemocratic" because of their opposition to the trusteeship plan. It became clear to the United States that the Soviet Union intended to establish a national Korean government dominated by the leftists, if not completely in their hands. Witnessing the difficulties which the Joint

Commission had faced, in October 1946 Kim Kyu-shik, a moderate nationalist, and Yo Un-hyong, a moderate leftist, organized the Coalition Committee for Cooperation between the Rightists and the Leftists in order to unite the strength of the middle groups and establish "a democratic transitional government" in accordance with the Moscow Agreement. In May 1947, the second session of the Joint Commission met in P'yongyang after a lengthy recess, but it failed to achieve any agreement, and in June the Commission's business was suspended indefinitely.

Realizing that the establishment of Korean unity and a national government by the Joint Commission was a remote possibility, the American occupation authorities adopted new plans for "Koreanization" of the American military government. In December 1946, the South Korean Interim Legislative Assembly (SKILA) replaced Korean advisory "Democratic Council," which had been set up in February 1946 by Gen. Hodge. Then in June 1947 the South Korean Interim Government (SKIG) was established to assist the American military administration. Meanwhile, the Soviet forces in the North, after arresting nationalist leaders, proceeded to establish a puppet regime under Kim Il-sung and began to implement economic measures to produce a socialist North Korea.

In September 1947, unilaterally discarding the Moscow Plan, the United States placed the Korean question before the United Nations. In November 1947, the United Nations General Assembly adopted a resolution establishing the United Nations Temporary Commission on Korea (UNTCOK). UNTCOK was authorized to conduct a national election in Korea to create a national government for the whole peninsula to end the Allied occupation.

This United Nations decision on Korea was welcomed by the United States and by most people in Korea, but the Soviet Union did not accept it and would not allow UNTCOK to function north of the 38th parallel. It soon became apparent that the United Nations plan would not work in the whole of Korea, and UNTCOK adopted an alternative plan to hold elections in those areas where it was possible, namely in South Korea only. It was assumed by UNTCOK that UN-sponsored and supervised elections would be held in the North in the near future, that a National Assembly created by two-thirds of the Korean people in the first democratic elections in Korea would represent the entire country, that the government would be that of all Korea, and that the people in the North would elect their representatives to the national assembly later.

While the right-wing nationalists in Rhee's camp welcomed this plan, moderate and progressive nationalists, such as Kim Kyu-shik, as well as extreme right-wing nationalists, such as Kim Ku, vehemently opposed it, fearing that it would turn the temporary division of Korea into a permanent political partition. In an effort to prevent such a development, they visited North Korea in April 1948 and talked with the communist leaders there. They failed, however, to achieve their objective, which was for Koreans themselves to solve the Korean question, primarily because of Kim Il-sung's refusal to cooperate.

The Soviet authorities in the North had already begun to transfer power to the Koreans and to introduce a Soviet-style government in North Korea. The North Korean Provisional People's Committee had been established in February 1946 as the central authority in the North and a People's Assembly was established in February 1947 as North Korea's legislative body. Unlike their counterparts in the South, these administrative and legislative organs exercised great authority. In 1948, a People's Army was formed in the North.

On 10 May 1948, a month after a communist-inspired rebellion broke out on Cheju Island, United Nations-sponsored elections were held in the South, electing members of a Constituent Assembly. About 7.5 million people, or 75 percent of the eligible voters, cast their ballots in the first democratic elections (although bloodshed accompanied the process) and elected 198 of 200 representatives to the National Assembly for the South, while 100 seats were left vacant to be occupied in the future by the representatives elected in the North.

The Constituent Assembly drew up a democratic constitution for the Republic of Korea. It elected Syngman Rhee as the first president of the Republic and Yi Si-yong as vice president for a four-year term of office. On 15 August 1948 the Republic and its government were inaugurated. Rhee took the oath of office as president, and the U.S. occupation of South Korea came to an end.

Meanwhile, in the latter part of August, the communists in the North held an election and established a new Supreme People's Assembly, which adopted a constitution, named the northern half of Korea as the Democratic People's Republic of Korea, and elected Kim Il-sung premier of North Korea. The communist Republic and its government were inaugurated on 9 September, ending the Soviet occupation of the North.

The rival regimes in divided Korea made conflicting claims for political legitimacy, each declaring that the entire Korean Peninsula was its national territory. South Korea's claim to legitimacy was based on the fact that the Republic of Korea was established by a majority of the Korean people under a United Nations resolution and UN supervision, and that the United Nations General Assembly recognized it in November 1948 as "the only and lawful government in Korea." North Korea, for its part, claimed that "all the Korean people" had established the Democratic People's Republic of Korea by elections North and South. It was claimed that in addition to the elections held in the North, underground elections were also held in the South. These "elections" had returned 360 delegates to the 572-member Supreme People's Assembly, in a turnout of 77.8 percent of the eligible voters in the South. Needless to say, no such elections had been held in the South.

The growing distrust and antagonism between the United States and the Soviet Union, which created the Cold War between East and West, together with the inability of the Allies to carry out their previous agreements, led to the establishment of two separate states in Korea with conflicting ideologies and systems, opening a tragic chapter in the history of the Korean people.

The Republic of Korea

The history of South Korea began in a turbulent domestic and international environment, and the many tragic events that took place in the Korean Peninsula shaped the particular character of South Korean society as it is today. The original aim of building a democratic country was soon overwhelmed by many unfortunate circumstances. These included the traditional bureaucratism that the government exercised, the Korean War, and the lack of experience in self-rule. The South Korean people's desire for democracy took a long time to be fulfilled; it was only in the 1990s, after a hard struggle, that South Korea could be described as a democracy. Despite that, various efforts made by the government and the people eventually brought about remarkable progress in cultural, economic, and social development, dramatically modernizing South Korean society.

The First Republic, August 1948–April 1960

The foundation of the Republic had hardly settled down when a communist-inspired military rebellion broke out on 19 October 1948 in the Yosu and Sunch'on areas in South Cholla Province, followed by another in Taegu, North Kyongsang Province, on 2 November. Both were crushed but they demoralized the nation and encouraged the repressive character of the government. Democratic aspirations suffered as the government became increasingly autocratic with the passage of the National Security Law in November 1948. Despite the growing fear of further communist uprisings and possible North Korean invasion, the United States troop withdrawal from South Korea was completed in June 1949, leaving behind an infant South Korean defense force of some 50,000 men. Although a group of 500 American military advisers remained in South Korea to help train South Korean troops, the latter were inadequately equipped, having neither fighter aircraft nor bombers, nor tanks, nor naval craft. They had been given only training aircraft and ships, and they were equipped with light arms, mostly those that had been surrendered by Japanese troops. The newly established Officers' Training School was yet to function fully, and the complete annihilation of communist guerrillas in the mountainous south central regions was yet to be achieved. As the new nation faced this difficult situation, tension mounted. An army officer's assassination of the rightist leader, Kim Ku, and the arrest in October of some 16 National Assemblymen under the recently passed National Security Law for alleged collaboration with communists, made the situation worse.

Although there was little publicity, military clashes between troops of North and South Korea had been taking place along the 38th parallel as both sides jockeyed for position. On 25 June 1950, a Sunday, North Korea launched a surprise attack at 04.00 hours. Some 80,000 well-trained North Korean troops, supported by Soviet-built tanks, crossed the 38th parallel and invaded South Korea to annex what North Koreans called "the southern half of the republic." Many South Korean army units were on weekend leave and were totally unprepared for the sudden attack. Three days later, the North Koreans captured Seoul and pushed southward. Neither the South Korea army nor small units of American troops, hastily sent back to Korea from Japan, were able to check the advance of the aggressors.

Responding to an appeal made by the United States, the United Nations Security Council, in the absence of the Soviet Union, condemned North Korea as an aggressor and organized a United Nations' force, consisting of troops contributed by 16 member nations, to assist South Korea. Meanwhile, North Korean troops occupied most of South Korea, leaving only the southeastern corner of the country along the Naktong River—the Pusan perimeter—unoccupied. After the arrival of United Nations' troops and the formation of the United Nations' Command (UNC) under General Douglas MacArthur, UN forces launched a counterattack, beginning with a seaborne landing at Inch'on in September 1950. At the same time, a breakout was organized from the Pusan perimeter. Seoul was recovered on 28 September, and the invaders were pushed back beyond the 38th parallel. United Nations troops then advanced into North Korea in pursuit of the fleeing enemy in early October, capturing the North Korean capital, P'yongyang, on 19 October. On 21 November, advance units of the United Nations forces reached the Chinese border on the Yalu River.

The People's Republic of China (PRC), established in October 1949, had begun life with a strong suspicion of United States' motives, deriving from American support for the Chinese Nationalists in the civil war. Tension between China and the U.S. increased at the outbreak of the Korean War when the U.S. announced that its Seventh Fleet would patrol the Taiwan Straits, thus preventing any attempt by either the PRC or the Chinese Nationalists now established on Taiwan to invade the other. After the Inch'on landing, the Chinese sent signals that if United Nations forces approached the Yalu, China would intervene. MacArthur discounted these signals, but in November 1950, China sent troops to the Korean Peninsula to save North Korea and to protect its border. By late November 1950, some 250,000 troops of the Chinese People's Liberation Army had crossed the Yalu. Officially described in the Chinese media as the "Chinese People's Volunteers" (CPV), they now struck hard at the United Nations forces.

MacArthur panicked, and the UN forces began a fast retreat. By December 1950, South Korean and UN troops had withdrawn from the North, and Seoul fell to the communist forces for the second time in January. Over a million Chinese troops participated in the Korean War, while Soviet pilots, in Chinese or North Korean uniforms, joined in air battles against the UN forces. The UN forces, under the local command of General Matthew Ridgeway, regrouped and mounted a counterattack, retaking Seoul on 12 March 1951. Thereafter, although many fierce battles would be fought, the war settled down in stalemate roughly along the 38th parallel, where it had begun.

At this point, the Soviet government called for truce negotiations. Talks began at Kaesong behind the North Korean lines in July 1951 but failed to end the fighting. They were later transferred to P'anmunjom, on the 38th parallel. Hostilities continued until an armistice agreement was finally signed at P'anmunjom on 27 July 1953 between the UNC and the North Koreans and the CPV. The South Korean government refused to sign the armistice, but did agree to abide by its terms. The 1953 cease-fire line became the military demarcation line, a new boundary between North and South Korea, with a narrow demilitarized zone (DMZ) separating the two countries. The war caused more than a million casualties in South Korea, as well as enormous property damage, and political and social conditions became chaotic as economic hardships multiplied. On 15 August 1953, the South Korean government returned to the war-devastated capital city of Seoul.

During the war, President Rhee and his Liberal Party, formed in 1951, acted high-handedly toward their opponents in the National Assembly. The Assembly refused to approve a series of constitutional amendments proposed by the government in January 1952, leading to a political crisis known as the "Pusan political disturbance" of May 1952. After proclaiming martial law in the Pusan area on 25 May, Rhee and his party forced the National Assembly in July 1952 to pass a constitutional amendment bill, instituting a direct, popular election of the president and the vice president.

Under the amended constitution, Rhee was reelected by popular vote in 1952, but the vice presidential candidate nominated by the Liberal Party was defeated by an aged, independent candidate, who was helped by the police under a secret instruction given by Rhee himself. In November 1954, the Liberal Party–dominated National Assembly adopted another series of constitutional amendments by dubious means, providing exemption to the incumbent president from the two-term limitation in office and abolishing the office of prime minister.

In the 1956 presidential election, a new opposition Democratic Party, founded in 1955, nominated candidates for the offices of president and vice president. The sudden death of its presidential candidate, Shin Ik-hui, assured victory for Rhee, but the Democratic Party's candidate for the vice presidency, Chang Myon, widely known as John Chang, defeated the Liberal candidate. Encouraged by this, Cho Pong-am, a socialist and former minister of agriculture, formed the Progressive Party in November.

As corruption among government officials and members of the Liberal Party became rampant and repression by the police increased, a widespread desire for change grew, particularly among the urban voters. In the general elections for the National Assembly in 1958, the Democratic Party increased its seats substantially. Aware of the danger of losing its absolute control, the Liberal Party repealed the local autonomy law and passed a new National Security Law, promulgated on 26 December 1958, so as to strengthen the government's control.

In the fourth presidential election, held in March 1960, Rhee and Yi Ki-bung ran as the presidential and vice presidential candidates of the Liberal Party. Three weeks before the election, the Democratic Party presidential candidate, Cho Pyong-ok, died while receiving medical treatment in the United States, once again assuring the election of Dr. Rhee. However, there were doubts about whether Yi would be elected. As a result, the ruling party resorted to corrupt and fraudulent means to elect Yi, who defeated Chang Myon, the vice presidential candidate of the Democratic Party, by a large margin. Popular reaction against the autocracy of President Rhee and the corrupt and fraudulent practices of the administration and the LP exploded immediately after the March election of 1960. Fierce student riots erupted throughout the country, particularly in the Pusan–Masan area, producing casualties among students and leading up to the Student Uprising of 19 April 1960 in Seoul. These incidents combined with mounting pressure from the U.S. forced President Rhee and his cabinet to resign *en masse* on 26 April.

The Second Republic, August 1960–May 1961

A caretaker government was set up under Foreign Minister Ho Chong, and in mid-June the National Assembly adopted constitutional amendments. In July, general elections for the new upper House of Councilors and the House of Representatives were held. In August, both houses of the National Assembly elected Yun Po-son as president and Chang Myon as prime minister, and the Second Republic emerged.

The Second Republic was handicapped from the start. It had no mandate from the people and both President Yun and Prime Minister Chang lacked determination and political skills. The Chang administration was indecisive in dealing with former leaders of the Rhee regime and seemed too tolerant toward left-wing radicals. It was unable to cope effectively with the ideological and social cleavage between political and social groups and failed to gain the confidence of the people. The ruling Democratic Party was badly split and it had no solutions for economic and social problems. Meanwhile, new student demonstrations erupted as left-wing influence grew among the students. Campuses were severely disrupted as students and some radical faculty members demanded more control over university affairs. Student agitation for direct negotiations with North Korean students, aimed at reunification of the country, created more problems. The danger to national security increased, as shortages of food and jobs became more acute. These developments set the stage for a military takeover that would usher in another important period in Korean history.

The Military Rule, May 1961–December 1963

On 16 May 1961 a military coup, led by a small group of young, disgruntled army officers headed by Major General Park Chung-hee, overthrew the Second Republic. Those involved claimed that their aims were to protect the country from Communist threats and reconstruct its political, economic, and social systems, establishing a clean government and social justice; however, there were also grievances within the officer corps about slow rates of promotion as a result of the rapid promotion of young officers during the Korean War, and other such issues.

The Military Revolutionary Committee (MRC), which emerged on 16 May and took over the government, declared martial law, dissolved the National Assembly, forbade all political activity, banned student demonstrations, and imposed press censorship. President Yun was persuaded to remain in office as the Second Republic fell on 18 May. Thereupon, the MRC, headed by Lieutenant General Chang To-yong, army chief of staff, who had not participated in planning of the takeover but became chairman of the committee, issued six pledges, and on the following day, acting as a legislative body, it adopted the Law Concerning Extraordinary Measures for National Reconstruction.

In late May 1961, the MRC was renamed the *Supreme Council for National Reconstruction (SCNR),* which became the supreme lawmaking organ of the nation. A new executive branch (cabinet), headed by the chairman of the SCNR, and a new judicial branch also in the hands of the military were established at the same time. Meanwhile, a Korean Central Intelligence Agency (KCIA) was established. In theory, this was modeled on the United States Central Intelligence Agency, but from the start its remit included domestic politics as well as external threats. Although not specified, part of its role was to ensure that no other group of soldiers followed Park's example. In November 1961 the General Alliance of the Laborers for Rapid Realization of Independence and the National Council of Labor Unions, which had been organized in October 1960, were compulsorily merged with the General Federation of Korean Labor Unions (*Han'guk Noryon*).

In July 1961, General Park Chung-hee became chairman of the SCNR. In August, he announced that political activity would be permitted in early 1963 to pave the way for a return to civilian government. Meanwhile, the activities of the Political Purification Committee, established under the Political Purification Law of 16 March 1962, created much controversy. In a bitter political dispute over the law, President Yun resigned, whereupon Park became acting president. The constitution, amended by the SCNR, was presented to the people, and it was approved in a national referendum in late December 1962. Meanwhile, a Political Party Law was promulgated on 30 December 1962, permitting the revival of political activities by those not purged.

In January 1963, as the ban against political activity was removed, military factions formed the Democratic Republic Party (DRP), and nominated Park as its presidential candidate. When, in mid-March, the discovery of an alleged plot to overthrow the military junta was announced, the acting president announced that a plebiscite would be held on a four-year extension of military rule. However, following a strong negative reaction against this proposal, Park withdrew it, once again promising the restoration of civilian rule. In August, Park retired from the army and ran for the four-year-term presidency.

The opposition forces were split into four parties, and in the presidential election held in October 1963, this allowed Park to defeat former President Yun, who ran as the presidential candidate of the Civil Rule Party, by a narrow margin. Park's DRP also won a majority in the

National Assembly elections held in November 1963, giving former military junta members control over the new civilian government. With the inauguration of President Park on 17 December, the Third Republic began.

The Third Republic, December 1963–December 1972

Theoretically civilian government had been restored, ex-military men occupied all major positions and the National Assembly was completely dominated by the military-based DRP.

Although considerable economic progress was achieved under the two consecutive Five-Year Economic Development Plans (1962–1966 and 1967–1971), and social stability was restored, the Third Republic failed to promote democracy. In March and April 1964, large student demonstrations broke out in Seoul against the normalization negotiations with Japan. As a result, the government declared an emergency decree in the Seoul area in June. Despite violent opposition, the government signed the treaty with Japan on 22 June 1965, establishing formal diplomatic and commercial relations. Matters were made worse when the National Assembly, without the participation of the opposition lawmakers, passed a bill authorizing the dispatch of South Korean troops to South Vietnam under a United States–South Korean agreement signed on October 1964. Violent demonstrations against these government actions broke out, and the government declared martial law in the Seoul area again in August 1965.

In order to promote a parliamentary democracy, if not to weaken the power monopoly of the ruling DRP, the opposition leaders formed a new party named the New Korea Party (NKP) in May 1966. However, formation of two new parties late in 1966 by two prominent dissident groups allowed the ruling party to maintain its control. In February 1967, the NKP and the Masses Party were united into the New Democratic Party (NDP), which nominated Yun Po-son as its presidential candidate. But in the May 1967 presidential election, the incumbent president defeated Yun again, this time by a large margin, and the ruling party won a substantial majority of seats in the National Assembly elections of July 1967.

At this point, there occurred a series of events that provided the government with ample excuses to tighten its control over the country, as well as increasing the sense of insecurity in South Korea. The first was the announcement in July 1967 of the arrest of an alleged pro–North Korean espionage team consisting of over 100 members, whose main operational base was located in East Berlin. This was followed in January 1968 by the attempt by a North Korean commando team to assassinate President Park; the capture off the coast of North Korea of a United States intelligence ship, the USS *Pueblo,* by North Korean naval vessels; and the arrest of an underground espionage group of the phantom "Unification Revolutionary Party" in August 1968. Partly in response to these developments, in April 1968, the government formed a 2.5 million-man Homeland Reserve Forces and in September introduced military training for college students.

In addition, and despite strong opposition, the ruling party amended the constitution in mid-September 1969 allowing the incumbent president to run for a third term of office while the members of the opposition party were boycotting the National Assembly sessions. A national referendum held in October approved the amendment.

A calmer political atmosphere prevailed in 1970. In September, seven months after former president Yun Po-son departed from the NDP, Kim Dae-jung was nominated as its presidential candidate. In December, the National Assembly revised the foreign trade law, allowing trade with "non-hostile Socialist countries."

In the presidential election held in April 1971, President Park defeated Kim Dae-jung by what many felt was a suspiciously narrow margin. However, in the National Assembly elections held in May, the ruling DRP won a larger majority. Shortly after President Park took the oath of office on 1 July for his third term, the government adopted the New Community Movement Plan (*Saemual Undong*), designed to prevent too big a gap developing between the urban and rural areas.

Hostile student demonstrations continued to plague the government. Their continuation, and the continued talks between the Red Cross societies of North and South Korea (the talks began in September 1971), led the government to declare a state of national emergency on 6 December 1971. This, it was claimed, would help the nation better meet the rapidly changing domestic and international situations. Meanwhile, the withdrawal of South Korean troops from South Vietnam began in early December. On 26 December 1971, the National Assembly adopted the Special Measures Law on National Defense, giving extraordinary power to the president.

The secret negotiations conducted between Seoul and P'yongyang in early 1972 led to the issue of an identical statement by the two Korean governments on 4 July 1972, recording their agreement on a Korean reunification formula. This momentous statement announced the opening of a dialogue to achieve national unification by peaceful means without outside intervention. Because two successive Five-Year Economic Development Plans (1962–71) had laid a good foundation for economic development, the future of the nation seemed brighter both politically and economically.

However, the sudden changes in the international situation, following the Sino–American détente, the new development in North–South relations, and changes in United States Asian policy that implied less commitment to preserving Asian security provided the ruling party with a convenient pretext to perpetuate President Park's rule. As a result, the government proclaimed a national emergency decree on 17 October 1972, dissolved the National Assembly, and suspended the constitution. This coup d'état, effectively staged by Park against himself, became known as the October *Yushin* (revitalizing) coup. The government proposed new constitutional revisions, including one that provided for the indirect election of the president, on 17 October. These revisions were approved in a national referendum held on 21 November 1972.

Martial law was lifted in mid-December. The new electoral college, known as the National Conference for Unification (NCU), whose 2,350 members were elected by popular vote on 15 December, was formally established and duly elected President Park as the eighth president of the Republic.

The Fourth Republic, December 1972–October 1979

The Fourth Republic began with Park's inauguration on 27 December 1972, and the new Yushin Constitution was officially proclaimed on 30 December, followed by the promulgation of the new National Assembly Election Law and the Political Party Law.

The elections for the National Assembly held in February 1973 under the new election law gave the ruling DRP a majority. Meanwhile, a new political society named the Political Fraternal Society for Revitalizing Reform (*Yushin Chong'uhoe*, or *Yujonghoe*) was set up as a companion political body of the ruling party, and 73 of its members were elected by the NCU, on the president's recommendation, to serve a three-year term in the National Assembly under the new constitution. This gave the ruling party a guaranteed built-in majority.

Soon the Fourth Republic began to encounter domestic and foreign problems. In August 1973, the kidnapping of Kim Dae-jung from Tokyo to Seoul, supposedly by agents of the Korean CIA, led to widespread protests. Increased antigovernment agitation and demands for the abolition of the 1972 Yushin Constitution produced political instability in 1974. As well as domestic problems, the government faced increased diplomatic tension with Japan and the United States over both the kidnapping of Kim Dae-jung and its increasingly repressive measures against civil liberties.

Park's response was more repression. To cope with the situation, a series of Presidential Emergency Decrees banned all antigovernment activities and agitation for constitutional reform, but these only added to the general air of instability. In this tense situation, a pro-North Korean from Japan attempted to assassinate President Park as he was addressing the audience at the National Theater on 15 August 1974 (National Day), but killed Park's wife (Yuk Yong-su) instead.

In late August, some of the Emergency Decrees were lifted, but the NDP and other groups relentlessly pressed for constitutional reform and the release of political prisoners. While college students of some 18 universities were engaged in violent antigovernment and anti-Japanese demonstrations in September and October, *Tong-A Ilbo* newspaper reporters and a group of 101 writers issued a "Declaration for the Realization of Freedom of Speech and the Press." In late November some 71 dissident leaders, including former President Yun, formed the National Conference for Restoration of Democracy.

Despite the national referendum held in February 1975, which reaffirmed the Yushin Constitution by some 73 percent of the vote, and the release of those who had violated the presidential decrees soon after that, antigovernment demonstrations and the demand for the revision of the constitution continued unabated.

To meet this situation, Park issued Presidential Emergency Measures No. 7 of April and No. 9 of May 1975, which imposed further restrictions on the opponents of the 1972 Constitution, banned student demonstrations, and outlawed public defamation of the government. However, political turbulence persisted as many dissidents were imprisoned. In

March 1976, the three major opposition political leaders issued a joint statement entitled the "Democratic National Salvation Declaration." They demanded the abolition of the 1972 Constitution and the complete restoration of human and civil rights. Further student demonstrations followed.

There were more difficulties for the Korean government as a result of the disclosure by *The Washington Post* in October 1976 of illegal lobbying activity by a Korean businessman, Park Tong-son, in Washington, D.C., followed by the investigation of Park and other Koreans, including a former ambassador to the United States, by the U.S. House of Representatives in the spring of 1977. Meanwhile, the reelection of President Park by the new members of the NCU in December 1978 only made the situation worse as student unrest, supported by the opposition, caused greater political turmoil.

After the National Assembly elections held on 12 December 1978, President Park took the oath of office as the ninth president on December 27 and released some 1,000 political prisoners, including Kim Dae-jung. However, the voice of the dissidents grew louder in March and May 1979 as Kim Young-sam, who became president of the NDP in May, initiated a new movement for constitutional revision. His antigovernment speeches and press interviews infuriated the government. This fury turned to savage attacks on all opposition, and following an incident in which riot police attacked the NDP headquarters where disgruntled workers had taken refuge, moves were taken to suspend Kim's party presidency and engineer his expulsion from the National Assembly.

Now the student protests became more intense and moved from the campuses to the streets. They also spread to other part of the country, including Kim Young-sam's hometown, Pusan. In Pusan, middle class citizens joined with the students in attacks on police boxes and government buildings in mid-October. The rioting then spread to the nearby city of Masan. The government's response was to impose martial law in the region. The situation became more critical toward the end of October as college students in Seoul prepared for a large-scale uprising, similar to that of April 1960. On 26 October 1979, in the midst of the crisis, Kim Chae-gyu, director of the Korean CIA, shot and killed President Park and his chief bodyguard and confidant, Cha Chi-ch'ol, in the course of a row over dinner about how to handle the growing demonstrations. As the country faced an unprecedented national crisis, Prime Minister Ch'oe Kyu-ha was named acting president and martial law was proclaimed, with Gen. Chong Sung-hwa as Martial Law Commander. Kim and his accomplices were executed in late May 1980.

The Interim Period, October 1979–March 1981

The NCU elected Ch'oe Kyu-ha as the new president on 6 December 1979, but Lieutenant General Chun Doo-hwan, commander of the Defense Security Command, overshadowed both the president and the government. On 12 December, Chun, aided by a fellow general, Roh Tae-woo, carried out a coup, arresting the Martial Law Commander Gen. Chong Sung-hwa, who was accused of complicity in Park's assassination. Both Chun and Roh were members of a secret military clique within the army, known as the *hanawoe*, or "One Association." The government restored the civil rights of former President Yun, Kim Daejung, and others in February 1980 and established a Constitution Revision Deliberation Committee in March, but both the opposition NDP and students became impatient with the slow progress in political reform.

Conditions deteriorated further when Chun was appointed as acting director of the Korean CIA in April without leaving his army post. Many campus rallies followed, demanding the immediate end of martial law, the adoption of a new constitution, and the resignation of Chun as acting director of the Korean CIA. Tens of thousands of students marched into the streets in Seoul and elsewhere in mid-May, clashing with riot police. Troops were mobilized, and on 17 May, the government proclaimed nationwide martial law. Martial Law Decree No. 10 followed. Under this, some 30 political leaders, including Kim Jongp'il, head of the DRP, Kim Young-sam, head of the NDP, and Kim Daejung were put under house arrest, and the National Assembly was closed, as were colleges. All political activities, assemblage, and public demonstrations were banned. In spite of these restrictions, demonstrations continued in Seoul and elsewhere. In Kwangju, capital of Kim Dae-jung's home province, and a city that had suffered much discrimination under Park Chung-hee, there were outbreaks of violence, with attacks on the police and public buildings. To take the city, Chun sent special forces trained to deal with North Korean infiltrators. They initially failed to do so, but Kwangju was eventually retaken, with heavy casualties, on 27 May 1980. It and nearby towns were put under military control.

Meanwhile, the cabinet tendered its resignation on 20 May, and a new cabinet emerged in an extremely unstable situation. A Special Committee for National Security Measures (SCNSM) was formed on 31 May to cope with the crisis with President Ch'oe as its chairman and Chun Doo-hwan as chairman of its Standing Committee. Chun resigned as acting director of the Korean CIA in June, but he and 15 other generals in the SCNSM exercised absolute power, instituting many changes, including a drastic educational reform in July.

President Ch'oe resigned on 16 August to be succeeded by Chun. When Chun was elected by the NCU as the president and took the oath of office on 1 September, he said that he would do his best to make his government an "honest and efficient one, which can win the confidence of the nation." He pledged that he would eradicate past ills and restore public faith in honest rule.

However, President Chun soon displayed dictatorial tendencies. In late September the police rounded up 13 NDP members on suspicion of playing a key role in the political melee in the 1976 NDP national convention. That same month, a military court sentenced Kim Dae-jung, charged with instigating the Kwangju Uprising even though he was in detention at the time, to death. On 22 October, new constitutional revisions proposed by the SCNSM were approved in a national referendum, replacing the Yushin Constitution and paving the way for the Fifth Republic. Meanwhile, Chun dissolved the National Assembly and replaced it by an 81-member "Legislative Council for National Security" (LCNS), whose members he appointed. In late October, all existing political parties were dissolved, and on 12 November, the government announced that a total of 835 persons were to be banned from political life for the next eight years. Meanwhile, the government forced the dismissal of 937 journalists (editors and reporters) and the consolidation of radio-TV broadcasting systems and newspaper presses, in what became known as "the massacre of the mass media" of October–November 1980. In essence, a new military revolution took place under the dictatorial leadership of Chun. In December, the Korean CIA was renamed the Agency for National Security Planning (ANSP) without losing any of its former power.

With the partial lifting of the Martial Law Decree No. 10 on 15 November 1980, political activity was renewed, and in January 1981 there emerged new parties with new leadership: President Chun's Democratic Justice Party (DJP), a Democratic Korean Party (DKP) led by Yu Ch'i-song, and the Korean National Party (KNP) of Kim Chong-ch'ol; all were government-funded in one way or another, as were a number of minor parties. On 25 February 1981, a 5,278-member Presidential Electoral College, which was popularly elected on 11 November and replaced the NCU, elected the incumbent president as the first president of the Fifth Republic for a non-renewable seven-year term of office under the new constitution.

The Fifth Republic, March 1981–February 1988

The Fifth Republic began on 3 March 1981 when Chun took the oath of office for a single seven-year presidential term. This was followed by the general elections for a new National Assembly in late March. The 11th National Assembly was inaugurated on 11 April, replacing the short-lived LCNS; the DJP was the majority party. Although Chun sustained the momentum of economic modernization and development that began in the 1960s, his government displayed little inclination to promote democracy and it failed to win the confidence of the people. It also misused power to strengthen government control and benefit the ruling party and those individuals and business firms that supported it. As a result, the people regarded the Chun administration as "a hotbed of illegality and irrationality," and the dubious financial dealings of President Chun's wife, his brother, and other relatives were widely known. Consequently, the democratic aspirations of the people suffered, and there occurred frequent student riots and labor unrest, accompanied by violence, as the demand for democratic reform increased.

President Chun made state visits to the five nations of the Association of Southeast Asian Nations (ASEAN) in June 1981, to Japan in September 1984, to the United States in February 1981 and April 1985, and to five European nations in April 1986, improving South Korea's diplomatic and commercial ties with them. However, his plan to visit six Southeast Asian nations in October 1983 was cut short by an assassination attempt by North Korean agents in Rangoon, Burma, on 9 October. Chun escaped, but many of his top advisers and cabinet ministers were killed.

In June 1981, Chun granted amnesty to some 1,061 political prisoners who had been imprisoned in connection with the Kwangju Uprising, reduced the death sentence given to Kim Dae-jung to life imprisonment, and allowed him to travel to the United States for "medical treatment" in December 1982. Between February 1983 and November 1984, Chun gradually removed 835 former political leaders from the political blacklist, restoring their political and civil rights. However, Chun and his government utterly failed to promote democracy, refusing to revise the constitution before 1989. Following the founding of an underground radical student organization named the "Committee for Promotion of Democracy" (*Minch'uwi*) in October 1984, a group of radical students occupied the headquarters of the ruling DJP, demanding further democratic reform. But Chun made no concession, except the removal of 84 names out of 103 persons who were still on the political blacklist in November 1984. A final group of 19 former political leaders, which included Kim Jong-p'il, Kim Dae-jung, and Kim Young-sam, did not regain political and civil rights until March 1985.

Those who regained their political and civil rights in November 1984 established the New Korea Democratic Party (NKDP) in January 1985 and agitated for an immediate revision of the constitution. At this juncture, Kim Dae-jung returned to Seoul from the United States.

In the general elections for the National Assembly, held in mid-February 1985, the opposition NKDP won the majority of urban votes, but the ruling DJP managed to maintain its overall majority. Shortly after, President Chun named Roh Tae-woo as new chairman of the DJP in order to strengthen the party, and also to indicate that Roh would be his successor. Meanwhile, the opposition party leaders, having formed a "Council for the Promotion of Democracy" (CPD), called for the merger of all opposition parties, named Kim Dae-jung and Kim Young-sam co-chairmen of the CPD, and demanded further constitutional revision. In mid-April 1985, radical students formed a "Committee for the Three People's Struggle" (*Sammint'u*) with the representatives of 23 universities and began to organize more violent protests. Students belonging to this and other radical groups occupied both the United States Information Center in Seoul in late May and the training institute of the ruling DJP.

In March 1985, Kim Young-sam officially joined the NKDP, becoming adviser to the party president. The NKDP thereupon launched a more determined movement for the revision of the constitution, demanding the direct election of the president, and a return to the system whereby the prime minister was responsible to the National Assembly.

In the turbulent political climate of the spring of 1986, the police placed 270 opposition politicians under house arrest to block a mass rally planned by the NKDP. Nonetheless, large mass rallies were held in Seoul, Inch'on, Kwangju, Taegu, and Pusan in support of the constitutional revision drive. It was the first time since 1981 that such large outdoor mass political rallies openly criticizing the current regime and its policies had been held in South Korea. While demonstrators even demanded the immediate resignation of Chun, several groups of university professors issued statements calling for the immediate revision of the constitution, while a group of 325 women leaders called for the promotion of social democracy and women's rights under a new constitution.

Political peace was restored temporarily when, following the meeting between the president and the opposition leaders, Chun agreed to form a Constitution Study Committee to prepare for the constitutional revision. However, Chun refused to revise the constitution before 1989 in order to enable his successor to be chosen by the Electoral College under the existing constitution. Thereupon, opposition groups such as the NKDP, the CPD, and Catholic and Protestant societies increased their demand for a constitutional revision in 1986 so that the 1987 presidential election would be held under a revised constitution.

The rise of radical groups and increasing demonstrations caused considerable problems for the government. In late October 1986, a group of young revolutionaries, whose aim was to form a Marxist-Leninist party, was arrested. This was followed in early November by a mass demonstration at Konguk University in Seoul of some 1,270 radical students from various universities. Meanwhile, the police cracked down on dissidents who organized a "Joint Masses Movement for Democracy and Unification" (*Mint'ongyon*) in mid-November, and the police also arrested the leaders of an alleged pro-North Korean "Anti-Imperialist League."

The political situation rapidly deteriorated as antagonism between the ruling DJP and the opposition NKDP grew following the adoption by the DJP in October 1986 of a resolution which would allow the police to arrest opposition Assemblymen. The passage of the 1987 national budget bill by DJP lawmakers in early December without opposition participation only worsened the situation. The death by police torture of a university student in December further radicalized antigovernment students, forcing the president to replace the home minister and the director of the National Police in January 1987.

President Chun's 13 April 1987 ban on any further talks for constitutional reform until after the 1988 Seoul Olympics precipitated violent reaction against the government and its party. Protestant ministers and Catholic priests and nuns carried out hunger strikes, demanding Chun's resignation, while professors at many universities and lawyers issued political statements, criticizing the policy of the president and his party. Meanwhile, hundreds of thousands of students and others staged antigovernment demonstrations throughout the spring and in early summer, regularly clashing with the paramilitary "combat"(riot) police. The city of Seoul became a battleground as tear gas filled the air over the city and traffic stoppage occurred day after day.

In this turbulent political situation, some 71 lawmakers defected from the NKDP and formed a new Reunification Democratic Party (RDP) on 1 May, with Kim Young-sam as its president and Kim Dae-jung as his advisor, declaring their determination to carry out their struggle for democratization.

The nomination on 10 June of Roh Tae-woo, chairman of the ruling DJP, hand picked by President Chun to be his successor as presidential candidate of the DJP, precipitated more violence. The opposition RDP demanded the following: an immediate revision of the constitution; restoration of full freedom of the press; release of all political prisoners; and the restoration of full civil rights for Kim Dae-jung. In the wake of this, some 500 persons, including the vice president of the RDP, were arrested on 10 June, in the midst of daily clashes between the riot police and protesters. A total breakdown of law and order seemed imminent.

On 24 June 1987, President Chun met with Kim Young-sam to seek a solution, but they failed to reach agreement because Chun would make no major concessions. Thereupon the opposition RDP mobilized the masses and carried out a "Grand Peace March" on 26 June. Hundreds of thousands of people took to the streets, clashing with the riot police. The police seized Kim Young-sam and others, while Kim Dae-jung, who had been freed the previous day after 78 days of detention in his home, was again placed under house arrest. The country seemed on the verge of a serious national crisis similar to that of April 1960.

Roh Tae-woo, backed by his loyal supporters in the party, now intervened. He announced his "Democratization Declaration" on 29 June, demanding that President Chun accept his proposals and indicating that he would resign the chairmanship of the party and candidacy for presidency if his demands were not met. The nation was stunned by this unexpected development but welcomed it with cautious optimism. Roh met with President Chun and convinced the latter that the only peaceful way to defuse the crisis was to implement his reform policy. Persuaded by Roh, President Chun announced on 1 July that he had accepted Roh's proposals, thus paving the way for a peaceful settlement of the most troublesome political issues that the nation had faced for years.

In an attempt at conciliation, the government granted amnesty on 10 July 1987 to some 2,335 political prisoners, including Kim Dae-jung, also restoring their civil rights. President Chun relinquished the presidency of the DJP to Roh in early August as the two major political parties agreed on the basic outline of a new constitution.

As the winds of democracy rose, labor unrest increased, while radical students continued their antigovernment demonstrations. More than 500 industrial disputes erupted, mainly in the motor, mining, and shipbuilding industries as striking workers demanded higher wages, better treatment, and better working conditions. Most of these were settled quickly, but violent clashes between striking workers and riot police took place at Hyundai Motors in Ulsan. By mid-October 1987, however, nearly all labor strikes ended when the government conceded a swift revision of labor laws. Workers were now guaranteed the right to form unions and to engage in collective bargaining, and minimum wages were raised.

On the political front, negotiations carried out between Kim Young-sam and Kim Dae-jung failed to result in selection of a single RDP presidential candidate. Kim Young-sam declared his candidacy for president in mid-October, and on 12 November, Kim Dae-jung, taking 27 of the RDP's lawmakers with him, formed his own Party for Peace and Democracy (PPD), becoming its head as well as its presidential candidate. With this, the two major existing opposition parties (the NKP and the NKDP) were virtually dissolved. Meanwhile, Kim Jong-p'il revived Park Chung-hee's old Democratic Republican Party (DRP), which had been defunct since early 1980, renaming it the New Democratic Republican Party (NDRP). He also became its leader and presidential candidate. For the first time in the history of South Korea, a woman, Hong Sook-ja of the Socialist Democratic Party, announced her intention to run for the presidency, although she later withdrew.

The democratization process moved ahead when on 12 October 1987, the National Assembly passed the ninth constitutional amendment providing for direct presidential election. The new Constitution was put to a national referendum on 27 October, to take effect on 25 February 1988. Some 20 million of the country's 25.6 million eligible voters cast their ballots, approving the constitution by 93.3 percent. Thus the stage was set for the establishment of the Sixth Republic.

The first direct popular presidential election in 16 years was conducted on 16 December 1987. Some 23 million, or 89.2 percent of the eligible voters, cast their ballots, electing Roh Tae-woo of the DJP as president for a non-renewable five-year-term of office with 36.6 percent of the votes. Kim Dae-jung received 28.1 percent and Kim Young-sam received 27.1 percent. It was clear that the two major opposition parties' failure to present a single candidate, "gave" the presidency to Roh. Kim Jong-p'il of the NDRP received 8.1 percent of the votes, while the fifth candidate received only 0.2 percent of the votes.

The Sixth Republic: 1st Stage Roh Tae-woo 1988–1993

On 25 February 1988 President Roh took the oath of office for a single five-year presidential term, the first truly peaceful transfer of power since 1948, thus beginning the Sixth Republic. In his inaugural address, Roh said that the era of "ordinary people" had arrived, and that the days when freedom and human rights could be suppressed "in the name of economic growth and national security has ended."

Looking forward to the National Assembly elections under the new National Assembly Election Law of 8 March 1988, which restored the single-member constituency for the first time in 17 years and increased the number of seats in the legislature from 276 to 299, Kim Young-sam resigned the presidency of the DRP, hoping to bring about the merger of the two major opposition parties. Kim Dae-jung refused to do likewise until criticism against him grew to such an extent that in mid-March he was forced to step down from the presidency of his party. Despite this move, the two opposition parties failed to merge, and both Kims resumed their respective party presidencies. In the general elections for the National Assembly held on 26 April, the ruling party failed to win a majority for the first time, as only 87 of its candidates were elected. Kim Dae-jung's PPD won 54 district seats, thus becoming the first opposition party, Kim Young-sam's RDP won 46 district seats, and Kim Jong-p'il's NDRP won 27 district seats. A minor party won one, and nine seats were taken by the Independents. The 75 national seats were distributed to each party according to the percentage of votes each received. Thus, the DJP received 38, the PPD 17, RDP 13, and the NDRP 8 seats.

The nature of politics remained undemocratic under the Sixth Republic. The uncooperative relationship between the ruling and opposition parties continued, the behavior of politicians and government officials remained dishonest and bureaucratic, and student, farmer, and worker unrest did not subside. Despite these unfavorable factors, the government of the Sixth Republic took several significant steps to promote democracy and restore harmony between the government and the people. First of all, in April 1988, the government redefined the May 1980 civil disturbances in Kwangju as "part of the efforts by students and citizens . . . for democratization of the nation," offered an apology to the people in Kwangju, and promised compensation for the victims. Secondly, in July it removed a longstanding ban on the published works of some 120 writers who had defected to North Korea after 1945, and in October it lifted another longstanding ban on the pre–Korean War songs and art works of some 100 musicians and artists who had either defected or were abducted to North Korea provided their material included no North Korean propaganda. The government also liberalized the press law, permitting the establishment of new newspaper presses and radio-television broadcasting corporations. It also allowed the sale of some books published in North Korea and elsewhere on communism and permitted the study of Marxism at colleges.

In May 1988, the Roh administration established the Administrative Reform Commission to study "future-oriented government systems" to help the country move forward with democratic development, including a plan to implement local autonomy in 1991. Roh made efforts to promote cooperative relationships between the ruling DJP and the opposition parties in solving domestic and foreign problems, especially those issues related to the Fifth Republic, and made some effort to meet the grievances of students and workers.

These and other measures brought about a temporary truce among conflicting groups for the primary purpose of hosting the 1988 24th Summer Olympics in Seoul as scheduled. As a result, between 17 September and 2 October 1988, Seoul witnessed the largest and the most peaceful Olympics ever held up until then. Following this success, the Roh administration was able to persuade former President Chun to make a nationwide television appearance on 23 November to apologize for the wrongdoings of his administration and its officials. Chun and his wife then left Seoul for self-imposed internal exile at a remote Buddhist temple where they stayed until December 1990. Three days later, on 26 November, Roh appealed for leniency for his predecessor, and in a five-point formula, he promised to launch a broad reform plan to ensure democratic rule and to end abuse of power by the government. His plan also included the reorganization of the government and the ruling party to realize "a spirit of a new era," institutionalization of an impartial method for raising and allocating political funds, and promotion of "liberal democracy."

In order to calm several months of political storm that engulfed his administration over the matters related to the Fifth Republic, as well as to improve public confidence in his administration's commitment to democratization, on 5 December 1988, Roh carried out a major cabinet reshuffle, appointing Kang Young-hoon as prime minister and replacing 20 of the 25 cabinet ministers and the mayor of Seoul. This was followed by the granting on 21 December of amnesty for more than 2,000 "politically motivated offenders" and release of 281 political prisoners, including those students who were serving 20-year sentences for firebombing the United States Cultural Center in Pusan in 1982.

While issues related to former President Chun and the Fifth Republic, as well as the alleged involvement of Roh as former commander of a military unit in the Kwangju incident, continued to trouble the Roh administration, a new outbreak of antigovernment demonstrations were triggered off when Roh announced on 20 March 1989 that he was postponing the national referendum on his administration that he had promised in 1987 during his presidential campaign.

The two most significant political developments in South Korea in the early 1990s were the emergence of the "super" ruling Democratic Liberal Party (DLP) and the restoration of partial local autonomy. The first was achieved when the interests of the ruling DJP, which had no majority in the National Assembly, and two opposition parties, the RDP and the NDRP, both of which badly needed to strengthen their positions, converged in January 1990. Following secret negotiations carried out among the presidents of these three parties during the month of January, in February 1990 the DJP, the RDP, and the NDRP merged, forming the Democratic Liberal Party as the "super" ruling party with 216 seats in the 299-seat National Assembly, making the lone opposition PPD with 70 seats in the National Assembly altogether powerless. Meanwhile, those former members of the RDP who refused to join the newly established DLP formed their own parties, such as the New Democratic United Party and the Democratic Party. Eventually these two parties merged with the PPD, forming a new viable opposition New Democratic Party (NDP) in 1991.

Shortly after the launching of the new ruling DLP, and facing a variety of economic problems in mid-March, President Roh carried out a major cabinet reshuffle, replacing all but one minister concerned with the economy. Premier Kang was retained then, but in December 1990, Ro Jae-bong replaced Kang in another major cabinet reshuffle.

New political problems soon hit the government. It was disclosed that government and party officials were involved in financial scandals, including one relating to an illicit allotment of a large tract of land in Seoul's Suso district to a developer. Riot police beat a college student to death. These developments and other political and labor problems led Roh to carry out the third major cabinet reshuffle in February 1991 when he replaced Premier Ro.

The most constructive political development during this period of the Sixth Republic was the partial restoration of local autonomy in 1991. It came about in two stages under a new local autonomy law adopted by the National Assembly in December 1990. In the first stage, members of small district councils were elected on 25 March 1991. The small districts included small cities, counties, and wards of large municipalities. In these elections, only 55.9 percent of the 24 million eligible voters cast their ballots. In the second stage, on 20 June members of the large district councils were elected. These included Seoul and five other special municipalities and nine provinces. In the large district council elections, only 58.9 percent of the 28 million eligible voters cast their ballots. The elections for provincial governors and mayors of the special municipalities, which would provide the new system with real authority, were to be held during the first half of 1992, but they were postponed until 1995. Real local autonomy was, for the present, aborted.

With National Assembly elections due in 1992, and in order to cope more effectively with the superior position of the ruling DLP, in September 1991, Yi Ki-t'aek's Democratic Party and the New Democratic Party led by Kim Dae-jung and Yi Wu-jong merged to form yet another Democratic Party (DP). This provided a stronger opposition party in the National Assembly. There was a surprising new development in January 1992 when Chung Ju-yung, founder and honorary chairman of the Hyundai Group who had no political experience, organized the Unification National Party (UNP). Soon after, Dr. Kim Tong-gil, professor of history at Yonsei University, reorganized his Asia-Pacific-Era Committee into the New Korea Party (*Saehandang*) in mid-January, while Pak Ch'an-jong formed the Party for New Political Reform (PNPR). On 7 February, the Unification National Party and the New Korea Party merged to form the Unification National Party (UNP), otherwise called the United Peoples' Party (UPP), with Chong as its president and Kim as its executive chairman.

In the general elections for the National Assembly held in March 1992, the ruling DLP, the DP, the UNP, and three other splinter parties competed for seats. Despite its size, the ruling DLP won only 38.5 percent of the votes, winning 116 district seats, while the major opposition DP won 29.2 percent of the votes (75 Assembly seats), and the newly formed UNP won 17.3 percent of the votes (24 Assembly seats). Independents won some 11.5 percent of the votes (21 Assembly seats). Even with 33 national Assembly seats allocated to the ruling DLP, it had failed to secure a majority. Only when seven Independents joined the DLP, and one assemblyman-elect from the UNP and another from the DP defected to the DLP did the ruling DLP gain a majority (159 seats). Meanwhile, the remaining Independents formed their own Fraternal Society. Only 71.9 percent (20.8 million) of the 29 million eligible voters cast their ballots, the lowest turnout of voters in the history of National Assembly elections, indicating voters' declining interest in politics.

President Roh's term of office was due to expire in February 1993. In preparation for the election, in May 1992 the major parties selected their presidential candidates. Thus the ruling DLP nominated Kim Young-sam, the DP nominated Kim Dae-jung, the UNP nominated Chung Ju-yung, and the PNPR nominated Pak Ch'an-jong as candidates. Only the DP selected its presidential candidate in a democratic manner, offering a choice of candidates. The leadership of the PNPR and the UNP nominated their presidential candidates without any contenders. The way in which the ruling DLP selected Kim Young-sam aroused not only bitter intraparty conflict, and eventually a party split, but also attracted criticism from the electorate.

At the December 1992 election, Kim Young-sam won with 42 percent of the votes, well ahead of Kim Dae-jung, the major opposition candidate. For the first time since 1961, South Korea had a democratically elected civilian president, albeit one who had thrown in his lot with the existing ruling party. Kim Dae-jung, his one-time fellow dissident and rival, announced his retirement from politics, retreating to the University of Cambridge in Britain, to reflect and write. The industrialist Chung Ju-yung, who had not done as well as he had expected, also moved out of the political arena. Kim Young-sam was therefore in a very powerful position, despite some lingering opposition from within his own party.

The Sixth Republic: 2nd Stage Kim Young-sam 1993–1998

Kim began well. In his inauguration speech, he pledged that he would fight both public and private corruption and revitalize the flagging economy. He called upon the people to help him build a "New Korea," in which Koreans would regain their former industriousness and regain their self-confidence. His first symbolic gesture was to open up the streets around the presidential palace, Chong Wa Dae, closed as a security measure since the 1960s. He introduced a series of short-term measures designed to get the economy moving, followed by a new Five-Year Plan, which provided a longer-term strategy for sustained economic development. He pledged also that he would clean out the money politics that had come to dominate the South Korean political scene. He made public his total assets and those of his immediate family. Corrupt officials were purged, and known corrupt lawmakers encouraged to leave the ruling party. A further weapon against corruption and financial irregularity was the introduction of the real name system in financial transactions, completed in August 1993, but prepared in great secrecy for the maximum effect. One personal contribution to honesty was that the president stopped dyeing his hair; instead of the jet-black locks he had hitherto worn, he now appeared in public and in his official pictures with a distinguished head of grey hair. At the end of his first year in office, he enjoyed an 80 percent approval rating in opinion polls.

The following year saw a further batch of reforms, mainly in the political field. These included a law against election malpractices, a law concerning political funds, and a local autonomy act. These were designed to strengthen and deepen the South Korean commitment to the democratic process. These were ambitious projects, often based on the best practice of more politically advanced countries, and some doubted whether they were really suitable for or likely to be successful in the particular circumstances of a country that had just emerged from a long period of military or quasi-military rule. Apart from such doubts, there was also some concern that, whatever the theory, there was a marked reluctance on the part of the South Korean ruling elite to give up power once obtained. In the case of the local autonomy law, for example, many powers that might have logically devolved to the locality were reserved to the center. The laws on election malpractices and political funds set high standards, perhaps even higher than the current level of South Korean political behavior could sustain. One area where radical reform had been expected from this first former opposition figure was in the national security apparatus. There were some changes. Kim Deok, a university professor, took over as head of the ANSP, with a mandate to downsize the organization and to end its role in domestic politics. There the reforms stopped. The National Security Law and the other means of repression used since the very beginning of the ROK continued in force, and before long, there was backtracking even on the modest reforms in the ANSP.

In addition to high standards of political behavior, South Koreans also found themselves expected to meet new international standards. From November 1994, President Kim committed South Korea to a new concept of "globalization," or in Korean, *segyehwa*. *Segyehwa* was from the beginning an imprecise concept. Building on the fact that the South Korean economy was the eleventh largest in the world, Kim appeared to claim that South Korea could teach the rest of the world about economic development. In the short term, however, much of the *segyehwa* rhetoric related to what some felt was a premature commitment to the opening of the South Korean economy to the world. This would culminate in South Korea's successful attempt to join the world's leading group of industrialized nations, the Organization for Economic Cooperation and Development (OECD). Ironically, this bid succeeded in November 1997, just as South Korea's economy faced its worst-ever economic crisis and as Kim Young-sam's term of office came to an end.

Well before that, however, Kim had begun to face major problems on several fronts, which would cast a shadow over his early successes. Just as he had taken up office, a crisis developed over North Korea's alleged nuclear weapons' program. Satellite evidence appeared to show that an experimental site at Yongbyon north of the North Korean capital, P'yongyang, contained more than the North Koreans admitted. There was also growing concern over the North Korean attitude toward the Nuclear Non-proliferation Treaty (NPT). The North had signed this in 1985, under Soviet pressure, but had failed to sign the required safeguards agreement or to provide a full list of its nuclear installations until 1992. Faced with international pressure, the North announced in March 1993 that it would withdraw from the NPT.

This was obviously a serious issue for South Korea, but it was the U.S. that dominated the attempts to persuade North Korea to conform to the terms of the NPT. Kim Young-sam's approach to the issue was very much in keeping with what was increasingly seen as his approach on most issues: he failed to pursue a consistent policy, sometimes being conciliatory, sometimes bellicose. Hostile press comment would quickly induce a presidential change of policy. Somehow, however, a dialogue with North Korea kept going, and there were plans for a summit meeting between the North's leader, Kim Il-sung and Kim Young-sam in July 1994. But to many in South Korea, their country seemed sidelined, especially when it was the former American President Jimmy Carter, still regarded with hostility in some circles in South Korea for his planned troop withdrawals in the 1970s, who appeared to save the day with his June 1994 negotiations in North Korea.

At this point, Kim Il-sung died, and the summit was postponed. Although Kim Young-sam had been prepared to meet Kim Il-sung, he now refused to express any form of condolence and the government took firm action against manifestations of sympathy that took place on a number of university campuses. The North retaliated with much hostile comment, and effectively ceased all dialogue with the South as long as Kim Young-sam remained president. A further sign of Kim's unsure touch where

North Korea was concerned came in 1996. When a North Korean infiltration/surveillance submarine went aground off the East Coast, the ROK security forces at first failed to capture those who went on the run, but subsequently they captured and killed them all. The North demanded the return of the bodies, and after it had agreed to apologize for the incident, the cremated remains were handed back on 30 December 1996. There had been no notification that the bodies were to be cremated, and this action increased the North's hostility toward Kim Young-sam.

Domestic issues also brought problems for Kim Young-sam. A series of fatal accidents during 1994–1995, while not the direct responsibility of the government, pointed to weak control of the construction industry and corruption in local and national government. The popularity of both the government and Kim Young-sam fell rapidly, a decline reflected in the antigovernment party vote in the June 1995 local elections.

More serious was the reopening of the issue of how Chun Doo-hwan had come to power and responsibility for the Kwangju incident. There had been high hopes among dissident groups and families of the Kwangju victims that Kim's election would lead to a reexamination of the events of 1979–1980. Kim Young-sam had declined to do so, saying that it should be left for history to decide. Some felt that this attitude had less to do with magnanimity on the president's part than with the fact that he had come to power with the support of Chun and Roh.

In 1995, the issue was taken out of Kim's hands. In 1993, the general whom Chun Doo-hwan had dismissed in 1979, Chung Sung-hwa, brought a case accusing Chun and Roh Tae-woo of mutiny on that occasion. The court agreed in July 1995 that 1979 had been something approaching a mutiny, but the prosecutors declined to take action. Chun and Roh had once again escaped an examination of their actions. As the real name financial reforms began to take effect, however, there was increasing speculation that some of the biggest borrowed-name accounts belonged to the two former presidents and their supporters. On 19 October 1995, an opposition legislator revealed in the National Assembly that Roh had about 400 billion won (U.S.$500 million) in a series of undisclosed bank accounts. Speculation was soon rife that Chun probably had similar amounts. On 27 October, Roh in tears revealed at a press conference that he actually held some U.S.$650 million in various funds.

This confession led to countrywide demonstrations and demands from the opposition that Kim Young-sam should indicate whether or not he had received money from Roh. The prosecutors also began their investigations into the source of the funds, which turned out to be mainly the big business conglomerates, and Roh was arrested on 25 November on suspicion of taking bribes. Before long, Chun too had been arrested.

Kim Young-sam, who hitherto had not been involved and indeed had refused to reopen the past, now effectively gave the go-ahead for a full investigation not just of the corruption and bribery issues, but also of the circumstances surrounding the 1979 coup and the Kwangju incident. A special law passed the National Assembly on 19 December 1995, and the way was open for the prosecution of Chun, Roh, and a number of their military and business associates.

The verdict came in August 1996. Chun was sentenced to death and Roh to 22 years and six months in jail, while both had large fines imposed. Other military figures received jail sentences but the industrialists who were convicted of bribery and corruption received suspended sentences. Both the former presidents had their sentences reduced on appeal, Chun to life and Roh to 17 years. Eventually, after the 1997 presidential elections, Kim Young-sam, with the agreement of the incoming president, Kim Dae-jung, released both men from prison; the heavy fines stood but have not so far (mid-2004) been paid.

There was much speculation as to why Kim Young-sam had changed his mind about prosecuting his predecessors. The public outrage at the extent of the corruption may have been a factor, but he had firmly resisted earlier calls for action. Some argued that he had allowed the prosecutions to go ahead to protect himself. Chun and Roh would not reveal what they knew about him since they might ultimately be dependent on him for presidential clemency. Others felt that he had acted to try and recoup some of his lost popularity and with a view to influencing both the April 1996 National Assembly elections and the 1997 presidential elections.

If these were his aims, they were unsuccessful. The April 1996 elections saw the government party failing to win an overall majority in the National Assembly. The defeat was soon remedied, with promises buying defections from other parties, but it was not a good omen. Soon there were other problems as well. The change of heart over prosecuting the former presidents brought little credit to Kim Young-sam, who was widely seen as having acted too late. Besides, there was soon clear evidence that corruption had by no means disappeared. Before the end of 1996, a former minister of health and a former minister of defense had been jailed for corruption. Early in 1997, the collapse of the Hanbo Iron and Steel Company not only had major economic repercussions, but brought the tide of corruption lapping at the president's own door. Another minister, a presidential aide, several parliamentarians, and various businessmen were caught up in the scandal, but so was one of the president's sons, Kim Hyon-ch'ol. In the event, no charges were levied against the younger Kim but again questions lingered as to the real reason for his activities.

Increasingly savage labor disputes and a new round of student demonstrations, during one of which a policeman was killed, added to Kim's difficulties. There were claims that pro–North Korean activists were behind the student demonstrations, and the North itself seemed to be more belligerent. To cope with these developments, Kim decided to restore many of the powers that he had taken away from the ANSP in his early days and to introduce tough new labor laws. Faced with opposition in the Assembly, in a move reminiscent of Park Chung-hee's day, the ruling party met at six in the morning on 26 December 1996 and passed the two bills.

The presidential election year of 1997 therefore began on a low note. Kim Young-sam's personal popularity in the opinion polls was below 20 percent, and falling. He was reluctant to name a successor as the ruling party candidate for the election, no doubt wishing to avoid an alternative center of power developing within the party. He also had to be careful in his choice if he wished to avoid the same fate as his two predecessors. The corruption issue would not go away, either, and in May Kim Hyon-ch'ol was arrested. The political parties traded allegations about the amounts of money political leaders had received. The year also saw increasing economic problems, beginning with the collapse of the Hanbo group in January. By the summer, several of the lesser *chaebol* appeared to be in serious difficulties. President Kim, preoccupied with the arrest of his son, and increasingly struggling to prevent his one-time associate and political rival, Kim Dae-jung, from becoming president, seemed oblivious to the major problems the country faced.

When the collapse of the Thai currency in July triggered the Asian financial crisis, Kim Young-sam seemed detached. He remained so as the crisis began to engulf the South Korean economy. It was true that the government stepped in when Kia Motors went bankrupt in October

1997, but that was to prevent the social dislocation likely to be caused by such a failure. As the won came under pressure, the government declined all outside assistance, only to see the currency fall to under 1,000 to the U.S. dollar. At this point, the government called on the International Monetary Fund (IMF) for assistance. By the end of November 1997, the IMF had advanced South Korea $57 billion, the largest such loan ever made. Koreans, used to success and fearful of the IMF's demands for the opening of the economy, seemed in despair.

This was the backdrop against which the 1997 presidential election was fought. The ruling party eventually settled on a respected High Court judge, Lee Hoi-chang as its candidate. He seemed to have good qualifications. He was notably younger than his main opponent, Kim Dae-jung, and enjoyed a reputation for honesty. However, there was opposition to his selection from within the party, and when news broke that both his sons had somehow avoided military service, his reputation suffered a setback.

Meanwhile, an unexpected alliance had emerged among the opposition candidates. In early November, just ahead of the election, Kim Dae-jung of the National Council for New Politics (NCNP), the party he had created in 1995, and Kim Jong-p'il, head of the United Liberal Democrats (ULD) and once Park Chung-hee's prime minister and founder of the KCIA, announced an electoral alliance, with Kim Dae-jung as their presidential candidate. Many predicted that what they saw as an unholy alliance would fail; the ruling party, using, as in the past, state powers, tried to ensure that it would. In any event, and following a split in the ruling party, it was Kim Dae-jung who won the 1997 presidential election on 18 December, albeit by just 400,000 votes out of 26 million. When he took office in February 1998 as the 15th president, it marked the first time since 1948 that power had passed from the ruling party to the opposition.

The Sixth Republic: 3rd Stage Kim Dae-jung 1998–2003

It was a formidable task that the new administration faced, as the economic crisis deepened. Kim Dae-jung appeared to begin badly, stating after receiving his first official briefings that he had no idea how bad things were. He later claimed that this was an attempt to bring home to the Korean people how serious a position they faced. If he had made an error, he quickly recovered. Kim had in fact given much thought to the economic needs of South Korea during his long years in opposition, and he now began to put some of these into practice. He also assembled a competent team of advisers, while making conciliatory moves toward both the labor unions and big business.

Clearly action was needed, as the economic crisis deepened, and the economy dominated Kim Dae-jung's first year in office. In the first six months of 1998, real GNP declined by 5.3 percent compared with the same period the previous year. The dollar/won ratio hovered around the 1,700 level. Unemployment increased as more and more companies became insolvent. This reflected a huge range of problems, including great over-capacity, a near bankrupt financial sector, and massive private debt.

Kim set out to persuade his countrymen that the IMF package, negotiated the previous year, had to be implemented, however hard that was. A Financial Supervisory Commission oversaw the shutting down of about 100 financial institutions and over 50 noncompetitive companies. The reform of the *chaebol* proved more difficult, but here too strenuous efforts were made, with most of the major companies agreeing to restructure around a set of core activities. At the same time, the South Korean capital markets were liberalized, and many areas hitherto closed to foreign investment were now opened. By the end of 1998, there were signs of hope.

Perhaps it was not surprising that in these circumstances, domestic politics seemed less important. Kim Dae-jung's links with the ULD and Kim Jong-p'il led to the latter's nomination as prime minister. Tensions between the ruling party and the opposition, so recently itself the ruling party, and Kim Jong-p'il's own past, meant that it was six months before the National Assembly approved his appointment as prime minister. There was little sign of the political reform that many had expected from a Kim Dae-jung government, although there was a swing toward new political blood as liberal scholars, former dissidents, and people from the hitherto neglected Cholla Provinces found themselves in positions of power. The catchall National Security Law remained, as did the powers of the ANSP, now renamed the National Intelligence Service (NIS). The NIS was given new leadership and once again there was a pledge that it would no longer operate on the domestic scene. In the event, the new leadership, while carrying out some reforms, appears to have made little difference to the overall ethos of the service, and it was not long before allegations of the organization's involvement in internal affairs were being made public.

Internationally, Kim Dae-jung enjoyed a high reputation for his long years of opposition to successive military regimes and for his democratic principles. Domestic problems to some extent limited his opportunities for travel, but when he did, such as his visit to London in April 1998 for the relatively new Asia Europe Summit Meeting, it made an impact.

Kim Dae-jung had long been an advocate of a new approach to North Korea, one that would avoid confrontation. Sometimes his advocacy of closer ties with the North had been seen as akin to treason. Now, as president, he was able to put his ideas into practice. Basically, Kim abandoned formally in public any idea of taking over the North. References to "unification policy" were dropped, in favor of a more general "policy towards the North." These new efforts at engagement of the North were named the "sunshine policy," and Kim Dae-jung would stick to it throughout his presidency, in the face of domestic attacks and the North's reluctance to engage.

Despite the latter, and despite what some saw as North Korean provocation, including a second submarine intrusion in June 1998 and a major naval clash in the Yellow Sea a year later, Kim Dae-jung continued to emphasize that his government was not planning to take over the North and that South Korea was willing and able to help the North out of its severe economic difficulties. He encouraged nongovernmental contacts with the North, including the Hyundai Corporation's tourist trips to the Kumgang (Diamond) Mountains. Eventually, in spring 2000, the North responded positively, and the first ever North–South summit took place in June 2000. When the North's *de facto* leader, Kim Jong-il appeared to be more human than expected, a short-lived wave of pro-North euphoria swept South Korea, to the chagrin of many South Korean conservatives.

Yet there were few who could deny that the summit was an outstanding achievement. The June 2000 summit, if it had done nothing else, seemed to secure Kim Dae-jung's place in history. The award of the Nobel Peace Prize later that year seemed to confirm this.

The euphoria did not last long. Contacts between North and South did flow from the June 2000 summit, and the North found itself being courted diplomatically by countries such as Great Britain and Germany that had hitherto been hostile. But even before the end of 2000, it was clear that the North–South relationship was not going to develop smoothly. The summit had envisaged a return visit by Kim Jong-il to South Korea, which did not materialize. Exchanges at lower levels could suddenly be halted by the North, usually on some perceived insult or another. Before long, the tone of the North Korean media had once again become critical of South Korea.

Many South Koreans, for their part, remained cautious about the growing links that were developing between North and South. Visitors to the North were watched carefully not only by the NIS, but also by the press and opposition parties, in case they appeared to be endorsing or supporting the North's position on unification or related matters. In August 2001, for example, some of those who had been allowed to attend the Liberation Day festivities in P'yongyang were much criticized for taking part in the ceremonies surrounding the opening of a monument to the late Kim Il-sung's principles for reunification. Others were questioned about what they had written at Mangyongdae, Kim's birthplace.

Despite such setbacks, North–South contacts moved forward, though at a painfully slow pace. Interfamily exchanges, though still involving painfully small numbers and subject to sudden cancellations, became more institutionalized, with an eventual agreement on a permanent meeting place. The Hyundai-organized tourist visits to Mount Kumgang continued, despite the huge financial burden they had become on the group and the inevitable loss of interest as few wanted to go for a second visit under the heavy restrictions that the North Koreans imposed. Work on connecting the cross-border roads and railways, also promised at the 2000 summit, made little progress. The North demanded help with earth-moving and other equipment but seemed unwilling to start the work. Yet by 2003, there was minor progress, and the once sealed DMZ had begun to see some cross-border traffic.

Kim Dae-jung stuck to his principle of engagement right to the end of his presidency. However, as time passed, it became clear that the events surrounding the 2000 summit had been rather murkier than they had first seemed. Allegations of large sums paid to the North to agree to the summit were heard almost as soon as it had been announced. Over the next three years, they would be confirmed. Even though this could be seen as money well spent as North Korea and its leadership were drawn out of their shells, the secrecy and denials tainted the image both of Kim Dae-jung and his sunshine policy.

Kim's domestic political legacy was also mixed. Despite Kim's personal reputation for probity, repeated corruption scandals marked his administration as they had that of his predecessor. A similar set of violent accidents to that which had rocked Kim Young-sam's government also showed that problems of shoddy work and evaded standards were not confined to one presidency. Neither did Kim Dae-jung move away from his predecessors' stand on civil rights issues as time passed. The NIS's role in domestic politics continued and the oppressive weight of the National Security Law (NSL) only began to be lifted, in very tentative fashion, when the apparent major change in North–South relations of June 2000 seemed to mark a possible permanent shift of approach by the North. When North–South rapprochement became more problematical, the will to change the NSL also faded.

Part of Kim Dae-jung's reluctance over changes in the security system may have been initially prompted by his political alliance with the ULD and Kim Jong-p'il. The latter, after all, was the original begetter of the KCIA, the forerunner of the NIS, and a man closely associated with the repression under Park Chung-hee. But if Kim Dae-jung conceded some ground to Kim Jong-p'il on the narrow area of security policy, he effectively broke his preelection pledge to introduce a cabinet system of government. To do so would have meant a major diminution of presidential power, and once he had obtained the office, Kim Dae-jung, again like his predecessor, showed no sign of being willing to do that. (In party matters too, Kim Dae-jung showed himself as determined as previous leaders to retain power as far as possible in his own hands.) Tensions over issues such as this led the ULD to withdraw from the coalition at the end of 1999. They would reenter it again, but in the long term, the strains between Kim Dae-jung and Kim Jong-p'il would lead the latter off on his own once again.

One area where Kim Dae-jung tried and failed to change South Korean attitudes was over the regional approach to politics. Although he himself had been elected largely on a regional vote, he tried to move politics away from such a base. However, the April 2000 National Assembly elections showed that regional differences were as strong as ever. Kim Dae-jung's party, now known as the *Minjudang* (literally the Liberal Party, but the party uses the name Millennium Democratic Party

[MLD] in English), came in second after the former ruling party, the Grand National Party, as the former Democratic Liberal Party became in 1997. Only by attracting some stray independents, and eventually renewing the alliance with the ULD, was the MLD able to command a majority in the assembly. The very low voter turnout on this occasion, at 57.2 percent, indicated a growing disillusionment with party politics. Another indication of the same trend was the emergence of "citizens' groups" who before and during the election took upon themselves to pass judgments on the suitability (or otherwise) of candidates for election. For most South Korean politicians, these signs of a growing political sophistication on the part of the electorate were not very welcome.

As though these problems were not enough, the last months of Kim Dae-jung's presidency were haunted by two old demons. One was corruption. Although Kim was regarded as personally incorrupt, the methods used to bring North Korea to the summit, the tax investigations of leading opposition newspapers, and the arrest of his sons on bribery charges tainted his image, as similar problems had done to his predecessors.

The other burden he faced in his last months was the return of the North Korea nuclear issue. Kim's sunshine policy toward the North had been paralleled by the willingness of the United States under President Bill Clinton also to engage with North Korea. By the end of 2000, while there clearly remained problems, the U.S. had moved to a point where it was seen as only a matter of time before North Korea was removed from the State Department's "terrorism list." The visit of U.S. Secretary of State Madeleine Albright to P'yongyang in 2000 seemed to hold out hope of major progress in U.S.–North Korean relations.

The election of President George W. Bush changed all that. The new administration from the start indicated that it did not agree with its predecessor's policies on a number of countries, including North Korea, and that these would be subject to review. The North Koreans reacted with hostility.

President Kim Dae-jung, feted in Washington under Clinton both as a great democrat and the man who had brought imagination to bear on the North Korea policy found on his visit early in 2001 that the new U.S. president was skeptical about the policy and, apparently, personally hostile to the North Korean leader, Kim Jong-il. President Bush announced that the Clinton policy of engagement would be put on hold while a review would be conducted of U.S. policy toward North Korea.

The review, when concluded, came to much the same view as had Clinton; whether one liked the North Koreans or not, it was necessary to engage. But although the United States continued to be the main supplier of food to North Korea through the World Food Program, and although some contacts between the two countries continued, the atmosphere between the United States and North Korea was increasingly one of hostility. Even North Korea's relatively quick move to express condolences to the American people and to condemn terrorism after the 11 September 2001 attack on the World Trade Center failed to shift the American stance. President Bush appeared to further undermine Kim Dae-jung's position when in his January 2002 State of the Union message to the United States Congress, he described North Korea, together with Iraq and Iran, as part of a worldwide "Axis of Evil." This was followed by references to the need for better verification of controls on the North Korean nuclear program than had been provided for by the 1994 Agreed Framework and suggestions that North Korea should also reduce its conventional weapons.

As 2002 progressed, relations between North Korea and the United States went progressively downward. Kim Dae-jung did what he could to keep his sunshine policy in place, but the struggle became harder as U.S. pressure built up and revelations about how the 2000 summit had been arranged indicated that the North Koreans had been only willing to move for payment. For their part, the North Koreans did little to help Kim, although contacts and exchanges between North and South continued.

In August 2002, a ceremony took place at Kumho to mark the first concrete pouring for the light water reactors promised under the 1994 Agreed Framework. But the atmosphere was already tense, with the North Koreans complaining that the project was years behind schedule, and the Americans hinting that before there could be more progress, the North Koreans would have to submit to a full inspection of their existing nuclear facilities. The U.S. continued to express willingness to talk to the North Koreans, however, and a visit by the State Department's assistant secretary of state for Asian affairs, James Kelley, was planned for October 2002. At the meeting, instead of discussing the broad range of subjects that the North Koreans expected, Kelley concentrated on one point, accusing the North Koreans of engaging in a second nuclear program, involving enriched uranium. When confronted with this allegation, according to the Americans, the North Koreans admitted that they were engaged in such a program, but argued that they were entitled to do so since the U.S. continued to target them with nuclear weapons. By the time that Kim Dae-jung left office in February 2003, the situation had deteriorated further. North Korea threw out the IAEA inspectors at Yongbyon and claimed to have restarted the plant there. North Korea had also announced its intention to withdraw from the Nuclear Non-proliferation Treat, which it formally did in April 2003.

Kim Dae-jung continued to stand by the policy of engagement, despite all the problems. It must also have struck a resonance with the South Korean people, for in November 2002, they elected as his successor a former lawyer, Roh Moo-hyun, who was both in favor of continued sunshine and came from a radical background, rather than the conservative Lee Hoi-chang of the Grand National Party. To many, this marked the end of South Korean politics as they had developed from the 1970s, sometimes known as the "era of the three Kims." In a sense, that era was not quite over. Kim Young-sam and Kim Dae-jung were indeed now gone from the political stage, but one Kim remained. Kim Jong-p'il was still leader of the United Liberal Democrats. In reality, however, there now seemed little chance that even that great survivor would again gain power. South Korea in February 2003 entered a new political stage, despite many old problems remaining.

ECONOMIC DEVELOPMENT

The background: Economic Development before 1945

The story of South Korea's economic development has been remarkable, and it still amazes many people. From being one of the poorest countries in the world, lagging even behind its rival in the north, South Korea by the mid-1990s was a member of the Organization for Economic Cooperation and Development, with the 11th largest economy in the world. Even though it was badly hit by the 1997 Asian economic crisis, and suffered briefly from negative economic growth, within two years, its economy had bounced back.

The Koreans began with much against them. The peninsula might be beautiful, but its mountains and steep valleys have always severely limited the amount of land available for dwelling and cultivation to about a fifth of the total. Traditional Korea before the days of Japanese colonization had been an agricultural society, with the main emphasis on rice growing. By all accounts, Koreans were good rice farmers, able to produce crops in the most difficult conditions. They also developed double cropping techniques that are still of value today. Korea was not as isolated from the mainstream of East Asian economic trends as is sometimes implied. The Korean court sent missions to both Imperial China and Tokugawa Japan that served the dual purpose of maintaining political links and allowing trade. The intrusion of the West into Asia in the 19th century also affected Korea in economic terms before the Japanese forced a reluctant Korean court to sign its first "unequal treaty" in 1876. The early Western merchants arriving in Korea found that simple Western goods such as matches were already on sale, brought in by enterprising Chinese and Japanese peddlers. That said, the opening up of Korea to Japanese and Western commerce after 1876 did have a major effect on Korea. Railways, roads, and modern buildings all now made their appearance.

The pace of economic change quickened under the Japanese after 1910. This is an area of much sensitivity in modern Korea, and one on which much work remains to be done. There have been many publications in recent years showing that there were benefits as well as disadvantages for the Koreans under colonial rule. The Japanese expanded the basic infrastructure that they inherited in 1910, adding new railways, tramways, and roads to those already in existence. By the mid-1930s, the peninsula was linked by air to Japan and China, and a broadcasting system was in place. Banks and financial institutions brought Koreans into the new world of capitalism, where they were also introduced to modern department stores and factories, even if such developments generally affected only a few. Japanese *zaibatsu*, or conglomerates, would later provide a model for South Korean economic development. Education, though severely limited at the upper levels, became a general part of Korean life. Of course, these developments were largely undertaken for the benefit of the colonial rulers, but there were gains for Koreans as well. But as Japan moved onto a war footing after 1937, Koreans found themselves called upon to work more and more for Japan. Pressures of war meant that by the Japanese surrender in 1945, many of the economic gains of the 1920s and 1930s had been lost. Factories and railways were worn out, the land suffered from lack of fertilizers, and there had been massive deforestation. The workforce, too, was exhausted by the unremitting demands of the war economy.

Economic Development 1945–1961

The division of the Korean Peninsula in 1945 dealt South Korea a severe blow. From 1910 onward, the peninsula had been developed on a unified model. Much heavy industry was in the northern part, which also supplied hydroelectric power and had the natural resources required for industrialization. The southern half of the peninsula was the agricultural center of the country as well as the home of much of the new light industry that developed in the Japanese period. Between 1945 and the emergence of separate states in 1948, the economic links between the two halves of the peninsula were steadily broken; they were to remain so until the late 1990s.

The departure of the Japanese also dealt Korea an additional blow. With the Japanese went their expertise in engineering, banking, and finance. There was also an outflow of capital. As the nature of the new regime in the northern half of the peninsula became clear, many fled to the South, while at the same time there was a huge inflow of Koreans returning from all over the defeated Japanese empire, pushing up what seemed an already large population. Estimates put the increase of the population of the southern half at between two and three million between 1945–1948.

The division had left South Korea's mostly light industries, depending entirely on North Korea's supply of electric power (95 percent) and chemical fertilizers (100 percent), as well as coal, the main source of fuel, and timber. When the supply of these vital commodities was cut off, the economic consequences were devastating. Almost all industrial establishments were forced to close down because of the shortage of electric power, and food production was sharply reduced due to the shortage of fertilizers. A 1948 World Bank report indicated that the South Korean economy was "close to the bottom of the international economic scale and without the benefit of sufficient supply of natural resources." South Korea had virtually no highly trained scientists, technicians, economic experts, or managerial personnel as a result of the Japanese policy that did not allow Koreans to be trained in these fields, and the American military government had done virtually nothing to bring about economic improvement.

The United States sent U.S. $525 million to South Korea between 1945–1948 in the form of essential goods, grants, and loans. This support, together with United Nations assistance, kept the population from starving and allowed some economic rehabilitation. The new South Korean government also made efforts to improve economic conditions. An economic reconstruction program began with land reform, which was carried out in June 1949, when all farmlands (excluding fields where special crops such as tobacco and ginseng were grown) not cultivated by the owners and holdings of more than 7.5 acres of farmlands owned by owner-cultivators were purchased by the government. The government, in turn, sold these lands to the farmers, charging lower prices than it had paid to the former owners and providing the opportunity to pay in a long-term installment scheme. Around 1.5 million farmers acquired some 1.2 million acres of land. With this the system of absentee landlordism was abolished, and the amount of grain produced rose from 4.6 million tons in 1948 to 5.2 million tons by 1950. The construction of three new railroads and the development of the coal industry helped manufacturing industries to operate their factories as the per capita gross national product (GNP) grew to $68 million in 1950.

The 1950–1953 Korean War wiped out such gains as were made. Millions died, and millions more were affected by the loss of family members. Two million additional refugees ended the war in South Korea. Schools, homes, and over 40 percent of industrial installations were destroyed. Total property damage from the war was estimated at U.S.$2 billion, the same as South Korea's Gross National Product (GNP) in 1949. Agricultural production in the South fell by 27 percent between 1949–1952, while total GNP fell by 14 percent during the same period. Inevitably, in the war and thereafter, expenditure on the military came to occupy a disproportionate share.

Once again, South Korea was kept going by economic assistance from the United States and the United Nations. By 1960, aid from these two sources amounted to over U.S.$2 billion dollars. Theoretically, a 1953 national plan, produced by the Office of National Planning, was originally established in 1948, but obviously not functioning during the war. In practice, Syngman Rhee's interest in economic matters was limited and little was done. Rhee was happy to concentrate on security issues and his own political survival. There was little industrial development and a heavy reliance on the import of foreign food and consumer goods. The result was rampant inflation and slow growth. By the end of the 1950s, despite the aid received, South Korean per capita income was still only about $74, making it one of the world's poorest countries. As with the colonial period, however, all was not as black as it is sometimes painted. Postwar reconstruction of new railroads, highways and roads, and power plants and an increased supply of fertilizer contributed to a formal growth rate that averaged 5.1 percent. Korean companies began to take the place left by the departing Japanese.

The government maintained the free enterprise system until 1962 when the military junta adopted various economic development plans and increased central control; the system remained nominally "capitalist," but owed much to Japan's prewar experiment in state-directed development in Manchuria. While the new military leaders had no ready-made blueprint for economic development, they were determined to make South Korea an economic success. Significant economic growth began following the implementation of the first Five-Year Economic Development Plan (1962–1966) by the military junta, accompanying sustained expansion of exports with large U.S. grants and foreign loans. The normalization of relations with Japan in 1965 brought additional economic assistance, contributing substantially to economic development.

South Korea's GNP grew annually by 7.4 percent between 1962 and 1981, during which period four successive Five-Year Economic Development Plans were successfully completed, bringing the nation's GNP to $66.2 billion with per capita GNP of $1,605 by 1981. The high rate of increase in GNP and personal income was accompanied by rising ratios of investment savings, exports, and by a basic structural change. Whereas the first Plan promoted import-substitution industries, the second Plan laid the foundation for a modern industrial structure, promoting exports; and the third Plan, achieving between 8.6 percent and 10.1 percent annual GNP growth, brought about the rise of an industrial structure, facilitating heavy industry and modernization of farm villages and rural areas with the Saemaul (New Community Movement). Finally, the fourth Plan established the foundation of a self-reliant growth structure and the advancement of high technology.

The share of agriculture/fisheries in the GNP decreased from 36.6 percent in 1962 to 18 percent in 1981 while that of mining and manufacturing industries increased from 16.2 percent to 30.9 percent during the same period. The manufacturing industry's share rose from 14.2 percent to 29.5 percent, and while the share of light industry decreased from 73.2 percent in 1962 to 44.6 percent in 1981, that of heavy industry and chemical industry increased from 26.8 percent to 55.3 percent during the corresponding period. The social service industry's share in the GNP also grew. All but the fourth Plan achieved the planned goals. The actual growth rate during this period of the fourth Plan was 5.8 percent per year. Among the factors responsible for this setback were the substantial increase in the price of imported petroleum and raw materials in the late 1970s, a worldwide recession, the rise of protectionist sentiments in the advanced countries, strong inflationary pressures, rising wage rates, and the chaotic situation that developed in South Korea following the assassination of President Park Chung-hee in 1979.

The fifth Economic and Social Development Plan (1982–86), which accompanied the liberalization of the domestic market and the strengthening of exports, was highly successful as South Korea attained a GNP growth rate of 10 percent per year during the period, the GNP reaching the \$95.1 billion mark in 1986 with the per capita GNP of \$2,300, despite the population increasing to 41 million. For the first time, South Korea's exports (\$34.7 million) exceeded its imports (\$31.6 million). In 1986, 8.2 million owner-cultivators cultivated some 5,300,000 acres of farmlands. The production of rice increased from three million tons in 1962 to 5.6 million tons in 1986, achieving near self-sufficiency in food supply. The total amount of grain production increased from 6.5 million tons in 1961 to 8.5 million tons in 1986. Other important accomplishments in the agriculture and forestry sector were the implementation of a ten-year Resources Development Plan (1972–1981), which included the planting of 186.6 million trees in 51,000 acres of land, rejuvenating hills and forest lands.

The most significant economic achievement of South Korea was industrialization, resulting in increasing production of anthracite, electric power, cement, chemical fertilizer, textiles, and the training of scientists and skilled workers. South Korea developed new industries such as automobile, electronics, iron and steel, petrochemical, oil refinery, and shipbuilding. The production of anthracite rose from three million tons in 1962 to 24 million tons in 1985, and that of cement increased from 790,000 tons in 1962 to 16.5 million tons in 1986. While increasing power production from 1,789 million kwh in 1962 to 67,639 million kwh in 1986, South Korea's chemical fertilizer production increased from 83,000 tons in 1966 to 3.5 million tons in 1986. The automobile, manufacturing, and shipbuilding industries made remarkable progress, as South Korea became one of the world's largest shipbuilders and automobile exporters.

These economic development plans brought about the rise of many industrial centers (tax-free industrial zones included), beginning at Kumi in the southeast of the country. Such industrial centers as shipbuilding at Ulsan and on Koje Island; iron-steel and petrochemical works at P'ohang; cement, coal, and fertilizer manufacturing at Samch'ok; and automobile manufacturing, electronics plants, and textile factories located at Inch'on and other places had a revolutionary effect on the Korean economy, increasing exports and changing the social life of the people. However, the heavy concentration of such development in Park Chung-hee's home area, the southeast, led to resentment in less-favored areas, such as the southwestern Cholla Provinces.

In 1987, a sixth Five-Year Economic and Social Development Plan began aimed to increase GNP by 7 percent and exports by 13.3 percent per year. In 1987 alone, the GNP grew to 128.4 billion with a per capita GNP of $3,110, and South Korea's exports ($47.2 million) remained greater than its imports ($41 million). In this way, South Korea managed to reduce its foreign debts from $45 billion in 1986 to $35.5 billion in 1987 as it showed its capacity to bring about continuous economic growth, despite many problems. By 1991, the GNP was $284.8 billion, or $6,498 on a per capita basis.

The political changes that marked Roh Tae-woo's presidency led to a relaxation of some of the hitherto tight controls on labor in South Korea. Yet despite various problems caused by labor disputes and appreciation of the won currency, South Korea achieved a 12.2-percent GNP growth in 1988. Per capita GNP jumped from $3,098 in 1987 to $4,040 in 1988 when the inflation rate of consumer goods was 7.5 percent. More than 500,000 new jobs were created in 1988 as the percentage of unemployment remained at 2.5 percent. South Korea's exports grew by 28.3 percent to $60.7 billion ($47.3 billion in 1987), while its imports rose by 26.3 percent to $51.8 billion ($41 billion in 1987), making South Korea one of the world's 10 largest trading nations. With the increase in exports, by the end of 1988, South Korea had reduced its foreign debts from $35.6 billion in 1987 to $31.2 billion.

South Korea's economic growth slowed down after 1988. Labor costs rose, as the average annual rate of wage increase between 1988 and 1991 reached 20 percent following the adoption of a minimum wage system and several labor strikes. The increasing wages of urban workers brought about a shift in income of urban and farm households; in 1988 the annual average urban household's income was $11,938 while that of farm households was $12,507. By 1991, the respective figures were $18,537 for urban households and $17,473 for rural. The dollar/won exchange rate was 1 to 680 in 1988, 1 to 700 in 1990, and 1 to 750 in 1991. The inflation rate of consumer goods in 1989 was 5.2 percent, but had jumped to 9.5 percent in 1991.

Mainly because of rising wages and importation of foreign goods, South Korea's GNP growth slowed down as its balance of trade shifted from plus to minus. Thus, in 1989 South Korea's GNP growth rate was 6.5 percent raising the GNP to $204 billion with the per capita GNP of $4,830. The downward trends in economic development continued in 1990 and 1991 as South Korea's overseas markets shrank due to growing competition from other Asian "Mini Dragons," as well as China. Despite this, South Korea's GNP growth rate in 1991 rose to 8.7 percent with the total GNP of $272.2 billion and per capita GNP of $6,498. South Korea's exports grew by 10.5 percent in 1991 reaching the $71.8 billion mark, but its imports jumped by 16.8 percent to $81.5 billion, producing a trade deficit of $9.7 billion, twice as large as the 1990 trade deficit of $4.8 billion. Of this, $759 million was with the United States and $8.8 billion with Japan. South Korea's two-way trade with China, the Soviet Union, and former socialist countries grew substantially from $3.7 billion in 1988 to $8.1 billion in 1991 with an annual rise of 40 percent. Exports jumped from $2 billion to $3.7 billion. However, the annual growth rate of imports from them was 49.8 percent, exceeding the annual growth rate of exports that was 30 percent.

As a result, the trade balance shifted from $329 million in favor of South Korea in 1988 to a deficit of $299 million in 1989, $159 million in 1990, and $591 million in 1991. Although the trade balance vis-à-vis the Soviet Union and Eastern European and other socialist countries was in favor of South Korea by $499 million in 1991, South Korea's trade balance with China created a deficit of $2.43 billion in 1991 ($1 billion in exports and $3.4 billion in imports), due primarily to the large amount of agricultural products and medicinal herbs imported from

China. Meanwhile, South Korea's market share in the United States shrank from 4.6 percent in 1988 to 3.5 percent in 1991 as a result of the growing Chinese market share of goods from 1.9 percent to 4.8 percent during the corresponding period.

GNP growth was sustained by the home market, with the population increasing from 41.9 million in 1988 to 43.9 million in 1991, creating more domestic demands for goods and services, especially in housing and transportation. However, in view of the declining rate of GNP growth, coupled with the growing trade deficit, the South Korean government reduced the share of military spending in the national budget from 33 percent in 1987 to 30 percent (4.37 percent of the GNP) in 1988. It was further reduced to 27.6 percent (3.77 percent of the GNP) in 1991, and 25.3 percent (3.71 percent of GNP) in 1992. The government announced in May 1992 that military spending would be further reduced to 24.4 percent of the national budget, or 3.69 percent of projected GNP, by 1997. By 1997, however, very different considerations would apply.

In November 1991, the South Korean government announced its seventh socioeconomic development plan for 1992–1997. Its targets were to achieve an average annual GNP growth rate of 7.5 percent and to raise the GNP to $492.6 billion and per capita GNP to $10,908 by 1996. There would also be a shift from what were by now the traditional heavy industry sectors toward new high-technology industries, such as computers, precision instruments, and electronic goods. But there were growing difficulties in the economy. Growth slowed, inflation grew, and the workforce became less and less amenable. Wages, under union pressure, rose rapidly; real wages doubled between 1986 and 1993, much faster than productivity, reducing the competitiveness of Korean goods internationally. There was also an increasing shortage of workers in many areas. South Koreans now refused to do many of the "dirty" jobs necessary in any economic system.

Yet by the mid-1990s, despite all the problems, South Korea seemed set for an indefinite period of single-digit high economic growth, with a balanced budget and a low current account deficit. The government continued to play a major role in directing the economy. President Kim Young-sam's proclaimed policy of "globalization," although somewhat imprecise in detail, was seen by many both in South Korea and abroad as a promise that the South Korean economy would, in due course, open up to foreign investment and would become more transparent in the process. Economic reform seemed to be promised in the decision to impose a real name system on the financial markets.

A few clouds appeared on the economic horizon early in 1997. The Hanbo group found itself at the center of a crisis as a result of taking on huge loans without proper collateral; the fact that one of the president's sons was implicated in the affair made what was originally a financial crisis into a potential political issue. Worse was to come. In the summer of 1997, international speculation against the Thai currency led to a collapse of the *baht*, and speculators turned their attention to other Asian currencies. At the same time, another major company, Kia Autos, found itself in difficulties and looked to the government to bail it out. There followed a run on the South Korean currency, which quickly showed up the problems of most of the country's financial institutions. The won fell from just over 800 to the U.S. dollar to around 1,700 to the dollar between October 1997 and January 1998. Unemployment soared. By the end of December 1997, foreign exchange reserves had fallen to $5 billion.

The government seemed paralyzed. President Kim Young-sam gave little indication of understanding the seriousness of the situation and did nothing to alleviate it. As the crisis persisted, it was clear that action was needed, and after much soul-searching, the government turned to the International Monetary Fund (IMF) for assistance. The IMF eventually came up with a $57 billion bailout package just before the 1997 presidential election. There was much dismay in the country at the apparent failure of "the miracle on the Han," and many protested at the "sell out" to the IMF and the forced opening of the South Korean economy that was part of the deal. Demonstrators smashed foreign goods (Japanese pens were one favored target) in protest, while some women donated their gold and jewels to help pay the nation's debts.

The incoming president, Kim Dae-jung, who at first seemed equally as overwhelmed by the enormity of what had happened as Kim Young-sam, pledged to implement the IMF package. In April 1998, the government formed the Financial Supervisory Commission to oversee the restructuring of the economy. By the end of 1998, this body had closed down about 100 financial institutions and more than 50 noncompetitive corporations. Organizations closed down included five commercial banks, five securities houses, and 16 merchant banks. Other major banks were forced to merge or were sold off to foreign companies. Even the *chaebol* did not escape; among liquidated corporations were 20 *chaebol* subsidiaries, though the big corporations generally resisted attempts to force them to undertake major structural reform.

Despite these efforts, 1998 was a bad year. GDP fell by over 6 percent. Unemployment continued to rise, reaching 6.8 percent by the end of the year and peaking at 8.6 percent in February 1999. By then, banks alone had dismissed some 39,000 staff. Over capacity, a near bankrupt banking sector, and huge private debt took their toll.

Difficulties continued into 1999, but before long, there were signs of improvement. Inflation dropped to 0.8 percent, the lowest since the days of Park Chung-hee. GNP bounced back, to around 10 percent over the year as a whole. Unemployment, while still high, began to fall and was down to 4.4 percent by November 1999. The won climbed back to about 1,150 to the dollar, and the IMF loan was paid off ahead of time. Inevitably, this led some to question the need for continued economic reform. The government continued to avoid a confrontation with the *chaebol* and showed the old willingness to bale out major companies in difficulties when Daewoo came near to bankruptcy. That the long-established links between the *chaebol and* the government continued in place was shown by the Hyundai group's involvement in North Korea. Although nothing was formally said, Hyundai could not have engaged in such a sensitive business without at least tacit government support.

The pace of recovery was maintained in 2000, though the opening up forced on South Korea by the events of 1997 altered the face of Korean industry and finance. Other problems remain. While the number of *chaebol* shrank, some of the remainder still have problems. The giant Hyundai group ran into financial difficulties in spring 2000 and sought government assistance. This was forthcoming but on condition that the group's founder, Chung Ju-yung and other members of his family, resign. There followed a hard struggle, but in theory this requirement was met. There was some disquiet in South Korean society that the pace of recovery had thrown a heavy burden on the poorer sectors of society who were not cushioned as they might have been in the West, but generally South Korea faced the economic future in mid-2000 with a degree of confidence that was remarkable, given the trauma of 1997.

This confidence continued for the remainder of Kim Dae-jung's term of office, despite the setbacks on the political scene. There was not, however, a totally smooth period of economic recovery. If GNP rose by 8.6 percent in 2000, it fell back to 3.6 percent in 2001. This was still respectable compared with other developed nations, but it was not what the Koreans had been used to, and it did not match the steady growth of the Chinese economy. The election year 2002 showed no sign of improvement in growth, which again slumped, from a projected 6.3 percent to 2.9 percent, over the course of the year. The *chaebol* began to go slow on reorganization. Kim Dae-jung, beset with other problems, now seemed as bemused about the economy as his predecessor had been in 1997.

Yet the positive outweighed the negative. The won slowly appreciated in value against the dollar; in May 2002, the exchange rate was Won 1,325 to the dollar, but a year later, it was at 1,200 and still rising. Foreign exchange reserves reached U.S.$121,41 billion in December 2002, the fourth largest in the world. The trade surplus for 2002 was $10.8 billion, with exports at $162.82 billion, and imports at $152.02 billion. Per capita income in December 2002 was $8,900 compared with $706 in North Korea. While the great growth days of the 1960s and 1970s might have been long past, all the signs were that the "miracle on the Han" was still in business.

EPILOGUE

The 20th century was hard on the Koreans. Loss of sovereignty, division, and war all took their toll. From time to time, hopes have been raised only to be dashed again. 1945 was one such moment; perhaps 1950 was another, when war seemed likely to end the division of the peninsula. The breaking of the long deadlock between North and South in 1971–1972 was certainly seen as hopeful, but it and subsequent North–South contacts ended as they had begun, with each side cut off from the other once more. The meeting between Kim Dae-jung and Kim Jong-il in 2000, however it was brought about, and however unrealistic some of the expectations that it raised, has nevertheless proved more productive than the earlier contacts. Substantive links between North and South now seem to have been forged that will be hard to break. South Korea's recovery from the economic doldrums of 1997 means that it can continue to afford to fund involvement in the North, and President Roh Moo-hyun seems keen to continue doing so.

The North Korean nuclear issue, of course, remains as a major problem, compounded by the ambiguous role of the United States under President George W. Bush. The signs are, however, that whatever President Bush's personal dislike of North Korea's Kim Jong-il, and whatever the wishes of the so-called neoconservatives, a peaceful solution will emerge, though it might take some time. In the meantime, South Korea's engagement efforts will continue to produce results. Unification is probably some way off, but all seem agreed that the best way to get there is peacefully. Perhaps then, the 21st century will be kinder to the Koreans.

The Dictionary

– A –

ACADEMY OF KOREAN STUDIES (*Hanguk jungsin munhwa yunguwon*). This academic institution was established in 1978 under President **Park Chung-hee**. Its formal purpose was to promote scholarship in the field of Korean studies, but it was also aimed at improving South Korea's international image. As well as publishing works on Korea and providing a center for scholars, the academy has had a graduate program since 1980. By 2003, this program had produced 400 master's and 110 Ph.D.s in Korean studies. It occupies an attractive campus just outside **Seoul**.

ACHESON'S STATEMENT ON KOREA. On 12 January 1950, Dean Acheson, then secretary of state of the **United States**, spoke on Asian policy at the Press Club in Washington D.C. Speaking "off the cuff" from notes, he said that the U.S. defense perimeter in the Pacific ran along the Aleutians to **Japan**, to the Ryukyus, and to the Philippine Islands, which must and will be held by the United States. In his statement, the Republic of Korea and the Republic of **China** on Formosa were conspicuously absent from the line of the U.S. defense perimeter, and some have seen this as the signal to **North Korea** that it would not have to deal with the United States in the event of a conflict on the Korean Peninsula. *See also* KOREAN WAR.

AGENCY FOR NATIONAL SECURITY PLANNING. *See* NATIONAL INTELLIGENCE SERVICE (NIS).

AGREEMENT ON RECONCILIATION, NONAGGRESSION AND EXCHANGES AND COOPERATION BETWEEN THE SOUTH AND THE NORTH. This Agreement was concluded at the fifth round of talks of the premiers of **North Korea** and South Korea in **Seoul** in December 1991.

The first three premier-level talks were held in September, October, and December 1990, and the fourth in October 1991. The Agreement was dated 13 December 1991. The principles set out in the document were reaffirmed by South Korea's **Kim Dae-jung** and North Korea's **Kim Jong-il** at their June 2000 summit and the text remains the main formal document in North–South relations.

In it, the two sides agreed to respect each other's political systems and to follow a policy of noninterference in each other's affairs. Until such time as a permanent peace agreement could be reached, each would abide by the terms of the 1953 armistice agreement. They also agreed to stop international competition with each other. The Agreement provided for a wide range of social and economic exchanges and for the reconnection of road and rail links severed since the **Korean War**.

The Agreement was approved by President **Roh Tae-woo** of South Korea on 17 January 1992 and by President **Kim Il-sung** of North Korea on 18 January 1992. The approved document was exchanged at the sixth round of the premiers talks, held in **P'yongyang** from 18–21 February 1992, in theory bringing the Agreement into force. In practice, it remained a dead letter until some of its precepts were re-affirmed in the June 2000 Inter-Korean Summit exchanges. Since then, there has been some progress on issues such **family reunions** and North–South transport links. *See* Appendix E for the full text of the Agreement.

AGRICULTURE. The southern half of the Korean peninsula was the traditional agricultural heartland of the country. Before the division in 1945, about 90 percent of the population in the southern part of the peninsula were engaged in agriculture. Agriculture was transformed as a result of two major land reform measures. The first was carried out in 1947, under the **United States Army Military Government in Korea**, and transferred land previously held by the Japanese to Korean farmers. The second, the **Land Reform Law** of 1949 under President **Syngman Rhee**, broke up large land holdings.

In the late 1950s, there were still well over two million families and 13.5 million people engaged in agriculture, out of a population of about 24 million. By the 1990s, agriculture contributed about 5.7 percent of the South Korean Gross Domestic Product (GDP), and accounted for about 11 percent of the workforce. There is nevertheless still a sizeable rural population and the agricultural sector is still important. Agricultural production is concentrated in the lowlands of the west and south coast of the peninsula, and in the major river valleys. Rice remains the main crop, accounting for some 30 percent of agricultural output. Other crops in order of importance include potatoes, barley, soybeans, maize, bananas, and wheat. South Korea is self-sufficient in rice but not in other food crops. Agricultural exports, including fish, amounted to $3.3 billion in 1997, while imports came to $10.8 billion. Changing eating patterns and the declining agricultural workforce have led some farmers to less labor-intensive crops, such as vegetables and fruit. A major project to create additional farmland in North Cholla Province, which began in 1991 but was stopped in 1999 as a result of the **IMF crisis**, resumed in 2002. The government has also encouraged farmers to use the **Internet** to increase outlets for farm produce. *See also* ECONOMIC DEVELOPMENT; NEW COMMUNITY MOVEMENT.

AIR-RAID DRILLS. From 1972 until 1993, regular daytime air-raid drills were held in South Korea on a monthly basis. From 1993 onward, they have been held only three times a year. Nighttime blackout drills, rigorously enforced, have also been held periodically. The **Civil Defense Corps**, created in 1975, was primarily charged with air-raid precautions.

AN CHAE-HONG (1891–1965). A progressive nationalist, An graduated from Waseda University in **Japan** in 1914. He was associated with the Korean Young Men's Christian Association (YMCA) and in 1919 was sentenced to three years of imprisonment for his activity in the March First Movement. (See the introduction.) In 1923, along with others, he founded a Korean-language newspaper, *Shidae Ilbo*, and served on its editorial board. Later, he became president and editor-in-chief of another Korean newspaper, *Chosun Ilbo*, a position he held for 10 years, but was imprisoned again in 1925, 1936, and

1942 for his nationalistic remarks. Upon Korea's liberation, An, a member of the **Korean Nationalist Party**, together with **Song Chin-u** and **Yo Un-hyong**, set up the **Committee for the Preparation of National Reconstruction**. When the **South Korean Interim Government** was established in 1947 by the **United States Army Military Government in Korea**, An became civil administrator. However, he opposed the **United Nations** plan to hold separate elections in South Korea. After the **Korean War**, he reappeared in **North Korea**, where he held a post in the Committee for the Peaceful Reunification of the Fatherland (*Chaebuk Pyonghwa Tongil Chokjin Hyopuihoe*).

AN HO-SANG (1902–1999). Educated at Jena University, Germany, An taught at Korea University (1933–1945) and Seoul National University (1945–1948). Dr. An served as the minister of education from 1948 to 1950. He was the author of South Korea's **Education Law** of 1949, which reflected his conservative philosophy.

AN IK-T'AE (1905–1965). Musician who pioneered Western-style music in Korea, and who composed the tune now used for the South Korean national anthem in 1936. An was born in **P'yongyang** and studied music in **Japan** and the **United States**. From the late 1930s until 1959, he spent most of his time in Europe, where he established a name both as a conductor and composer. In 1959 he returned to South Korea, and remained active in musical circles until his death in Majorca, Spain. The current South Korean national anthem, the *Aegukka* ("Love country song") adopted in 1948, may have been originally written in the late 19th century. There were earlier anthems, including one sung to the tune of the Scottish melody "Auld Lang Syne" and another composed by the German bandmaster Franz Eckert. An is credited with drawing on traditional musical forms for the current version.

AN SU-GIL (1911–1977). Born in Hamhung, now in **North Korea**, An went to school in **Seoul** and was briefly detained at the time of the 1929 **Kwangju** incident before going to **Japan** to study at Waseda University. After graduation, he went to Manchuria, where he worked as a teacher and a journalist. After 1945, he returned to **North Korea**

but reached Seoul in 1948. Thereafter An worked as a journalist on the *Kyonghyang Sinmun* and as a teacher, while producing many novels and short stories. The best known of his novels is *Pukkando* (North Jiandao), published in five volumes between 1959–1967, which describes life from the 1860s to 1945 in an area that was famous for its resistance to the Japanese.

ANTI-COMMUNISM LAW. Promulgated on 3 July 1961 by the **Supreme Council for National Reconstruction**, the purpose of the law was to strengthen the anticommunist posture of the nation, to block the activities of communist organizations, and to secure the safety of the nation and freedom of the people. It consisted of 11 articles, barring the affiliation and solicitation of affiliation with antistate organizations, praising, encouraging, or cooperating with antistate organizations, or escape to or secret entry from regions under control of antistate organizations, offering assistance to persons who had committed offenses in violation of this law or the **National Security Law**. Those who violated the law or failed to report to the authorities any criminal offenders under it would be punished. In December 1980, the Anti-Communism Law was consolidated with the National Security Law. *See also* EAST BERLIN CASE; NATIONAL INTELLIGENCE SERVICE.

ANTI-TRAITOR LAW. *See* LAW CONCERNING PUNISHMENT OF THOSE WHO COMMITTED CRIMES AGAINST THE PEOPLE.

APRIL 1960 STUDENT UPRISING. This refers to popular antigovernment demonstrations, led by students, which forced President **Syngman Rhee** and his cabinet to resign in April 1960, ending the problem-ridden First Republic. It is also known as the *April Student Righteous Uprising* or *student "revolution."*

It began immediately after the 15 March 1960 presidential and vice presidential elections when the opposition **Democratic Party** and students protested the "rigging" of elections by Rhee's **Liberal Party** in collusion with the **police**. The protesters clashed with the police, several persons were killed, and many more were wounded by the shots fired by the police. The discovery in **Masan** on 11 April of the body of a student who had been shot and killed by the police provoked even more violent antigovernment demonstrations. Police stations, the Liberal Party headquarters, and some public buildings in Masan were wrecked.

Students in **Seoul** and other cities and towns began their demonstrations, demanding the nullification of the 15 March election results, as well as the resignation of President Rhee and his cabinet members. On 18 April, some 3,000 students of Korea University in Seoul staged a mass rally and marched to downtown Seoul. On their way back to the campus, they were attacked by hundreds of thugs, presumably hired by the Liberal Party. A new wave of student demonstrations, joined by professors and thousands of citizens, erupted on 19 April, resulting in clashes with the police. The demonstrators marched toward the presidential mansion, while police fired upon the demonstrators. Further provoked, students burned down police stations, sacked the building of the government newspaper, the *Seoul Shinmun*, and broke into the headquarters of the Liberal Party in Seoul.

Greatly outnumbered and facing a dangerous situation, many police officers fled, but others continued to fire at the demonstrators, killing 125 persons and wounding some 1,000. President Rhee declared martial law on the afternoon of 19 April, and mobilized army troops accompanied by tanks, but the troops refused to act against the demonstrators. In an attempt to save the president, all cabinet members submitted their resignations en masse. Under pressure from the **United States**, and facing impossible odds, President Rhee himself resigned on 26 April. *See also* STUDENT MOVEMENT.

ARCHITECTURE. Little of Korean architecture before the 17th century has survived the wars and invasions that followed. Because wood featured prominently in many buildings, even those that claim a long ancestry have often been rebuilt several times. Many modern buildings draw on what are believed to be traditional principles, especially in roof design.

Western-style architecture was introduced in the last years of the 19th century. Surviving examples include the Roman Catholic Myongdong Cathedral in **Seoul** and a number of other churches, as well as the ambassador's residence and a former office and residential building at the British Embassy. Under the Japanese **Government-General of Korea**, Korean cities acquired many modern buildings. In Seoul, these included the **Capitol Building**, demolished in 1997, the City Hall, the **Bank of Korea**, a number of department stores, and Seoul Railway Station. The **Korean War** saw much destruction, and postwar building was often hastily erected and of poor quality. As South Korea became wealthier in the 1970s and 1980s, new buildings drawing on a wide range of traditions began to appear in the capital and elsewhere. They included a number of branches of the **National Museum of Korea**, the Sejong Cultural Center in Seoul, the 1988 Olympic Stadium, and a number of related buildings. The late 1980s and 1990s saw a further wave of new buildings, including Seoul Arts Center and the spectacular new **Inch'on** International Airport, opened in 2001.

ARMED FORCES. *See* NATIONAL DEFENSE FORCES.

ASIANA AIRLINES. South Korea's second airline, after **Korean Air**, founded in 1988 when air transport was deregulated. By 2000, Asiana owned 54 aircraft, flying on both domestic and international routes. The company then flew to 51 destinations in 17 countries.

ASSASSINATION AND ASSASSINATION ATTEMPTS. The history of the use of assassination to eliminate opponents in Korea began well before the colonial period, and was also used against the **Japanese**. It recommenced against prominent political leaders soon after the division of Korea in 1945, with the assassination on 28 December by a leftist of **Song Chin-u**, a major leader of the **Korean Democratic Party** in the midst of antitrusteeship protests. The killing of Song was followed by the assassination on 19 July 1947 by a refugee from North Korea of **Yo Un-hyong**, a prominent moderate left-wing nationalist who was the head of the **Working People's Party**. On 2 December 1947, a leftist assassinated another key leader of the Korean Democratic Party, **Chang Tok-su**. On 26 June 1949, **Kim Ku**, an ultra-rightist leader and the head of the **Korean Independence Party**, was assassinated by a South Korean army lieutenant, who charged him with being an obstacle to the Republic and to the promotion of democratic government in South Korea.

On 28 September 1956, a would-be assassin shot and wounded vice-president-elect **Chang Myon** at the Citizen's Hall in **Seoul**.

There was then a gap until the evening of 26 October 1979, when President **Park Chung-hee** was fatally wounded by pistol shots fired by the director of the Korean Central Intelligence Agency (now the **National Intelligence Service**), Kim Chae-gyu, and died early the next morning. The assassin allegedly said that he killed the president to promote democracy in South Korea. On that occasion, President Park's security service chief was also killed.

North Korea has also made assassination attacks. On 21 January 1968, a 31-man team of North Korean commandos infiltrated the northern part of Seoul in order to gain access to the **Blue House** and assassinate President Park Chung-hee. All but one of the commandos were killed by the **police**.

On 15 August 1974, a Korean resident from Japan, believed to be associated with pro–North Korean groups, made an attempt to assassinate President Park at the National Theater in Seoul. President Park escaped the assassin's bullets but his wife, Madame Yuk Yong-su, who was sitting on the platform, was shot and died shortly thereafter at a hospital. On 9 October 1983, North Korean agents attempted to assassinate President **Chun Doo-hwan** in the **Rangoon bombing**. They placed remote-controlled bombs at the Martyr's Mausoleum, in Rangoon Burma but detonated them before Chun's arrival. Chun, who was on a state visit tour in Southeast Asia, was behind schedule because of traffic congestion, thus escaping certain death. However, Chun's top advisors and several cabinet ministers were killed.

AUSTRALIA, RELATIONS WITH. These date back to the late 19th century, when Australian Presbyterian missionaries arrived in Korea. Until 1941, Australian diplomatic and consular interests in Korea were handled by **Great Britain**. After 1945, Australia played a prominent role in the 1947 **United Nations Temporary Commission on Korea** (UNTOK) and its successor, the 1948 United Nations Commission on Korea (UNCOK). Australia recognized the Republic of Korea in 1948, although an Australian Embassy was not established in **Seoul** until 1962. During the **Korean War**, Australian forces from all three services participated. Australian forces eventually formed part of the 28th British Commonwealth Brigade, and later the First Commonwealth Division. Australian forces remained in South Korea until 1957, though in decreasing numbers. In 1974,

Australia established diplomatic relations with **North Korea** and the two countries exchanged embassies. This link was broken in 1975, and not renewed until 2000. Australia is a major trading partner of South Korea, and in 1994 briefly overtook the **United States** as the country's second largest export market. Although Australia did not hold that position for long, it has continued to be important, with two-way trade at the turn of the century reaching over $10 billion annually.

– B –

BANK OF KOREA (*Hankuk unheung*). Another bank had this name during the **Japanese** protectorate period (1905–1910), but this became the Bank of Chosen during the colonial **Government-General of Korea**. The modern Bank of Korea dates from 1950. The Bank of Korea Act of 12 June 1950 established this bank as the country's central bank. Originally, it had a capital of 1.5 billion won, all subscribed by the government, but under another Bank of Korea Act passed in 1962, it became a state juridical person with no capital. It issues banknotes and coins, formulates monetary and credit policy, and acts as the bank for both the government and other banks. It also manages the foreign exchange reserves and is the bank of settlement for South Korea. It occupies the premises built in the Japanese colonial period for the Bank of Chosen. *See also* BANKING SYSTEM.

BANKING SYSTEM. South Korea's modern banking system can be traced back to the foundation of a **Japanese**-owned bank, the First National Bank, established at **Pusan** in 1878. This later became the first note-issuing bank in Korea. In 1909, a central bank, called the **Bank of Korea**, took over the note-issuing function. This bank became the Bank of Chosen during the Japanese **Government-General of Korea**. Several other banks were also established under the Japanese, some of them, such as the Chosen Industrial Bank, highly specialized.

The Bank of Chosen became the Bank of Chosun in 1945, but the whole banking system was thrown into disarray by the split between the Japanese and Korean economies that occurred then. On the eve of the **Korean War**, a new banking act created the current Bank of Korea and also provided for the organization of commercial banks. However, the outbreak of the war prevented the implementation of this section of the act. Only with the end of the war did new banks emerge. The Korea Development Bank, wholly government funded, was established in 1954, followed by the Korea Agriculture Bank in 1956. As their names implied, these were specialized banks, aimed at economic development.

Following the **Military Revolution of May 1961**, the government reorganized financial institutions to facilitate the operation of its economic plans. Various specialized banks were created to meet the needs of areas such as fisheries and housing. Regional banks also emerged, to assist local development. Although the 1960s and 1970s saw the creation of private banks, the whole financial sector was very close to, and very influenced by, government policies. In particular, the government encouraged the banks to support the *chaebol*, or industrial conglomerates. The 1970s saw the development of merchant banking, and foreign banks began to open in **Seoul**.

In theory, the government began to withdraw from the banking sector as early as 1972, when the Commercial Bank of Korea, originally government-owned, was privatized. Further privatizations took place in the 1980s, but in reality, a close relationship continued between the banks and the government, with the latter still directing much of the banks' lending. This created some of the problems that emerged during the **IMF crisis** of 1997, when a number of banks were brought down by the burden of their nonperforming loans. A massive banking reorganization took place, with strong, healthy banks taking over a number of weaker ones. Many workers were laid off as a result. In the end, however, the banking sector came through the crisis stronger than before. *See also* ECONOMIC DEVELOPMENT; BANK OF KOREA.

BLUE HOUSE (*Chong Wae Dae*). The official residence in **Seoul** of the president of the Republic of Korea. In both English and Korean, the name has come to symbolize the highly centralized system of presidential government that has characterized South Korean politics for most of the period since 1948. The term "Blue House" comes from the color of the roof tiles. The site was originally that of a Koryo (918–1392) palace that was much built over in the Yi dynasty (1392–1910). In 1927, the **Japanese** demolished all the then extant buildings to erect a residence for the Japanese governor-general; office accommodation was erected below this, in the **Capitol Building**. After 1945, the former Japanese governor-general's residence was first used by U.S. General **John R. Hodge**, and then by the Republic of Korea's first president, **Syngman Rhee**. Under Rhee, the building was known as *Kyongmudae*. In 1993, President **Kim Young-sam** had all the Japanese-era buildings removed and a Korean-style building, supposedly in the original palace style, erected on the site. *See also* ARCHITECTURE.

BROADCASTING. Radio broadcasting in Korea began from a station in **Seoul** in 1927 during the **Japanese** colonial period. At liberation in 1945, the **United States Army Military Government in Korea** reorganized this station into the Korea Broadcasting System (KBS). Until 1954, this remained the sole broadcasting station in South Korea. In that year, however, the Christian Broadcasting System (CBS) began to broadcast news, entertainment, and religious and educational programs. Another religious station, the Far East Broadcasting Station, started at **Inch'on** in 1956, broadcast in Korean, English, Chinese, and Russian. The first commercial service, provided by the **Pusan** Munwha Broadcasting Station (MBC), dates from 1959. Many others followed. FM broadcasting began in 1966 from Seoul, and was followed quickly by others in Pusan and **Taegu**. Both the Republic of Korea **national defense forces** and the U.S. forces in Korea had their own radio (and later television) broadcasting systems. KBS has maintained an overseas broadcasting service since 1953, providing programs in a variety of languages.

Television began in South Korea in 1956 from a privately owned station, which closed down in 1959. In 1961, the existing radio broadcasting system was renamed KBS-Radio, and KBS-TV began operating. Cable TV started in 1970. At first its use was mainly confined to areas of difficult reception but later it became much more widespread as people sought a greater variety of channels. By 2000, 30 Korean, as well as a number of foreign, channels were available to South Korean viewers. Satellite TV began in the mid-1990s, and has also enjoyed widespread popularity. Cable TV is also popular; by July 2002, 92 operators provided 211 channels. Of these, 114 were video and 97 audio. Digital broadcasting began in 2001. TV set ownership has risen from about 25,000 in 1961 to some 15.8 million in 1998.

Both radio and television broadcasting have attracted the attention of several governments. In 1980, under the growing authoritarian regime of **Chun Doo-hwan**, the state-owned KBS, and MBC, absorbed the private radio and television networks. Until 1989–1990, KBS-TV featured four channels and MBC-TV had one channel with 20 local stations. Then, under **Roh Tae-woo**, there was a major liberalization of broadcasting, and many new stations emerged. By 2000, South Korea had 86 FM and 59 AM radio stations, in addition to its variety of TV stations.

BUDDHISM. Arriving in 372 A.D. from **China**, Buddhism (Mahayana sect) became the religion of the masses, including the upper class. Although it was introduced to Koguryo first, it did not flourish there. However, it became the state religion of Paekche in the fourth century and that of Shilla in the sixth century, contributing greatly toward the development of art, **architecture**, crafts, music, scholarship, and sculpture, as well as metallurgical technology. Several sects, including Son (Zen in **Japan**), rose in Shilla. From the Korean Peninsula, Buddhism was also transmitted to Japan.

During the Koryo period, as in the latter half of the Shilla period, Buddhism reached its golden age in Korean history as many books, including the massive *Tripitaka Koreana*, were printed in the 13th century. During the Yi period, the government and the ruling class rejected Buddhism. It survived among the rural population.

Buddhism revived somewhat during the Japanese colonial period, encouraged by the **Government-General of Korea**, which saw it as a counterweight to **Confucianism**. However, at the time of liberation in 1945, relatively few people claimed to be Buddhist. As with all **religions**, numbers claiming to be Buddhists have grown enormously since the 1960s. Among several current sects, the most prominent one is the Chogye Sect, which combines Son practices with evangelistic drive. Two other important sects are the T'aego and the Won sects. By the mid-1990s, more than 10 million South Koreans described themselves as Buddhists. By 2000, the number had reached 11 million Buddhists, representing some 20 percent of the population.

However, not all those who claimed to be Buddhist were necessarily familiar with Buddhist scriptures or practices.

– C –

CAIRO AGREEMENT. In November 1943, a summit conference of the **United States**, **Great Britain** and **China** was held in Cairo, Egypt, to adopt an Allied plan to deal with **Japan** during and after World War II. Regarding Korea, the communiqué issued on 1 December 1943 by the Allies stated that "the . . . great powers, mindful of the enslavement of the people of Korea, are determined that in due course Korea shall become free and independent." This decision was made in accordance with the decision that Japan be stripped of all the islands in the Pacific that it had seized or occupied since 1914, that all the territories which Japan had "stolen" from China be returned, and that Japan be expelled from all other territories that had been taken by violence and greed.

CAPITOL BUILDING. The most prominent colonial-era building in **Seoul**, erected by the Japanese **Government-General of Korea** in the 1920s as the center of government, it was taken over by the **United States Army Military Government in Korea** in 1945. It was on its steps that **Syngman Rhee** proclaimed the Republic of Korea in 1948. Although badly damaged in the early stages of the **Korean War**, General **Douglas MacArthur** made it the setting for the formal return of Seoul to Rhee's government in September 1950. However, Rhee disliked it as a symbol of Japanese imperialism and refused to devote funds to its repair. After the 1961 military coup, the new government of **Park Chung-hee** had no compunction about using it, and it once again became the center of government. In 1986, after three years' work, it reopened as the **National Museum.** In 1996, President **Kim Young-sam** decided to demolish it because of its links with the Japanese. The ground on which it stood has been reincorporated into the **Kyongbok Palace.** *See also* ARCHITECURE.

CARTER, JAMES (JIMMY) EARL (1924–). President of the **United States** from 1977–1981, Jimmy Carter began his presidency with a pledge to withdraw United States forces from the Korean Peninsula. He also disliked the authoritarian policies of President **Park Chung-hee**, and was strongly critical of South Korea's human rights record. After a visit to South Korea in June 1979, Carter agreed to postpone the proposed troop withdrawal, though he remained highly critical of Park and his regime. One of his last acts as president was to intervene with Park's successor, **Chun Doo-hwan**, to persuade him not to execute the opposition leader **Kim Dae-jung**. Carter continued to take an interest in Korea after leaving office, and it was his intervention in June 1994 that is credited with helping to bring about a temporary solution to the **North Korean nuclear program**.

CATHOLICISM. *See* CHRISTIANITY; RELIGIONS.

CENSORSHIP. From the beginning of the Republic of Korea until 1987, successive governments engaged in repressive measures against the press and other media. Newspapers and journals have been suspended or closed, and **broadcasting** restricted in 1948–1949, 1962, and 1980, with the dismissal of many journalists. Of particular concern to the censors was material portraying **North Korea** and other communist states in a favorable light, or reproducing material published by them. Criticism of the government could also lead to trouble; the Seoul daily, *Tong-a Ilbo*, fell foul of President **Park Chung-hee** in the mid-1970s, and suffered the loss of most of its advertising revenue under government pressure. When **Chun Doo-hwan** came to power, his government carried out a major purge, known as the **"massacres of the mass media,"** to curtail both print and **broadcasting** journalists. After **Roh Tae-woo** became president in 1987, there was a marked reduction in government interference with the media, and a consequent big increase in the numbers of newspapers and magazines published and in the number of radio and TV outlets. *See also* CINEMA; DECONTROL OF THE PRESS; PRESS CODE.

CENTRAL ELECTION MANAGEMENT COMMITTEE. Under the amended **Constitution** of 1960, this committee was established "for the purpose of conducting fair elections." It included three members elected by the justices of the Supreme Court and six members recommended by the political parties. This committee decided upon all disputes over the results of elections.

CENTRAL INTELLIGENCE AGENCY (KCIA). *See* NATIONAL INTELLIGENCE SERVICE.

CHAEBOL. These large business conglomerates are a distinct component of the South Korean economy, which bear some resemblance to the pre-World War II **Japanese** *zaibatsu*, in that they often began as family firms, and some still remain so. Some go back to small beginnings in the Japanese colonial period, and a number have become internationally known, including **Hyundai**, Samsung, LG (formerly Lucky Goldstar) and Daewoo. During the rapid industrialization of the 1960s and 1970s, they diversified into many areas of manufacturing and trade, while working closely with the government to build up the South Korean economy. The **IMF crisis** of 1997, however, revealed that severe management problems occurred even among the most successful *chaebol*, and that the close relationship with the government and the financial system had often resulted in poor financial and managerial control. By 2000, a number of the smaller ones had gone into liquidation and even the big groups faced major difficulties. Hyundai, for many years the largest of the groups, broke up in 2001 after the death of its founder, **Chung Ju-yung**, and the Samsung group became the leading group. *See also* BANKING; ECONOMIC DEVELOPMENT.

CHANG MYON (1899–1966). Educated in the **United States**, Chang taught at a secondary commercial school in **P'yongyang** during the **Japanese** colonial period. Following the liberation of Korea in 1945, he served as a member of the **Representative Democratic Council** and a member of the **South Korean Interim Legislative Assembly**. He was elected to the Constituent Assembly in May 1948 as a moderate nationalist. Chang was sent to the United States by President **Syngman Rhee** as ambassador in 1949. In 1950 he served as head of the South Korean observer mission to the **United Nations**. After serving as prime minister in 1951, he resigned from the post and became a prominent opposition leader, forming the **Democratic Party** in 1955 in cooperation with **Shin Ik-hui**. Elected in 1956 as vice president of the Republic, Chang was shot and slightly wounded by a would-be assassin in September, in one of many political **assassination and assassination attempts** during this period.

Chang was nominated by the Democratic Party as vice presidential candidate for the March 1960 presidential elections, but was defeated. In the heat of the **April 1960 Student Uprising**, Chang resigned the vice presidency although his term of office did not expire until May. When the First Republic fell, and the **National Assembly** adopted a new **constitution**, in August 1960 Chang was chosen as prime minister by the National Assembly. The **Military Revolution of 16 May 1961** forced him to resign on 18 May 1961. Chang was purged by the military junta and retired from politics.

CHANG T'AEK-SANG (1893–1969). Educated at Edinburgh University, he was appointed as chief of the **Seoul** Metropolitan **Police** in 1945 by the **United States Army Military Government in Korea**. He became a legislator in 1950, and then was appointed as prime minister in 1952. Reelected to the **National Assembly** in 1954 and 1958, he served as chairman of the Anti-Communist Struggle Committee. Again elected in 1960 to the National Assembly, he was purged in 1961 by the military junta. In 1963 he reconstituted former President **Syngman Rhee**'s **Liberal Party**, but he and the new party played no significant role.

CHANG TO-YONG (1923–). Born into a Christian family in a village near Shinuiju, North P'yongan Province (now **North Korea**), he enrolled at Toyo University in **Japan**, but his education was interrupted by student mobilization that the Japanese government carried out in January 1944. Drafted into the Japanese Imperial Army, Chang served as an instructor of the Nanjing Officers' Candidate Training School in **China**, toward the end of World War II. When the war ended, he returned to his hometown and became a high school teacher. Following an anticommunist uprising by his students in November 1945, he fled to South Korea.

Graduating in 1946 from the Military English School, which was established by the **United States Army Military Government in Korea** to train Korean officers in the constabulary, the forerunner of the South Korean armed forces, Chang was commissioned as lieutenant. He remained in the military after the Korean armed forces were established in 1948, and during the **Korean War**, he commanded combat divisions and an army corps.

Chang received further military training at the Command and General Staff College in the **United States** in 1953, and rising in rank rapidly, Chang became army chief of staff in February 1961. When the **military revolution of 16 May 1961** began, he went along with it. Hoping to avoid large-scale bloodshed, believing that many commanders of army divisions were behind the revolution, mindful of the persistent military threats from North Korea, and with the idea of "guiding" the revolutionaries, he accepted the chairmanship of the **Military Revolutionary Committee** (MRC). In late May, the MRC was renamed the **Supreme Council for National Reconstruction** (SCNR), and as chairman of the SCNR, he served as head (prime minister) of the cabinet until July 1961 when he was charged with an alleged antirevolutionary plot. Chang was tried and was given a death sentence by a lower military court, later reduced to a life term by a higher military court. The case then went to the highest military court, but, while the case was being reviewed, Chang received a pardon from General **Park Chung-hee**, who had become chairman of the SCNR, and dismissed the case in May 1962. Shortly thereafter, Chang was allowed to leave Korea and go into exile in the United States.

CHANG TOK-SU (1894–1947). A prominent right-wing nationalist, who was educated at Tokyo's Waseda University, who later received a Ph.D. from Columbia University. He served as chief editor of the *Tong-a Ilbo* newspaper from 1920, and championed the Korean cause. He was an important founding member of the **Korean (Han'guk) Democratic Party** and chairman of its Political Committee. He was shot by a **police** officer on 2 December 1947 because of his support for the **Moscow Agreement**, despite his party's opposition to it. *See also* ASSASSINATION AND ASSASSINATION ATTEMPTS.

CHARTER FOR NATIONAL EDUCATION. On 5 December 1963, the **Park Chung-hee** government promulgated this charter to set the goal and standard of Korean education. It called for the promotion of a "posture of self-reliance . . . by revitalizing the illustrious spirit of our forefathers" with a keen sense that "we have been born into the land, charged with the historic mission of rejuvenating the nation." *See also* EDUCATIONAL DEVELOPMENT.

CHEJU ISLAND. Cheju is the Korean Peninsula's largest island, lying some 60 miles (80 km.) off the south coast. It is some 45 miles long and 17 miles wide (72 km. by 17 km.). Its total land area is 718 square miles (1,845 square km.). It contains South Korea's highest mountain, Mount Halla, which reaches a height of over 6,000 feet (1,950 meters). Cheju was under Mongol control for over 100 years in the 12th and 13th centuries. During the Chosun dynasty, it was a place of exile. The Japanese **Government-General of Korea** administered it as part of South Cholla Province, but it became a separate province in 1946. Cheju has a national university, established in 1982, based on a long-existing national college. The island's main sources of revenue are **agriculture**, fisheries, and **tourism**—it has always been a popular Korean honeymoon destination; there is no industry. Its population, 366,000 in 1970, is now (2003) some 530,000. In 1948, it was the scene of a major uprising against the growing political dominance of right-wing groups based around President **Syngman Rhee**. *See also* CHEJU REBELLION.

CHEJU REBELLION. On 3 April 1948, some 3,000 communist guerrillas, in collusion with communist elements in the Korean Constabulary units, began a rebellion on **Cheju Island** in opposition to the planned 10 May general elections. Their main targets were the **police** force and right-wing youth groups on the island.

The rebellion started in the northern part of the island, spreading as other islanders joined the rebels. After reinforcements of police and constabulary arrived from the mainland, a counterinsurgent campaign began, leading to a large number of rebel casualties. The rebellion lasted until May 1949, although some guerrilla activities continued well into 1953.

During the rebellion, 15,000 persons were reported to have been killed by the communists, 300 to 400 villages were ravaged, 20,000 houses were burned down, 34 schools and 15 town halls were destroyed, and 65,000 islanders were left homeless. Between 20,000–30,000 rebels were reported killed. Of some 2,000 captured insurgents, 250 were executed and the remainder were given prison terms, ranging from seven years to life. Allegations of atrocities by government forces during the suppression of the rebellion have regularly surfaced, and recent years have seen demands that the government reopen the issue.

On 10 May 1949, one year after the general elections were held on the mainland, elections were held on Cheju Island to elect the two Cheju representatives to the Constituent Assembly.

CHI CH'ONG-CH'ON (1888–1959). Born *Chi Tae-hyong*, he was also known as *Ji Ch'ong-ch'on* and *Yi*. He graduated from an army cadet school in **Japan** in 1913. In 1919, he fled from Korea after taking part in the March First Movement and joined an anti-Japanese military group of Koreans in Manchuria. When the **Korean Independence Party** was organized in **China** in 1930, Chi became chairman of its military committee, establishing the Korean National Restoration Army. In 1940, he became its commander. Chi returned to Korea after liberation and organized the **Taedong Youth Corps**, an extreme rightist organization. He later became minister without portfolio, one of the founders of the **Korean Nationalist Party**, and in 1950 a member of the **National Assembly** loyal to President **Syngman Rhee**.

CHINA, RELATIONS WITH. Historic links between China and Korea are of long-standing, with Korea deriving much of its cultural and political inheritance from its huge neighbor. The Chosun dynasty, Korea's last independent rulers, had a particularly close relationship with China. Following Japan's takeover of Korea from 1905 onward, many Korean exiles went to China. Some organized political parties and a government in exile based in Shanghai. Others, such as, **Kim Il-sung**, later leader of **North Korea**, organized guerrilla bands that fought with Chinese groups against the Japanese.

Given the staunch anticommunism of South Korea's first president, **Syngman Rhee**, it is not surprising that he developed early links with General Chiang Kai-shek and the Chinese Nationalists after the establishment of the Republic of Korea in 1948. These links would persist after Chiang lost the Chinese Civil War and was forced to flee to Taiwan in 1949. From then until the 1980s, anticommunism was a strong binding force between the Republic of Korea and the

"Republic of China," as the Chinese Nationalists continued to style themselves.

South Korea's leaders therefore viewed with much suspicion the establishment of the communist-run People's Republic of China (PRC) in 1949. This was partly the natural Korean suspicion of any strong government in China, given the past tendency of such governments to take an active interest in Korea. But in the case of the PRC, such suspicions were reinforced because of the PRC's communism and the Chinese Communist Party's past support for Kim Il-sung and his followers.

It is not surprising therefore, that there were no contacts between the two sides until they met on the battlefield during the **Korean War**. After the end of the war, successive South Korean governments continued to view the PRC with suspicion. Chinese hostility to the Republic of Korea was made clear at the 1954 **Geneva Conference**, and by its continued support for North Korea. It was not until 1973, when President **Park Chung-hee** announced that South Korea would no longer oppose contacts with "nonhostile" communist regimes, that the first low-level contacts between the two countries took place. These were mostly at the sporting or cultural level for several years, though some commercial links also developed. In the mid-1980s, the Chinese imposed restrictions on trade with South Korea, allegedly because of the latter's dealings with Cambodia and **Vietnam**. A more positive sign was the growing Chinese willingness during the 1980s to allow contacts between Chinese **Overseas Koreans** and South Korea.

By the later 1980s, Sino–South Korean trade had recovered and was growing steadily. South Korean manufactured goods found a ready market in China, while Chinese raw materials and traditional products, such as medicines, were welcomed in South Korea. Despite North Korean protests, PRC athletes attended the Asian Games in **Seoul** in 1986, and also the 1988 **Olympic Games**. Finally, in 1992, South Korea and the PRC established full diplomatic relations, again despite strong North Korean objections. Since then, relations have generally continued to develop to the mutual satisfaction of both sides. Problems have arisen because of the increased numbers of Chinese visiting South Korea, some of whom have overstayed their permitted visiting time. The question of North Korean refugees in China has also put some strain on the relationship, as has South Korean activity in China's **Yanbian Korean Autonomous Region.**

CHO PONG-AM (1898–1959). After serving a one-year prison term in 1919 for his participation in the March First demonstrations, he went to Tokyo to study, joining a radical leftist group there. Cho went to Shanghai in 1919, and then to Moscow to study at the Communist University of Toilers of the East. Upon returning to Korea, he became a founding member of the **Korean Communist Party** in 1925, and he collaborated with other Socialists in forming the General Federation of Farmers and Laborers. Cho played an active role in promoting social revolution, as a result of which he served several prison terms. After his release from prison in August 1945, Cho was active in the labor movement and, in September 1945, in cooperation with other Communists, he reestablished the Korean Communist Party. However, in 1946, he left the Korean Communist Party following a disagreement with the head of the party, Pak Hon-yong.

Elected in 1948 to the Constituent Assembly, Cho became the first minister of agriculture, forestry and fisheries of the **Syngman Rhee** administration, and advocated radical land reform and a progressive economic policy that led to his dismissal by President Rhee. He was reelected to the **National Assembly** in 1950, and ran for the presidency in the 1952 election. In 1956, Cho formed the **Progressive Party** and in the same year ran for the presidency.

In January 1958, he was arrested and sentenced to a five-year prison term for illegal possession of firearms and a minor violation of the **National Security Law**. He was found guilty of "treason against the state in collaboration with the Communists," and was executed on 30 July 1959.

CHO PYONG-OK (1894–1960). Born to a Christian family, Cho was educated at Christian schools in Korea and then studied at Columbia University, where he was strongly influenced by liberal and democratic ideas. After earning a Ph.D. in 1925, he returned to Korea, becoming a professor of economics at Yonhui College (now Yonsei University). He joined a pan-national society of men named the *New Shoots' Society* (*Shinganhoe*), and in 1929 he was imprisoned for three years for his involvement in the **Kwangju** student incident.

After his release from prison, Cho became a staff member on a vernacular daily paper, *Chosun Ilbo*. In 1940, he was again imprisoned for his nationalistic activity. In September 1945, Cho was one of the founders of the **Korean (Han'guk) Democratic Party**, serving briefly as director of the Department of Public Security of the **United States Army Military Government in Korea**. On the inauguration of the Republic of Korea, Cho became minister of home affairs. In 1952, he visited the **United States** and other democratic countries as a presidential envoy, campaigning for membership of the Republic in the **United Nations**. From 1951, Cho, as secretary-general of a small **Democratic Nationalist Party**, struggled to promote democracy. He was elected to the **National Assembly** in 1954 and again in 1958, and in 1955 he became a cofounder of the **Democratic Party**. In 1959, the Democratic Party nominated Cho as its presidential candidate, but he died on 15 February 1960 while receiving medical treatment in the United States.

CH'OE KYU-HA (1919–). Born to the family of a Confucian scholar in Wonju, Kangwon Province, he graduated from Tokyo High Normal School in 1941, taught at National Taitung Institute in Manzhouguo (Manchukuo) from 1943 to 1945, and Seoul National University from 1945 to 1950. After serving as director of the Bureau of Trade of the Ministry of Agriculture, Forestry and Fisheries, he became consul general in the Korean mission to **Japan** from 1952–1957, becoming counselor and minister from 1957–1959. Other posts he held included vice-minister of foreign affairs (1959–1960), advisor to the chairman of the **Supreme Council for National Reconstruction** (1961–1963), ambassador to Malaysia (1964), minister of foreign affairs (1967–1971), special assistant to the president in foreign affairs (1971), acting prime minister (1975), chairman of the **National Conference for Unification** (NCU) (1979), and prime minister (1976–1979). Following the death of President **Park Chung-hee**, he became acting president from October to December 1979. In December 1979, the NCU elected him president. He resigned in August 1980, paving the way for **Chun Doo-hwan** to become president. Ch'oe then virtually disappeared from public life. In 1996, when Chun and **Roh Tae Woo** were tried for treason, Ch'oe refused to testify against the former presidents. *See also* DECEMBER 1979 COUP.

CH'OE NAM-SON (1890–1957). Ch'oe was born in **Seoul**, and began publishing while still a child. He was educated at Waseda University in **Japan**. On his return, he set himself up as a publisher. He soon established a reputation as a poet and as one of the early leaders of the new culture movement in Korea. He was publisher of magazines for Korean youth, such as *Sonyon* (Children, 1908) and *Ch'ongch'an* (Youth, 1914). With his poem, "From the Sea to Children," he established a new form of Korean poetry. Ch'oe authored the Declaration of Independence of 1919, and after serving a prison term in connection with his activity in the March First Movement, in 1924 he and others organized a vernacular newspaper named *Shidae Ilbo*.

In 1949, Ch'oe was imprisoned as a traitor for his alleged collaboration during the Japanese colonial period. Released from prison in 1950, he published many historical works, including *Korean People's History*, *Korea's Culture*, and *Korea's Mountains and Rivers*. In 1954, Ch'oe published a new edition of the historical work, *Samguk Yusa*. He edited the *Korean Historical Dictionary* in 1955. In 1955, he became a Roman Catholic.

CHOI HONG-HI (1918–2002). Born in the northern half of the peninsula, Choi went to **Japan** during the Pacific War. He joined the new South Korean armed forces after independence, and quickly made a name for himself, rising to the rank of general. In 1948, he was one of the panel of officers that condemned the future president, **Park Chung-hee** to death in 1948 for his part in the **Yosu–Sunch'on Rebellion**. As a result, although he was one of those who supported the 1961 **Military Revolution of 16 May 1961**, he was forced to resign from the armed forces. He became ambassador to Malaysia from 1962–1965, and settled in Canada from 1972.

Choi's main interest, however, was martial arts, which he introduced into the South Korean armed forces in 1952. Choi was instrumental in having the type of martial arts practiced in Korea renamed **Taekwondo**. In 1966, he founded the International Taekwondo Federation (ITF), and he wrote a number of books about the sport. When he moved to Canada, he took the ITF with him. Park Chung-hee responded by creating the World Taekwondo Federation. Choi's last years were spent in **North Korea**, which further alienated him from the South Korean government.

CH'ONDO-GYO (Teaching of the Heavenly Way). Ch'oe Che-u founded a native **religion** named Tonghak ("Eastern Learning") in 1860. This quickly became a religion of the oppressed. Combining superstitious religious beliefs in a better future with the concept of the unity of god and man, as well as the equality of man, it became an antiestablishment and antiforeign (particularly anti-Christian) force in the late 19th century. Its followers took part in the Tonghak Uprising in 1893–1894, which led both **China** and **Japan** to intervene in Korea.

In 1906, its leaders changed the name to *Ch'ondo-gyo,* which asserted that, through self-discipline and cultivation of mind, one could obtain the divine virtue of being able to influence everything without conscious effort of volition. The leaders of Ch'ondo-gyo played an important part in the March First Movement in 1919 and in other Korean independence movements. Its followers were active in the opposition to the division of the peninsula in 1945, insisting that Korea was one nation. The division of the peninsula also affected its membership because in 1945 the majority of its followers were in the northern half of the peninsula.

Today, it is a minor religion in South Korea. It was reported as having about 53,000 followers in 1985, but that figure had fallen to 28,184 by 1995. (Some sources give figures in the hundreds of thousands, based on claims made by the governing body of Ch'ondo-gyo, but this is probably a major overestimation or the result of people claiming to belong to more than one religious group.) Since the end of military rule in South Korea in 1993, the Tonghak Rebellion has become less of a taboo subject than it was in the past, and some of the sites of the various battles in the 1890s have become national monuments. A Ch'ondo-gyo church and political party also exists in **North Korea**, where it supposedly represents the interests of those of peasant origin.

CHONG IL-GWON (1917–1994). A graduate of **Japan**'s military academy in Manzhouguo (Manchukuo) in 1940, he joined the Japanese army there. After the liberation of Korea, Chong returned to South Korea, joining the newly established Korean army. He played a prominent role in the suppression of the **Yosu–Sunch'on Rebellion**. It has been claimed that he saved the life of the then major, and future president, **Park Chung-hee**, who was accused of communist sympathies at that time.

Chong rose in rank during the **Korean War**. After serving as head of the Command and Staff College (1954–1956), he became chairman of Joint Chiefs of Staff. Retiring from the army as a lieutenant general in 1975, he served as ambassador to Turkey (1957), France (1959), and the **United States** (1960–1963). In 1963, he became minister of foreign affairs. Appointed to the premiership in 1964, he served the Third Republic until 1970. He was elected to the **National Assembly** in 1971 and 1979, and served as acting chairman of the ruling **Democratic Republican Party** (1972–1979).

With the fall of the Fourth Republic in 1979, Chong's political fortune declined, but he remained active during the 1980s as a member of the advisory council of state affairs to President **Chun Doo-hwan**.

CHONG SUNG-HWA. (1926–). In October 1979, when the then head of the Korean CIA (now the **National Intelligence Service**) assassinated President **Park Chung-hee**, Chong Sung-hwa was army chief of staff. Moving quickly to maintain order, acting President **Ch'oe Kyu-ha** appointed Chong as martial law commander. However, when General **Chun Doo-hwan** staged the **December 1979 coup**, Chong was arrested and charged with complicity in Park's murder. He was imprisoned but later released.

In 1993, Chong brought a charge of mutiny for his arrest in 1979 against Chun and his accomplice and successor as president, **Roh Tae-woo**. The court agreed that their action in 1979 had been mutiny, but declined to take the issue further. But Chong's action began a wave of popular protest that eventually led to the arrest and eventual conviction of both former presidents in 1996.

CHONMINYON. *See* NATIONAL COALITION FOR A PEOPLE'S DEMOCRATIC MOVEMENT.

CHOSUN ILBO **(Korea Daily).** This prominent South Korean newspaper was founded in March 1920 by Sin Sogu (1894–1953). At first it supported the **Government-General of Korea**, but like the *Tong-a Ilbo*, it soon became an advocate of Korean independence. It supported the use of the Korean alphabet (*han'gul*), encouraged the study of Korean culture and organized art exhibitions. Closed down, along with other Korean newspapers in 1940, it reappeared in 1945. The *Chosun Ilbo* has always had a reputation for conservatism, and since 1998, it has taken a very skeptical line on President **Kim Dae-jung**'s **"sunshine policy"** toward **North Korea**. It has come under heavy criticism and threats from the North as a result.

CHRISTIANITY. Both Catholicism and Protestantism have flourished since their introduction to Korea. Catholicism was first introduced to Korea in the 17th century from **China**, and it grew in the 18th century, despite many difficulties and several anti-Catholic persecutions. It was called *Sohak* ("Western Learning") before 1900. In the anti-Catholic persecution of 1866, some 7,000 faithful, including several French priests, were executed. Although persecution ended after 1868, Catholics tended to remain in hiding—even after the Franco-Korean Treaty of 1886 allowed them to practice their **religion** legally.

The Roman Catholic Myongdong Cathedral was built in **Seoul** in 1892, and Catholicism continued to grow in the 20th century. In May 1984, Pope John Paul II visited Korea and canonized 93 Korean and 10 French martyrs as he celebrated the bicentennial of the founding of the first Catholic church in Korea; this was the first time a canonization ceremony was held outside the Vatican. John Paul II made a second visit to South Korea in October 1989. The modern Korean hierarchy was established in 1962, and the first Korean cardinal, Kim Souhwan (Stephan Kim), was appointed in 1969. There are 15 Catholic dioceses in South Korea, with 3,000 priests. In 1998, 3,500,000 Catholics were in South Korea. Since the end of the **Korean War**, Catholics have been frequently associated with the political opposition.

Protestantism was introduced to Korea in the late 19th century, first by Scottish missionaries working in Northeast China and then by American and other missionaries who arrived after the conclusion of the **United States**–Korean Treaty in 1882 and later treaties with Western nations. The main missionary groups were from the United States, and included both Methodists and Presbyterians. Later, there were also Canadian and **Australian** Presbyterians, but all worked together to establish one Korean Presbyterian Church. Together with a small group of Anglicans from 1890, and the Holiness Church from

1907, all the Protestant missions worked together on Bible translation under the auspices of the British and Foreign Bible Society, which became the Korea Bible Society after 1945. The Salvation Army, established in Korea in 1908, did much to meet social welfare needs with the provision of orphanages and homes for homeless children.

Protestantism played an important role in modern **education** and in the establishment of a modern health system. Koreans identified Protestantism with modernization. Since the liberation, members of Protestant churches have become political and social leaders of South Korea as the membership of Protestant churches increased rapidly. The original missionaries were usually of a conservative nature, and this was reflected in the attitudes of Korean Protestants until the late 1960s. As of 2000, there were more than 10,000,000 Protestant church members in 168 denominations, forming a clear majority of Korean Christians.

CHUN DOO-HWAN (1931–). Born in a small village in South Kyongsang Province, Chun enrolled at the **Taegu** Technical Middle School in 1950, but in 1951, he transferred to the Korean Military Academy, graduating in 1955 as a member of the "Class of '55," and served in various posts in the army.

After serving as a member of the Civil Affairs Section of the **Supreme Council for National Reconstruction** in 1961 and as Personnel Section chief of the Korean Central Intelligence Agency (now the **National Intelligence Service**) in 1963–1967, Chun became battalion commander of the Capital Garrison Command in 1967. Between 1969 and 1970, he served as senior aide to the army chief of staff. In 1970, he went to **Vietnam** as commander of the 29th Regiment of the Korean Army.

Returning home in 1971, Chun became commander of the First Paratrooper Special Force. After serving as assistant deputy chief of the **Blue House** security force from January 1973, he rose to the rank of major general in February 1978, commanding the First Army Division. In March 1979, he became commander of the **Defense Security Command**.

Following the assassination of President **Park Chung-hee** in October 1979, Chun and a number of his fellow officers, including **Roh Taewoo**, began plotting to seize power from the weak civilian government that succeeded Park. On 12 December 1979, Chun and his fellow officers carried out the **December 1979 coup**, arresting **Chong Sung-hwa**, the army chief of staff and martial law commander, and other officers on charges of treason connected with the murder of Park Chung-hee. In 1980, Chun became acting director of the Korean CIA and chairman of the Standing Committee of the **Special Committee for National Security Measures**. When President **Ch'oe Kyu-ha** resigned in August 1980, the **National Conference for Unification** elected Chun as president. In February 1981, he was reelected president of the Fifth Republic by the newly created electoral college. When the **Democratic Justice Party** was formed by his supporters, many of whom were members of the "Class of '55," he was made its head, a post he held until June 1987.

During his presidency, Chun made much of the fact that, under the terms of the eighth **Constitutional Amendment**, he was limited to a single term in office. Although there were occasional rumors that he would try to extend his period to include the 1988 **Olympic Games**, in any event, he made no attempt to do so. His presidency began with a purge of most political figures from Park Chung-hee's day, and a wide-ranging **"massacres of the mass media."** Many journalists lost their jobs, and forced amalgamations reduced the number of newspapers and TV stations. The veteran opposition leaders **Kim Young-sam** and **Kim Dae-jung** were particularly singled out for attack.

Chun spent much time traveling and taking part in summit meetings with other heads of state. In 1983, he negotiated a major aid and loan agreement with **Japan**, arguing that Japan should reimburse South Korea for the latter's role in the frontline against communism. He made a number of attempts to open a dialogue with **North Korea**, without much success. He was the presumed target of the 1983 **Rangoon bomb attack**, apparently carried out by North Korean agents. Despite this attack, in which he lost many of his most capable advisers, Chun accepted a 1984 offer from North Korea of materials for flood relief. This rare imaginative gesture came to nothing, however.

In the latter part of Chun's period in office, there was some relaxation of the tight controls of the early years. Kim Young-sam was freed from house arrest in 1984, and Kim Dae-jung returned from the **United States** the following year, though he was subject to strict controls at first. Faced with strong opposition demands for political reform, Chun agreed in April 1986 to a debate on constitutional revision. This failed to produce results by April 1987, and Chun announced the suspension of debate, arguing that the existing constitutional arrangements, which provided for the indirect election of the president, would apply to the 1987 presidential election. He also indicated that his preferred successor was Roh Tae-woo. These attempts to control the outcome of the presidential election sparked off a series of protests, which eventually included many middle-class voters. The protests, and the worldwide attention that they attracted, seemed to threaten the 1988 Olympic Games. At this point, Roh intervened, saying that he would not stand as president unless Chun accepted a package of political reforms, including direct election of the president. Chun agreed to do so, and the crisis passed.

Chun's term of office expired on 25 February 1988, but he got little credit for the peaceful transfer of power that his action represented. A wave of criticism of Chun and of his family for alleged corruption, led him to make a nationwide television appearance in which he admitted many wrongdoings during his administration. Chun and his wife retired to a **Buddhist** temple in a remote mountain region, staying there until December 1991.

But the issue of how he had come to power in the first instance would not go away. Following the 1992 election of Kim Young-sam as president, there were renewed calls for an investigation of the events of December 1979 and the **Kwangju Uprising**. In December 1993, former General Chong Sung-hwa brought a case of mutiny in the courts against both Chun and Roh. The courts accepted that there had been a mutiny in 1979 but declined to take the matter further. Pressure continued, however, and in December 1995, both Chun and Roh were arrested and charged with bribery and corruption. Soon, charges of treason and mutiny were added, and in 1996 both were convicted. Chun was sentenced to death and ordered to pay a heavy fine. On appeal, Chun's sentence was reduced to life imprisonment. After the 1997 presidential election, President Kim Young-sam, with the agreement of president-elect **Kim Dae-jung**, released both, though the fines still stood.

CHUNG JU-YUNG (1915–2001). Chung was South Korea's leading businessman from the 1950s until his death in 2002. Originally from **North Korea**, in 1946, he started a company called **Hyundai** Auto

Services that would eventually became the basis of South Korea's biggest conglomerate. He worked closely with family members, and apparently found the tough approach to labor and other issues favored by President **Park Chung-hee** to his liking. In the 1960s and 1970s, Hyundai worked closely with Park's government to bring about the economic transformation of South Korea. In the process, Hyundai became the biggest of the *chaebol*, leading in such fields as construction, shipbuilding, and automobiles.

In the late 1980s, Chung decided to enter politics, as Hyundai found itself less in favor with the government. In 1992, he formed his own party, the **Unification National Party**, but failed to achieve his goal of becoming president. Instead, he found that the government turned against him, with President **Kim Young-sam** launching a series of tax audits and other probes. Chung was prosecuted for using Hyundai funds in his presidential campaign, and received a three-year prison sentence, suspended because he was already 80. These moves drove him out of politics, but also set in motion the eventual breakup of Hyundai.

Before that took place, however, Chung had begun to open links to North Korea. In 1998, he was allowed to go to the North, taking 500 head of cattle with him. He repeated this gesture later in the year. Out of this gesture, which reflected the intentions of President **Kim Dae-jung**'s **"sunshine policy,"** would eventually emerge Hyundai Asan (Asan was Chung's home village), which developed tourist links with the North. It also seems to have transmitted funds that helped to pave the way for the **June 2000 Inter-Korean Summit**.

Chung died in March 2001, and his death prompted the breakup of the Hyundai conglomerate. Revelations about payments and undercover transactions seem to have prompted his son Chong Mong-hun, head of Hyundai Asan, to commit suicide in August 2003. *See also* ECONOMIC DEVELOPMENT.

CINEMA. The first known moving picture show in Korea was given at the **Kyongbok Palace** in **Seoul** in 1899. The first Korean films appeared in the early 1920s. Sound films arrived in 1928, but the first Korean sound film was *Ch'unhyang* in 1936; until 1945, however, Japanese films predominated. After 1945, a number of silent films were made, and the first color film appeared in 1949.

The **Korean War** disrupted the industry until the mid-1950s. It then revived, with American assistance. Soundtracks added specially composed Korean music from the early 1960s, which also saw the emergence of a star system and Cinemascope in 1968. By then, however, the cinema was facing strong competition from both foreign films and increasingly, from television. Cinema attendance peaked at 173 million in 1969, but declined to about a quarter of that number in the mid-1990s. Successive Korean governments exercised **censorship** over imported films until the late 1980s, banning those such as *Gandhi*, which it was thought could incite civil disobedience. Restrictions on Japanese films continued until **Kim Dae-jung** became president in 1997.

CIVIL DEFENSE CORPS (*Minbanguidae*). It was established in September 1975 to protect lives and property in times of enemy attack or national disasters, as well as to provide support to rescue and rehabilitation activities and to augment military operation. All male citizens between the ages of 17 and 50, except members of constitutionally established government agencies, **police**, firefighters, military and civilian personnel serving in the armed forces, members of the **Homeland Reserve Forces**, and members of the **Student National Defense Corps**, were obliged to serve in the corps.

The government designated the 15th day of each month as a civil defense day, with mock **air-raid drills** and other exercises under the direction of the Civil Defense Headquarters. In June 1988, the government revised the minimum age from 17 to 20, benefiting some 300,000 youths in that age group.

CIVIL DEFENSE FORCE SCANDAL. The Civil Defense Force (*Kukmin bangwigun*) was a paramilitary force organized to augment the regular armed forces against the communist aggressors in the heat of the **Korean War**. Able-bodied Korean males between the ages of 18 and 40 who were not in regular military services were obliged to join the force and fight in the war. This case, in the early stages of the war, involved embezzlement of a large amount of funds and misappropriation of supplies allocated for the force by General Kim Yun-gun, commander of the force, and a former bodyguard of President **Syngman Rhee**, and his coterie. The investigations conducted by the

National Assembly found the commander and other officers in the force guilty, and they were executed in August 1951. The Civil Defense Force was abolished at the end of the Korean War.

CIVIL RELIEF IN KOREA. This **United Nations** program began during the **Korean War** to provide assistance for civilian relief efforts. Under a resolution of the UN Security Council on 31 July 1950, the **United Nations Command** determined the requirements for civil relief, and a military unit known as the *United Nations Civil Assistance Command* (later reorganized as the *Korean Civil Assistance Command*) was delegated to make necessary requests for civil relief in South Korea.

CIVIL RULE PARTY (*Minjongdang*). In May 1963, this political party emerged with **Yun Po-son** as its president, advocating the promotion of democracy. In May 1965, however, it and the **Democratic Party** (formed in August by **Pak Sun-chon**) were united into the **Masses Party** (*Minjungdang*). Eventually, in February 1967, the Masses Party and one other party were united, forming the **New Democratic Party**.

CIVIL SERVICE. In the Chosun and earlier periods, the civil service was a highly respected occupation, reserved for the educated nobility. The myth of the honest man serving the king and the people was strongly entrenched. With the beginning of Western influences in the 1880s, new concepts of the role of the civil service began to take hold in Korea, but these developments had not gone very far by the time **Japan** established total control over the country in 1910.

Under the Japanese **Government-General in Korea**, the civil service was organized on more modern lines, similar to those introduced into Japan after the Meiji Restoration in 1868. The result was to create a powerful bureaucratic machine that penetrated into all sections of the country. This did involve Koreans but important positions were reserved for Japanese officials and most Koreans were confined to low-ranking positions in the colonial civil service.

With the disappearance of the Japanese in 1945, Koreans tried to take over the immediate running of the country, but the establishment of the **United States Army military Government in Korea** meant that once again, senior positions were held by foreigners. Gradually, however, a South Korean civil service began to emerge. From the start, although the civil service was held in high regard as a proper occupation for a well-educated Korean, some of the old deference toward government officials from precolonial days had disappeared.

After the establishment of the Republic of Korea in 1948, the Law on Public Officials of August 1949 classified Korean government officials into two main categories. A "special category" included military personnel, members of the **National Assembly**, cabinet ministers, presidential staff, judges, and senior diplomats were and still are regarded as noncareer public servants. They are either elected or appointed by the president. The "general category," which constituted the civil service proper, included bureaucrats in various branches of the government who were classified into five ranks. All "general category" officials were appointed according to the results of a civil service examination that had two categories, the higher and the ordinary. Both were open to all who met certain required educational standards. The 1949 law was amended in 1950, 1961, and 1962, but basically remained the same.

Following the **Military Revolution of 16 May 1961**, many civil servants were purged for corruption. A National Civil Service Act passed in 1963 reaffirmed the principle of a career civil service, which was divided into a national and a local service. The act also confirmed the continued existence of the special and general categories. Later acts would provide separately for those in **education** and for foreign service officers. Management of the civil service was in the hands of the Ministry of Government Administration. There were nine grades. Ministers appointed grades one to five, while grades six to nine were presidential appointments. The main criteria for promotion were efficiency and merit.

An extensive purge of the civil service took place in 1980–1981, after **Chun Doo-hwan** became president. As with **Park Chung-hee**'s 1961 purge, this was widely seen as politically inspired. Under Chun's successor, **Roh Tae-woo**, a far less politically motivated anticorruption campaign netted some of Chun's family and advisers, as well as a number of regular bureaucrats.

In 1998, the government of President **Kim Dae-jung** amalgamated the Ministries of Home Affairs and Government Administration, but the new ministry continued to be responsible for civil service matters. However, the following year, the government created a Civil Service Commission, which took over all responsibility for recruiting and managing the civil service.

CLARK, MARK WAYNE (1896–1984). Born in New York, Clark saw service in World War I and World War II, which he ended as commander of **United States** forces in Italy. In May 1952, Clark became commander in chief of the Far Eastern Command and commander in chief of the **United Nations forces** in Korea, succeeding General **Matthew Bunker Ridgway**. Clark faced a tough period in the **Korean War**. Fighting was fierce but with little progress, and there were problems in the prisoner of war camps, with the prolonged armistice discussions and obstruction from South Korean President **Syngman Rhee**.

Although Clark shared some of Rhee's views about the conduct of the war, he kept to his orders and was prepared to remove Rhee if required. This proved unnecessary, and Clark signed the 27 July 1953 **Korean Armistice Agreement**, claiming later that he did so with a heavy heart, as the first United States military commander to end a war short of victory. In retirement, he was noted for his anticommunist views and for his belief that the Korean War led to the war in **Vietnam.**

COALITION COMMITTEE FOR COOPERATION BETWEEN THE RIGHTISTS AND THE LEFTISTS. In October 1946, **Kim Kyu-shik**, representing moderate right-wing nationalists, and **Yo Un-hyong**, representing moderate leftists, organized this committee as the extreme rightists and the hard-line leftists, including the communists, were engaged in bitter controversy in connection with the implementation of the **Moscow Agreement**. The aims of this committee were to promote the strength of the moderates by unifying them, and to establish "a democratic transitional government" in Korea in accordance with the Allies' Moscow plan. Both Kim and Yo accepted the inevitability of a trusteeship, and neither of them wished to see the establishment of absolute control over the government by either conservative rightists or radical leftists.

COMBINED ECONOMIC BOARD. An agency set up under the Economic Coordination Agreement signed between the South Korean and **United States** governments in 1952 "to ensure effective support of the military forces . . . to relieve the hardships of the people of Korea, and to establish and maintain a stable economy." Its membership included both Koreans and Americans. It was abolished in 1960.

COMBINED FORCES COMMAND. Established in 1978, this brought together the South Korean and the **United States** forces in Korea under the control of the commander of the U.S. forces in Korea, who is also the commander of the **United Nations Command** in Korea. A South Korean general was appointed as the deputy commander. In theory, this arrangement placed all South Korean forces under U.S. command, just as U.S. President **Jimmy Carter** announced the planned withdrawal of such forces from the peninsula. In practice, American control over South Korean forces has been limited.

COMFORT WOMEN. Name given to Korean and other women who were used as military prostitutes by **Japan**'s military forces from about 1932 onward. After decades of silence, a number of women came forward in the early 1990s in South Korea and other areas of Japanese occupation, arguing for a formal Japanese apology and for compensation. There were claims that between 100,000–200,000 Korean women had been forced into military prostitution by the Japanese. Many had died or had been killed during World War II, and most had been prevented by shame from coming forward. When the first comfort women had emerged in the early 1990s, the Japanese government at first argued that the program had been an entirely private one. Later, as evidence emerged that in fact there had been official involvement, the Japanese position shifted to argue that all claims involving South Koreans had been settled by the 1965 Normalization Treaty. Subsequent Japanese proposals for privately funded compensation have met with a hostile response in South Korea, where the government of **Kim Young-sam** said that it would provide compensation. However, few if any of the women concerned appear to have claimed the offered sums. A number of former comfort women also appeared in **North Korea**, where the government also demanded that Japan acknowledge their claims.

COMMITTEE FOR ASSISTING THE RETURN OF DISPLACED CIVILIANS. Authorized by paragraph 59 of the 1953 **Korean Armistice Agreement**, this committee dealt with the needs of two groups. One was those who had been resident on one side of the **Military Demarcation Line** before 24 June 1950 and who found themselves on the other side at the end of the **Korean War**. The other was civilians of foreign nationality who found themselves north or south of the line at the end of the war. Two military officers from each side made up the committee. In any event, only 37 from the South in the first category went to **North Korea**. The North put forward no Koreans, but instead released 19 foreign nationals (11 Turks, one large family, and nine stateless Russians) who had been captured in 1950. After these exchanges, the committee was disbanded on 1 March 1954. Subsequent movements of population were clandestine.

COMMITTEE FOR REPATRIATION OF PRISONERS OF WAR. Authorized by the 1953 **Korean Armistice Agreement**, this committee consisted of three officers from each side, whose task was to supervise the handing over by both sides of prisoners of war. Large numbers were involved, with some 66,900 from **North Korea** and **China**, and 12,700 from South Korean and **United Nations forces**. The committee was tasked to complete repatriation of prisoners of war within 60 days of the signing of the armistice, and was then disbanded.

COMMITTEE FOR THE PREPARATION OF NATIONAL RECONSTRUCTION (*Konguk Chunbi Wiwonhoe*). This committee was established at the suggestion of the last head of the Japanese **Government-General of Korea**, General Abe Nobuyaki, on 16 August 1945 by **Yo Un-hyong** with **An Chae-hong**, a prominent moderate right-wing nationalist as the vice-chairman, and **Song Chin-u**, to function as a transitional government of all Korea. As soon as it was established, branches were organized throughout the country, functioning as local governmental units. Under these committees were formed security maintenance units, performing the role of the **police**. When the **Korean People's Republic** and its government were established by the "National Assembly" on 6 September 1945, the committee went out of existence.

COMMITTEE FOR THE THREE PEOPLE'S STRUGGLE (*Sammint'uwi*). A committee formed in the spring of 1985 by radical students, with an anti-imperialist and antifascist line. It advocated popular struggle for national unification, people's liberation, and democratization. *See also* STUDENT MOVEMENT.

COMMITTEE TO PROMOTE A DEMOCRATIC COALITION (*Minju Yonhap Ch'ujin Wiwonhoe,* or *Minyonch'u*). This political organization was formed in April 1990 by leaders of the dissident forces who represented a broad national coalition composed of such radical groups as the National Association of Laborers (*Chonnohyop*), formed in January 1990, the National Federation of Farmers' Unions, the National Federation of Teachers' Unions (*Chon'gyojo*) formed in May 1989, and the National Council of Representatives of University Students (*Chondaehyop*). The main purpose of the founders was to create a progressive party in cooperation with the **Party for Peace and Democracy** of **Kim Dae-jung** and the newly formed **Democratic Party** of Yi Ki-t'aek. Their aim was to establish a large, united opposition party of all dissidents. However, the leaders of the committee were split between those who advocated the creation of their own party and those who favored the formation of a united opposition party with other opposition groups. In the end, those who belonged to the former group set up their own **Masses (People's) Party** in November 1990.

COMMUNICATIONS. *See* TRANSPORTATION AND COMMUNICATIONS.

CONFUCIANISM. A Chinese secular philosophy, which was introduced to Korea in the second century A.D., and which gained strength during the Three Kingdoms period, exerting its influence on political, cultural, and social development. The Koryo dynasty maintained Confucian influence, but it did not strengthen it, other than by its promotion of an educational system in Confucian tradition. The Yi dynasty adopted the Chu Xi school of Neo-Confucianism as a state creed, building a Confucian temple and establishing Confucian academies such as *Songyunkwan* as a national university and other colleges collectively known as *Sahak* in **Seoul**.

Along with the Confucian bureaucracy that the Yi dynasty strengthened, certain social institutions such as "ancestor worship" (*chesa*) were transplanted to Korea and became firmly entrenched there. The number of those claiming to be "Confucianists" has steadily declined, so that by 1998, there were only about 200,000 in this category. But certain moral and ethical standards, including respect for those in authority, educational philosophy, cultural patterns, and social institutions, which developed in Korea under Confucian influence, are still evident in South Korea. *See also* EDUCATIONAL DEVELOPMENT; WOMEN'S MOVEMENT.

CONSTITUENT ASSEMBLY. *See* NATIONAL ASSEMBLY.

CONSTITUTION. The Constitution of the Republic of Korea was adopted on 12 July 1948 following a perfunctory debate by the Constituent Assembly. It was promulgated on 17 July. It showed traces of both the principles of responsible parliamentary democracy and of the **United States** concept of an independent executive. Although displaying the outward form of responsible parliamentary government, it granted much power to the presidency. No constitutional provision was made for the dissolution of the **National Assembly**, but Article 48 gave the president an extraordinary power, stating that "in time of civil war, or a dangerous situation arising from foreign relations, in case of a national calamity, or on account of a grave economic or financial crisis, it is necessary to take urgent measures for the maintenance of public order and security, the President shall have a power to issue orders having the effect of law . . . if time is lacking for convening of the National Assembly."

The 103-article Constitution was divided into 10 chapters, followed by a preamble that stated that "We the people of Korea at this time engaged in reconstructing a democratic and independent society," are determined to (1) "consolidate national unity by justice, humanity, brotherly love, and the elimination of all kinds of social evils," (2) "offer equal opportunity to every person," (3) "provide for the fuller development of an equality of each individual in all the fields of political, economic, social and cultural life," (4) "permit every person to discharge his duties and responsibilities," and (5) "promote the welfare of the people, to maintain permanent internal peace, and thereby to assure Security, Liberty and Happiness of ourselves and our posterity." Chapter I (Articles 1–6) included general provisions. It stated that Korea shall be a democratic republic (Article I) and the territory of Korea shall consist of the Korean Peninsula and its accessory islands (Article 2). Chapter II (Articles 8–30) enumerated rights and duties of citizens. Chapter III (Articles 31–50) dealt with the National Assembly established on the principle of universal, direct, equal, and secret votes. Chapter IV (Articles 51–75) covered the structure of the government, making the president the head of the executive branch. The president and the vice president were to be elected by the National Assembly, and the prime minister was to be appointed by the president with the consent of the National Assembly. Under Articles 46 and 47, they, together with the members of the cabinet and judges, were subjected to impeachment by the National Assembly.

Chapter V (Articles 76–83) dealt with the judicial branch of the government. It specified that the chief justice and justices of the Supreme Court were to be appointed by the president with the consent of the National Assembly. Article 80 designated the Constitution Committee, consisting of the vice president as its chairman and five members of the National Assembly, as having the power to determine the constitutionality of a law. Chapter VI (Articles 84–89) established the principle of the economic order of the nation, recognizing citizen's private ownership of property.

Chapter VII (Articles 90–95) related to financial matters of the government. Chapter VIII (Articles 96–98) dealt with local autonomous organizations. Chapter IX (Article 98) spelled out the procedure for **constitutional amendments**. Finally, Chapter X (Articles 99–103) included supplementary rules concerning the National Assembly and enactment of the special law dealing with the punishment of those who committed malicious antinational acts prior to 15 August 1948. *See also* CONSTITUTIONAL COMMITTEE; CONSTITUTIONAL REVISION DELIBERATION COUNCIL.

CONSTITUTIONAL AMENDMENTS. The **Constitution** has been amended nine times since its adoption. The first amendment made on 4 July 1952, which was forced upon the **National Assembly** by then President **Syngman Rhee** and his **Liberal Party**, instituted the system of a direct popular election of the president and vice president. It also included the right of the National Assembly to pass a vote of nonconfidence against cabinet members and the decision (not carried out by the president) to establish a bicameral legislative body by adding the **House of Councilors** as upper house of the National Assembly. The lower house was to be named the **House of Representatives**.

The second amendment was voted on 27 November 1954, eliminating any limit on the term of office of the incumbent president. It received 135 votes, one vote short of the required two-thirds majority. Nevertheless, the Liberal Party declared it passed applying a dubious mathematical principle known as *Sa-sa o-ip* (round off), or the practice of knocking off fractions under 0.5. It instituted the system of national referendum on constitutional amendments, and abolished the office of the prime minister. The National Assembly adopted the amendment after the fall of the Rhee administration in April 1960.

The Constitution of the Second Republic, adopted on 15 June 1960, strengthened fundamental civil rights and freedom of the press, and established a new **Constitutional Court** and a **Central Election Management Committee**. At the same time, it reinstalled the system of election of the president as a figurehead chief-of-staff by the National Assembly, eliminated the office of the vice president, and established a responsible cabinet system, giving the prime minister full responsibility for the administration responsible to the National Assembly. It also created an upper house (House of Councilors) of the National Assembly.

The fourth constitutional amendment adopted on 23 March 1960 by both houses of the National Assembly provided for an exception to the principle of no retroactive punishment so that those involved in the rigging of the 15 March presidential and vice presidential elections would be punished. The fifth amendment was adopted following the **Military Revolution of 16 May 1961**. For the first time, the amended constitution was put to a national referendum on 17 December 1962, and became the Constitution of the Third Republic in 1963. It revived the presidential power, abolished the upper house of the National Assembly, downgraded the cabinet to a consultative body, and authorized the president to appoint the prime minister without the consent of the National Assembly.

The sixth amendment was approved by a national referendum on 17 October 1969, eliminating the two-term restriction on the president.

The amendment also authorized members of the National Assembly to concurrently serve as cabinet ministers and increased the membership of the National Assembly to no less than 150 and no more than 250.

With the seventh amendment approved by a national referendum on 21 November 1972, the Constitution became known as the *Yushin* (Revitalizing) Constitution, which provided extraordinary power to the president. With the removal of the restriction on the term of office, the incumbent president, **Park Chung-hee**, was reelected on 23 December 1972, an event that marked the beginning of the Fourth Republic. The amended constitution introduced a new system of presidential election by establishing the **National Conference for Unification (NCU)**, whose members were popularly elected, as an electoral college. It also authorized the president to recommend 73 members of the National Assembly to form a new political society named **Political Fraternal Society for Revitalizing Reform**, to be appointed by the NCU as members of the National Assembly. In February 1975, the voters confirmed their acceptance of the Yushin Constitution in a national referendum.

The eighth amendment was adopted on 22 October 1980 in a national referendum and was promulgated on 27 October. It formally ended the Yushin rule and laid the legal foundation for the launching of the Fifth Republic in 1981. The amended constitution strengthened the legislative and judiciary branches and limited the term of office of the president to a single seven-year term. Upon its promulgation, the National Assembly and all existing political parties were dissolved, and the **Legislative Council for National Security** was set up to function as a legislative body.

The ninth amendment, adopted by the National Assembly on 12 October 1987 and approved in a national referendum on 28 October, limited the term of office of the president to a single five-year term, laying the foundation for the establishment of the Sixth Republic. Under the amended constitution, the system of a direct, popular election of the president was restored, civil rights and freedoms of the press and speech were expanded, and the power of the National Assembly was strengthened.

CONSTITUTIONAL COMMITTEE. Under the **Constitution** of 1948, questions involving the constitutionality of laws were decided by this committee headed by the vice president of the Republic. It included five justices of the Supreme Court and five members of the **National Assembly**. Under the 1960 Constitution, the Constitutional Court, consisting of three members of the National Assembly, three justices of the Supreme Court and three others appointed by the president, was set up, replacing the Constitutional Committee. The Constitutional Court adjudicated the constitutionality of laws; impeachment trials; the dissolution of a political party; and litigation on election of the president, chief justice, and justices of the Supreme Court.

CONSTITUTIONAL COURT. See CONSTITUTIONAL COMMITTEE.

CONSTITUTIONAL REVISION DELIBERATION COUNCIL. Under great pressure, the government established this committee in March 1980. It consisted of 69 individuals drawn from political, academic, business, legal, journalistic, and other circles, and was chaired by the prime minister. The new **constitution** it drafted was approved in a national referendum on 22 October 1980, replacing the **Yushin** Constitution.

COOPERATIVES. Korea has a long history of cooperatives. The traditional format of the indigenous cooperative, or *kye*, was a small nonfamily group operating a circulating credit system. Since the end of the colonial period, one of the main areas of cooperative development has been in **agriculture**, especially since the government began promoting cooperatives in the early 1960s, but others can be found in fisheries and for credit and savings purposes.

Some 3,744 agricultural cooperatives of various categories were organized throughout the country in February 1958 as mutual aid associations, while some 2,200 others were being formed. The number of these cooperatives grew to about 20,000 by 1960. But the membership in individual cooperatives remained small.

In July 1961, the **Supreme Council for National Reconstruction** promulgated a new Agricultural Cooperatives Law, establishing a semigovernment agency, the National Agricultural Cooperative Federation (*Nong'op Hyoptong Chohap,* NACF) in August 1961. Newly combined agricultural cooperatives were organized, one in each district (*myon*), throughout the country to promote the welfare of the farmers, increase production, and advance cooperative spirit and efforts. To further these aims, a national cooperative training center for agricultural cooperatives was set up in 1962. It was followed by other training centers covering fisheries, livestock, and savings and credit. By the early 1980s, there were some 1,473 agricultural cooperatives with 2,099,720 members, 1,138 credit societies with 833,173 members, 72 fisheries cooperatives with 137,038 members, and 126 others with 76,071 members. By 1997, there were 5,886 cooperatives with a total membership of 19,802,406; this amounted to 43.5 percent of the population. Agricultural cooperatives suffered during the 1997 **IMF crisis** and the NACF took on a lobbying role. This led to the Agricultural Cooperative Law of 13 August 1999, which brought the livestock and ginseng cooperative groups into the NACF. *See also* NEW COMMUNITY MOVEMENT.

COUNCIL FOR THE PROMOTION OF DEMOCRACY (*Minjujui ch'oksong Hyopuihoe*). Organized by opposition leaders in 1984 to promote a united movement of all dissident groups to bring about a constitutional reform and democratization, it was led by two co-chairpersons (**Kim Young-sam** and **Kim Dae-jung**). The organizers of the council were disillusioned when the two Kims failed to work together, making the council an almost meaningless entity. When the two Kims formed their own political parties in 1987, the council was effectively dissolved.

CROSS-RECOGNITION. The idea that South Korea's principal international supporters (the **United States** and **Japan**) and those of **North Korea** (the then **Soviet Union/Russia** and **China**) should each establish diplomatic relations with the "other Korea" seems to have been first suggested by a U.S. official, Morton Abramovitz, in a paper published in 1971. It began to gain ground internationally after South Korea's President **Park Chung-hee** announced in June 1973 that South Korea would no longer break off diplomatic relations with countries that established relations with the North. U.S. Secretary of State Henry Kissinger was one proponent of the idea, and it regularly reemerged during the late 1970s and the 1980s.

However, the Eastern European countries recognition of South Korea beginning with Hungary in 1989, followed by the Soviet Union in 1990 and by China in 1992, was not matched by Western diplomatic relations with North Korea. Only at the end of the 1990s, with Italy's decision to establish relations with North Korea, followed in 2000 by **Australia**, Canada, New Zealand, and the Philippines, did the original concept of cross-recognition appear to be taking shape. This new trend was confirmed at the Asia–Europe Meeting (ASEM 3) in Seoul in October 2000, when a number of other countries, including **Great Britain**, Germany, and the Netherlands announced their intention of establishing diplomatic relations with North Korea.

CURFEW. Because of fear of **North Korean** infiltration by night, a wide-scale midnight to four A.M. curfew operated throughout most of South Korea, with the exception of **Cheju Island**, from 1945 until January 1982. Theoretically, curfews on the same basis can still be imposed on a local basis.

CURRENCY. *See* MONETARY SYSTEM.

– D –

DECEMBER 1979 COUP. On 12 December 1979, Major General **Chun Doo-hwan**, commander of the **Defense Security Command**, an army intelligence unit charged with preventing internal subversion in the army, carried out a coup with the aid of the 9th Army Division troops under Lieutenant General **Roh Tae-woo**. The official purpose of the coup was to "ensure a joint investigation into the assassination of the late President Park." Chun claimed there was sufficient evidence of possible complicity of some senior army officers in the conspiracy against the late President **Park Chung-hee**.

Chun arrested General **Chong Sung-hwa**, army chief of staff and the martial law commander, and several other generals, charging them with involvement in the death of the president, and at the same time, took control of the armed forces. The coup placed the real power in the hands of Chun and a small group of army officers who cooperated with him. As a result, acting President **Ch'oe Kyu-ha** became a puppet of the military. His resignation in August 1980 paved the way for Chun to make himself president.

DECLARATION OF DEMOCRATIC NATIONAL SALVATION.
A declaration adopted by opposition leaders, including **Yun Po-son**,
Kim Dae-jung, and Ham Sok-hon, on 1 March 1976 at the Roman
Catholic Myongdong Cathedral in **Seoul**, and which led to what became known as the "Myongdong Incident." Many dissident leaders
were arrested following this declaration. At the same time, staff dismissed from the *Tong-a Ilbo* newspaper formed the "Tong-a Committee for the Struggle for Protection of Freedom of the Press and
Speech."

DECONTROL OF THE PRESS. The government of President **Roh
Tae-woo** in July 1988 lifted the ban on the publication of literary and
artistic works by some 80 **defectors** who had gone, either voluntar-
ily or not, to **North Korea**. At the same time, the government allowed the circulation of books on socialism and communism, as well
as North Korean publications, thereby encouraging the rise of studies
on North Korea and other socialist countries.

DEFECTORS. Since the end of the **Korean War**, there has been a
steady trickle of defectors from **North Korea** to the South, matched
by a much smaller number who have gone from South to North. The
volume of defectors to the South has been rising since the 1970s. In
October 1998, the South Korean Unification Ministry said that from
July 1953 to October 1998, 923 defectors had come from the North.
In 1999, the number was 148 and in 2000, it rose to 312. In 2001, 583
made their way to South Korea. In 2002, the number reached 1,140.

Since the late 1980s, an increasing number of defectors have come
via **China**. Some reports speak of tens of thousands of North Koreans
hiding out in China. From 2002, groups of North Koreans made persistent attempts to seek asylum in embassies in Beijing. Most defectors
appear to have left for economic or social reasons, or because of personal problems; a 1994 survey in South Korea found that only about a
quarter of the defectors questioned had left for ideological reasons.
Some, such as North Korean agents discovered in South Korea or a few
fishermen who drifted into South Korean waters had originally been
involuntary defectors; some of these have been returned. Prominent
North Korean defectors have included the deputy head of the North
Korean Central News Agency, Yi Su-gun, who fled to the South while

covering a **Military Armistice Commission** meeting at **P'anmunjom** in 1967, who was later accused of being a spy and executed, and **Hwang Jang-yop**, supposed architect of North Korean political philosophy, the *juche* philosophy, and tutor to the North Korean leader, **Kim Jong-il**, in 1997. Most defectors have not found adjustment easy, and a few have gone back to North Korea, to meet an uncertain fate.

The number of defectors from South to North since the end of the Korean War is believed to be very small, but it includes some prominent figures, such as **Choi Hong-hi**, a former military officer and later sportsman. From time to time, there are reports of South Koreans being kidnapped and taken to the North. One such case was that of a South Korean missionary, Kim Tong-shin, who disappeared from North China in 2000, and was allegedly taken to North Korea. Fishermen and farmers in the **demilitarized zone** have also been taken North from time to time.

DEFENSE SECURITY COMMAND. A military intelligence organization of the Ministry of Defense, primarily responsible for security within the armed forces. However, it has also handled civilian subversive activities.

DEMILITARIZED ZONE (DMZ). With the signing of the **Korean Armistice Agreement** on 27 July 1953, a 150-mile (225 kilometer) zigzagging **military demarcation line** across the Korean Peninsula established a new boundary between South and **North Korea**. At the same time, a demilitarized zone was established along the military demarcation line. This zone is 2.5 miles (4 km) wide, 1.25 miles (2 km) on each side of the line. A 10-foot high fence was erected on each edge of the zone, guarded by heavily armed guards posted outside it. All civilian dwellings inside the DMZ were removed, but some farmers were allowed to farm there. The truce village of **P'anmunjom** is located at the point in the western DMZ, where the main north–south highways meet. At the end of 2000, administrative jurisdiction over the southern half of the zone passed from the **United Nations Command** to the South Korean military.

DEMOCRATIC JUSTICE PARTY (*Minju Chong'udang*). In January 1981, the supporters of President **Chun Doo-hwan** formed this new political party with Chun as its president. It became the ruling party in the **National Assembly**. In April 1988, Chun's successor, **Roh Tae-woo** replaced Chun as president. In February 1990, it merged with the **Reunification Democratic Party** and the **New Democratic Republican Party** to become the **Democratic Liberal Party**.

DEMOCRATIC KOREA PARTY (*Minju Han'gukdang, or Minhandang, DKP*). In January 1981, a group of dissidents formed a new political party with Yu Ch'i-song as its president. In 1984, it was absorbed into the **New Korea Democratic Party**.

DEMOCRATIC LABOR PARTY (*Minju nodondang*). The Democratic Labor Party began in 2000, bringing together various "progressive forces," and claiming to represent labor, students, peasants, and other dispossessed groups. The party enjoyed some success in the 2002 local elections, winning two mayoral slots in the industrial city of **Ulsan**. In October 2002, it claimed 30,000 members, of whom 13,000 were trade unionists. It is close to the Korean Confederation of Trades Unions.

DEMOCRATIC LIBERAL PARTY (*Minju Chayudang*). The merger of the ruling **Democratic Justice Party** (DJP) and two minor parties—the **Reunification Democratic Party** (RDP) and the **New Democratic Republican Party** (NDRP)—created this new party. The agreement to form a "grand alliance" of the three parties was announced on 22 January 1990. The formal decision to form a new party was made on 9 February. By doing so, the new party secured an absolute majority in the **National Assembly** by including 127 lawmakers of the former DJP, 54 lawmakers of the former RDP, and 56 lawmakers of the former NDRP, having 18 more seats than the opposition, thus allowing the government to pass any bills. Only five lawmakers of the former RDP refused to join the new party. When the representatives of the three parties met on 9 February and made a formal decision to form a new party, they chose **Roh Tae-woo**, **Kim Young-sam**, and **Kim Jong-p'il** as supreme representatives of the new-party, forming the party leadership of a troika. In 1996, the party was renamed the **New Korea Party**.

DEMOCRATIC NATIONALIST PARTY (*Minju Kungmindang*). In February 1949, the **Korean (Han'guk) Democratic Party** merged with several other conservative groups to form an anti-**Syngman Rhee** political party under the leadership of **Shin Ik-hui**. Its leadership group boasted many prominent individuals, including **Cho Pyong-ok**. Among its aims was to institute a responsible cabinet system in order to strengthen parliamentary democracy. Its opposition to **constitutional amendments** in 1952 and 1954 failed. Many of its members were involved in the **Pusan Political Disturbance** of 1952. After suffering much under the repressive measures of the government, it was reorganized into the **Democratic Party** in September 1955.

DEMOCRATIC PARTY (*Minjudang*). Shortly after the **constitutional amendments** in November 1954, the members of the **Democratic Nationalist Party** formed the "Society of the Comrades for the Protection of the Constitution," and solicited wider support among the people. In order to strengthen their antiautocracy struggle, in September 1955 they reorganized their party in an enlarged Democratic Party with **Shin Ik-hui**, **Cho Pyong-ok**, and **Chang Myon** as its supreme committee members. It became the majority party in the aftermath of the fall of the First Republic, and the **National Assembly** elected its leaders, **Yun Po-son** and Chang Myon, as the president and prime minister respectively of the Second Republic.

The party was badly split into the "old" and the "new" factions, and when the new faction gained prominence under Chang Myon's leadership, the old faction broke away, forming the **New Democratic Party** (*Shin Minjudang*, or *Shinmindang*) in October 1960. The Democratic Party, along with others, was dissolved following the **Military Revolution of 16 May 1961**. However, when a dozen new political parties emerged in the spring and summer of 1963, **Pak Sun-chon** established a new Democratic Party in July. In May 1965, this party and the **Civil Rule Party** (*Minjongdang*) were united into the **Masses Party** (*Minjungdang*). In order to strengthen the opposition group, in February 1967, the Masses Party and the **New Korea Party** (*Shin Hankukdang*) formed in May 1966 were united into another **New Democratic Party** (*Shin minjudang*), which became the main opposition party under the leadership of **Yu Chin-o**.

The third Democratic Party was formed in June 1990, by Yi Kit'aek and others who refused to follow **Kim Young-sam**, who united his **Reunification Democratic Party** (*T'ongil Minjudang*) with the **Democratic Justice Party** (*Minju Chong'udang*) and the **New Democratic Republican Party** (Shin Minju Konghwadang) to form the **Democratic Liberal Party** in February 1990. In September 1991, Yi Ki-t'aek of the Democratic Party and **Kim Dae-jung** of the New Democratic Party agreed to merge their parties, bringing the fourth Democratic Party into existence with Kim and Yi as copresidents.

DEMOCRATIC PEOPLE'S REPUBLIC OF KOREA. *See* NORTH KOREA.

DEMOCRATIC REPUBLICAN PARTY (*Minju Konghwadang*). A political party established in February 1963 by the leaders of the **Military Revolution of 16 May 1961**, with General **Park Chung-hee** as its president. It became the ruling party, remaining as such until 1979. It was dissolved along with other political organizations in May 1980, but in 1981 it was revived as the **New Democratic Republican Party** (*Shin Minju Konghwadang*) under the leadership of **Kim Jong-p'il**.

DEMOGRAPHICS. *See* SOCIAL AND CULTURAL DEVELOPMENT.

DIPLOMATIC RECOGNITION. With the emergence of two separate states on the Korean Peninsula in 1948, it was natural that they should compete against each other for diplomatic recognition. At first, there was a clear division. The **Soviet Union/Russia** and its allies recognized **North Korea**, while the **United States** and most western countries recognized South Korea, on the basis of **United Nations** resolutions, although relatively few established diplomatic missions in **Seoul**.

The emergence of newly independent states in the late 1950s as decolonization began to take effect prompted the two Koreas into a competition for diplomatic recognition. The South Korean government operated a "Hallstein Doctrine," similar to that of West Germany from where the name came, whereby it would break off relations with countries that established links with the North. This worked well for some years. By 1965, South Korea had diplomatic relations with 64 countries, the North with 24. Following the North–South dialogue in 1972, the South announced that it would no longer oppose the establishment of diplomatic relations with the North. This announcement, and the abolition of the **United Nations Commission for Unification and Rehabilitation of Korea** in 1973 led to a steady increase in diplomatic recognition of both North and South. By March 1973, 86 countries recognized the South and 47 the North; 11 recognized both. By December 1976, recognition was almost equal, with 94 for the South, 90 for the North, and 46 recognizing both. Thereafter, the competition rather petered out until the end of the 1980s, when, following President **Roh Tae-woo**'s policy of **Nordpolitik**, the South began cultivating the East European countries. Diplomatic relations were established with Hungary in 1989, and most of the socialist countries followed.

The North, faced with increasing economic problems, began closing posts in the 1990s (the South would do the same after the 1997 **IMF crisis**), while some of those that remained were involved in illegal activities such as drug smuggling in order to support themselves. Only in late 1999 did the North, with the establishment of diplomatic relations with Italy, once again appear to be expanding its diplomatic contacts, though this time with the positive encouragement of South Korea. Australia and the Philippines soon followed Italy, and in October 2000, **Great Britain**, the Netherlands, and Germany announced their intention of establishing relations with North Korea. The trend continued into 2001, with New Zealand establishing relations in March that year. *See also* CROSS-RECOGNITION; FOREIGN POLICY.

– E –

EAST BERLIN CASE. On 8 July 1967, the Korean Central Intelligence Agency (now the **National Intelligence Service**) announced that 107 Koreans had been arrested in connection with an alleged antistate espionage (pro–**North Korea**) team based in East Berlin, then the capital of the German Democratic Republic. Seventeen leaders of the East Berlin–based spy ring were abducted to **Seoul** via West Germany, and they, along with those who were arrested in South Korea, were tried under the **Anti-Communism Law**. This was known as "Case of East Berlin." Of 34 of those who were indicted, two were given the death sentence, one a life term, and the rest received various prison terms. Five of those who were abducted from East Berlin were allowed to return to West Germany in March 1969. The death sentence given to two was later commuted to life imprisonment. *See also* NATIONAL SECURITY LAWS.

EAST SEA/SEA OF JAPAN. The East Sea/Sea of Japan are names given to the stretch of water that lies between the Korean east coast and **Japan**. During the Japanese colonial period, the name "Sea of Japan" was formally registered with the International Hydrographic Organization in 1929. Since the establishment of the Republic of Korea in 1948, successive South Korean governments have sought at least to have both names accepted, arguing that "East Sea" or even "Sea of Korea" have a much longer pedigree than "Sea of Japan," which it is claimed, only came into general use from the end of the 18th century. As well as taking its case to the Sixth (and subsequent) United Nations Conference on the Standardization of Geographical Names in 1992, and to the Fifteenth International Hydrographic Conference in 1997, South Korea has conducted a campaign to persuade commercial map publishers and others to use "East Sea." **North Korea** also claims that "East Sea" is the correct name.

EC 121, DOWNING OF. On 15 April 1969, a **United States** naval reconnaissance aircraft with 31 crew onboard was shot down by North Korean MiG fighter planes over the **East Sea/Sea of Japan** at a point some 95 miles (165 kilometers) south of the port of Ch'ongjin on **North Korea**'s east coast. The U.S. claimed that the incident took place over international waters. The aircraft was equipped to monitor both ELINT (electromagnetic intelligence) and SIGINT (signals intelligence), and had been engaged in reconnaissance activity along the eastern coast of North Korea from its home base at Atsuki, **Japan**.

ECONOMIC DEVELOPMENT. The Introduction gives an account of South Korea's economic development up to the early stages of the recovery from the 1997 **IMF crisis**. To widespread international surprise, this recovery has generally continued, though internal and external factors have had adverse effects. Reform of the *chaebol* has perhaps not gone as far as many expected, but it has continued. Reform of the banks and opening up of the **banking** sector to the outside world has also continued. In 2001, estimated Gross Domestic Product (GDP) was U.S.$865 million, with per capita GDP at $18,000 (These are purchasing power parity, or PPP, rates). Real growth was 3.3 percent, much lower than in the two previous years, inflation 4.3 percent, and unemployment down to 3.9 percent. The labor force numbered 22 million. Of this number, 69 percent were in services, 21.5 percent in industry, and 9.5 percent in **agriculture**. Domestic consumption continued strong, helped by the low unemployment rate. Main industries included electronics, automobile production, chemicals, shipbuilding, steel, textiles, clothing, footwear, and processed foods. Trade was down, but the trade balance improved in South Korea's favor. Total exports were $1,504.4 billion, imports $1,411 billion. The country's main trading partners were the **United States**, **Japan**, **China**, Hong Kong, Taiwan, Saudi Arabia, and **Australia**.

In 2002, growth was estimated at 5.8 percent, despite low economic activity world wide, and the dampening effects of the **World Cup 2002** on production. On the same PPP terms, GDP reached $931 billion, and per capita GDP $19,400. Unemployment fell slightly to 3.1 percent. The division of labor remained more or less the same as in 2001. Trade figures were $159.2 billion exports, and $146.6 billion imports, with the same pattern of trading partners. The United States remains South Korea's main trading partner, followed by Japan and China. *See also* NATIONAL DEVELOPMENT PLANS.

EDUCATION LAW. Promulgated on 31 December 1949, this law set forth the basic direction and objectives of education and delineated the fundamental policy directions for education in the country. Education, according to the law, was to inculcate in everyone a sense of national identity and respect for national sovereignty. The law emphasized the development of the spirit of universal fraternity and ability to work for the common prosperity of all humankind. *See also* EDUCATIONAL DEVELOPMENT.

EDUCATIONAL DEVELOPMENT. Korea's educational development began with the introduction of **Confucianism** in the second century A.D. and **Buddhism** in the fourth century A.D. Since then, Confucian learning, along with studies in Chinese culture, developed rapidly under state sponsorship, particularly during the Yi period. Buddhism also contributed toward the development of scholarship.

Modern education began in 1883 when a Western-style private school was established in Wonsan by a Korean. This was followed by the establishment of schools by foreign missionaries in 1885 and 1886, and a palace school by the government in 1886. The founding of girls' schools by foreign missionaries from 1886 was the first time in Korean history that girls were given an opportunity to receive formal education. Many private schools were established from the 1890s up to 1906, increasing educational opportunity for young Koreans.

When **Japan** annexed Korea in 1910, the Japanese educational system was introduced. The Japanese built public primary and secondary schools, as well as professional schools, although the number of the latter was small. Meanwhile, foreign mission boards established four colleges. However, educational development was restricted by the **Government-General of Korea**, and only a small number of Koreans received a modern education. The illiteracy rate of Koreans at the end of Japanese colonial rule was a staggering 75 percent.

Korea's liberation from Japan in 1945 provided a turning point for educational development although the progress was slow because of a shortage of funds and trained teachers. Those Korean colleges, which had been closed down by the Japanese, were reopened, and private schools began to appear slowly. The **United States Army Military Government**, while maintaining the Japanese centralized national education system, introduced the American school system of six years primary school, followed by three middle and three high school years, with a four-year college period. They also published new textbooks and trained teachers at various institutes.

When the Republic was inaugurated, the American system was kept. The **Constitution** of 1948 guaranteed equal opportunity for education, making elementary education compulsory and free. The **Education Law** of December 1949 laid the cornerstone of national education, setting out the purposes of education. Although all public primary schools were coeducational, separate public middle and high schools were established for boys and girls.

The **Korean War** delayed the implementation of the six-year plan for compulsory education, originally planned to begin in 1950, until 1954. By the end of 1959, 95 percent of all school-age children were enrolled in primary schools that operated in two shifts. Meanwhile, a five-year plan for vocational education was implemented in 1958, and the Industrial Educational Promotion Law followed in 1963. A significant step was taken in 1969 with the extension of compulsory education to the ninth grade, and abolition of the entrance examination for middle schools. With this, the ratio of primary school graduates advancing to middle schools reached 98.7 percent in 1987. In that year, 91.9 percent of middle school graduates went on to academic and vocational high schools. In 1992, three-year compulsory middle school education was extended to rural areas. There has been a steady decline in the number of primary schools in rural areas as more people have moved to cities.

The government paid particular attention to the promotion of secondary vocational and technical schools, as well as higher education. Meanwhile, many private colleges and **universities** were established along with primary and secondary schools of various kinds, contributing toward rapid educational development and an increase of skilled workers. In April 1974, two years after the nongovernmental **Korean Educational Development Institute (KEDI)** was founded, the government established the National Institute of Education to carry out comprehensive research for the development of educational theories and practice in the sociocultural context of Korea and improvement of educational programs. In March 1985, a Presidential Commission for Educational Reform was established, with a mandate to formulate a comprehensive set of reform measures for educational policy and administration to promote education for the 21st century.

The government began the introduction of computers at all educational levels in the 1990s. By April 2001, all primary and secondary schools in the country were equipped with personal computers and access to the Internet. There are also plans to extend administrative links between the Ministry of Education and schools via computer links.

Special schools exist for handicapped children. By 1997, there were 109 special institutions, with a total enrollment of 22,569. This had increased to 134 institutions, with 23,769 students by 2002. Of these, 47 were public and 87 private. In 2002, there were 12 schools for blind children, 19 for the deaf, 18 for the physically handicapped, 85 for the mentally handicapped, and four for the emotionally handicapped.

Preschool education is not compulsory, but has been steadily expanded in recent years. In 1965, 19,466 children attended kindergarten. By 1997, the number had risen to 586,000 children enrolled in over 9,000 kindergartens throughout the country. However, the numbers in kindergarten have dropped in recent years, possibly a reflection of the country's economic problems. In 2001, the number was down to 545,912, though this represented a slight increase over the previous year. The Ministry of Education plans to have 90 percent of kindergarten-aged children admitted to such schools by 2005.

Less-formal education has also developed, under both the government and private organizations. Until the early 1960s, nonformal education consisted of literacy campaigns, civil education, agricultural extension, and adult education. These programs not only reduced the rate of illiteracy among the adult population, especially in rural areas, but also provided practical knowledge and technology for life in a rapidly changing world. Rapid cultural, economic, and social transformation of Korean society from the 1960s onward increased the need for a more organized and systematic form of continuing or lifelong education. As a result, the government created a Non-formal Education Division in the Bureau of Social and International Education of the Ministry of Education (since 2001, renamed the Ministry of Education and Human Resources Development), and expanded and strengthened nonformal educational programs. Civic schools were established for young people who had not completed a primary school education, and civic high schools for those who were unable to attend formal middle and high schools. Trade schools at primary and secondary levels were also established for those who had primary education but did not go on to secondary schools.

In 1972, the Air (radio-TV) and Correspondence High School system was adopted to provide educational opportunities to those who had to start making their livelihood early. In 1974, junior college level courses

Educational Growth in South Korea, 1945–2001* (1945 figures include both North and South Korea; 2001 figures latest available as at mid-2003.)

	Number of Schools					
	1945	1960	1970	1980	1991	2001
Primary	2,834	4,496	8,961	6,487	6,245	5,322
Middle Schools	166	1,054	1,608	2,121	2,498	2,770
High Schools*	640	889	1,353	1,624	1,730	1,969
Colleges/ Universities**	19	85	168	236	244	415

	Number of Students					
	1945	1960	1970	1980	1991	2001
Primary	1,366,024	3,622,685	5,739,301	5,658,002	4,758,505	4,089,429
Middle	80,828	528,593	1,318,808	2,476,997	2,232,330	1,831,152
High—	273,434	590,382	1,696,792	2,233,894	1,911,173	
Colleges/ Universities	7,819	101,041	201,436	501,994	1,427,208	1,729,638

* Includes vocational/technical high schools such as agricultural, commercial, fishery and marine, and technical high schools. All secondary schools were middle schools in 1945.
** Includes private, national universities, national teachers colleges, junior and senior colleges.

were added when the Korean Air and Correspondence University was established, offering 12 bachelor's programs in 13 departments. Subsequent years saw a steady expansion of distance learning through these programs. In 1977, a program of special evening classes for young workers, and evening secondary schools attached to industry, began, to be followed in 1982 by the open college programs. These national and private open colleges offered industrial workers with a high school education the chance to earn a college degree while working.

ELECTIONS. *See* APPENDIX C; APPENDIX D; CONSTITUTION; CONSTITUIONAL AMENDMENTS; LOCAL AUTONOMY; NATIONAL ASSEMBLY.

EMERGENCY DECREES. President **Park Chung-hee** issued Emergency Decrees Nos. 1–3 in January 1974, banning criticism of the **Yushin** system. Decree No. 1 prohibited any agitation for constitutional revision, Decree No. 2 established an Emergency Court Martial, and Decree No. 3 was concerned with security of lives. These three were followed by Decree No. 4, issued in April 1974, which prohibited activities of Democratic Youth and Student Federations. These decrees were cancelled in August 1974, following the killing of Madam Yuk Yong-su, wife of President Park. But new Emergency Decrees Nos. 5–9 were proclaimed in April and May 1975, dealing with campus unrest and the growing demand for constitutional revision. *See also* ASSASSINATION AND ASSASSINATION ATTEMPTS; STUDENT MOVEMENT.

EQUALITY LAW OF MALE AND FEMALE EMPLOYEES. *See* LABOR MOVEMENT.

– F –

FAMILY COURT (*Kajong Popwon*). This court, set up in 1963, marked a new departure in South Korea's judicial development, and a new stage in the **Women's Movement.** The court deals with matrimonial and juvenile issues, and meets in private. In matrimonial cases, the court attempts mediation first. Only if that fails does it proceed to adjudication.

FAMILY LAW. South Korea's 1948 **Constitution** provided for formal equality between the sexes. The reality, however, was that Korea remained a very male-oriented society, and this was reflected in practice and in the family law. The first formal introduction of a family law was in 1957, under President **Syngman Rhee**. This essentially took over the Japanese **Government-General of Korea**'s legal provisions dealing with the family. The law firmly laid down the role of the husband/father as head of the family, in accordance with the principles of **Confucianism.** However, the 1957 law did allow married women to function legally separate from their husbands. Women were also allowed to inherit property, and to be treated equally in divorce hearings. These concessions did not satisfy the growing **Women's Movement**, which pressed for a much fuller set of rights.

A further revision took place in 1977. From then on, a wife's share of the inheritance from her husband was equal to that of the eldest son, other inheritance rules also changed to improve the position of women, the age for marriage without parental consent became equal for men and women, and a provision for divorce by agreement under the auspices of the **Family Court** was introduced.

In the 1980s, pressure continued for reform as women played a more active role at all levels of society, leading to a further revision of the law in 1989. This effectively marked the legal end of male dominance of the family. Men and women now had equal rights over their children, inheritance rules no longer discriminated in favor of husbands/male heirs, and the definition of relatives, for marriage purposes, was much curtailed. Campaigners continue to press for further legal reforms, such as the abolition of the "crime" of adultery, in order to bring about full legal equality.

FAMILY REUNIONS. The **Korean War** left families divided, and the hostility between the two sides meant that few people either in **North Korea** or South Korea had any contact or news of relatives in the other part of the peninsula after 1953. Only with the beginning of the first North–South dialogue in 1971 was the possibility of some form of direct contact raised. With the collapse of the dialogue in 1976, the desultory exchanges on the subject came to a temporary halt. Discussions revived in the mid-1980s, however, and two small-scale reunions took place. Following an agreement reached in August 1985 between the Red Cross societies of North and South Korea, on 20 September 1985, members of separated families and folk art troupes numbering 151 members from each country arrived in **Seoul** and **P'yongyang**, respectively, for four-day visits.

Although this relaxation was widely welcomed, contacts between North and South broke off in January 1986, and there was no follow-up on visits until August 2000. Then, following the historic **June 2000 Inter-Korean Summit** between the South Korean president, **Kim Dae-jung**, and the North Korean leader, **Kim Jong-il**, a further exchange was arranged. On 15 August 2000, 200 elderly people from each side visited P'yongyang and Seoul. The visit was also remarkable in that aircraft from each side were involved in the exchange. A further exchange took place in February 2001, and more are planned. There have also been some unofficial family reunions in **China** and in **Japan**. *See also* NORTH KOREA–SOUTH KOREA RELATIONS; REUNITING OF SCATTERED FAMILY MEMBERS.

FARMERS' DEMONSTRATION. Although South Korean farmers were often not happy with the policy of successive governments toward **agriculture**, they carried out no public demonstrations until the emergence of the democratic movement after 1987. Thus, on 13 February 1989, some 15,000 farmers from various parts of the country held a violent rally in front of the National Assembly building, clashing with riot **police**. It was led by the Preparation Committee for the Federation of Farmers Movement, a branch of the **National Coalition for a People's Democratic Movement** that included many dissident groups. Other demonstrations followed.

FEDERATION OF KOREAN EDUCATION ASSOCIATIONS (*Taehan Kyoyuk Yonmaeng, or Kyoryon*). *See* GENERAL FEDERATION OF KOREAN TEACHERS' ASSOCIATIONS.

FEDERATION OF KOREAN TRADE UNIONS (FKTU). *See* GENERAL FEDERATION OF KOREAN LABOR UNIONS.

FLAG, NATIONAL. The South Korean National Flag, known as the *T'aegukki*, consists of two interlocking commas, one red and one blue, which represent *yang and yin*, symbolizing the universe. They are surrounded by four trigrams or bars, variously representing, heaven-earth-sun-moon, father-mother-daughter-son, and benevolence-justice-propriety-wisdom. The flag in its present form dates from 1949, and derives from a royal flag of the 1880s.

FOREIGN POLICY. Two features have characterized the foreign relations of the Republic of Korea. Foreign affairs from the earliest days of the Republic have been dominated by the views of successive presidents. Although a number of capable people have occupied the post of foreign minister, foreign policy has essentially always been made in the presidential secretariat, known as the *Blue House*. Just as important was the fact that until the late 1980s at least, foreign policy issues were dominated by the perceived need to combat attempts by **North Korea** to secure international recognition.

When the Republic of Korea was established in August 1948, the **United States** and other Western countries recognized the new nation and established diplomatic relations with it. However, neither the **Soviet**

Union/Russia and its allies, nor most of the small number of independent Middle Eastern and African states did so. Even after the **United Nations** General Assembly in December 1948 recognized the South Korean government as the only legitimate government on the Korean Peninsula, South Korea was unable to obtain UN membership, and its diplomatic ties with the nations of the world remained limited. Negotiations to establish normal relations with **Japan** began after the Japanese Peace Treaty came into force in April 1952, but brought no results, partly because of President **Syngman Rhee**'s dislike of Japan. However, a South Korean mission, with diplomatic status, began to operate in Tokyo from 1952.

Following the **Korean War**, the United States and South Korea signed a **South Korea-United States Mutual Defense Treaty**, which further tied the latter to the U.S. Until the 1970s, South Korea had a very clear policy on **diplomatic recognition**, refusing to establish relations with countries that had diplomatic relations with North Korea. If relations were already established with a country and that country recognized the North, then South Korea broke off relations. This practice, similar to that of West Germany toward East Germany, was known as the "Hallstein Doctrine."

During the 1960s, South Korea's diplomatic relations expanded following the adoption of a more active foreign policy. As a result, the number of countries with which South Korea maintained diplomatic ties increased from 22 to 93; the number of resident missions abroad rose from 17 to 97; membership in international organizations increased from 26 to 476, and the number of international agreements signed grew from 127 to 598. The president of South Korea made only four state visits (mainly to the U.S.) up until 1961, but between 1961 and 1970, 13 such visits were made, followed by many more in the 1980s. The foreign policy goals of South Korea were to improve its image in the international community and gain a greater share of world markets through a program of modernization, thereby strengthening her own economic position.

One of the most significant achievements in foreign relations was the conclusion, on 22 June 1965, after 13 years' negotiations, of the **South Korean–Japan Normalization Treaty**, establishing diplomatic relations between the two countries. In addition, South Korea secured a large loan and a large sum of monetary reparations from Japan.

Other major achievements included the conclusion in July 1966, of a **United States-South Korea Status-of-Forces Agreement** with the U.S., the strengthening of ties with the U.S. by dispatching South Korean troops to **Vietnam**, and the establishment of the Asian and Pacific Council (ASPAC) in 1966, at South Korean initiative, to promote cultural ties with Asian nations.

In the 1970s, South Korea continued to expand its diplomatic links, particularly in Africa, Latin America, and the Middle East. Hoping to establish relations with the Soviet Bloc nations, on 3 June 1973, President **Park Chung-hee** said that South Korea would "open its doors to all the nations of the world on the basis of the principle of reciprocity and equality." In turn, he urged those countries whose ideologies and social institutions were different from South Korea's "to open their doors" to South Korea. Although Park and his successors would continue to make efforts to prevent countries from developing relations with North Korea for some years longer, this was the effective beginning of the end of the Hallstein Doctrine. Efforts to establish diplomatic relations with socialist countries did not bring results until late in the 1980s, but the number of other countries that established diplomatic ties with South Korea rose to more than 103, including 50 full members of the group of nonaligned nations, and the Holy See. Although South Korea supported countries that had been struggling for independence, the elimination of racial discrimination, national sovereignty, and territorial integrity, it failed to become a member of the nonaligned movement, although North Korea did.

Meanwhile, South Korea concluded bilateral cultural treaties with 35 countries (28 between 1965 and 1977) and multilateral cultural agreements with several consortiums. By 2001, South Korea maintained a network of embassies, consulates, and other diplomatic missions in 183 countries, with a total of 100 embassies, 38 consulates, and 7 other missions. It was a member of 91 international bodies, including 16 United Nations agencies, as well as a host of nongovernmental bodies.

Although cordial and amicable relations developed between South Korea and many countries, some incidents created friction. The **Military Revolution of 16 May 1961** and subsequent suppression of civil liberties by the South Korean government caused tension in

Korean–American relations, as did President **Jimmy Carter**'s plan, later abandoned, in the late 1970s, to withdraw all American ground troops from South Korea, the investigation of the House of Representatives of the U.S. Congress of the so-called **Koreagate**, and General **Chun Doo-hwan**'s **December 1979 coup**.

The 1967 **East Berlin case** involving the abduction of an alleged pro–North Korean espionage team from West Germany to **Seoul** by South Korean agents likewise created diplomatic tensions between Seoul and Bonn for some years. The relationship between South Korea and Japan was strained when Korean agents kidnapped Kim Daejung from Tokyo to Seoul in August 1973. Since the early 1980s, there have been regular disputes between South Korea and Japan because it was claimed that Japan's revised high school history textbooks white-washed Japanese aggression in Korea. The **East Sea/Sea of Japan** issue has also soured relations from time to time. Under Chun Doo-hwan, South Korean demands that Japan should provide more aid in return for South Korea's role as a shield against communism, while ultimately successful, also caused tension in relations with Japan.

One of the most significant developments in foreign relations was the steady development of links with communist countries from the 1970s onward. The Soviet Union's decision to allow South Korean diplomats to attend the UNESCO conference in Moscow in 1976, and the participation of the Soviet Union, Hungary, East Germany and Yugoslavia in the International Athletic Association Federation (IAAF) meeting in Seoul in 1978, paved the way for the establishment of new relations between South Korea and these socialist countries. After the adoption of the policy of *perestroika* by Mikhail Gorbachev, South Korea increased commercial and cultural ties with the Soviet Union. At the same time, South Korea developed cultural and economic contacts with the People's Republic of **China** and East European countries.

In March 1988, Hungary became the first socialist country to open a trade office and mission in Seoul, followed by the Soviet Union and China. After the 1988 Seoul **Olympic Games**, South Korea's foreign relations with socialist countries grew rapidly. In February 1989, South Korea established diplomatic relations first with Hungary and then with Poland. Yugoslavia followed, while South Korea and the

Soviet Union concluded an agreement to establish consular relations in early December 1988. Meanwhile, South Korea established new trade relations with Vietnam, which eventually led to diplomatic ties in 1992.

In November 1989, President **Roh Tae-woo** strengthened the new links with Hungary by a state visit. It was the first time that a South Korean president had made an official state visit to a socialist country, marking a significant turning point in South Korea's foreign relations. Following the meeting between President Roh and Soviet President Mikhail Gorbachev in San Francisco on 4–5 June 1990, the Soviet and South Korean Foreign Ministers, meeting in New York on 30 September 1990, announced the establishment of full diplomatic relations between the two nations. After that, President Roh made a state visit to Moscow in December, and in April 1991 President Roh and President Gorbachev held a summit meeting in **Cheju Island**.

One of the features of the normalization of relations with the Soviet Union was a large aid package. South Korea agreed to provide U.S.$3 billion in aid over three years. A "tied" loan of $1.5 billion that included a $1 billion bank loan and $472 million in export credits was provided to Moscow. The long-hoped-for diplomatic relations with the Soviet Union came just as the Soviet system was on the point of collapse, and there was much domestic criticism of what was regarded as the high price paid for diplomatic relations. There were problems over the repayment of loans to Russia, and a row over the activities of diplomats in each country in 1998.

Diplomatic relations with China came in 1992, following the steady development of economic links between the two countries, as did the entry of both Koreas to the United Nations that autumn. By the mid-1990s, South Korea had effectively won the diplomatic competition with North Korea, as more and more of the latter's former supporters established relations with the South. South Korea played a prominent role in the establishment of the Asia–Europe Movement (ASEM) in 1997, and the second meeting of this forum was held in Seoul in 2000.

The relationship with China was at first more satisfactory than that with Russia, but here, too, there were soon problems over the activities of South Koreans in China's **Yanbian Korean Autonomous Region**, and over the influx of Chinese to South Korea.

During the presidencies of **Roh Tae-woo** and **Kim Young-sam**, the question of the **North Korean nuclear program** increasingly came to the fore, and led to close coordination with the U.S. on the issue. Both paid frequent visits to Washington.

Under President **Kim Dae-jung**, the Foreign Ministry became the Ministry of Foreign Affairs and Trade. Kim's diplomatic debut was to attend the second Asia–Europe Summit (ASEM) meeting in London in April 1998; the third meeting was in Seoul in October 2000. Kim Dae-jung's international prestige as a champion of democracy and as the advocate of the **sunshine policy** toward the North remained high, as testified by the award of the Nobel Peace Prize to him in 2000.

By 2000, South Korean foreign policy had ceased to be a "one-issue" matter. New difficulties emerged as South Korea continued to face a hostile North Korea, and a large United States presence continued to be in South Korea. But South Korea was also playing a larger role internationally, and was facing new issues. Better relations with China were complicated, for example, by the question of North Korean refugees in northeastern China. A more confidant South Korea was able to face such issues head on, in a way that had not been possible in the past. *See also* CROSS-RECOGNITION; NORDPOLITIK; NORTH KOREA–SOUTH KOREA RELATIONS.

– G –

GENERAL ALLIANCE OF LABORERS FOR RAPID REALIZATION OF KOREAN INDEPENDENCE. A group formed in March 1946 by right-wing labor leaders to combat the leftist labor movement, represented by the **National Council of Labor Unions**. **Syngman Rhee** was its honorary president and **Kim Ku** its honorary vice president. It was renamed the **General Federation of Korean Labor Unions** (*Taehan Nodong Chohap Ch'ongyonmaeng*, or *Taehan Noch'ong*) in 1948 when the Republic was inaugurated. In this role, it was essentially a political front for the conservative regime of President Rhee, although it did also claim to represent workers' rights. In 1949, it became a founder member of the anticommunist International Confederation of Free Trade Unions (ICFTU).

In 1960, following Rhee's downfall, it merged with the National Council of Labor Unions to form a new General Federation of Korean Labor (or Trade) Unions. See also LABOR MOVEMENT.

GENERAL FEDERATION OF KOREAN LABOR UNIONS (*Han'guk Nodong Chohap Ch'ongyonmaeng, or Han'guk Noryon*). In November 1960, the **National Council of Labor Unions** joined the General Federation of Korean Labor Unions, forming the new General Federation of Korean Labor Unions (*Taehan Nodong Chohap Ch'ongyonmaeng*, or *Taehan Noryon* for short), claiming a total membership of three million. From the start, it was generally known in English as the *Federation of Korean Trade Unions (FKTU)*. However, it was disbanded following the **Military Revolution of 16 May 1961**.

It was reestablished in August 1961 as the *General Federation of Korean Labor Unions*. During the **Park Chung-hee** era, it was widely seen as close to the government and as a means of curtailing rather than enhancing workers' rights. Despite this reputation, it was one of the targets of **Chun Doo-hwan** in 1980, when under the martial law regime. Its president and those of 11 industrial unions were dismissed, local branches were closed, and their leaders sacked. As tight governmental controls relaxed, the Federation again began to play an active role in labor matters, though during the 1990s, it faced increasing competition from the more radical Korea Confederation of Trade Unions. In 1996, its total membership was reported as 1,100,000. *See also* GENERAL ALLIANCE OF LABORERS FOR RAPID REALIZATION OF KOREAN INDEPENDENCE; LABOR MOVEMENT; NATIONAL COUNCIL OF LABOR UNIONS.

GENEVA POLITICAL CONFERENCE. A conference of 19 nations was held in April–June 1954 at Geneva to deal with issues arising from conflicts in Korea and **Vietnam**. In addition to the 16 nations that had fought on the **United Nations'** side in the **Korean War**, **North Korea**, **China**, and the **Soviet Union/Russia** participated in the Korean conference. In the Korean case, this was regarded as the political conference provided for in the July 1953 **Korean Armistice Agreement**. The conference "solved" the Vietnam problem by dividing Vietnam into two, but it failed to reach agreement on the Korean issue.

The North Korean delegation rejected proposals made by the South Korean government and the United States to bring about a peaceful unification of Korea. Following the conference, those countries that had fought in the Korean War issued the **16 Nations Declaration on Korea**. This stated that the UN was fully empowered to take collective action to repel aggression, to restore peace and security, to extend its good offices, and to seek a peaceful settlement in Korea. The declaration also said that genuinely free elections should be held in Korea under United Nations supervision to unify the country. The declaration has never been invoked. A South Korean attempt to do so at the time of the **USS *Pueblo*** incident met with no response.

GOVERNMENT-GENERAL OF KOREA (*Chosen Sotokufu*). When **Japan** annexed Korea in August 1910, the Japanese established a Government-General of Korea as the colonial administration. The government seat was in **Seoul**, renamed *Keijo* by the Japanese. Korea was called *Chosen*. The colonial government was headed by a governor-general of Korea (*Chosen Sotoku*) who was assisted by the director-general of administration (*Seimu Sokan*). All the governors-general were Japanese army generals on active duty, except for a retired admiral installed after the 1 March 1919 incident. The governor-general was appointed by the Japanese emperor himself and was directly responsible to the emperor as well as to the Japanese prime minister. He also exercised military power and was authorized to mobilize Japanese armed forces in Korea.

All chiefs of bureaus and sections in the Government-General were Japanese, as were most of the top-ranking officials. The governor-general appointed provincial governors as well as provincial **police** superintendents. The Government-General of Korea was abolished following Japan's surrender to the Allies on 15 August 1945.

GRAND NATIONAL PARTY (*Hannara-dang*). The Grand National Party (GNP) was formed in November 1997 by a merger between the **New Korea Party** and one of South Korea's many **Democratic Parties**. The party, which has campaigned on a platform of "progressive conservatism," became the main opposition party in South Korea following **Kim Dae-jung**'s election as president in 1998. It performed well in parliamentary and local elections, but its candidate (and party president), **Lee Hoi-chang**, failed to win in both the 1997 and 2002 presidential elections. In June 2003, Choe Byung-yul (1938–), a former lawyer and journalist who was elected mayor of **Seoul**, became the party chairman following Lee Hoi-chang's resignation from politics.

GREAT BRITAIN, RELATIONS WITH. Great Britain took an interest in Korea in the 19th century mainly because of the peninsula's strategic importance. But Korea was never a primary British interest. Britain's main interests were in **China** and **Japan**, and by the 1902 Anglo–Japanese Alliance, Britain effectively allowed Japan a free hand in Korea. There was some British concern about the policies of the Japanese **Government-General of Korea**, especially at the time of the uprising in March 1919, and there were always a few Britons in Korea as traders and missionaries until the late 1930s.

Britain played a minor role in the World War II discussions of Korea's future and was a party to the 1943 **Cairo Agreement**, but took no part in the postwar occupation of Korea. Following the 1948 elections in South Korea, Great Britain recognized the government of the Republic of Korea, establishing diplomatic relations in 1949.

At the outbreak of the **Korean War** in June 1950, Great Britain responded to the **United Nations** call for assistance. The Royal Navy was in operation off the coast of Korea within a week and ground troops arrived at the end of August 1950. The Royal Air Force was also present. In 1951, British ground forces became part of the First Commonwealth Division. British troops remained in Korea until 1957, and a British general, representing the Commonwealth forces, sat on the **Military Armistice Commission**.

After the war, Britain played a role in the economic reconstruction of South Korea, and was a firm supporter of South Korea's international position, especially at the United Nations. Although the legal obstacles to British recognition of **North Korea** were removed with the abolition of the **United Nations Commission for the Unification and Rehabilitation of Korea** in 1973, Great Britain did not recognize North Korea until the two Koreas entered the United Nations in 1991. When **Kim Dae-jung** became president in 1998, he encouraged countries supporting South Korea to establish relations with the North. Britain was at first reluctant to do so, but on 12 December

2000 signed an agreement on the establishment of diplomatic relations with North Korea. A British embassy opened in **P'yongyang** in July 2001.

– H –

HAM SOK-HON (1901–1989). A 1924 graduate of Tokyo High Normal School, Ham joined the Korean Quaker movement in 1960, becoming the voice of Korean pacifists and a champion for peace and democracy. He published a monthly named *Voice of a Prayer*, became an uncompromising crusader for human rights, and played the role of spiritual leader, gaining the respect and love of the people until his death. He was arrested, tried, and imprisoned many times in the 1970s.

HAMP'YONG–KOCH'ANG INCIDENTS. These two separate bloody incidents refer to the massacre of villagers in the Hamp'yong and Koch'ang areas by South Korean troops during the **Korean War**. Both of these incidents involved the 9th Regiment of the 11th Division of the South Korean army. They occurred during the mopping-up campaign following the beginning of the counterattack of the **United Nations forces** in October 1950. The first incident took place in the Hamp'yong area in South Cholla Province between December 1950 and early January 1951, in the aftermath of an attack on the local **police** station by communist guerrillas. Troops of the 5th Battalion launched an antiguerrilla assault in which they killed 500 people in several villages in the Hamp'yong area, charging them with collaboration with the enemy.

The second incident took place in the Koch'ang area in South Kyongsang Province, from 9–11 February 1951, when troops of the 3rd Battalion launched a mopping-up campaign, killing 700 villagers and burning down over 700 houses in several villages, charging them with harboring fugitives. *See also* NOGUN-RI MASSACRE.

HANAHWOE **("One" Association).** Soon after **Park Chung-hee**'s 1961 military coup, a group of junior army officers led by then Captain **Chun Doo-hwan** organized a secret military association called the *Ch'ilsongwoe* (Seven Star Association). In 1964, it changed its name to *Hanahwoe* or "One" Association, referring to the fact that its original members were all graduates of the first four-year (South) Korean Military Academy (KMA) course. Gradually, it recruited carefully chosen members of other KMA classes, and it operated as a mutual support and advancement body within the military. Its members played an important role in paving the way for Chun's road to power after Park's assassination. When **Kim Young-sam** became president in 1993, he set about controlling and ultimately eliminating the association's influence in the military leadership.

HIJACKING OF SOUTH KOREAN AIRPLANES. The first hijacking of a South Korean plane took place in February 1958, when a passenger plane belonging to Korean Airlines (KAL, now **Korean Air**), on its way to **Seoul** from **Pusan**, was hijacked to **North Korea**. All passengers and crew were returned to South Korea in March 1958. The second took place in December 1969, when a passenger plane belonging to KAL was hijacked en route from Kangnung on the east coast to Seoul and also diverted to North Korea. Of the 47 passengers on board, 35 were returned to South Korea in February 1970 along with four crew members.

HO CHONG (1896–1988). A graduate of Posong College (now Korea University), he became a nationalist. Elected to the **National Assembly** in 1948, he served as minister of transportation (1948–1950), minister of social affairs (1950–1959), acting premier (1950–1951), and minister of foreign affairs (April–Aug. 1960). He became acting president following the fall of the First Republic in April 1960, bringing in the Second Republic in August 1960. After 1961, he served as adviser to the National Unification Board (1969–1984), as a member of the Advisory Council on State Affairs (1980–1988), and was chairman of the National Unification Advisers' Conference (1980–1984).

HODGE, JOHN REED (1893–1963). Hodge was born in Golconda, Illinois in 1893. He joined the **United States** Army and served in France in World War I. He served on the General Staff before Pearl Harbor, and acquired a reputation as a brave and competent soldier during the Pacific War. At the end of the war, he was a lieutenant general, in command of the XXIV Corps of the 10th Army. In this capacity, he was ordered to move his troops to Korea to take the Japanese surrender south of the **38th parallel** and also to take over the day-to-day running of South Korea. Nothing in Hodge's previous experience had prepared him for this task, and he was more or less left without orders for the next six months.

Hodge and his colleagues arrived in Korea unprepared for the revolutionary fervor that they found. Hodge's main concern was to preserve law and order, and at first he made little distinction between Koreans and Japanese, using the latter for a short period to control the former. This, and his decision to suppress the People's Committees and other popular movements, led to opposition from the Koreans. In addition, Hodge had few Korean-speaking staff and instead became increasingly reliant on a small group of English-speaking Koreans. These tended to come from wealthy backgrounds and some had close links to the former Japanese **Government-General of Korea**, which added to popular resentment. At the same time, Hodge did not get along with **Syngman Rhee** after the latter's return from exile in October 1945. All in all, under Hodge, the **United States Army Military Government in Korea** seemed to be less responsive to the Korean people's wishes than the Soviet forces in **North Korea**.

Hodge also had to represent the United States in the **Joint United States–Soviet Union Commission on Trusteeship** set up in December 1945. He did not find it easy working with the Soviet representatives, and was happy, when the Commission proved unworkable, to see the matter referred to the **United Nations** in 1947. Hodge left Korea in August 1948, as two separate regimes emerged on the peninsula. He retired from the army in 1953 and died in 1963.

HOMELAND RESERVE FORCES. The 2.5 million (191 reserve battalions with 2,018 companies) Homeland Reserve Forces were established in April 1968. The reservists were under the operational control of the regular army and they received part of their training at regular military installations. All veterans remained in the reserve units until the age of 35 in the case of enlisted men, and until 45 in the case of officers. In June 1975, a Combat Land Reserve Corps was set up under the Homeland Reserve Forces. In 2002, there were 4.5 million members of these forces.

HONG SUK-CHA (1933–). A graduate of Ewha Woman's University and holder of a doctoral degree, she served as assistant to the minister of foreign affairs in 1959, vice consul in New York in 1965, and chairman of the **Korean National Council of Women** (1980–1987). In the 1987 presidential election, she ran as a candidate for the presidency for the Social Democratic Party, but, like a number of other small party nominees, she withdrew from the race in favor of the **Democratic Justice Party** candidate, **Roh Tae-woo.**

HOUSE OF COUNCILORS (*Ch'amuiwon*). Under the revised **Constitution** of 1952, the Election Law for an upper house, named House of Councilors, was promulgated in January 1958 after a long period of bickering among the lawmakers. According to this law, each city and province constituted an electoral district; between two and eight councilors were to be elected from each district, each representing 600,000 constituents; and the total number of the councilors was to be not more than 70. The elections for the upper house were to be held within a year after the promulgation of the law, but President **Syngman Rhee** failed to implement the law.

When the First Republic fell, and the Constitution was amended in June 1960, it was decided that the upper house be established according to the previous Election Law for the House of Councilors, which was modified. According to the new law, only the city of **Seoul** and each province would constitute an electoral district, each electing between two and eight councilors to serve a three-year term. In June 1960, 58 councilors were elected from ten electoral districts (Seoul plus nine provinces). However, following the **Military Revolution of 16 May 1961**, the **National Assembly** was abolished, and the House of Councilors was never reestablished.

HOUSE OF REPRESENTATIVES (*Minuiwom*). The **National Assembly** established in 1948 had one house until the upper house, named the **House of Councilors**, was established in July 1960 under the revised **Constitution**. At that time, the lower house was designated as the *House of Representatives*. As before, each member of the lower house represented 100,000 constituents, serving a four-year term. Under the new National Assembly Election Law of 1962, the country was divided into 131 single-member districts and 44 additional at-large districts.

Each single-district representative was elected by popular vote, and at-large seats were distributed to each party according to the percentage of popular votes it received. When the unicameral legislative system was restored under the Constitution of 1963, the South Korean legislature was simply called the *National Assembly.*

Currently, the total number of seats is 299, of which 253 are elected from single-member electoral districts, and 46 are national constituency seats that are distributed to political parties winning five seats or more in the direct election. All members of the National Assembly are elected for four-year terms of office.

HWANG JANG-YOP (1923–). In February 1997, Hwang Jang-yop, a secretary of the Central Committee of the North Korean ruling Korean Workers' Party (KWP), became the highest-ranking **defector** from **North Korea** to the South since the 1950–1953 **Korean War**. The importance of the defection was not confined to Hwang's current party role. He was widely credited with being the main theorist of the KWP's *juche* (self-reliance) philosophy, and had been tutor to **Kim Jong-il**, the son and heir of North Korea's first leader, **Kim Il-sung**. Hwang's defection, which took place in Beijing following a visit to **Japan**, and which appears to have been arranged by the South Korean Agency for National Security Planning (now the **National Intelligence Service**), was at first seen as indicting major problems within the North Korean regime.

However, although the defection was denounced by the North, and Hwang revealed some details of how the North Korean political structure operates, it soon became clear that he had long been away from the center of political power in North Korea and that personal as well as political reasons had played a part in his defection. Since moving to South Korea, Hwang has spent much time complaining that his views are not listened to and that he has not been allowed to travel abroad.

HYUNDAI. Hyundai was originally one of the biggest of the *chaebol*, South Korea's industrial and business conglomerates. **Chung Ju-yung**, who came originally from **North Korea**, founded Hyundai Auto Services, largely dealing in spare parts, in 1946. The following year, Chung established Hyundai Civil Works Company. These merged into the Hyundai Construction and Engineering Works in 1950. By 1960, this was the largest construction company in South Korea.

During the next 20 years, Hyundai expanded into engineering, petrochemicals, shipbuilding, and finance. Hyundai Construction built most of the new roads and tall apartment blocks that became a symbol of South Korea's rapid **economic development** under **Park Chung-hee**. South Korea's first modern ships came from Hyundai yards, while the country's first indigenous automobile, the Pony, was produced by Hyundai in 1976. Later, the group would branch out into new industries, such as computers. Chung and his brothers remained firmly in control of the various companies that made up the Hyundai group, and Chun became group chairman in 1971, a post he held until 1987, when he began to take an interest in politics.

Because of his North Korean background, Chung also used Hyundai to develop links with North Korea. Following a visit to the North with 500 cattle in June 1998, he returned with more cattle in the autumn. This eventually led to the creation of Hyundai Asan, a company that developed tourist links with the North, but which also seems to have acted as a channel for the South Korean government to pass funds to the North, as part of President **Kim Dae-jung**'s **"sunshine policy."**

By that stage, Hyundai was already in trouble. Chung's political career attracted the wrath of President **Kim Young-sam**, and the group was subject to a series of tax audits and probes. Family disputes over control of the group, as a second generation came to the fore, did not help. When Chung died in March 2001, Hyundai broke up. The individual components were still important; although only one part of the original group, Hyundai Motors was still the fourth largest *chaebol* in 2002, but it was a long way from the number one position that the group had held for many years.

– I –

IMF CRISIS. Popular name given to the economic crisis that rocked South Korea in autumn 1997. The crisis, triggered by the devaluation of the Thai *baht* in July 1997, hit South Korea in October of that year, with a massive run on the currency. The decision to seek assistance from the International Monetary Fund (IMF) was received with much bitterness by many in South Korea and wry jokes along the lines of "I'MF fired" became common. *See also* ECONOMIC DEVELOPMENT.

INCH'ON. This is the major port and industrial center on South Korea's west coast, 25 miles (40 kilometers) from the capital, **Seoul**.

It was a small fishing village in 1882, with a population of around 5,000, when the first treaties between Korea and western countries led to the establishment of a foreign settlement at Chemulp'o, now a suburb of Inch'on. The city developed as a port under the Japanese **Government-General of Korea**, though high tides limited its use. In 1947, the population was 260,000. During the **Korea War**, Inch'on was the scene of General **Douglas MacArthur**'s spectacular landing, which played an important role in turning the tide of the war.

After the war, Inch'on was rebuilt and developed as an important industrial and educational center as well as a port. Its population reached one million in 1979, and 2.5 million by 1999. The city was placed under the central government in 1981, and became a metropolitan city in 1995. The port area has continued to expand, and ambitious new developments are in hand. South Korea's newest airport, located in the harbor, opened in March 2002, and the city was an important center for the **World Cup 2002** competition. In August 2003, the city was designated a free economic zone.

INFILTRATION TUNNELS. The first two infiltration tunnels were discovered in 1974, the third one in 1975, and the fourth one in 1989. The **United Nations Command** charged **North Korea** with digging the tunnels for the purpose of invading South Korea, and it is suspected that they may have dug at least 10 more such tunnels. Three of the tunnels were found in the western part of the **demilitarized zone** and the fourth in the eastern part. The North Koreans have always denied the charge, claiming that the tunnels were old mine workings and had nothing to do with them. Some of the tunnels have been opened up for **tourism** purposes.

INTERNET. Use of the Internet in South Korea began to take off in the mid-1990s. Korea Telecom's Internet services date from 1994, and the real boom in use began the following year. There were then about one third of a million users. By February 2001, South Korean Internet users had reached 22 million, rising to 26.2 million at the end of 2002. This makes South Korea one of the world's leading users of broadband facilities. The government has encouraged this development by providing Internet facilities for farmers and other groups and by encouraging the use of the Internet for recreational and similar bookings.

– J –

JAPAN, RELATIONS WITH. South Korea's relations with Japan have been complicated by the long historical involvement between the Korea Peninsula and the Japanese islands. The harsh rule of the Japanese **Government-General of Korea** during the 1910–1945 colonial period left a bitter legacy in both South and **North Korea**. Since liberation in 1945, both Koreas have struggled to come to terms with their relationship with Japan.

In South Korea from 1948–1960, under President **Syngman Rhee**, relations with Japan were formally very distant. Although kept secret at the time, the **United Nations Command** did use former Japanese imperial forces during the **Korean War**, especially in actions such as the naval landings at **Inch'on** in September 1950. Negotiations began in 1952 to normalize relations between the two countries, but Rhee's personal antagonism to the Japanese prevented much progress during his presidency. The former Japanese military officer turned president, **Park Chung-hee**, had no scruples about South Korea's need for Japanese assistance for **economic development**, and in 1965, despite domestic opposition, he concluded the **South Korea–Japan Normalization Treaty**. This treaty, and a second in 1970, brought much needed Japanese finance for South Korea's growing economy.

Difficulties remained on a number of issues. These included some perennial problems such as the status of Koreans in Japan, relations between Japan and North Korea, the **East Sea/Sea of Japan** issue, **comfort women**, and the Japanese treatment of the historical relationship. But they also included events such as the attempted kidnapping of the South Korean opposition leader, **Kim Dae-jung**, from

Tokyo in 1973. Under President **Chun Doo-hwan**, there was much popular South Korean support for his demand that Japan should provide additional economic assistance because of South Korea's forward role in defense against communism.

In 1992, Japanese Prime Minister Kiichi Miyazawa visited South Korea and apologized for Japan's colonial past. Other Japanese leaders have made similar apologies on numerous occasions, but even younger Koreans often remain unsatisfied. At the same time, Japan is a major economic partner of South Korea, and things Japanese such as popular songs and fashion are readily accepted in South Korea, except when prevented by government action. The joint staging of the **World Cup 2002** competition in Japan and South Korea helped to bridge some of the gaps, but there was much rejoicing in South Korea when the Koreans did better than the Japanese, indicating that old antagonisms continue. *See also* DIPLOMATIC RECOGNITION; FOREIGN POLICY; RHEE (PEACE) LINE.

JOINT DECLARATION OF THE NON-NUCLEARIZATION OF THE KOREAN PENINSULA. Representatives of the two Koreas initialed this Declaration on 31 December 1991. It provided for the total end of nuclear weapons development and deployment on the Korea Peninsula and for full mutual inspection. South Korean President **Roh Tae-woo** approved the Declaration on 17 January 1991, and the North Korean President **Kim Il-sung** did so on 18 January 1991. The signed document was exchanged at the sixth round of talks between the premiers of two Koreas held in **P'yongyang**, 18–21 February 1992. Despite numerous attempts by the South Korean government to persuade **North Korea** to act on it, the Declaration has remained a dead letter. *See also* NORTH KOREAN NUCLEAR PROGRAM.

JOINT UNITED STATES–SOVIET COMMISSION ON TRUSTEE-SHIP. Under the **Moscow Agreement** signed by the foreign ministers of the **United States**, **Great Britain**, and the **Soviet Union/Russia** in December 1945, the occupation authorities of the Allies in Korea were mandated to form a commission to establish a Korean national government to end the occupation of Korea. The Joint Commission was formed in January 1946. The head of the Soviet delegation was Colonel General Terenti Shtykov, and his American counterpart was Major General A.V. Arnold.

The first meeting of the Joint Commission was held in March–May 1946, briefly interrupted in April, but on 8 May was adjourned *sine die*, without reaching any agreement on the establishment of a new Korean government. The second commission meeting was held in June–August 1946, and the third in May–August 1947, without achieving any of its goals. This was the last meeting of the commission, which was effectively dissolved when the **United Nations**, at the U.S. request, took over the Korean question in November 1947.

JUDICIARY. The judicial branch of the government is headed by the Supreme Court, whose chief justice is appointed by the president with the consent of the **National Assembly**. The Supreme Court justices are appointed by the president on the recommendation of the chief justice and with the consent of the National Assembly. Below the Supreme Court are the High (Appellate) Courts, District Courts, and a **Family Court**. The chief justice can serve only one term of six years under the 1987 **Constitution**. The other ten Supreme Court justices can serve ten years, which can be renewed. The chief justice of the Supreme Court appoints all judges of the High Courts, District Courts, and the Family Court.

JULY 1972 STATEMENT ON KOREAN UNIFICATION. On 4 July 1972, following a series of secret negotiations that began in May of that year between the director of the Korean Central Intelligence Agency (now the **National Intelligence Service**) and his counterpart from **North Korea**, the governments of North and South Korea each issued an identical statement announcing an agreement to end hostility and work together toward peaceful unification of the country without outside interference. The seven-point statement included the following three principles for national unification:

(1) Unification shall be achieved through independent Korean efforts without being subjected to external imposition or interference;
(2) Unification shall be achieved through peaceful means, and not through the use of force against each other; and
(3) As a homogeneous people, a broad national unity shall be sought above all, transcending differences in ideas, ideologies, and systems.

The statement pledged "to ease tension and foster an atmosphere of mutual trust between the South and the North." Both sides agreed not to "slander or defame each other" or "undertake avowed provocative measures to prevent inadvertent military incidents," and that each side would carry out "various exchanges in many fields" to "restore severed ties, to promote mutual understanding and to expedite independent peaceful unification." In order to achieve these objectives, the statement said that a political dialogue between the two sides would begin. *See also* NORTH–SOUTH POLITICAL COORDINATING COMMITTEE; NORTH KOREA–SOUTH KOREA RELATIONS.

JUNE 29th DEMOCRATIZATION DECLARATION. Issued in June 1987 by **Roh Tae-woo**, then chairman of the ruling **Democratic Justice Party** and its presidential candidate, this declaration defused the political crisis that had been building up under President **Chun Doo-hwan** since April 1986. It included the following points:

1. The **constitution** should be expeditiously amended to adopt a direct presidential election system, and presidential elections should be held under a new constitution to realize a peaceful transfer of power in February 1988.
2. The Presidential Election Law should be revised so that freedom of candidacy and fair competition are guaranteed.
3. Antagonisms and confrontations must be resolutely eradicated not only from our political community, but also from all other sectors to achieve grand national reconciliation and unity. **Kim Dae-jung** should be given amnesty and his civil rights restored, and all those who are being detained in connection with the political situation should also be set free, except those who have committed treason.
4. Human dignity must be respected even more greatly and the basic rights of citizens should be promoted and protected to the maximum.
5. The freedom of the press and the relevant systems and practices must be drastically improved.
6. Freedom and self-regulation must be guaranteed to the maximum . . . Colleges and **universities** . . . must be made self-governing and educational autonomy in general must be expeditiously put into practice.
7. A political climate conducive to dialogue and compromise must be created expeditiously, with healthy activities of political parties guaranteed.

8. Bold social reform must be carried out to build a clean and honest society.

At the end of his speech, Roh Tae-woo said he was confident that President **Chun Doo-hwan** and the DJP members would accept his proposals. But he added: "If they fail to be accepted, however, I want to make it very clear that I will resign from all public duties, including the presidential candidacy and the chairmanship of the Democratic Justice Party." Chun accepted the proposals, and the crisis passed.

JUNE 2000 INTER-KOREAN SUMMIT. In June 2000, a summit meeting between the South Korean president, **Kim Dae-jung**, and the North Korean leader, **Kim Jong-il**, took place in **P'yongyang**, the capital of **North Korea**. The two leaders held a series of wide-ranging talks and reached agreements that held out much hope for a reduction of tension on the peninsula.

Although Kim Dae-jung's government had pledged to maintain its **"sunshine policy"** (engagement policy) however North Korea reacted, it had come in for much domestic criticism for so doing, especially following naval clashes in the West Sea in 1999. Aid flowed to the North, and there was some trade, but until 2000, no spectacular breakthrough seemed likely. In March 2000, Kim Dae-jung made a speech in Berlin that offered assistance to the North, together with a pledge that the South's policy was not aimed at the overthrow of the northern regime. The North made no immediate public response, but in April 2000, it emerged that the two sides had almost immediately begun talking, despite the rhetoric, and had agreed that the leaders of North and South would meet in P'yongyang in June.

Such a summit was not in itself a new idea. There had been many proposals in the past for such a meeting, and as recently as 1994, a summit had been planned between **Kim Il-sung** and the then South Korean president, **Kim Young-Sam**. Kim Il-sung's death intervened, however, and the two sides lapsed into their customary hostile mode. So there was some skepticism about this latest proposal. Planning continued, however, and, despite an unexplained one day postponement just before the meeting, on 13 June, Kim Dae-jung flew North in the first direct civil flight between North and South since 1948, to become the first South Korean president to visit North Korea.

From the start, it was Kim Jong-il who dominated the summit. He appeared at the airport to greet his guest, according the older man all the deference Koreans would expect, and over the next few days, he became the unlikely star of the media coverage of the visit. The formal talks were conducted on the North Korean side by the chairman of the Standing Committee of North Korea's parliament, the Supreme People's Assembly, and Kim Yong-nam, the nearest to a head of state. However, Kim Jong-il appeared at several informal sessions. After two days of talks, the two sides pledged in a joint declaration to work for national unification, accepted that there were common elements in each sides proposals about some form of federated state, agreed to work together for a balanced national economy, promised to promote exchanges and cooperation, and agreed to work toward further humanitarian exchanges by 15 August, the anniversary of Korea's liberation from **Japan** in 1945.

Implementation of the summit agreements began almost immediately. Red Cross meetings led to two rounds of separated **family reunions**. These were stilted affairs, with the North's choice of participants carefully chosen from among the most loyal groups. Attempts to agree on more regular exchanges, with a permanent meeting place, led to much wrangling between the two sides.

In South Korea there is a widespread belief that the North gained more than the South from the summit, especially as details emerged of how much the South had paid to persuade the North to attend the meeting. Not only has there been continued aid and economic assistance to the North, but the South also agreed to release and repatriate a number of long-term unconverted prisoners to the North. Despite claims to the contrary, the North denied that it held any similar prisoners. In other areas, too, the North appeared to be moving more slowly than the South. Work to reconnect the **Seoul–P'yongyang** railway began on the southern side of the **demilitarized zone**, but there was no corresponding work on the northern side.

Talks between military leaders of both sides were held, but again, the South felt that these lacked substance, and in particular, failed to begin the implementation of confidence-building measures that would reduce the military standoff on the peninsula. Despite these problems, the sunshine policy, increasingly referred to as the "engagement policy," continued under Kim Dae-jung until his retirement in February 2003. His successor, **Roh Moo-hyun**, pledged to continue a similar policy toward North Korea.

– K –

KAESONG. The capital of Korea during the Koryo dynasty (918–1392), Kaesong was on the southern side of the **38th parallel** at the division of Korea in 1945. It was swiftly captured in the early days of the **Korean War** and has remained in **North Korea** ever since, the only major South Korean city to do so. It was the site of the first truce talks in 1951, but was soon abandoned in favor of the nearby village of **P'anmunjom**. Today, it has an estimated population of about 200,000–300,000 and produces porcelain and ginseng. Visitors to the North Korean side of P'anmunjom often visit the city as well, which has an old quarter and a Koryo museum. Since the late 1990s, the South Korean **Hyundai** group has been interested in developing an industrial free-trade area at Kaesong. A groundbreaking ceremony for this park took place in July 2003.

KANG YOUNG-HOON (1922–). Born in Ch'angsong, North P'yongan Province, now in **North Korea**, Kang graduated from the Manzhouguo (Manchukuo) National University. Returning home at the end of the World War II, he joined the Korean army. Rising in rank during the **Korean War**, he served as a division commander in 1953. In 1958, he studied at the Army Command and General Staff College in the **United States**.

In 1959, he became a corps commander, becoming the commandant of the Korean Military Academy in 1960. He was critical of the **Military Revolution of 16 May 1961**, and retired from the army as a lieutenant general in 1961. He then went to the U.S. for graduate studies, receiving a doctoral degree in political science from the University of Southern California. He established the Research Institute on Korean Affairs in Silver Spring, Maryland, in 1970.

Returning to Korea in 1976, Kang became dean of the graduate school of Han'guk University of Foreign Studies in 1977, and from 1978 to 1981 he served as director of the Ministry of Foreign Affairs training institute, the Institute of Foreign Affairs and National Security. He then became ambassador to **Great Britain** (1981–1984) and to the Holy See (1984–1987), and, after leaving the Foreign Ministry, he was elected to the **National Assembly** in 1988 as a member of the ruling **Democratic Justice Party**. In December 1988, Kang was appointed prime minister, serving in that office until December 1990.

He was subsequently president of the Korean National Red Cross from 1991–1997, during which period he was involved in negotiations between the Red Cross Societies of the two Koreas. Kang has also served as president or chairman of a number of academic and social organizations and societies.

KCIA. *See* NATIONAL INTELLIGENCE SERVICE (NIS).

KEDO. *See* KOREAN PENINSULA ENERGY DEVELOPMENT ORGANIZATION.

KIM CHANG-RYONG (1916–1956). Kim was born to a peasant family in South Hamyong Province, now in **North Korea**. He became a Japanese military **police** officer, working mainly in counterintelligence in **China**, in 1940. It is alleged that in this role, he pursued many Korean patriots. After the defeat of Japan in 1945, he returned to North Korea. Later, he claimed to have been twice arrested and sentenced to death in the North but to have escaped each time, before finally escaping to South Korea. There, Kim joined the constabulary, the forerunner of the South Korean army, as a corporal, the same rank he had under the Japanese. However, after attending officer school, he became a lieutenant in April 1948.

He again began to work in counterintelligence, and was involved in the extensive enquiries launched after the **Yosu–Sunch'on Rebellion**. During this period, he was promoted to major. Kim was noted for the fervor of his anticommunist activities and some have linked him to the assassination of **Kim Ku** in 1949. He was also closely associated with President **Syngman Rhee**, and was widely believed to have eliminated a number of Rhee's opponents. Promoted to colonel on the eve of the **Korean War**, Kim was also believed to have masterminded the massacre of the members of the **National Rehabilitation and Guidance League** in the early days of the Korean War.

During the war, Kim became the formal head of South Korea's military Counter Intelligence Corps (CIC, *Dukmudae*). In 1953, he became a brigadier, and in 1955 a major general. On 30 January 1956, a group that included members of his own organization assassinated him. *See also* ASSASSINATIONS AND ASSASSINATION ATTEMPTS.

KIM CHI-HA. *See* KIM YONG-IL.

KIM DAE-JUNG (1924–). In December 1997, after three previous attempts, Kim Dae-jung became president of South Korea. Born in **Kwangju**, South Cholla Province, Kim graduated from high school in 1943, and later became a clerk in a Japanese-owned shipping company, which he took over in 1945. In 1950, he became president of a daily newspaper in Mokp'o, in South Cholla. He graduated from Konguk University in 1953, and later earned graduate degrees from Korea and Kyunghee Universities. After several attempts, he was elected to the **National Assembly** in 1960. Reelected to the National Assembly in 1963, Kim became spokesman for the newly formed **Masses Party** in 1965, and when the **Democratic Party** and the Masses Party merged into the **New Democratic Party** (NDP) in 1967, he became the spokesman of the new party.

Kim ran for the presidency in 1971 as the nominee of the NDP, narrowly losing the election to **Park Chung-hee**. Kim thereafter became a strong critic of Park and his government. In August 1973, while on a visit to **Japan**, Kim was abducted by agents of the Korean Central Intelligence Agency (now the **National Intelligence Service**) to **Seoul** from Tokyo. Kim claimed that the KCIA intended to kill him, but that he was saved by **United States** intervention. Although he was released from prison, he was arrested many times for his alleged antigovernment activities, and in 1979 he was given the death sentence for alleged espionage activity. The death sentence was reduced to a life term, but Kim was purged in May 1980, again put on trial, and again given the death sentence, this time for his alleged instigation of the **Kwangju Uprising**. His sentence was reduced to life, and he was allowed to travel to the United States for medical treatment in December 1982.

Returning home in February 1985, Kim served as cochairman of the **Council for the Promotion of Democracy**, and after a brief period of collaboration with **Kim Young-sam** as a member of the **Reunification Democratic Party**, he organized his own **Party for Peace and Democracy** in 1987, becoming its head as well as its presidential candidate. After losing the election, Kim successfully ran for the National Assembly in 1988. In the spring of 1991, he merged his party with the Democratic Party, forming another New Democratic

Party. In September of that year, his party merged with the Democratic Party, keeping the title New Democratic Party (NDP). In May 1992, he was nominated as the NDP presidential candidate.

Once more, he lost, this time to Kim Young-sam, who had thrown in his lot with the ruling party under **Roh Tae-woo**. Kim Dae-jung then announced his retirement from politics, and left for a period of study at the University of Cambridge in England. However, on his return to South Korea in 1993, he resumed his political career, founding the **National Congress for New Politics** (NCNP). In 1997, he and another veteran politician, **Kim Jong-p'il**, joined forces to fight the presidential election. Kim Dae-jung became the candidate, winning the election by a narrow majority; Kim Jongp'il eventually became premier. Despite the narrow margin of his victory, it had great symbolic importance, marking the first ever South Korean peaceful transfer of political power from the government to the opposition. Kim's most immediate task on becoming president in February 1998 was to tackle South Korea's economic problems, but he also introduced a new approach to North Korea, the **"sunshine policy."** In 1999, the NCNP changed its name to the **Millennium Democratic Party.** Following a falling-out with Kim Jongp'il, the coalition split up in 2000, but when both parties did badly in the April 2000 elections, the coalition reformed in May 2000.

At the **June 2000 Inter-Korean Summit** in the North Korean capital, **P'yongyang**, Kim Dae-jung and the North Korean leader, **Kim Jong-il**, held the first ever such meeting. For a brief moment, Kim Dae-jung enjoyed huge domestic and international prestige, winning the 2000 Nobel Peace Prize. The high hopes of June 2000 quickly faded however, and during 2001, Kim's domestic popularity steadily declined, as did that of his party. Corruption scandals involving his sons, and the lack of progress in relations with North Korea also added to his political problems. By the time he left office in January 2003, Kim was a sick man, and his political reputation had suffered badly as a result of these scandals and growing revelations about clandestine payments to North Korea in order to bring about the 2000 summit.

KIM HWALLAN (KIM, HELEN) (1899–1970). Born to a Christian family in **Inch'on**, Kyonggi Province, her childhood name was

Kiduk, but she became better known among Westerners in Korea as *Helen Kim.* Educated at Ewha Girls' School in **Seoul**, where she took up the nationalist cause in 1919, she received her higher education in the **United States** at Columbia University. She obtained her doctoral degree in 1931, the first Korean woman to do so.

Kim taught at Ewha Woman's College (now Ewha Woman's University) while promoting Korean women's modernization and the nationalist movement during the 1920s and 1930s. In 1939, she became president of her alma mater, serving in that position until 1961. Kim was a cofounder of the Korean Young Women's Christian Association (YWCA) in 1922, a dedicated educator, a devout Christian, as well as a social reform advocate. After retiring from the presidency of Ewha Woman's University, she devoted her life to the Christian and social reform movement, receiving five honorary doctorate degrees. She was the recipient of the Magsaysay Prize in 1963. Since the 1980s, however, there has been some criticism in South Korea of her role in the Japanese colonial period. *See also* UNIVERSITIES; WOMEN'S MOVEMENT.

KIM HWAN-GI (1913–1974). After study in **Japan**, Kim returned to Korea in 1937 and became the leading Korean experimenter with abstract art. Picasso influenced his early work, but after 1945, he concentrated on Korean themes, executed in circles and curved and straight lines. He worked hard to promote art appreciation in South Korea. He later moved to New York, where he died.

KIM IL-SUNG (1912–1994). Born Kim Sung-ju in a village near **P'yongyang**, Kim was taken by his parents to Manchuria in 1925. He became active in anti-Japanese guerrilla groups from about 1929 and campaigned against **Japan** until forced to retreat into the **Soviet Union/Russia** about 1941. Kim remained in the Soviet Union until 1945, where he served in the army, and became one of a number of Koreans brought into **North Korea** to effect the Soviet occupation in the summer and autumn of 1945. By 1948, and the establishment of separate governments in North and South Korea, Kim was in effect the main leader in North Korea.

With the agreement of both Josef Stalin and Mao Zedong, Kim launched the **Korean War** in June 1950 in the belief that he could unify the country. The attempt almost succeeded but the North was defeated by **United Nations** intervention, and only saved by **China**. After the 1953 **Korean Armistice Agreement**, Kim remained the undisputed leader of North Korea until his death in 1994. From 1953 to the late 1960s, Kim concentrated on the elimination of his domestic opponents and on postwar reconstruction, but then set about attempts at destabilizing the South under President **Park Chung-hee**.

Nevertheless, in 1972, both Kim and Park agreed on the **North–South Red Cross talks**, and the further contacts that flowed from them. Later Kim seems to have sanctioned both the 1983 **Rangoon bomb attack** and the 1991 North–South rapprochement. Kim died in July 1994, just before a planned summit with the South Korean President, **Kim Young-sam**. By then much of the day-to-day responsibility for running North Korea had passed to his son, **Kim Jong-il**. The elder Kim, still referred to as the "Great Leader," however, remains formally the president of North Korea.

KIM JONG-IL (1942–). Eldest son of the North Korean leader, **Kim Il-sung**, whom he succeeded as *de facto* leader of **North Korea** in 1994. His main formal title is chairman of the National Defense Committee and he is also secretary general of the Korean Workers' Party (KWP). According to official North Korean accounts, he was born on 15 February 1942 on Mount Paektu, the sacred mountain on the Sino–Korean border, but other reports say that he was born in 1941 in the **Soviet Union/Russia**, where his father had taken refuge from the Japanese. During the **Korean War**, he was sent to **China** for safety.

Kim attended Kim Il-sung University in **P'yongyang**, and on graduation in 1963, joined the KWP secretariat. In 1973, he became KWP secretary in charge of organization and propaganda, and seems to have been selected as his father's successor. He was not named publicly, but was referred to as "The Party Center." From 1980 onward, he began to make public appearances, and was referred to as the "Dear Leader," while his father remained the "Great Leader." In South Korea, Kim was described as a hard-drinking playboy, and also blamed for incidents such as the **Rangoon bomb attack**.

After his father's death in 1994, Kim turned increasingly to the military for support, and played down the role of the KWP. Although described in the South Korean press as reclusive, he proved a capable host during the **June 2000 Inter-Korean Summit**, deferring to the South Korean President, **Kim Dae-jung**. The high hopes raised then for improved **North Korea–South Korea relations** proved abortive, however, and Kim Jong-il did not pay the promised return visit to the South.

KIM JONG-P'IL (1926–). Popularly known as *J.P.*, he was born in Kongju, South Ch'ungch'ong Province. After graduating from Seoul National University in 1947, he enrolled at the Korean Military Academy, graduating as a member of the 8th graduating class in 1949. Rising in rank to lieutenant colonel, he served in the Army Headquarters G-2 Intelligence Section, and married a niece of Major General **Park Chung-hee**. In December 1960, Kim and other rebellious army officers, who had been contemplating a military coup for some time since early 1960, advocated the purification of the army. As a result, he was forced to retire from active military service for his insubordination to his superiors. After that, he became a more determined plotter of a military coup, bringing about the **Military Revolution of 16 May 1961**.

Following the 1961 military takeover, Kim established the Korean Central Intelligence Agency (now the **National Intelligence Service)**, becoming its first director, and when he and his comrades in arms established the **Democratic Republican Party (DRP)** in early 1963, he became one of its key leaders. He was elected to the **National Assembly** in 1963 as chairman of the DRP. Reelected to the National Assembly in 1967, he served as senior adviser to president Park Chung-hee, who was also president of the DRP. Kim himself became vice president of the DRP in 1971.

He served as Park's premier from June 1971 until December 1975. In March 1973, when he and his close associates formed a new political party named the **Political Fraternal Society for Revitalizing Reform**, Kim became one of its key leaders. Reelected to the National Assembly in 1979, he became the president of the DRP when president Park was assassinated in October.

Following the **December 1979 coup**, Kim was purged in May 1980, and was often under house arrest. Depurged in 1987, he reconstructed the defunct DRP into the **New Democratic Republican**

Party, becoming its head as well as its presidential candidate. He lost the election in December 1987, but in 1988 he was elected to the National Assembly once again. When the party merged with the **Democratic Justice Party** and the **Reunification Democratic Party**, forming the **Democratic Liberal Party** (DLP) in February 1990, Kim became one of its three supreme leaders.

Kim survived in the leadership of the DLP until early 1995. By then he was party chairman, but he was forced out of this position in January 1995. Undaunted, he proceeded once more to form a new political party, the **United Liberal Democrats (ULD)**, with himself as leader. It claimed to be the only genuine conservative party in South Korea. It enjoyed modest electoral success, with 50 members elected in the 1996 National Assembly elections.

How deep its political convictions were was not clear. In a surprise move, the party joined with **Kim Dae-jung**'s **National Congress for New Politics** in 1997, in order to contest the presidential election. Despite their long years in opposition to each other, the two Kims agreed that Kim Dae-jung would be the presidential candidate. After his narrow win in 1997, Kim Dae-jung made Kim Jong-p'il his prime minister, though not without a great deal of opposition from within his own party. As prime minister, Kim Jong-p'il advocated a cabinet system of government, to replace the executive president system. Early in 2000, the coalition broke up, and Kim resigned as prime minister, to contest the April 2000 general election as ULD leader. However, his party did badly in the election, and by May 2000, he was once again in a coalition with Kim Dae-jung.

The election of **Roh Moo-hyun** as president in 2002, and the passing from the political scene of Kim Dae-jung in 2003 has left only Kim Jong-p'il from the era of the "three Kims," as the period since the early 1970s has come to be known. How much longer he can survive as an active politician is now a matter of speculation.

KIM KU (1876–1949). Born in Haeju, Hwanghae Province, Kim Ku joined the Tonghak movement in 1893. Fleeing to Manchuria in 1895, he joined the contingent of the Righteous Armies there, but he returned to Korea to fight the Japanese. Imprisoned for his killing of a Japanese army officer in 1895, he managed to escape from the prison in 1898. He was briefly a Buddhist monk until he became a

Christian in 1903, teaching at a mission school. In 1911, he was arrested in connection with the so-called 105 Persons Incident, serving a prison term until 1914. After that, he was involved in the Rural Enlightenment Movement until he joined the March First Movement in 1919.

Fleeing from Korea to Shanghai in 1919, Kim became one of the founders of the **Korean Provisional Government** in exile, serving as its chief of security, minister of home affairs, and then premier. In 1930, he and others formed the **Korean Independence Party** and directed terrorist activities against the Japanese. In 1935, he established the Korean National Restoration Army in **China**, and he served as the president of the Provisional Government in Chongqing from 1944. Returning to Korea in October 1945, as head of the Provisional Government with his Korean Independence Party, Kim and **Syngman Rhee** collaborated as leaders of the rightist movement for a while. Kim served as vice president of the **National Council for Rapid Realization of Korean Independence**, and vice-chairman of the **Representative Democratic Council**.

As the controversy grew over the implementation of the **United Nations** (UN) plan to establish a Korean government by having general elections only in the South, Kim opposed the UN plan, becoming a bitter political rival and critic of Rhee. He and others made vain efforts to solve the Korean question by Koreans themselves and prevent the permanent division of Korea. Kim and some of his supporters even went to **P'yongyang** and met the North Korean communists, but were unable to reach an agreement.

Kim refused to take part in the founding of the Republic of Korea. An army officer, Ahn Du-whi, assassinated him on 26 June 1949. Ahn was sentenced to life imprisonment, but soon released. Ahn lived under a false name until he was murdered in **Seoul** in October 1996. *See also* ASSASSINATION AND ASSASSINATION ATTEMPTS; NORTH KOREA–SOUTH KOREA RELATIONS.

KIM KYU-SHIK (1881–1950). Born into a poverty-stricken family near **Pusan**, he became an orphan at the age of nine when his widower-father died. With the help of Dr. Horace G. Underwood, an American Presbyterian missionary and member of the **Underwood family**, he was able to study at Roanoke College in Virginia from

1896. Returning home in 1904, Kim worked as Dr. Underwood's private secretary while teaching at the Korean Young Men's Christian Association (YMCA) in **Seoul** and at a mission school.

Kim became an elder in a Presbyterian church in Seoul, and worked for Korean independence from **Japan** while teaching English at Paejae College in 1911–1912. Fleeing from the Japanese **police**, he went to Manchuria in 1912, and then to Shanghai in 1918. There, he met many Korean nationalists and became one of the leaders of the Korean Independence Movement. In Paris in January 1919, as a representative of the Korean YMCA, he solicited the help of Western powers for the Korean cause, and when the **Korean Provisional Government** in exile was established in April that year, he was appointed as foreign minister, continuing his work for Korea in Paris.

In May 1919, Kim presented the "Petition of the Korean People and Nation for Liberation from Japan and for the Reconstitution of Korea as an Independent State" and the "Claims of the Korean People and Nation" to the Paris Peace Conference. When the Korean Provisional Government was reorganized, he was named the minister of education and was sent to Washington as chairman of the Korean Commission to work with Dr. **Syngman Rhee**, who as president of the Provisional Government, created the Korean Commission in Washington in 1919.

Kim Kyu-shik arrived in Washington D.C. in September 1919 and remained in the **United States** until early 1921. After his return to Shanghai, he served in the Provisional Government in various capacities while endeavoring to bring about the unity of the Korean nationalists. In 1930, he and his colleagues formed the Anti-Japanese United League of Koreans in **China**, and in 1935, they organized the Nationalist Revolutionary Party to lead the united Korean anti-Japanese struggle. In 1944, he became vice president of the Provisional Government in Chongqing, China.

Kim and other members of the Provisional Government returned to Korea in November 1945. A moderate nationalist, Kim and a moderate liberalist leftist formed the **Coalition Committee for Cooperation between the Rightists and the Leftists**. When the **United States Army Military Government** established the **South Korean Interim Legislative Assembly** in 1946, Kim was appointed its chairman. Meanwhile, his opposition to Rhee's plan to establish a separate government in South Korea, when it became apparent that the **United Nations** plan would not work in all Korea, led to a growing antagonism between him and Rhee. Kim, along with others who were determined to prevent the permanent partition of Korea, visited **P'yongyang** in April 1948 to solve the Korean question in cooperation with the North Korean Communists, but they failed to achieve their aims.

During the **Korean War** he was abducted by the North Koreans and taken to **North Korea** where he died in 1950.

KIM SANG-HYOP (1920–1995). A graduate of Tokyo Imperial University in 1942, he taught at Korea University (1957–1962, 1963–1970, 1972–1982). He served as the minister of education (1962) under President **Park Chung-hee**, and president of Korea University (1970–75). Elected to the **National Assembly** in 1980, he was named prime minister in 1982, resigning in 1983. He became president of the Korean Red Cross Society in 1985.

KIM SANG-MAN (1910–1994). Son of **Kim Song-su**, whose memory he made great efforts to preserve, and a cousin of **Kim Sang-hyop**, Kim spent his entire public career as a newspaperman with the *Tong-a Ilbo*. He was educated at the London School of Economics, for which he retained a life-long affection, and at Waseda University in **Japan**. He received many honors, and was for several years chairman of the Press Foundation of Asia.

Although Kim was conservative in his political views, he opposed President **Park Chun-hee**'s **Yushin rule**. In particular, he fought against press censorship, and the presence in newspaper offices of agents from the Korean Central Intelligence Agency (now the **National Intelligence Service**). The *Tong-a Ilbo* suffered as a result, with all government advertising removed for a time; Kim published the paper with blank spaces. Many of its staff were singled out for attack, but Kim did his best to defend them.

The *Tong-a Ilbo* also suffered following the **December 1979 coup**. The company's **broadcasting** assets and provincial publications were suppressed, and staff members were once again targeted. Many lost their jobs, but Kim Sang-man made sure that as many as possible were given backstage or unofficial positions. Eventually, government opposition waned, and Kim was treated like an elder statesman in his later years.

KIM SONG-SU (1891–1955). Born into a wealthy landlord family in Koch'ang, North Cholla Province, he graduated from Waseda University in **Japan** in 1914. In 1915, he took over a secondary school for boys in **Seoul**, becoming its principal in 1917. He and his brothers established a textile firm named *Seoul Spinning and Weaving Company* in 1919, contributing to the development of nationalistic entrepreneurial ventures.

In 1920, Kim established a new Korean-language newspaper press, publishing the *Tong-a Ilbo* and other Korean language publications for the purpose of maintaining Korean nationalistic spirit. After taking over Posong College (later Korea University) in 1932, Kim became its president, training Korean youths in modern law and commercial studies. In 1947, he and other right-wing political leaders established the **Korean (Han'guk) Democratic Party**. He served as vice president of the **National Council for Rapid Realization of Korean Independence**, and when his party and another party merged into the **Democratic Party** in 1949, he became one of its top leaders.

In May 1951, Kim was elected by the **National Assembly** as vice president of the Republic, replacing vice president **Yi Si-yong**, who resigned after disputes with President **Syngman Rhee**, but Kim, too, resigned from the position in May 1952 after bitterly criticizing Rhee's autocratic rule. After that, he served as adviser to the **Democratic Nationalist Party**.

KIM SOU-HWAN (1920–). Cardinal Kim Sou-hwan (Stephen Kim) was the leader of the Roman Catholic Church in South Korea from 1968 until he retired in 1998. He was ordained a priest in 1951, and became pastor of the parish of Andong in the archdiocese of **Taegu** the same year. Kim studied at Munster in Germany from 1956–1963, and became bishop of **Masan** in 1966, moving to be archbishop of **Seoul** in 1968. He became a cardinal in 1969.

During the 1970s, many Roman Catholics, including **Kim Dae-jung**, opposed the increasingly authoritarian **Yushin rule** of President **Park Chung-hee**. Seoul's Roman Catholic cathedral in Myong-dong was the scene of major protests against the regime in 1976. Although Cardinal Kim did not confront the Park regime head-on, he and the church provided support for the dissidents and their families.

Later, during the presidency of **Chun Doo-hwan**, Kim became a more outspoken critic of government suppression of democracy. In particular, he opposed Chun's attempt to stifle the debate on reform of the **Constitution**. See also RELIGION.

KIM YONG-IL (1941–). Kim Yong-il, who writes under the pen name, Kim Chi-ha, became the best-known South Korean dissident writer under President **Park Chung-hee**. A Roman Catholic, and supporter of radical theology, Kim attacked Park's regime for its oppression of the poor and promotion of elite groups in a series of poems, essays, and plays. In 1972, he was tried under the 1961 **Anti-Communism Law**, and was sentenced to death in 1974.

Following national and international protests, however, Kim was reprieved, and released briefly with a suspended sentence. He was reimprisoned in 1975, and held, mostly in solitary confinement, until 1980. Since then, his work has been published in South Korea, and Kim has also worked on environment and human rights issues. *See also* NATIONAL SECURITY LAWS.

KIM YOUNG-SAM (1927–). Born in **Pusan**, South Kyongsang Province, Kim graduated from Seoul National University in 1951. He joined the **Liberal Party**, and served as secretary to the prime minister in 1951. Deserting the Liberal Party, Kim joined the **Democratic Party** and was elected to the **National Assembly** in 1954 and 1960. He was reelected to the National Assembly in 1963 as a member of the **Civil Rule Party**, and in 1967 as a member of the **New Democratic Party**, serving in the National Assembly until 1980. He was then banned from politics under President **Chun Doo-hwan**, but by 1984, was again active in political circles.

Kim served with **Kim Dae-jung** as cochairman of the **Council for the Promotion of Democracy** in 1984, and when the **New Korea Democratic Party** was established in 1986 he became its adviser. In 1987, he founded the **Reunification Democratic Party**, becoming its president, as well as its candidate in the 1987 presidential election. He lost the election, but was elected to the National Assembly in 1988. In June 1989, he visited the **Soviet Union/Russia**, contributing to the development of South Korean ties with Moscow. In February 1990, when his party merged with the Democratic Justice and the

New Democratic Republican parties, forming the **Democratic Liberal Party** (DLP), he first became one of the three supreme leaders of the new party, and then its executive chairman. In May 1992, the DLP nominated him as its presidential candidate for the December 1992 presidential election.

His presidency, which broke away from the military dominance that had prevailed since **Park Chung-hee**'s coup in 1961, aroused high hopes. He began well, with a series of reforming measures. But faced with the issue of the **North Korea nuclear program** and domestic pressure to reopen the issue of the **Kwangju Uprising**, he seemed to lose his touch. His policy toward **North Korea** swung back and forth as events developed, and while he authorized the trials of Chun Doo-hwan and **Roh Tae-woo**, he gained little credit, since he only did so under growing popular pressure. His last months in office were marred by his son's alleged corruption and tax evasion, by attempts to prevent **Kim Dae-jung** from succeeding him as president, and eventually by his failure to respond to the financial crisis that hit South Korea in the autumn of 1997. In retirement, Kim made occasional references to returning to politics, but these came to nothing.

KO HUI-DONG (1886–1965). A Korean artist, who pioneered the application of Western painting techniques to the traditional Korean approach to painting. He was the first Korean student to learn Western-style oil painting during his study in **Japan** from 1908 onward. He returned to Korea in 1915 but found little interest in his new skills, and he devoted most of his time thereafter to more traditional painting. In 1945, he became chair of the Korean Association of Artists, and in 1955 chair of the Korean Academy of Arts. In his later years, he became involved in politics as a supporter of President **Syngman Rhee**, but retired following Rhee's overthrow in 1961.

KOCH'ANG INCIDENT. *See* HAMP'YONG–KOCH'ANG INCIDENTS.

KOREA ADVANCED INSTITUTE OF SCIENCE AND TECHNOLOGY (KAIST). A research body, the **Korea Institute of Science and Technology (KIST)** was established in 1966 for the promotion of science and technology through the conduct and encouragement of scientific research and development

In 1971, the South Korean government, feeling the acute need for a pool of experts in the field of science and technology, established the Korea Advanced Institute of Science (KAIS). KAIS, while expanding its research programs, established a graduate school exclusively for physical science and engineering, training a large number of high-level scientists and engineers.

In 1981, these two bodies merged to form the Korea Advanced Institute of Science and Technology, which came under the control of the Ministry of Science and Technology. It was not a wholly successful merger, with the two institutions pulling in different ways. In June 1989, therefore, the former KIST demerged to become an independent research center once again. At the same time, KAIST, which was solely devoted to postgraduate and advanced research, merged with the Korea Institute of Technology, founded in 1984, where the main remit was to teach science and technology to undergraduates.

KAIST was relocated to the "Science Town" at Taedok, where it aims to become a world-class research university. In 2001, it had more than 20,000 students, three-quarters of whom were studying for master's or doctor's degrees.

KOREA/COREA CONTROVERSY. After the establishment of the Yi dynasty in 1392, the name "Chosun" was used by Koreans to refer to their country, until the Yi kingdom became the "Taehan" (Great Korean) empire in 1897. Under the Japanese **Government-General of Korea** from 1910, the Japanese used "Chosen," while Koreans continued to use "Chosun." In the early colonial years, however, the Japanese often used "Korea." After the division of the peninsula in 1945, **North Korea** continued to use Chosun, while South Korea eventually revived "Han," in the form of "Han'guk." Neither side now uses the other term.

The Western name for the Korean Peninsula derives from the Koryo dynasty (918–1392) either through Chinese *Gaoli* or Japanese *Korai*. The first known Western reference to "Caule" is in the Franciscan friar William of Rubruck's account of his visit to Mongolia in 1253. Until the 18th century, most mapmakers appear to have used variations of the country's name spelled with "C", and "Corea," which first appeared in 1596, became the norm. However, "Korea" is found as early as 1738. During the 19th century, both were common, but in the 20th century, "Korea" became the more usual form in English, though "Corea" was not uncommon until about 1940. Latin languages continue to use variations of "Corea."

In the late 1990s, a number of South Koreans began to claim that the Japanese had deliberately fostered the use of *Korea* rather than *Corea* so that **Japan** would be listed before Korea in country lists. This movement received a boost during the **World Cup 2000**. There is no evidence that Japan actually did this, and, since Korea was not an independent country from 1910 until 1945, it rarely appeared in country lists. However, the movement gained some momentum, and in 2003, the issue was also taken up in North Korea. This was largely in the context of opposition to Japanese colonialism, and there were no signs that North Korea intended to change its usage. In August 2003, 22 South Korean **National Assembly** members introduced a bill to make the use of "Corea" compulsory, since this was the "historically correct" way to refer to the peninsula until changed by the Japanese. Some of those involved attended a conference in **P'yongyang** in September 2003, to discuss the proposed use of "Corea."

KOREA DEVELOPMENT INSTITUTE (KDI). A private think tank, funded by the government but with considerable independence in operation, was established in 1971 under a charter to conduct research and analysis on a systematic basis on matters relating both to the national economy as a whole and to specific problems of particular sectors. While making studies on past performances of the economy, the institute provided professional advice to the government's Economic Planning Board and provided economic forecasts. It had a large number of foreign-trained, economic specialists on its staff and published various reports on the economic performance of the nation.

With the move away from government direct involvement with the economy in recent years, KDI's emphasis has also shifted. It now provides expert analysis and advice on all aspects of long- and short-term policies in a wide range of areas from domestic economic policy to international investment. In addition, it has played an increasing role in international economic cooperation.

KOREA FOUNDATION (*Han'guk kukje koryu chedan*). Established in 1991, the Korea Foundation resembles the Japan Foundation and the British Council. It encourages scholarship on Korea by funding Korean studies overseas, including museums and art galleries, by inviting scholars of things Korean to South Korea, by publishing under its own imprint and assisting the publication of books and journals. Although separate from the Ministry of Foreign Affairs and Trade, and essentially nonpolitical, the Foundation works closely with the ministry, and the senior leadership is drawn from former diplomats.

KOREA INSTITUTE OF SCIENCE AND TECHNOLOGY (KIST). Under an agreement signed in 1965 between the **United States** and South Korean governments, a nonprofit research organization named the *Korea Institute of Science and Technology* was established in 1966 for the promotion of science and technology through the conduct and encouragement of scientific research and development. A major portion of the KIST funds was provided by the U.S. government, and, with a large number of well-trained scientists and technicians, most of whom were educated abroad, KIST contributed much toward South Korea's industrial development through its research and technology transfer in cooperation with the United States.

In 1981, this institution and the **Korea Advanced Institute of Science and Technology** merged, with the new body taking the *KAIST* name. In practice, KIST maintained its separate structure and purpose, and in 1989 a demerger took place, with the KIST title being revived. KIST is a research institute, working in the field of developing all areas of technology for domestic use. It works closely with similar bodies in other countries.

KOREA STOCK EXCHANGE. Established in **Seoul** on 3 March 1956, with 12 corporations listed, the Korea Stock Exchange initially traded mainly in government bonds. Computerization started in 1977, and in July 1979, the Exchange moved to its present location on Yoido Island. In March 1988, it was privatized. Direct foreign investment was allowed for the first time in January 1992, with a 10 percent foreign investment ceiling set for any single stock by the government. From 1 September 1998, the trading system became fully computerized, and in May 1998, the ceiling on foreign investment was lifted.

KOREA TRADE PROMOTION ASSOCIATION (KOTRA). A government agency established in 1962 for the purpose of promoting exports. It participates in international trade fairs, sends trade missions overseas, provides information to foreign business people and firms, and displays Korean products at the World Trade Center in **Seoul**. It has branch offices around the world.

KOREAGATE. Name given, in ironic reference to the Watergate scandal, to a major lobbying exercise carried out by South Korea in the **United States** following the decision under President Richard Nixon to reduce the U.S. military commitment in Asia. South Korean President **Park Chung-hee** sanctioned the exercise, which involved the Korean Central Intelligence Agency (KCIA, now the **National Intelligence Service**), **Moon Sun-myong** and the **Unification Church**, and a businessman, Park Tong-sun. When the introduction of the **Yushin** Constitution in 1972 led to widespread U.S. criticism, efforts were also made to counteract this development. The main target was the U.S. Congress, and it was claimed that a number of Congressmen took bribes from the Koreans. The exercise became public in 1976, and led to a series of Congressional hearings between 1977–1978. Although Park testified in exchange for immunity, there were no convictions. Moon left the United States when summoned for questioning, and the KCIA was immune from prosecution. But the case left a shadow over South Korea's relations with the **United States** for many years.

KOREAN AIR. Originally Korean Air Lines, but the company changed its name after the disastrous **Korean Air Lines flight KE007.** Founded in 1962 as **Korean National Airlines**, a government-owned company, Korean Airlines was privatized in 1969 and became part of the Hanjin Corporation. This move turned the company from a loss-making enterprise, mainly flying domestic routes, into a major Asian airline. It remained the sole carrier in South Korea until 1988, when air transport was deregulated, and a second carrier, **Asiana Airlines**, was licensed. At the end of 2000, Korean Air owned 112 civil aircraft and flew to 28 countries. The company also served a variety of domestic routes.

KOREAN AIR FLIGHT KA 858. On 29 November 1987, while flying over the Andaman Sea near Burma, Korean Air flight KA 858 traveling from the Middle East to **Seoul** blew up in midair, killing all 115 passengers and crew. A Korean man and woman who had left the aircraft during a fueling stop in the Gulf came under suspicion. The man committed suicide before he was caught, but Kim Hyon-hui failed to kill herself. Taken to South Korea, she eventually admitted that she was from **North Korea** and a member of a special task force that had carried out the attack, which was designed to dissuade people from attending the 1988 Seoul **Olympics Games**. Kim was sentenced to death, but was subsequently given amnesty. She later gave lectures and wrote an account of her role in the attack, married, and settled in South Korea.

KOREAN AIR LINES FLIGHT KE007. In the early hours of 1 September 1983, Korean Air Lines flight KE007 from New York to **Seoul** via Anchorage, Alaska, was shot down in Soviet airspace off the west coast of Sakhalin by fighter aircraft of the **Soviet Union/Russia**, with the loss of all 269 passengers and crew. The Boeing 747 should have been on a heavily used flight path, well away from the Soviet Union, but appears to have been some 360 miles (580 kilometers) off course. According to later Soviet claims, the aircraft displayed no navigation lights and failed to respond to warning shots. There was widespread international condemnation of the Soviet action, and the incident immediately became part of the ongoing dispute between the Soviet Union and the **United States**. Despite many claims and counterclaims about what really happened, there has never been a satisfactory explanation of why the aircraft was so far off course.

KOREAN ARMISTICE AGREEMENT. An agreement signed on 27 July 1953 between the **United Nations Command** and representatives from **North Korea** and **China**, ending the **Korean War**. It established the existing line of control as a cease-fire (**military demarcation) line** and designated a 1.5-mile (2.4 kilometers) area on each side of the line as a **demilitarized zone (DMZ).** A **Neutral Nations Supervisory Commission** was established to investigate violations of the cease-fire. The cease-fire line is some 150 miles (240 kilometers) long, zigzagging from sea to sea. Although South Korea refused to sign the agreement, on the grounds that it perpetuated the division of the peninsula, **Syngman Rhee** agreed not to oppose it.

It remains the only agreement governing the cession of hostilities on the peninsula. In February 2003, however, North Korea threatened to denounce the agreement, as tension rose over the **North Korean nuclear program.**

KOREAN ASSOCIATION OF WOMEN'S STUDIES. An umbrella organization for women's organizations, established in October 1984. *See also* WOMEN'S MOVEMENT.

KOREAN AUGMENTATION TO THE UNITED STATES ARMY (KATUSA). Name given to South Korean military recruited to augment United States Army units during the **Korean War**. KATUSAs, as they are known, remained subject to South Korean discipline and received South Korean rates of pay, but received U.S. rations, weapons, and training. They acted in many capacities, but were especially important as interpreters and in liaison roles. So useful have both parties found the system that it continues to survive. During the War, there were similar arrangements with the British Commonwealth Division and with the Belgian forces.

KOREAN CENTRAL INTELLIGENCE AGENCY (KCIA). *See* NATIONAL INTELLIGENCE SERVICE (NIS).

KOREAN COALITION FOR THE FUTURE (KCTF). A short-lived political party established in 2002 by **Park Geun-hye**, the daughter of the former president, **Park Chung-hee**, following her falling out with the **Grand National Party (GNP)** and its leader, **Lee Hoi-chang**. Park was nominated as the party's presidential candidate in the 2002 presidential elections, but withdrew. She then rejoined the GNP, and acted as a campaign manager for Lee Hoi-chang.

KOREAN COMMUNIST PARTY (*Chosun Kongsandang*). In September 1945, Pak Hon-yong and others reconstituted the Communist Party that had been broken up by the Japanese soon after it was founded in 1925. On its revival, it formed many subordinate labor and social organizations to promote socialism in South Korea.

In November 1946, the Korean Communist Party was reorganized into the South Korean Workers' Party *(Namchosun Nodongdang)* by uniting two other leftist parties under the leadership of Ho Hon and Pak Hon-yong. This occurred after the North Korean Bureau of the Korean Communist Party and the New People's Party in North Korea merged to form the North Korean Workers' Party in July. In 1947, the **American Army Military Government in Korea** organized a crackdown against the South Korean Workers' Party (SKWP) and its affiliated organizations. This was partly because of their illegal activities, including the printing of counterfeit money, and the leadership group of the party fled to **North Korea**.

Many of its members went underground in the South in order to continue their activity. Their subversive actions led to the rebellion on **Cheju Island** and the **Yosu–Sunch'on Rebellion**. Under the control of the Korean Communist Party (later SKWP) were the **National Council of Labor Unions**, the General League of Korean Women, the National Federation of Farmers' Unions, and the General Federation of Democratic Korean Youth.

In October 1949, the South Korean government outlawed the SKWP and its subordinate organs. However, many communists, who went underground, continued their subversive activities. *See also* NATIONAL ASSEMBLY SPY RING CASE.

KOREAN DEMOCRATIC PARTY *(Chosun Minjudang)*. In September 1945, right-wing nationalists in **North Korea** formed this party. Under the leadership of Cho Man-shik, an elder in the Presbyterian Church in **P'yongyang**, they struggled against the communists, opposing the trusteeship proposal. When the Soviet military forces put Cho under house arrest and cracked down on the rightist organizations because of their opposition to the **Moscow Agreement**, its leaders brought the party to South Korea. Eventually it broke up as its members joined other opposition parties in South Korea.

KOREAN DEMOCRATIC PARTY *(Han'guk Minjudang)*. In September 1945, conservative right-wing leaders in South Korea formed a political party under the leadership of **Song Chin-u**, **Chang Tok-su**, and **Kim Song-su**. The list of its leadership included nearly all prominent right-wing leaders in the South. After the assassination of

Song in 1945 and Chang in 1947, Kim led the party as the major opposition party in 1948. In February 1949, it merged with another party, forming the **Democratic Nationalist Party**.

KOREAN EDUCATIONAL DEVELOPMENT INSTITUTE (KEDI, *Hanguk Kyoyuk kaebalwon*). Established in 1972 with government funding as an autonomous educational research and development organization. Its purpose was the development of high-quality **education** in South Korea by undertaking comprehensive and systematic research and development activities on educational goals, content, and methodology, and formulating education policies and recommending them to the Ministry of Education and Human Resources Development. A number of other educational research bodies exist, including one for children with special needs, the Institute for Special Education (Kuknip Toksuyokwon), founded in 1994.

KOREAN FEDERATION OF TEACHERS' LABOR UNIONS (KFTLU). Following the fall of the First Republic, labor unions of all kinds were formed. In May 1960, some 300 primary and secondary school teachers and college professors formed this federation in order to launch a more aggressive movement to promote the welfare of the teachers and protect their rights. The Ministry of Education immediately outlawed these unions and their federation, but it was not until the **Military Revolution of 16 May 1961** that the unions and the federation were dissolved by the military junta. *See also* FEDERATION OF KOREAN EDUCATION ASSOCIATIONS; LABOR MOVEMENT; NATIONAL TEACHERS' UNION.

KOREAN FOLK VILLAGE. In the 1960s and 1970s, under President **Park Chun-hee**, a series of national monuments were either refurbished or constructed, to emphasis Korea's history. As part of this process, and to record traditional housing and customs, which were disappearing, a Korean Folk Village was established at Suwon, some 25 miles (40 kilometers) south of **Seoul** in 1973. This brought together types of building and crafts from all over the peninsula, in a re-creation of a Korean community of about 1900. The village has steadily expanded since its foundation, becoming a major **tourism** attraction, immensely popular with both domestic and foreign visitors.

The term "Folk Village" is also sometimes used for Hahoe, on the Naktong River in North Kyongsang Province, but that is a genuine survival from the past. In addition, a number of folk museums have been established in various parts of the country. In addition to one in Seoul, there are important museums in Andong and **Cheju Island**. The Korean folklorist, **Zo Zayang**, tried to counteract what he believed was the ersatz nature of such enterprises with a more robust presentation of Korean popular customs.

KOREAN HISTORICAL ASSOCIATION (*Hanguk yoksa hakhoe*). The oldest organization of South Korean historians, founded in 1952, and dominated by conservative historians. It has faced challenges at regular intervals in recent years from younger historians who desired to throw off the restraints imposed by a conservative view of Korean history, and to study Korean history based on a "scientific methodology" and in particular to study the masses (*minjung*) as the agents of social transformation and progress. These have included the Korean History Research Society (*Hanguk yoksa yonguhoe*), established in 1988, and several others. Most do not survive very long.

KOREAN INDEPENDENCE PARTY (*Chosun tongnipdang*). This extreme right-wing political party formed in **China** by **Kim Ku** in 1930, advocated violent struggle for Korean independence against the Japanese. It relocated to South Korea when Korea was liberated, but after the assassination of Kim Ku in June 1949, its members abandoned it for other parties. The party name was revived in October 1963, without success.

KOREAN NATIONAL AIRLINES. South Korea's first airline company, founded in 1962. It was government owned, and lost money heavily on both its domestic and the few international routes that it flew, mainly to Japanese cities. In 1969, the government sold it to the Hanjin group, which renamed it **Korean Air Lines** (now **Korean Air**). Under this new management, the company became one of Asia's leading airlines.

KOREAN NATIONAL COUNCIL OF WOMEN (KNCW). *See* WOMEN'S MOVEMENT.

KOREAN NATIONAL WRITERS' UNION. Formed in September 1987 by 500 liberal playwrights, novelists, and poets, its aim is to promote what it called *people's* or *masses (minjung) literature* to bring about national unification.

KOREAN NATIONAL YOUTH CORPS (*Chosun Minjok Ch'ongayondan, or Chokch'ong*). An ultra-rightist youth organization organized in October 1946 by General **Yi Pom-suk**, a military leader who returned from **China** in 1945. Its primary aim was to combat those who supported the **Moscow Agreement**. Dr. **Syngman Rhee** and **Kim Ku** were its honorary chairmen, and at one point, the corps claimed more than one million members. When the Republic of Korea was inaugurated, it changed its name to *Taehan Minjok Ch'ongnyondan*, and it gave strong support to Dr. Rhee until 1956 when Yi Pom-suk withdrew from the **Liberal Party**.

KOREAN NATIONALIST PARTY (*Chosun Kungmindang*). In September 1945, **An Chae-hong** and other moderate nationalists brought several small political parties together and formed this party. Most of its members had broken away from the **Committee for the Preparation of National Reconstruction**. However, gradually, its members drifted away to join other parties. When An became the civil administrator of the **South Korean Interim Government** in July 1947, the party was virtually dissolved.

KOREAN NATIONALIST PARTY (*Taehan Kungmindang*). In November 1949, several small groups of politicians who supported President **Syngman Rhee** formed a new political party, which they called the *Nationalist Party*, creating intense rivalry with the **Democratic Nationalist Party**. The Nationalist Party was composed of right-wing politicians led by Yun Ch'i-yong. It was dissolved in March 1952, when the **Liberal Party** was formally established.

KOREAN PENINSULA ENERGY DEVELOPMENT ORGANIZATION (KEDO). An organization set up in March 1995 by the Governments of South Korea, **Japan**, and the **United States**, following the 1994 "Agreed Framework" between **North Korea** and the United States, which froze the **North Korean nuclear program**. Subsequently, a number of other governments also joined.

KEDO's purpose was to provide for the financing and supply of 1,000-megawatt light water reactors (LWRs) to North Korea; to provide interim energy resources to North Korea before the LWRs are operational; and to carry out any other measures that would help implement the Agreed Framework. The LWRs were to be built at Kumho on North Korea's east coast, and were scheduled to be ready by 2003, but it was clear by the end of 2001 that they would not be, although the first concrete laying for them took place in August 2002. North Korea began to demand additional compensation for lost power. However, North Korea's apparent admission to a visiting United States delegation in October 2003 that it had been trying to develop an enriched uranium program threw the future of both the Agreed Framework and KEDO into doubt, and revived tension over the North Korean nuclear program.

KOREAN PEOPLE'S PARTY (*Chosun Inmindang*). Following the outlawing of the **Korean People's Republic** by the **United States Army Military Government in Korea** in October 1945, in November **Yo Un-hyong** and other moderate leftists organized the Korean People's Party. To do this, they united several small moderate left-wing political and social groups. The party advocated socialistic economic reform, and supported the **Moscow Agreement**. After joining the **Coalition Committee for Cooperation between the Rightists and Leftists** in May 1946, in October the Korean People's Party and two other moderate leftist parties were united into the Socialist Labor Party (*Sahoe Nodongdang*), pursuing democratic socialism. When the **Korean Communist Party** was expanded into the South Korean Workers' Party in November by incorporating two other radical leftist parties, many of the members of the Socialist Labor Party deserted, joining the radical Communist Party. Consequently, Yo and other moderate leftists reorganized their party into the Working People's Party (*Kullo Inmindang*) in May 1947, pursuing a middle-of-the-road policy, and seeking cooperation with the moderate rightists. With the death of Yo Un-hyong in July 1947, the party collapsed.

KOREAN PEOPLE'S REPUBLIC. This organization and its associated "government" were established on 6 September 1945 by the "National Assembly," convened under the auspices of the **Committee for the Preparation of National Reconstruction**. The "National Assembly" appointed Dr. **Syngman Rhee**, who was still in the **United States**, as chairman of the republic, and **Yo Un-hyong** as vice-chairman. It elected Ho Hon, a prominent leftist, as premier, and it named cabinet ministers. The key cabinet members were: **Kim Ku** (internal affairs), **Kim Kyu-shik** (foreign affairs), Cho Man-shik (finance), **Kim Song-su** (education), Kim Pyong-no (justice), Ha P'il-won (commerce), and **Shin Ik-hui** (communications).

The republic's main program included the establishment of a politically and economically independent nation, the elimination of Japanese collaborators, the realization of a democracy based on fundamental human rights, implementation of social and economic reforms, and maintenance of international peace in close cooperation with friendly nations. However, the **United States Army Military Government in Korea** outlawed both the republic and its government.

KOREAN PROVISIONAL GOVERNMENT (*Taehan minguk imsi chongbu*). Established by Korean exiles in Shanghai, **China**, in April 1919, following the 1 March 1919 uprising against the Japanese in Korea. Later, it followed the Chinese Nationalists to Nanjing and then to the wartime capital, Chongqing, where it remained until 1945. **Syngman Rhee**, then living in the **United States**, was elected president and a socialist, Yi Tong-hwi, premier. It also had a newspaper, *Tongnip Sinmun* (Independence News).

A split occurred in 1921, when Yi and some others left, and there was a more serious division in the late 1930s, because of the split between the Chinese Nationalists and the communists, but the "government" continued to exist. In 1943, it was organized with the right-wing **Kim Ku** as president and **Kim Kyu-shik** as his deputy. However, when **Japan** was defeated in 1945, the Provisional Government failed to make the transition to actual rule. The **United States Army Military Government in Korea** refused to deal with it, and its members were forced to return to Korea as private individuals.

KOREAN WAR. The Korean War began on 25 June 1950 when **North Korea** launched a well-prepared attack against South Korea across the **38th parallel**. **Kim Il-sung**, premier and chairman of the Korean

Workers' Party of North Korea, had been scheming to overthrow the government of the Republic of Korea and annex South Korea ever since the establishment of the two Korean states.

In early 1949, Kim Il-sung proposed to the Soviet leader, Josef Stalin, that the North should launch a war against South Korea, but it was only when Kim realized that communist uprisings and other subversive activities would fail to topple the South Korean government that he finally decided to go to war against the South. He consulted Stalin in February 1950, seeking support for an attack. Following Stalin's agreement, sometime in March or April 1950, to such a move, and the arrival of new Soviet military advisors, Kim began the war with massive Soviet military aid.

The North Koreans called this attack the "war to liberate the southern half of the Republic from American imperialists and their puppets." Initially, some 80,000 of 165,000 North Korean troops, supported by Soviet-built tanks, crossed the 38th parallel. Three days later, on 28 June, the North Koreans captured **Seoul**, the South Korean capital. The South Korean government fled first to **Taejon**, then to **Taegu**, and finally to **Pusan**. North Korean troops pushed southward, encountering minor resistance. When South Korea, which was taken by surprise with only 67,000 ill-equipped and poorly trained troops and faced with the threat to its very existence, requested military assistance of the **United States**, the American government ordered U.S. troops in **Japan** to go to Korea in support of South Korean troops. The U.S. forces that arrived in July were lightly equipped and ill-prepared, and could not stop the southward push of North Korean troops. Both South Korean and U.S. troops took up defense positions in the southeastern corner of the peninsula known as "the Pusan perimeter."

In response to the North Korean attack, South Korea and the U.S. brought the matter to the **United Nations (UN).** The Security Council, in the absence of the **Soviet Union/Russia**, condemned North Korea as an aggressor and mounted a collective defense action in support of South Korea. When 16 UN member states, including **Great Britain**, France, **Australia**, New Zealand, Greece, and Turkey, in addition to the United States, provided military forces, a **United Nations Command (UNC)** was set up. American General **Douglas MacArthur** was named supreme commander of the UN forces. The South Korean government put its defense forces under his command as UN troops arrived in growing numbers. Following a seaborne landing by the UN forces at **Inch'on** on 15 September 1950, Seoul was recaptured on 26 September, and in early October the UN forces moved across the 38th parallel in pursuit of the fleeing enemy, capturing **P'yongyang**, the North Korean capital, on 20 October. At the same time, UN troops reached the Yalu River, the border between Korea and **China**.

At this juncture, troops of the Chinese People's Liberation Army, described officially by the Chinese as the "Chinese People's Volunteers," which had been preparing to enter Korea from Manchuria for some time, joined the North Korean forces in combat, bringing "an entirely new war" as General MacArthur called it. Initially, some 250,000 Chinese troops entered North Korea in mid-October, but before long, more than one million Chinese troops were engaged in military actions in Korea.

Soviet forces also took part in the Korean War, although not as openly as the Chinese. After the fall of the Soviet Union in 1991, hitherto classified reports confirmed that some 70,000 Russian airmen were also involved in the Korean War from November 1950, flying MiG-15 and other Soviet aircraft, wearing Chinese uniforms, and with air bases in Manchuria.

The massive counterattack launched by the Chinese forces in late October 1950 against the UN forced the withdrawal of the UN forces from the Yalu River region as well as other areas. As UN troops withdrew southward, the communist forces came across the 38th parallel. Seoul fell for the second time on 4 January 1951, as the UN forces set up their defense line just south of the city of Wonju, some 100 miles (160 kilometers) south of Seoul. UN counterattacks launched in February pushed the enemy northward, and on 15 March 1951, Seoul was recovered.

The UN forces crossed the 38th parallel once again in early April. Although there was a series of seesaw battles, stalemate now developed. Meanwhile, Lieutenant General **Matthew B. Ridgway** was appointed supreme commander of the UN forces, replacing MacArthur, who was dismissed by President Harry S. Truman.

In April 1951, the Chinese launched a ferocious attack to end the war, but it failed to achieve its objective. Meanwhile, the United

States, which was unwilling to invite the Soviet Union and China into the Korean conflict directly, wished to end the fighting somehow, despite Rhee's wish to destroy North Korea completely and unify Korea. Thus, when Yakov Malik, the Soviet ambassador to the UN, called for a cease-fire on 23 June 1951, and when the Chinese also voiced their desire for a cease-fire two days later, the U.S. government welcomed the opportunity to initiate truce talks, and instructed Ridgway to arrange meetings with the communists to achieve this.

Armistice negotiations began on 10 July 1951, at **Kaesong**, formerly a South Korean city but captured by the North Koreans in the early stages of the war. The talks dragged on until the communists suspended negotiations on 23 August. Talks resumed at **P'anmunjom** on 25 October 1951 but various issues prevented any progress toward an armistice. Meanwhile, fighting continued as the two sides argued over issues relating to prisoners of war and the location of a truce line. As the U.S. indicated that it was anxious to end the "wrong war in the wrong place at the wrong time," President Rhee expressed his strong feelings against a cease-fire, advocating a complete victory against the communists. Rhee's vehemence led the U.S. government even to contemplate his removal from the presidency by a military coup.

General Dwight D. Eisenhower, who became the new U.S. president in January 1953, was anxious to end the fighting, but he was not in favor of the U.S. taking drastic action against Rhee. As a result, he agreed with Rhee on a **South Korea–United States Mutual Defense Treaty**, and also that the Korean question be solved by political means at a political conference after an armistice. In spite of this agreement, in June 1953 President Rhee ordered South Korean guards at prisoner-of-war camps at Pusan and other places to release North Korean prisoners of war who did not wish to be repatriated. Some 25,000 of them were freed without the knowledge or approval of the UN Commander.

This action not only angered the Americans, but also the North Koreans and the Chinese. However, the threat made by President Eisenhower that the United States might use atomic weapons to end the war, together with the death of the Soviet leader Stalin in March 1953, led the communists to resume cease-fire negotiations. On 27 July 1953, General William K. Harrison, representing the UNC, General Nam Il, representing North Korea, and General Peng Dehui, representing the

"Chinese People's Volunteers" signed the **Korean Armistice Agreement**, and the fighting stopped. Syngman Rhee refused to sign, however.

With the signing of the truce, a **military demarcation line** was established across the peninsula, based on the respective lines of actual control at the time of the armistice, with a **demilitarized zone (DMZ)** either side. At the same time, P'anmunjom, where the truce was signed, was designated as a neutral zone where the **Neutral Nations Armistice Supervisory Commission (NNSC)** and the **Military Armistice Commission (MAC)** established their headquarters. The NNSC, drawn from UN member nations that had not taken part in the Korean War, was to supervise observance of the terms of the armistice, while the MAC, composed of the representatives of North Korea, China, and of the UN Command, was to deal with any problems rising between the two former belligerents.

With the armistice, North Korea lost a sizeable amount of mountainous area in the east while gaining a small but fertile rice growing area in the west, including the city of Kaesong. When the truce was signed, the sixteen UN member states that fought the war issued a **16 Nations Declaration on Korea**, which indicated that they would fight again if the communists renewed their aggression.

Exchanges of prisoners of war were carried out under supervision of a UN Neutral Nations Repatriation Commission in an exercise called "Operation Big Switch" that began on 5 August 1953. It saw the handing over of 75,823 communist prisoners of war (5,640 Chinese), who wished to be repatriated. The communist side turned over 12,773 UN prisoners of war (3,597 Americans, 7,862 South Koreans, and 1,112 other UN troops). The remaining 22,606 prisoners of war were held under the custody of the Neutral Nations Repatriation Commission pending their decision on repatriation. Of these, some 22,118 communists (mostly Chinese) who did not wish to be repatriated elected to settle either in South Korea or Taiwan. The "Chinese People's Volunteers" withdrew from North Korea toward the end of 1958 while a sizeable number of UN troops (mainly American) remained in South Korea.

The Korean War caused heavy property damage and a large number of casualties on both sides. Of some 1.3 million U.S. troops who served in the Korean War, 33,625 were killed, 105,785 were wounded, and several hundred were reported missing. The South Korean army lost 225,784 men and 717,170 were wounded. Some 2,186 other UN troops were killed and 10,117 were wounded. In South Korea, some 373,500 civilians were killed, more than 225,600 wounded, and over 387,740 were listed as missing. The war produced one million orphans and 600,000 war widows in South Korea alone. During the occupation of Seoul, the communists massacred 128,936 civilians and 84,523 were taken captive to North Korea. When the communists retreated from Seoul, a large number of artists and writers who were pro–North Korean defected to the North. The casualties on the part of North Korean troops were some 294,151 dead, 229,849 wounded, and 91,206 missing. It was estimated that some 900,000 Chinese troops were either killed or wounded. Some 406,000 North Korean civilians were reported killed, 1,594,000 were wounded, and 680,000 were missing. Over 1.5 million North Koreans fled to the South during the war.

The Korean War was a national tragedy for the Korean people. It achieved nothing other than causing property destruction, loss of life, and great human suffering. It made peaceful settlement for Korean unification more difficult as it fostered deep hatred between the North and the South.

KOREAN WOMEN'S ASSOCIATION OF WOMEN'S STUDIES. *See* WOMEN'S MOVEMENT.

KOREAN WOMEN'S DEVELOPMENT INSTITUTE (KWDI). A government body, established in 1983, under a law passed the previous year. It first came under the Ministry of Health, but in 1991, with the appointment of the Minister of Public Affairs II, KWDI transferred to that department. Following a further government restructuring in 1998, it moved to the Presidential Commission for Women's Affairs, but the following year, it was again moved, this time to the Council for Humanities and Social Research under the Prime Minister. It has played an important role in promoting gender equality in Korea.

KOREAN WOMEN'S NATIONALIST PARTY. *See* WOMEN'S MOVEMENT.

KOREAN WOMEN'S SOCIETY. *See* WOMEN'S MOVEMENT.

KOREAN YOUTH CORPS. *See* KOREAN NATIONAL YOUTH CORPS.

KWANGJU. Capital of South Cholla Province and a special city with a population (2003) of 1.36 million, it has been a major market town and communications center since the early 20th century. Early industry included textile production and breweries, and in the 1960s, it became a center for automobile production.

Kwangju has a long revolutionary tradition. It was the scene of a serious anti-Japanese outbreak of violence in 1929, which spread nationwide. During the **Korean War**, it was an important military training center. Kwangju is also closely associated with the opposition leader, later, president, **Kim Dae-jung**, and it was his arrest in May 1980 that sparked off the **Kwangju Uprising** that same month. A monument to those killed in 1980 was erected in the city during **Roh Tae-woo**'s presidency.

KWANGJU UPRISING. Following violent student demonstrations in **Seoul** on 14 May 1980 against the growing power of General **Chun Doo-hwan**, the government extended martial law, which had been declared on 26 October 1979, to the entire country on 17 May 1980; banned all political activities; and arrested many prominent political leaders, including **Kim Dae-jung**. Kim Dae-jung was charged with inciting the students. Angered by such government action, dissident groups in the city of **Kwangju** in South Cholla Province rose in violent protests, clashing with the **police**.

When the situation in Kwangju got out of control and demonstrations against the government spread into other nearby cities and towns, troops were sent in to crush what the government regarded as a rebellion, but this only provoked people in Kwangju more. A violent protest movement became an open uprising as the demonstrators attacked police stations, other government buildings, and small military units, confiscating weapons. A bloody conflict ensued.

A special paratrooper unit was sent in to put down the rebellion, causing many deaths. Although the official estimate of the number of people killed was around 200, the local people claimed that more than 2,000 were killed. The uprising ended on 27 May 1980. In April 1988, following the fall of the Fifth Republic, the government of the Sixth Republic under President **Roh Tae-woo** redesignated the 1980 Kwangju Uprising as a "part of the democratization efforts of the students and citizens in Kwangju" and publicly apologized for failing to provide a satisfactory solution for the uprising. In June 1988, the **National Assembly** set up the Special Committee for the Investigation of the Kwangju Incident, and eventually the government agreed to provide monetary compensation to the families of the victims and erect a proper monument in honor of the dead. However, the issue has not gone away, and there are regular calls for further investigations into the role of the government forces and allegations that the **United States** could have stopped the suppression but failed to do so.

KYONGBOK PALACE. One of the four major palaces constructed after **Seoul** became the capital of Korea in 1392. It was destroyed during the Imjin Wars (1592–1597), and rebuilt with much splendor in the 1860s. Following the annexation of Korea by **Japan** in 1910, many of the main buildings were again destroyed. In 1923, the Japanese began building the **Capitol Building**, the administrative center for the **Government-General of Korea** in front of the palace. Although many regarded the Capitol Building as a fine example of neoclassical building, to some Koreans, these additions to the palace site symbolized Japan's domination of Korea.

After 1945, the Capitol Building was used as offices. The whole area was badly damaged in the **Korean War**. After the war, the Capitol Building remained a burned-out shell, though some attempt was made to rehabilitate the Kyongbok Palace, which was used for government receptions and later as the site of various museums. Under president **Kim Young-sam**, a decision was made to pull down the Capitol Building and to reconstruct some of the original Kyongbok Palace buildings as a demonstration of nationalist sentiment.

KYONGJU. A small city in North Kyongsang Province, 34 miles (55 kilometers) east of the provincial capital, **Taegu**, with a population of some 140,000. It was once the capital of the Shilla kingdom and has become one of the most important centers of **tourism** in South Korea, following an imaginative program of reconstruction of some of its ancient buildings at the direction of President **Park Chung-hee** in the 1960s and 1970s. These include the Pulguk temple, one of the greatest architectural remains of **Buddhism** in the peninsula, and the seventh-century observatory, the Chomsongdae. There are also important royal tombs of the Shilla period, some of which have been excavated.

– L –

LABOR MANAGEMENT COUNCIL. *See* LABOR MOVEMENT.

LABOR MOVEMENT. The first Korean organized labor movement, developed in the mid-1920s by left-wing groups, was crushed by the Japanese colonial regime after 1931. When Korea was liberated from **Japan**, left-wing groups quickly took the initiative in developing the labor movement by forming labor unions. In November 1945, they established the **National Council of Labor Unions** (*Chon'guk Nodong Chohap P'yongyuihoe*, or *Chonp'yong*). In order to combat the leftist labor movement, right-wing labor unions were organized, and in March 1946 the **General Alliance of Laborers for Rapid Realization of Korean Independence** (*Taehan Tongnip Ch'oksong Nodong Ch'ongyonmaeng*, or *Taehan Noch'ong*) was formed with Dr. **Syngman Rhee** as its president and **Kim Ku** as its vice president.

The Korean labor movement was highly politicized because of the colonial situation in which Korea was placed during the Japanese colonial period, the partition of Korea, and the growing antagonism between left and right. The 1945 **Moscow Agreement** only made the labor movement more political with the rightists opposing it and the leftists supporting it. When the leftists brought about a general railway workers' strike in the fall of 1946, bloody clashes took place between the members of the *Taehan Noch'ong* and the *Chonp'yong* throughout the fall and winter of 1946 and in the spring of 1947. It was followed by a nationwide railway, factory, and communication workers' strike sponsored by the Communists in March 1947.

Following the emigration of the leaders of the **South Korean Workers' Party** to the north in the fall of 1947, and the implementation of antileftist measures by the new government after August

1948, the left-wing labor movement was drastically weakened. The rightist labor federation became badly split between those who were allies of the Rhee administration and those who advocated a pure labor movement. The conflict between these two groups grew more vicious when the head of the *Taehan Noch'ong*, Chun Chin-han, became minister of social affairs in 1948 and the top leadership of the *Taehan Noch'ong* consisted of pro-Rhee elements. Meanwhile, the name of the *Taehan Noch'ong* changed to the **General Federation of Korean Labor Unions**, claiming over 3 million members. But the *Taehan Noch'ong* had become a tool of the government first, and then of the **Liberal Party** after 1952, playing more a political role rather than promoting the welfare of the laboring class.

The labor strikes of the workers at Chosun Spinning and Weaving Company in **Pusan** in March 1952, followed by the dock workers' strike in Pusan in July, led the **National Assembly** to enact four labor laws: a labor standards law, a labor dispute mediation law, a labor commission law, and a labor union law. But strikes, and labor unions entering into separate negotiations with the management, were banned. Nonetheless, the growing labor unrest brought about the strikes of the workers at Taehan Spinning and Weaving Company in **Taegu** in May 1955 and February 1956, the cement factory workers in Samch'ok in December 1956, the workers at Chosun Spinning and Weaving Company in Pusan in January 1958, and the workers at the Taehan Shipbuilding Corporation in November 1958.

In October 1959, those who advocated the development of a pure and democratic labor movement formed a new National Council of Labor Unions (*Chon'guk Nodong Chohap Hyopuihoe*, or *Chon'guk Nohyop*) in Pusan, and brought about a labor strike at Chosun Spinning and Weaving Company in Pusan in March 1960. There followed the emergence of the **Korean Federation of Teachers' Labor Unions** (dissolved in May 1961), of primary and secondary school teachers and college professors in May 1960, and the establishment of the National Labor Union of Bank Employees in July. In order to unify the labor movement and strengthen it, in November 1960 the *Taehan Noch'ong* and the *Chon'guk Nohyop* merged into the **General Federation of Korean Labor Unions** (*Han'guk Nodong Chohap Ch'ongyonmaeng*, or *Han'guk Noryon*), which included 1,000 labor unions. It was dissolved following the **Military**

Revolution of 16 May 1961, but was reestablished in August 1961 as a new federation of labor unions commonly known as *Han'guk Noryon*, composed of some 1,035 separate trade unions. Meanwhile, in August 1961, the government established the Association of Agricultural **Cooperatives** (*Nongop Hyoptong Chohap*, or *Nonghyop*).

The **Supreme Council for National Reconstruction** revised the labor union law in December 1963, making labor unions self-supporting and restricting their activity. As before, strikes were banned. South Korean labor laws prohibited the development of a true labor movement, and as a result many unions went out of existence, reducing the number to 420 and the membership to 260,000 by 1965. The government tightened its control over the labor movement even more after 1965, further weakening it following a protest made by the *Han'guk Noryon* against the labor law and a wage dispute in the government monopoly industries (ginseng and tobacco) in December 1963.

The *Noryon* leaders made various efforts to bring about the revision of the labor law without much success. In November 1970, in a dramatic gesture of protest, Chun Tae-il, a labor leader demanding higher wages and improvement of working conditions, set himself alight and died. The incident was followed by violent labor strikes at the **Hyundai** shipyard in September 1974, that of the Tongil Spinning and Weaving Company in Pusan of February–March 1978, and that of the female workers of the YH Trading Company in **Seoul** in August 1979. Then in April 1980, some 700 coal mine workers at Sabuk and over 1,000 workers at Tongguk Steel Works in Pusan carried out violent strikes, demanding higher wages. Subsequently, some 500 disputes erupted until the declaration of martial law on 17 May 1980, when a large number of union leaders were purged.

During the Fifth Republic (1981–1988), the government continued suppressive measures against the labor movement, but beginning with the strike of the workers at Kuro Industrial Estate in 1985, labor unrest continued to grow with an increasing number of wage disputes. The watershed in the labor movement came in July and August 1987, immediately following the publication of the **June 29th democratization declaration** by the presidential candidate **Roh Tae-woo**. A strike that began at Hyundai Motors at **Ulsan** on 5 July 1987 was followed by some 3,200 strikes during the months of July

and August. The largest-ever number (3,749) of labor disputes occurred in 1987, some 3,500 of them after 29 June. This represented
18 times as many as there had been in the 12 years since 1975. After
June 1987, the number of unions increased from 2,658 to 4,086 in
1987, 6,142 in 1988 and 7,500 in 1989. The number of union members increased from 900,000 before 1987 to 1,800,000 in 1989.

The major issues in these disputes were those of wages and working conditions. In order to deal with the rapidly growing labor problems, the **National Assembly** adopted the new Labor Standard Law,
the Labor Union Law, and other laws concerning labor in October
1987. These laws allowed the formation of unions and simplified the
procedures for establishing a union. These developments led to the
establishment of a new General Federation of Korean Trade Unions
(*Han'guk Nodong Chohap Ch'ongyonmaeng, or Noch'ong* – FKTU).

Meanwhile, the government of the Fifth Republic in its twilight encouraged the establishment of labor-management councils for the better relations between the two. As a result, 6,596 such councils were established by the end of November 1987, reducing the number of labor
disputes to 1,686 in 1988 and 1,560 in 1989 following the establishment of the Sixth Republic in 1988. In order to reduce labor problems,
the National Assembly adopted a two-tiered Minimum Wage Law in
January 1988 and the Equality Law of Male and Female Employees,
effective 1 April, to ensure equal opportunity and equal treatment for
female workers. At the same time, labor wages rose by 10.1 percent in
1987, 15.5 percent in 1988, and 18.8 percent in 1989.

Radical labor leaders, who advocated the development of a genuine union movement, regarded the General Federation of Korean
Trade Unions as a government-manipulated organization. Consequently, they launched a "democratic labor movement." This led to
the emergence of the National Headquarters for Labor Law Reform
in 1988, and the National Council of Regional Trades Unions in
1989. In 1989, the latter organized the first workers' May Day rally
since the Japanese period. It also supported the establishment of a
new National Teachers' Union in 1989 despite the government ban
against the organization of such unions by schoolteachers. Radical labor leaders formed a new federation tentatively named **National
Council of Labor Unions** (*Chon'guk Nodong Chohap Hyopuihoe,
or Chonnohyop*) in January 1990. This eventually became the Korean

Confederation of Trade Unions (*Minju Noch'ang,* KCTU) in 1994. It claimed membership of 862 enterprise unions and 418,000 members. A year after its founding, it organized a General Strike in December 1996, in protest at the railroading through the National Assembly of bills including the National Security Agency Planning Act. It pressed for the legalization of all trade unions, a campaign that was eventually successful with the recognition of the teachers' union (*Chun'gy-ojo*) in 1999, the same year that the KCTU was also officially recognized by the government. Both the FKTU and the KCTU are affiliated to the International Labour Organisation (ILO). The South Korean government became a member of the ILO in 1991.

Korea's progress toward democracy in the 1990s led to a more sympathetic environment for labor activity. However, labor suffered a severe setback in 1997–1998, as a result of the economic crisis that hit the country in 1997. Unemployment rose dramatically; from 556,000 in 1997 to 1,436,000 in 1998. New legislation passed early in 1998 allowed massive layoffs and in other ways reduced employment security. Both wages and hours worked fell as the recession deepened.

The picture changed again as Korea came out of recession from late 1998 onward. Unemployment levels fell steadily, so that by mid-2001, numbers of unemployed were back at the level of December 1997, though some structural problems remained. Numbers of unions and members grew; by 2000, there were some 5,698 unions, with 1.52 million members, which represented about 12 percent of the workforce. Strikes were frequent, with the KCTU being generally more militant than the FKTU. Many disputes, however, were settled by arbitration. The government took active measures on a number of labor issues, including the formal introduction of a five-day week and protection for casual and part-time workers. Such moves were severely criticized by employers and by the opposition for giving too much power to the labor movement. *See also* KOREAN WORKERS' PARTY; WOMEN'S MOVEMENT.

LAND REFORM LAW. Promulgated on 12 June 1949, it provided for government purchase of all, except half an acre (0.2 hectares), of farmland not cultivated by the owners themselves and all holdings of more than 7.5 acres (3 hectares), irrespective of whether they were cultivated by the owners or not. Certain lands (special crop-growing areas such as orchards, sapling gardens, and mulberry trees) were exempt from the 7.5 acre limitation as were lands cultivated by religious and educational institutions. The government paid 150 percent of the current market price to the sellers, and sold the land to farmers at 125 percent of the current land price. Those who could not pay for the land could purchase on an installment plan, paying in cash or in crops.

The **Korean War** interrupted the land reform program, but it was completed in 1964. Some 25 million acres (10 million hectares) of farmlands were sold to the farmers who had little or no land. Whereas small farmers who sold land to the government received an additional 30 percent compensation, poor farmers who bought the land were given a 30 percent subsidy by the government. With the implementation of this law, traditional absentee landlordism was abolished.

LAW CONCERNING EXTRAORDINARY MEASURES FOR NATIONAL RECONSTRUCTION. This law, divided into four chapters and 22 articles followed by a supplementary provision, was promulgated on 6 June 1961. Chapter I dealt with the establishment of the **Supreme Council for National Reconstruction** "for the reconstruction of the Republic of Korea as a genuine, democratic republic, in order to safeguard the Republic of Korea against communist aggression, and to overcome the national crisis resulting from corruption, injustices, and poverty." It defined the council as having the status of the supreme ruling organ of the Republic, pending the establishment of a civilian government following the recomposition of the **National Assembly**. The basic rights of the citizens were allowed only when they did not conflict with the fulfillment of the tasks of the revolution.

Chapter II dealt with the composition of the Supreme Council, Chapter III dealt with the authority of the Supreme Council, and Chapter IV covered "miscellaneous provisions," including the methods of amendment to this law.

LAW CONCERNING PUNISHMENT OF THOSE WHO COMMITTED CRIMES AGAINST THE PEOPLE (*Panminjok haengi ch'obolbop*). Commonly known as the antitraitor law, this law was passed by the Constituent Assembly in September 1948, despite strong opposition from President **Syngman Rhee**. Its purpose was to seek out and punish those who were alleged to have collaborated with Japan between 1910 and 1945. It remains the only South Korean attempt to deal with the issue of collaboration by legal means.

Under the law, a Special Investigation Committee for Acts Against the People was established in October 1948, and it began work in January 1949. From the start, it continued to face opposition from Rhee and from those who had, for whatever reason, worked with the Japanese **Government-General in Korea**. In June 1949, the **police** ransacked its offices, and all members of the investigative committee resigned the following month. Although a new more compliant committee was appointed, the Constituent Assembly abolished the law and the committee in August 1949.

The committee investigated 682 cases. Of these, 559 were referred to the prosecutor's office, but only in 221 cases were any charges laid, and only 38 cases went to court. Twelve were given prison sentences, five of them suspended. There was one life sentence and one death sentence. The death sentence was not carried out, and by the outbreak of the **Korean War** in June 1950, all those concerned had been released.

LAW CONCERNING THE RESTRICTION OF THE CIVIL LIBERTIES OF THOSE WHO COMMITTED ANTIDEMOCRATIC ACTS. This law No. 587, of 31 December 1960, was adopted by the **National Assembly** to deprive those who performed "notably anti-democratic acts" prior to 26 April 1960 of their civil rights. Many political leaders (most of whom were supporters of disgraced President **Syngman Rhee**'s **Liberal Party**), **police** officers, and high military personnel who were investigated, lost their civil rights as a result.

LEAGUE FOR THE PROTECTION OF WOMEN'S RIGHTS. *See* WOMEN'S MOVEMENT.

LEE HOI-CHANG (1935–). Born in South Hwanghae province (now in **North Korea**), in 1935, Lee grew up in South Korea. He graduated in law from **Seoul** National University in 1957. He spent many years as a judge in **Inch'on** and Seoul, becoming in 1981 the youngest-ever Supreme Court judge at the age of 46. In 1988, Lee was appointed head of the **Central Election Management Committee**. In 1993, he became prime minister under President **Kim Young-sam**. However, he found the position lacked power, and he resigned in 1994, returning to his law practice. In 1996, he entered the **National Assembly** as a member of the ruling **New Korea Party** (NKP). The following year, he became the party's chairman.

Following the creation of the **Grand National Party** (GNP) by the merger of the NKP and the **Democratic Party**, Lee was the new party's candidate in the 1997 presidential election. However, he failed to beat **Kim Dae-jung** by a narrow margin. He remained at the head of the GNP, pursuing a conservative agenda against the reforming government of Kim Dae-jung. In particular, Lee and his party expressed much skepticism about Kim's policy toward North Korea. Although he had a personal reputation for being incorrupt, there was some scandal surrounding the circumstance in which neither of his sons had done military service. Lee was again the GNP's candidate for president in 2002, and was widely expected to win, especially given the party's success in other elections.

To widespread surprise, however, he again failed, loosing to **Roh Moo-hyun**. Following this defeat, Lee resigned from the GNP (and from politics) in December 2002, and in February 2003, announced that he would spend a year at Stanford University in the United States.

LEE HU-RAK (1924–). Lee was born in **Pusan** in 1924, and served as a noncommissioned officer in the Japanese army during the colonial period. After liberation, he attended the South Korean Military Academy. From 1963–70, he was private secretary to President **Park Chung-hee**. Lee was briefly ambassador to Tokyo in 1970, but that same year, he became director-general of the Korean Central Intelligence Agency (KCIA, now the **National Intelligence Service**). In this capacity, he visited **North Korea** twice in 1972, thus beginning Park's dialogue with the North. However, in 1973, Lee was blamed for the KCIA's attempt to kidnap the opposition leader, **Kim Dae-jung**, in **Japan**, and resigned as director-general on health grounds. He then disappeared from view, resurfacing in 1978 as an independent member of the **National Assembly**. When **Chun Doo-hwan**

came to power in 1979, Lee was one of those purged from politics, after being accused of embezzlement. *See also* NORTH KOREA–SOUTH KOREA RELATIONS.

LEGISLATIVE COUNCIL FOR NATIONAL SECURITY (LCNS). Shortly after the public referendum on a new **constitution** in October 1980, an 81-member Legislative Council for National Security, whose members were appointed by President **Chun Doo-hwan**, replaced the **National Assembly**. It served as the legislative arm of the Special Committee for National Security Measures, and after adopting various crucial laws, including the revised **National Security Laws** which incorporated the **Anti-Communism Law**, and following the general elections for the National Assembly on 25 March 1981, the LCNS was dissolved on 31 March.

LIBERAL PARTY (*Minjudang*). Two pro-**Syngman Rhee** conservative political groups emerged in December 1951, each calling itself the Liberal Party. One was based in the **National Assembly** members, and the other belonged to those outside the assembly. However, in March 1952, these two were united into a single Liberal Party, exercising enormous power in collusion with the Rhee administration. The united party elected Rhee as its president and **Yi Pom-suk** as its vice president.

The Liberal Party was crippled when the **April 1960 Student Uprising** occurred, and after the fall of the First Republic it barely maintained its existence. Following the **Military Revolution of 16 May 1961**, it was dissolved. In January 1963, the party was reestablished under the leadership of **Chang T'aek-sang**. It made no attempt to win the presidency in the 1963 and 1967 presidential elections. Its members ran for the National Assembly, but all failed to win seats.

LIM WON-SIK (1919–2002). A major figure on the modern South Korean musical scene, Lim was a conductor who studied in **Japan** before attending the Julliard School of Music in the **United States**. In 1946, he established the Koryo Symphony Orchestra, the first postliberation orchestra. He created the Korean Broadcasting System (KBS) Orchestra in 1956, and served as its resident conductor until 1971. He was later appointed honorary conductor of the orchestra.

Lim became the **Inch'on** Symphony Orchestra's principal conductor in 1984, a post he held until 1992. During the **Korean War**, he was a founder of the **Seoul** Arts School, in **Pusan**, and was later its principal from 1961–1975. Although Lim was devoted to the German classical composers, he introduced much modern music to Korean audiences as well. He also defended his fellow musician, **Yun I-san**, and tried to arrange for his return to South Korea.

LOCAL AUTONOMY. Although Articles 96 and 97 of the July 1948 **Constitution** stated that local autonomy would be operated under local assemblies, President **Syngman Rhee** was reluctant to proceed with its implementation. Instead, Rhee decided to appoint all provincial governors and the mayor of the Special City of **Seoul**. However, on 17 June 1949, the **National Assembly** adopted the local autonomy bill (revised in December), and elections for the establishment of local governments and their councils were planned for December 1950.

The 1949 law governing local autonomous organizations specified that the mayor of Seoul and provincial governors were to be appointed by the president; mayors of other cities, chiefs of towns and townships were to be elected by respective local councils; and provincial councils, councils of Seoul and other cities, and of towns and townships were to be established by direct elections of the inhabitants. County chiefs were to be appointed by governors in the respective provinces. Limited elections were conducted in 1950 in Seoul and one other city, three towns, and 140 townships in northern districts.

Because of the **Korean War**, it was not until spring 1952 that elections for autonomous organizations of provinces, cities, towns, and townships were held in the rest of South Korea. The local autonomy law was revised twice in 1956 abolishing the previous system of indirect election of mayors of cities, towns, and chiefs of townships. However, the system of appointment of the mayor of Seoul and provincial governors was retained. Under the revised law, elections were held in August 1956 to elect new councilors of all municipalities, including Seoul, provinces, towns, and townships as well as heads of local governmental units, except the mayor of Seoul. Fearing the election of Rhee's opponents in the forthcoming local elections in August 1960, in December 1958 the Rhee administration and its ally, the **Liberal Party**, engineered the railroading of an amendment to the local autonomy bill whereby provincial governors, mayors of municipalities and towns, as well as chiefs of townships were to be appointed by the central government. With this, any chance for the development of genuine local autonomy was destroyed.

The amended local autonomy law went into effect in January 1959. In February and May that year, the central government appointed all provincial governors, the mayor of Seoul and other cities, and county chiefs. The county chiefs in turn appointed township heads while mayors of cities appointed ward chiefs. Local councils could only elect the chiefs of the precincts in small cities, towns, and townships. Under such a system, local government bodies enjoyed little or no independence. Their financial situation did not allow them to promote local autonomy while the control of the central government increased. The bureau of political affairs of the Ministry of Home Affairs controlled virtually all local affairs, including the allocation of grants in aid and the collection of local taxes and fees.

The short-lived Second Republic took measures to establish meaningful local autonomy under the amended Constitution. Thus, it enacted in November 1960 a new local autonomy law, and elections for new councils of Seoul, provinces, cities, towns, and townships were held in early December. The elections for mayors of cities, excluding Seoul, and chiefs of towns and townships were then held, followed by the elections for the mayor of Seoul and provincial governors at the end of December. The **Military Revolution of 16 May 1961** "temporarily" suspended the local autonomy law, abolishing all local councils. However, Article 110 of the 1963 Constitution stated that "The local government authority shall have a council," while Article 109 stated that "The local government authorities shall deal with matters pertaining to the welfare of local residents, manage properties, and may establish, within the limit of laws and ordinances, rules and regulations regarding local government." In spite of these provisions, the central government of the Third Republic steadfastly refused to reestablish local councils and hold elections to elect local government heads on the grounds that the local areas in South Korea did not have financial self-sufficiency to institute true local autonomy.

Undoubtedly, the real reason for the central government's attitude was its unwillingness to decentralize power. Chapter X of the Constitution of the Fourth Republic, amended and approved in a national referendum in November 1972, retained those features regarding local autonomy included in the Constitution amended in 1963, but it decided to postpone the restoration of local autonomy "until reunification" was achieved. **Chun Doo-hwan**'s Fifth Republic made no attempt to restore local autonomy.

It was the Sixth Republic that began the process of reestablishing local autonomy. In December 1990, the National Assembly enacted three laws related to local autonomy. Accordingly, President **Roh Tae-woo** announced in early March 1991 that elections for councils of small districts (small cities, counties, towns and townships, and wards in cities) would be held in late March, and that elections for councils of large districts (six special cities and nine provinces) would be held in June.

In the 26 March 1991 elections for small district councils, 10,102 candidates from 3,562 electoral districts ran for 4,304 council seats. In these elections, the new ruling **Democratic Liberal Party** (DLP) won a total of 2,142 seats whereas its major opponent, the **Party for Peace and Democracy** (PPD), won only 785 seats, and another minor party won only 33 seats. Some 1,343 seats were won by Independents. In the large district council elections conducted on 20 June, 2,873 candidates ran for 866 seats in six special cities and nine provincial councils. As was the case of small district council elections, the ruling DLP won victory when 564 of its candidates were elected while only 165 of the **New Democratic Party** (a party that emerged in April when the PPD and the **New Democratic Alliance** were united) won. Only 21 New Democratic Party candidates and one **Masses Party** candidate were successful. Some 115 Independents won council seats in all areas, except Seoul and **Pusan**.

In both these elections, the voters showed marked disinterest. In the small district council elections, 13.2 million (55.9 percent) of 24 million eligible voters cast their ballots. Only 42.3 percent of eligible voters in Seoul cast their ballots in ward council elections. In the elections for large district councils (municipal councils of the special cities of Seoul, Pusan, **Taegu**, **Kwangju**, **Inch'on**, and **Taejon** and nine provincial councils), 16.5 million (58.9 percent) of 28 million eligible voters cast their ballots. In Seoul 52.4 percent of the eligible voters participated in the elections for the Seoul Municipal Council.

Complete local autonomy was still not achieved. In May 1992, the mayoral and gubernatorial elections due in mid-1992 were postponed because of "financial constraints." These elections were finally held in June 1995, the first time that local government moved out of central control since 1948. The 1995 elections were followed by the second comprehensive local elections in June 1998. From 1998 onward, local elections were scheduled to take place every five years. Local autonomy has not been without its critics, who allege that it encourages regionalism and favoritism. In November 2000, for example, a group of lawmakers from the ruling and opposition parties proposed, unsuccessfully, a return to the appointment system. This move was fiercely opposed by many of those involved in local government.

In theory, local governments have a wide range of functions, including property management, provision of local services, assessment and collection of local taxes and fees, and some responsibility for **education**. In practice, Central government still retains considerable powers over local governments, and seeks to control them. Thus the ministry of Government Administration and Home Affairs carried out a major reform of local government staff matters in 2000.

LONG-TERM PRISONERS, REPATRIATION OF. In February 1999, South Korea's president, **Kim Dae-jung** released the world's longest serving political prisoner, 71-year-old Woo Yong-gak, an alleged North Korean spy, and 16 other North Korean prisoners. These were either people captured during the post–**Korean War** guerilla campaigns in South Korea, or spies from **North Korea**. They had all refused to admit their alleged crimes and had therefore remained in detention.

Although released from prison, they were not allowed to go to North Korea, as they demanded. In August 2000, following the historic **June 2000 Inter-Korean Summit** meeting in **P'yongyang** between Kim Dae-jung and the North Korean leader, **Kim Jong-il**, the South Korean government allowed a number of these long-term prisoners to return to North Korea. On their return to North Korea, they were decorated and acclaimed as heroes. They were provided with apartments, and for those who wished it, spouses.

There was some criticism in the South of the decision to free them, on the grounds that they should have been used as bargaining chips to obtain the release of a number of South Koreans who have allegedly been abducted by North Korea over the years.

– M –

MACARTHUR, DOUGLAS (1880–1964). Douglas MacArthur, general of the army from 1944, commander-in-chief of the **United States** forces in the Pacific at the end of World War II, was appointed supreme commander for the allied powers in **Japan** after the Japanese surrender in 1945. Following the outbreak of the **Korean War** in June 1950, U.S. President Harry S. Truman appointed him commander of the **United Nations Command** (UNC). On 14 July 1950, South Korea's President **Syngman Rhee** also put the South Korean armed forces under MacArthur's command.

In September 1950, MacArthur planned and executed "Operation Chromite," whereby **United Nations forces** captured the port city of **Inch'on**, opening the way for the recapture of the South Korean capital, **Seoul**, and for the crossing of the **38th parallel** into **North Korea**. Meeting little opposition, the UNC swept north, with MacArthur discounting rumors that **China** would intervene if the UN forces approached the Yalu River. When Chinese forces did intervene in November 1950, MacArthur panicked and demanded that the war be extended to China. This was refused, and under General **Matthew Ridgeway**, who was given battlefield command in Korea, the line of battle stabilized around the 38th parallel, although a war of movement would continue until mid-1951.

By then MacArthur had been dismissed for insubordination. He had privately criticized the decision not to attack China, and in a public letter in April 1951 called for the use of Chinese Nationalist forces from Taiwan against the Chinese mainland. As a result he was relieved of his command on 11 April, and Ridgeway took over.

After retirement, MacArthur continued to blame those he believed had prevented him from winning the war in Korea. In South Korea, he is remembered as the savior of the country, and a statue of him stands on Freedom Hill in Inch'on.

MARINE CORPS. Established in April 1949 and patterned after that of the United States Marines, this corps played a crucial role in the **Military Revolution of 16 May 1961**. In October 1973, it was disbanded and incorporated into the South Korean navy but in November 1987, the Marine Corps regained its former status as a separate entity within the South Korean **national defense forces**.

MASAN. This is a major industrial and port city in South Kyongsang province, originally opened for foreign trade in 1899, but closed in 1908 because it was close to a fortified naval zone. It was reopened as a port in 1967 and has developed rapidly since then. It was the scene of massive student rioting in 1980. Its population is about 500,000.

"MASSACRES OF THE MASS MEDIA." In October–November 1980, under pressure exerted by the **Defense Security Command**, the **Special Committee for National Security Measures** forced the publishers of newspapers and magazines to dismiss 298 journalists and bring about "voluntary resignation" of some 635 others who were deemed to have defied the ruling party and the government. They were also forced to accept a series of compulsory closures and mergers.

Part of the *Tong-a Ilbo* group was taken over by the pro-government *Kyonghyang Daily News*. The measures also affected **broadcasting**. The government-run Korean Broadcasting System (KBS) radio and TV absorbed the Tongyang and the Tong-a radio-TV broadcasting systems as well as three others, leaving only two (KBS and the Munwha Broadcasting Corporation) radio-TV broadcasting systems and one (Christian) radio broadcasting system in operation. Several local newspapers were either abolished or forced to merge with other progovernment presses. The two national news agencies, Hapdong News Agency and Orient Press, were merged to form **Yonhap News Agency**. *See also* CENSORSHIP; DECONTROL OF THE PRESS.

MASSES PARTY (*Minjungdang*). In May 1965, the **Democratic Party** of **Pak Sun-ch'on** and the **Civil Rule Party** merged, forming the Masses Party, playing a key role as an opposition party. In February 1967, this party united with the **New Korean Party** to form the **New Democratic Party** with **Yu Chin-o** as its president.

MASSES (PEOPLE'S) PARTY (*Minjungdang*). This left-of-center party was formed in November 1990 with Yi Wu-jae as its leader. It was organized by former members of the **Committee to Promote a Democratic Coalition** who refused to become associated with the regionally based **Party for Peace and Democracy** (PPD) of **Kim Dae-jung** when the leaders of the committee advocated its merger with the PPD.

MILITARY ARMISTICE COMMISSION (MAC). The Military Armistice Commission owes its origins to the **Korean Armistice Agreement** signed on 27 July 1953, which ended the **Korean War**. It was composed of five officers on each side from **North Korea** and **China** on the one hand, and the **United Nations Command** (UNC) on the other, of which three on each side should be of general rank, to deal with issues related to violations of the neutrality of the **demilitarized zone (DMZ)** or territorial rights of North and South Korea by another party.

A conference building for the MAC was erected at **P'anmunjom**, where the armistice was signed and designated as a free zone. The conference building is half located in the northern side and half in the southern side of the **military demarcation line**. A table covered with green cloth in the center of the conference room straddles the border. The MAC is a joint organization with no chair, and is supported by a secretariat and 10 joint observer teams.

During the Cultural Revolution in China (1966–1976), the Chinese representatives withdrew; however, they returned in the 1970s. In March 1991, the UN side appointed a South Korean general to replace the American head of the UNC members on the Commission. **North Korea** refused to recognize such a change, charging that South Korea had no right to represent the UNC because it had not signed the armistice agreement. As a result of this move, the 460th meeting that was due to take place on 29 May 1992 failed to materialize.

In 1994, the North Korean side announced that it was withdrawing from the MAC, and persuaded the Chinese to make a similar announcement. However, in June 1998, the North Koreans agreed to resume general officer-level meetings at P'anmunjom, providing that an American officer headed the UNC side. The full MAC has not met since 1991.

MILITARY DEMARCATION LINE. The boundary between the opposing forces drawn up along the line of actual control when the **Korean Armistice Agreement** was signed on 27 July 1953, ending the

Korean War. The 150-mile (240 kilometer) line runs a course from sea to sea. A 1.5-mile (2.4 kilometer) wide **demilitarized zone** (DMZ) was established on each side of the line, and the small hamlet named **P'anmunjom** on the line, where the armistice negotiations had taken place after being moved from **Kaesong**, was designated as a "truce village."

The armistice agreement made no mention of a boundary at sea. On the east coast, the line is simply projected out into the **East Sea/Sea of Japan**, which has caused few problems. On the west coast, however, soon after the armistice, the **United Nations Command** introduced unilaterally a maritime division line, which became known as the "Northern Limit Line" that ran north of the logical extension of the MDL. This was designed to secure important fishing grounds for South Korean fishermen, and to ease access to certain South Korean controlled islands. Although such an extension had no legal force, and is rejected by **North Korea**, South Korea has insisted that this is a legal boundary. There have been frequent clashes between the South and North Korean navies in the area, especially during the crab fishing season in May–June.

MILITARY REVOLUTION OF 16 MAY 1961. As early as February 1960, young army officers, under the leadership of Major General **Park Chung-hee**, then logistic base commander in **Pusan**, formulated a plan to carry out a coup. This group included Major General Yi Chu-il, chief of staff of the Second Army, Major General Kim Tong-ha, commander of the Marine Corps, Lieutenant Colonel Kim Chong-ch'ol, commander of the 33rd Anti-Aircraft Artillery Battalion, and Lieutenant Colonel **Kim Jong-p'il** of the Army Headquarters G-2. They decided to stage the coup on 8 May 1960, three days after the scheduled departure of Army Chief of Staff General Song Yo-ch'an for a visit to the **United States**.

The plan adopted by this disgruntled and rebellious group, which was dominated by the 8th graduating class of the Korean Military Academy (1949), included the following demands:

1. Punishment of top military officers who collaborated with the **Liberal Party** in rigging the 1960 presidential elections.
2. Punishment of military officers who amassed wealth illegally.
3. Elimination of incompetent and corrupt commanders.

4. Establishment of political neutrality of the armed forces and elimination of factionalism within the armed forces.
5. Improvement of treatment for military servicemen.

The planners were particularly unhappy with three things: politicization of the armed forces, particularly the army; incompetent generals who occupied top army posts and blocked the advancement of younger army officers (mostly of the rank of colonel); and corrupt and illegal means by which these top-ranking army generals enriched themselves.

The **April 1960 Student Uprising** interrupted their plan. After the fall of the First Republic, the group decided to wait and see how the new president, **Yun Po-son**, and the new **Chang Myon** administration would handle domestic problems, including the problem that existed within the military establishments. They were disappointed, although they were able to pressure army chief of staff General Song to resign in May 1960, as well as obtain the resignation of the new army chief of staff, Lieutenant General Ch'oe Yong-hui, who had replaced General Song. The appointment of Lieutenant General **Chang To-yong** in early 1961 as army chief of staff did not fully satisfy the core group of revolutionaries whose number had grown to some 250 officers. The planners of the military revolution succeeded in securing the pledge of many commanders of various units of the army, as well as those of the **Marine Corps** before they launched the revolution.

In the predawn hours of 16 May 1961, 1,600 troops, spearheaded by the Marines, struck and seized key government buildings, banks, the Metropolitan **Police** headquarters, and communications centers. Some 2,000 more troops entered the city, putting **Seoul** under siege. On 16 May, the Military Revolutionary Committee (MCR) quickly formed from a handful of generals, declared martial law, along with a **curfew** from 1900 to 0500. It froze all banks, closed airports and harbors, placed the media under strict **censorship**, and forbade assembly. At the same time, it dissolved both houses of the **National Assembly** as well as provincial councils.

Although both President Yun and General Chang To-yong were urged by the Americans to launch a counterrevolution in cooperation with American troops, they did not wish to bring about possible large-scale bloodshed by doing so, for they believed that many army commanders were behind the revolution. They were also keenly mindful of the ever-present threat from **North Korea**. Moreover, it was the opinion of President Yun that, although a military revolution was not desirable, it was perhaps inevitable in view of the domestic situation. Had they followed American advice, there is no doubt that it would have resulted in a civil war. General Yi Han-lim, commander of the First Army Corps, which was stationed near Seoul, could have mobilized at least three divisions under his command against the revolutionaries, but he did not, although he himself was not a member of the core group of the revolutionaries. In the late afternoon of 17 May, his headquarters announced that General Yi supported the revolution.

The plotters succeeded in persuading President Yun to remain in office and he approved the declaration of martial law. At the same time, they persuaded General Chang to join and lead the revolution. Chang, with the idea of controlling and leading the revolutionaries so as to preserve the constitutional system, accepted the chairmanship of the Military Revolutionary Committee on 18 May. That same day, Premier Chang returned to Seoul from his hiding place, and held his last cabinet meeting, submitting the resignation of cabinet members en masse, ending the Second Republic. Meanwhile, also on 18 May, the Military Revolutionary Committee issued its six pledges of military revolution.

Efforts made by General Chang brought about the American recognition on 19 May of the military takeover as a *fait accompli*. Following this, on 6 June, the revolutionaries promulgated the **Law Concerning Extraordinary Measures for National Reconstruction**, and the next day, they renamed the MRC the **Supreme Council for National Reconstruction** (SCNR) as the nation's supreme governing organ. All administrative, judicial, and legislative functions were now in the hands of the 30-member SCNR. It appointed the head of the cabinet (prime minister), who in turn appointed cabinet members with the approval of the SCNR. The judicial branch was also placed under the control of the members of the SCNR, as were the armed forces. The SCNR functioned as a legislative organ as well. Thus, the junta rule began.

MILITARY REVOLUTIONARY COMMITTEE. *See* SUPREME COUNCIL FOR NATIONAL RECONSTRUCTION.

MILLENNIUM DEMOCRATIC PARTY (MDP, *Minjudang*, or *Saechonyonminjudang*). In 1999, **Kim Dae-jung**'s party, the **National Congress for New Politics** renamed itself the Millennium Democratic Party, or MDP. Although its formal Korean name included Millennium in the title, in fact most Koreans saw it and referred to it as the *Minjudang* or **Democratic Party**, thus emphasizing the continuation of the opposition tradition. The party selected **Roh Moo-hyun** as its candidate in the 2002 presidential elections, where he beat **Lee Hoi-chang**. In autumn 2003, the MDP split, and thus ceased to be the official ruling party.

MONETARY SYSTEM. Until the establishment of the Japanese **Government-General of Korea** in 1910, Korean currency consisted solely of coins. During the colonial period, the Bank of Chosen issued various notes, and these continued in use, together with **United States** dollars, under the **United States Army Military Government in Korea** after liberation from **Japan** in 1945.

Following the establishment of the Republic of Korea in 1948, the **Bank of Korea** replaced all colonial era monies. The smallest unit was a copper coin called *chon*, and 100 *chon* equaled one *won* (paper money). There were five, 10, and 50 *chon* coins. In February 1953, a monetary reform replaced the *won* currency by the *hwan* currency at the rate of 100 *won* to one *hwan*. In June 1962, the second monetary reform was implemented, returning to the *won* system at the rate of 10 *hwan* to one *won*, and new paper monies of larger monetary units were issued by the Bank of Korea. The *chon* has long since ceased to be used.

MOON SUN-MYONG (1920–). Charismatic founder of the **T'ongilgyo** or Unification Church (popularly known as the "Moonies"), who was born in **North Korea**. At 16, he claimed that he had a divine mission to reform the Christian Church; he would later claim to be the younger brother of Jesus Christ. His religious activities around **P'yongyang** led to his imprisonment by the communists in 1945. Released by the UN forces in 1950, he fled to South Korea.

In 1954, he organized the Unification Church in the **Pusan** area, and by 1959, he was able to send the church's first missionary overseas.

Thereafter, the Unification Church's main strength was overseas, and Moon moved to the **United States** in the 1970s, later leaving after being charged with tax evasion during the **Koreagate** affair. Moon was staunchly anticommunist and provided support for South Korea under President **Park Chung-hee**, but even in South Korea, there has been concern over his church's recruiting methods and business practices. Later South Korean presidents have tended to keep Moon and the Unification Church at a distance, although sometimes using the church's cultural groups, such as the Little Angels dance troupe, for formal entertainment. During the 1990s, and despite his earlier anticommunism, Moon became a frequent visitor to North Korea, where the Unification Church has a number of business interests.

MOSCOW AGREEMENT. To deal with the postwar problems among the Allies, the foreign ministers of the **United States**, **Great Britain**, and the **Soviet Union/Russia** met in Moscow from 16–26 December 1945. Regarding Korea, they reached the following agreement, which was made public on 28 December:

1. To set up a provisional Korean democratic government;
2. In order to do so, a **Joint United States–Soviet Commission on Trusteeship** drawn from the U.S. and the Soviet occupation authorities in Korea would be established, and this commission, in consultation with Korean democratic parties and social organizations, should establish a provisional Korean government; and
3. A four-power trusteeship of the U.S., **China**, Great Britain and the Soviet Union should oversee Korean affairs for a period of up to five years following the establishment of a Korean government and the national independence of Korea.

When news of this agreement reached Korea, there was an outpouring of opposition from all political groups to the continued division of the peninsula and to the postponement of national independence.

MOUNT KUMGANG TOURS. During 1998, the veteran South Korean economic leader, **Chung Ju-yung** of the **Hyundai** group, reached agreement with the North Korean authorities for tourist visits from South Korea to the Kumgang (Diamond) Mountains in

North Korea. The Kumgang Mountains have long been famed for their natural beauty. Tours began in November 1998, and by November 1999, some 140,000 South Koreans had been to the Kumgang Mountains.

The tours continued despite clashes between the North and South Korean navies in the West Sea in June 1999 over the Northern Limit Line, and the detention for five days, also in June 1999, of a South Korean tourist. At the end of 1999, the tours were opened to some non-Korean participants. According to published statistics, the Hyundai Group lost over U.S.$257 million in the first year of operation, and continued to lose heavily thereafter. But it was widely believed that the South Korean government had tacitly underwritten the venture as a means of furthering the **"sunshine policy"** of President **Kim Dae-jung.**

MURDER OF RIOT POLICE. On 3 May 1989, when riot **police** invaded the campus of Tongui University in **Pusan** to break up a large and violent antigovernment student demonstration, the rioting students confined some of the police in a corridor, and then doused them in flammable liquid, which they set on fire. Seven police officers died and six others were badly burned. Seventy-one students were arrested, and in October 1989, one was sentenced to life imprisonment. Thirty others were given various prison terms. About half of them were released on suspended sentences. The incident proved to be a major setback for the **student movement**, which took some time to recover from public hostility to such a use of violence.

– N –

NAEWOE NEWS AGENCY. The Naewoe ("Home and Abroad") News Agency was a South Korean government-affiliated organization, established in the mid-1970s. Its task was to publish information and analysis about **North Korea** from a South Korean perspective, which it did in books and in journals such as the monthly *Vantage Point: Developments in North Korea*. From 1996, it has also been available via the **Internet**. Its products became less partisan since the late 1980s, and are often a useful source of information on North Korea. On 1 January

1999, Naewoe merged with the **Yonhap News Agency**. This continues to produce the same materials, but no longer uses the Naewoe imprint for its monthly summary of developments in North Korea. It also announced that it will charge for Naewoe publications, hitherto often distributed for free as part of the government's propaganda effort.

NATIONAL ALLIANCE FOR DEMOCRACY AND UNIFICATION (*Minjujuui minjok t'ong'il chon'guk yonhap* or *Chon'guk yonhap*). An alliance of radical opposition groups, organized on 1 December 1991. It included some 21 radical organizations. It advocated "the rejection of interference of outside (foreign) powers, the winning of the autonomy of the people, and the establishment of a democratic government." *See also* NATIONAL COALITION FOR A PEOPLE'S DEMOCRATIC MOVEMENT; NATIONAL COUNCIL OF FARMERS' UNIONS; NATIONAL COUNCIL OF REPRESENTATIVES OF UNIVERSITY STUDENTS; NATIONAL TEACHERS' UNION.

NATIONAL ANTHEM. *See* AN IK-T'AE.

NATIONAL ASSEMBLY. The National Assembly of the Republic of Korea emerged as a unicameral Constituent Assembly in June 1948, following the 10 May general elections under the supervision and sponsorship of the **United Nations Temporary Commission on Korea** (UNTCOK). Of the 300-member assembly, 198 were elected from mainland South Korea, each representing 100,000 constituents. Two more members were elected from **Cheju Island** later in May 1949 when the rebellion on that island was subjugated. One hundred seats allocated for **North Korea** were left vacant.

The members of the Constituent Assembly were elected for a two-year term of office, and the assembly opened on 31 May 1949. It elected Dr. **Syngman Rhee** as chairman, and on 12 July, it adopted the **Constitution** of the Republic of Korea. In accordance with the Constitution, Rhee was elected as president and **Yi Si-yong** as vice president for four-year terms of office. Thus, the Constituent Assembly acted as a legislative assembly, as well as an electoral college.

In May 1950, the second general elections were held, a new legislative National Assembly of 210 members was established, and the term of office of each assemblyman was extended to four years. It remained a single-house legislature until July 1960, when, with a **con-**

stitutional amendment, a bicameral legislature was established with the **House of Councilors** as the upper house and the **House of Representatives** as the lower house. Following the **Military Revolution of 16 May 1961**, the Assembly was dissolved.

It was reestablished in November 1963 as a unicameral legislative assembly. The seventh constitutional amendment of 1972 introduced a new system of legislative assembly, whereby 73 of its 219 members, or one-third of its total membership, were appointed by the newly established **National Conference for Unification** upon the nomination of the president. Thus, the 9th, 10th, and 11th National Assemblies had one-third of the total number of seats occupied by members of the **Yujonghoe** (Political Fraternal Society for Revitalizing Reform), a political group closely associated with the ruling **Democratic Republican Party**. With the fall of the Fourth Republic in 1979, this system was abolished.

In October 1980, the National Assembly was again dissolved, replaced by the **Legislative Council for National Security** whose members were appointed by the president. When the Fifth Republic emerged in March 1981, the new National Assembly Election Law stipulated that 184 of the 276-member National Assembly were to be popularly elected from 184 electoral districts, and the remaining 92 seats (proportional representation) were to be distributed among parties winning five seats or more in the National Assembly according to the age of the number of candidates each party elected in the direct election. The National Assembly Law was revised after the proclamation of the Constitution of the Sixth Republic. According to the new law, 224 members of the 299-member National Assembly were to be elected through popular vote, and the remaining 75 seats were to be proportionally distributed among parties winning five or more seats.

The National Assembly has one speaker, two vice-speakers, 16 standing committees, and a secretariat. It holds one regular session per year (up to 100 days), extraordinary sessions (up to 30 days), and occasional special sessions requested by the president. The 16th National Assembly elections were held on 13 April 2000. The next National Assembly elections will be held in April 2004.

NATIONAL ASSEMBLY SPY RING CASE. In May–June 1949, Kim Yak-su, No Ik-hwan, and eight other **National Assembly** members were arrested in connection with an alleged conspiracy in collaboration with communists, most of whom were underground members of the **South Korean Workers' Party**. The accusation was based on their advocacy of the withdrawal of **United States troops in South Korea** and negotiations with **North Korea** for national reunification. On 10 February 1950, they were given prison terms of between four and 12 years for violating the **National Security Laws**.

NATIONAL CEMETERY. Originally designed for those killed in the **Korean War**, this cemetery is situated on the south bank of the Han River in **Seoul**. It contains an impressive memorial to the Korean War dead, the tombs of former presidents including **Syngman Rhee** and **Park Chung-hee**, and a section devoted to those killed under the Japanese. Those of President **Chun Doo-hwan**'s advisors and cabinet members killed in the 1983 **Rangoon bomb attack** are buried together in an area reserved for meritorious civilians.

NATIONAL COALITION FOR A DEMOCRATIC CONSTITUTION. A loose alliance formed in June 1987, to protest at the attempts by President **Chun Doo-hwan** to prolong the military dominance of the South Korean political scene. As an umbrella organization of the opposition intellectuals and religious leaders, it provided a leadership for popular opposition outside the established opposition parties.

NATIONAL COALITION FOR A PEOPLE'S DEMOCRATIC MOVEMENT. Formed in January 1989 by some 200 dissident social, labor, and religious organizations, it launched a new grassroots democratization movement and struggle against dictatorship and foreign influence under the slogan "Social Movement in an Age of Masses."

NATIONAL CONFERENCE FOR UNIFICATION. An electoral college established in December 1972 under the revised, or **Yushin rule, constitution** of 1972. Its members, not less than 2,000 and no more than 5,000, were to be popularly elected. In 1972, 2,359 members were popularly elected. Under the revised constitution of 1980 a new 5,278-member **Presidential Electoral College** replaced it in February 1981. When the revised constitution was approved in a national referendum in October 1987, the electoral colleges were replaced by direct presidential elections from December 1987.

NATIONAL CONGRESS FOR NEW POLITICS (NCNP). Party founded by veteran opposition leader, **Kim Dae-jung**, on his return from self-imposed exile in **Great Britain** in 1993. This was the vehicle that brought Kim to the presidency in 1997. In 2000, the party changed its name to the **Millennium Democratic Party**.

NATIONAL COUNCIL FOR RAPID REALIZATION OF KOREAN INDEPENDENCE (*Tongnip ch'oksong kungmin hyopuihoe*, or *Tokch'ok*). On 25 October 1945, 50 right-wing political and social organizations formed this council, with Dr. **Syngman Rhee** as its head. Its purpose was to launch a united movement to end the Allied occupation as quickly as possible and restore Korean national independence. However, many moderate nationalists, as well as moderate and radical leftist organizations, declined to join the council.

NATIONAL COUNCIL OF KOREAN WOMEN'S ORGANIZATIONS. A body formed in 1959 by some 64 women's societies to strengthen the campaign for full women's rights in Korea. It became a major factor in the **Women's Movement**.

NATIONAL COUNCIL OF LABOR UNIONS (*Chon'guk Nodong Chohap P'yonguihoe*, or *Chonp'yong*). Formed in November 1945 by leftist groups, following the emergence of the **labor movement** after August 1945, this council included some 500,000 members belonging to various trade unions. Following a railway strike in October 1946 and a general strike of laborers in November 1947, the movement declined under the suppressive measures taken by the **United States Army Military Government in Korea** against violent, illegal labor movements, and it was closed down in June 1948.

NATIONAL COUNCIL OF LABOR UNIONS (*Chon'gak Nodong Chohap Hyopuihoe*). In October 1959, progressive labor leaders formed this council for the purpose of promoting a more efficient and moderate **labor movement** in South Korea. However, in November 1960 it was forced to merge with the **General Federation of Korean Labor Unions**.

NATIONAL COUNCIL OF LABOR UNIONS (*Chon'guk Nodong Chohap Hyopuihoe*, or *Chonnohyop*). An organization of radical labor unions formed in late January 1990. Some 190,000 members belonging to 600 local chapters of various unions joined the new group.

The organizers of this radical council charged that the existing **General Federation of Korean Labor Unions** was "progovernment" and "promanagement" rather than working for the rights of the workers. The government immediately declared that the council was an illegal body. *See also* LABOR MOVEMENT.

NATIONAL COUNCIL OF REPRESENTATIVES OF UNIVERSITY STUDENTS (*Chondaehyop*). A national federation of radical university students, established in June 1988. Spearheaded by the Federation of Seoul Student Associations, its member groups numbered some 115, and it promoted socialistic democratization, an anti-American national reunification movement, and North–South student talks. *See also* STUDENT MOVEMENT.

NATIONAL COUNCIL OF TEACHERS' LABOR UNIONS. Shortly after the formation of the Secondary School Teachers' Labor Union in **Seoul**, on 1 May 1960, some 300 elementary and secondary teachers, as well as college professors, met in Seoul and established this council. The government immediately declared that it was in violation of the Public Employees Law, and therefore an illegal body. It was dissolved in late May 1961, when the **Military Revolutionary Committee** dissolved all political and social organizations under its Decree No. 6. *See also* LABOR MOVEMENT; NATIONAL TEACHERS' UNION.

NATIONAL DEFENSE FORCES. On 29 August 1948, the Law on Organization of the National Defense was promulgated. Under this law, the Korean Constabulary and the Coast Guard, established in January and September 1946 respectively by the **United States Army Military Government in Korea**, were reorganized into the army and the navy. The army and navy chiefs of staff were installed on 30 November 1948. A **Marine Corps** was established in April 1949, followed by the establishment of the air force in October. In 1973, the Marine Corps was absorbed into the navy, but it again became a separate force in 1987. Up to September 1952, members of the armed forces consisted of volunteers. However, in September 1952 a military conscription law was implemented, and all able-bodied men between the ages of 20 and 40, except students and only sons, were obliged to serve in the armed forces for two years in the army or the navy and three years in the air force.

The army was ill prepared for the outbreak of the **Korean War** in June 1950, and suffered badly in the early stages of the conflict. However, with **United States** assistance, the army was rebuilt. By the end of the war, it had become a formidable fighting force. Army units served in **Vietnam** in the 1960s.

In 2000, the army was organized into Army Headquarters, three armies, and Aviation, Special Warfare, and Capital Defense Commands. It has 11 corps, some 50 divisions, 20 brigades, 560,000 troops, 2,200 tanks, 4,850 field artillery pieces, and 2,200 armored vehicles. Weapons production for the army began in 1971, with the assembly of U.S.-designed Colt M-16 rifles. The army is also responsible for the ground air defense network.

The navy, which played an important role in the Korean War, is a small force, primarily concerned with coastal defense. The main naval base is at the former Japanese naval base at Chinhae. It began with patrol and torpedo boats, and acquired destroyers in the 1960s.

The air force, which scarcely existed at the time of the Korean War, has developed into a major fighting force. It is organized into three commands: a Combat Air Command, which controls the jet fighting forces; a small Air Transport Command; and an Air Training Command. The air force has a number of large air bases spread around the country, and there are also small air bases. Civilian airfields and specially designated sections of some highways can also be used in time of war. The air force works closely with United States units based in South Korea. *See also* CIVIL DEFENSE CORPS; HOMELAND RESERVE FORCES; STUDENT NATIONAL DEFENSE CORPS.

NATIONAL DEMOCRATIC FRONT (*Minjujuui Minjok Chonson***).** Organized in February 1946 by **Yo Un-hyong**, Ho Hon, Pak Hon-yong, and other leftists in order to counter the rightists and establish a socialistic Korean nation. However, Yo withdrew from the front, leaving it in the hands of more radical leftists. It collapsed when Ho and Pak fled to **North Korea** in 1947. *See also* DEFECTORS.

NATIONAL DEVELOPMENT PLANS. Five Five-Year Economic Plans were completed between 1962 and 1986, and the sixth national development plan was implemented in 1987. The First Five-Year

Plan (1962–1966) was aimed at developing social overhead capital, such as electricity, railroads, ports, and communications in order to build a firm basis for subsequent **economic development**.

In the Second Five-Year Economic Development Plan period (1967–1971), the government sought to upgrade industrial structures by developing electronic and petrochemical industries while promoting exports and increasing farm income. The Third Five-Year Plan (1972–1976) marked a turning point in the expansion of heavy industries such as shipbuilding, iron and steel production, and petrochemical manufacturing. During this period, the **New Community Movement** played an important role in modernization of the rural environment and reconstruction of farm economy.

The Fourth Five-Year Plan (1977–1981) included both economic and social development plans. It paid particular attention to the development of technology and skilled labor-intensive industries such as machinery and electronics. Shipbuilding was stressed and industrial consolidation was carried out. At the same time, urban renewal accompanied a comprehensive and systematic social development plan. After suffering a sharp economic decline in 1980, the Fifth Economic and Social Development Plan (1982–1986) was implemented with the basic goal of achieving stability, efficiency, and balance in economic growth. During this period, the Gross National Product (GNP) growth rate rebounded from 3.7 percent in 1980 to 12.9 percent in 1986 with the GNP increasing from $60.5 to $102.7 billion.

In 1987, the Sixth Economic and Social Development Plan (1987–1991) was launched with the aim of achieving an average GNP growth of 7.2 percent and raising the GNP to $166 billion and the per capita GNP to $3,800. Despite many problems, the plan moved ahead, achieving the GNP growth of 13 percent in 1987, 12.2 percent in 1988, and 6.6 percent in 1989. In 1989, the GNP reached the $204 billion mark and the per capita GNP increased to $4,830. There was also some progress on the plan's proclaimed agenda of liberalizing markets and removing restrictive regulations.

A revised Five-Year Plan was introduced in 1993. The aim now was to prepare South Korea for membership with the Organization for Economic Cooperation and Development (OECD), and the targets were structural reform of the economy and eliminating official corruption. To this end, three subplans targeted deregulation, financial liberalization, and the management of foreign exchange and capital flows. The OECD targets were achieved, and South Korea became the 39th member in December 1996. Unfortunately, this moment of success came just before the breaking of the **IMF crisis**, which hit the country in 1997. *See also* ECONOMIC DEVELOPMENT; LABOR MOVEMENT; NEW COMMUNITY MOVEMENT.

NATIONAL HISTORY COMPILATION COMMITTEE (*Kuksa py- onchaan wiwinhoe*). Established in 1946 as the National History Office (*Kuksagwan*), and theoretically tracing its roots back to the Chosun dynasty's Annals Compilation Office (*Chunchugwan*), this government organization is charged with preserving the Korean cultural and historical heritage. Until it was settled at its new purpose-built headquarters at Kwachon city near **Seoul** in 1987, the committee suffered from frequent moves that disrupted its work. Since then, and aided by new laws on the preservation of historical records, its work has steadily expanded. It has a strong publication record, covering both original materials and works of interpretation, including a 25-volume *History of Korea* (*Hanguksa*) published between 1971–1979, and a major study of the Korean independence movement in the Japanese colonial period. It produces regular bulletins in Korean and English, recording historical works published in Korea, and has encouraged historical research by the provision of research grants for scholars since 1988. Increasingly, its products are available in electronic form. *See also* KOREAN HISTORICAL ASSOCIATION.

NATIONAL INTELLIGENCE SERVICE (*Kukka chongbowon*, NIS). Originally, the Korean Central Intelligence Agency (KCIA), which was established in June 1961 following the **Military Revolution of 16 May 1961** by a law of 10 June 1960 "for the purpose of countering indirect aggression of the communist forces and to remove obstacles to the execution of the revolutionary tasks." The first director was **Kim Jong-p'il**. It was to "coordinate and supervise activities of government ministries, including armed forces, concerning information and investigation of matters at home and abroad related to the ensuring of national security and the investigation of criminal activities." It not only dealt with external threats, but was also involved in domestic affairs, providing valuable services to the administration in exercising its autocratic power. In 1979, its then director,

Kim Jae-kyu, shot and killed President **Park Chung-hee**, following a dispute about how to handle the **student movement**.

In December 1980, it was renamed the Agency for National Security Planning (*Kukka Anjon Kihoekpu*, usually abbreviated to *Angibu* in Korean, or ANSP in English) without losing any of its power. Under President **Kim Dae-jung**, the ANSP was renamed the National Intelligence Service in January 1999, again with little change in either its powers or its apparent remit. Various attempts over the years to restrict its domestic operations have not been successful. For many years, it had offices on Namsan hill in **Seoul**, and in the city's eastern suburbs, but in 1995, it moved to new purpose-built offices south of the capital. Many of its staff work overseas under diplomatic cover.

NATIONAL LABOR FEDERATION OF BANK EMPLOYEES. *See* LABOR MOVEMENT.

NATIONAL MUSEUM OF KOREA (*Kuknip chongang bakmulgwan*). In 1908, the Yi dynasty government opened a museum in the Changgyonggung Palace in **Seoul**; it is from this event that the modern National Museum of Korea dates its foundation. In 1915, the Japanese **Government-General** reorganized the museum as the Japanese Government-General Museum and moved it to the **Kyongbok Palace**; this became the National Museum of Korea in 1945. The exhibits were packed up at the beginning of the **Korean War** in 1950, to be moved south. Unfortunately, Seoul was taken before this could happen and they fell into enemy hands. **North Korea** clearly intended to take the collection to the north, since it was moved from its original location to the basement of the Museum of Modern Art in the Toksu Palace, closer to Seoul Railway Station. However, the recapture of the city in September 1950 saved the collection.

As the communist forces swept south again at the end of 1950, the South Korean government moved the exhibits to **Pusan**, where they remained until the end of the war. The collection then returned to Seoul, where part of it was put on display in the Stone Palace in the Toksu Palace. The bulk of materials, however, remained in storage until a new National Museum was opened in the grounds of the Kyongbok Palace in 1972. There the museum remained until August 1986, when the former Japanese Government General Building, known since 1945 as the **Capitol Building**, was converted into a new museum. For the first time ever, all the museum's collection, including a small number of foreign artifacts, could be displayed. However, the government of President **Kim Young-sam** decided that the Capitol Building was too great a reminder of the colonial past and determined to remove it; there was no consultation with the museum authorities, who once again found themselves homeless.

A temporary museum was subsequently erected in the grounds of the Kyongbok Palace, and it is planned to open a new museum on the former **Yongsan military base** in 2003. The museum's collection covers all aspects of Korean art and artifacts, and is particularly strong in bronze ornaments and pottery.

There are branches of the National Museum in a number of other cities; the foremost of these is that at **Kyongju**. There are also numerous private museums in Seoul and elsewhere.

NATIONAL REHABILITATION AND GUIDANCE LEAGUE (*Kukmin bodo rungmaeng*). An organization established by the **Syngman Rhee** government in June 1949 to reform the views of left-wing sympathizers, who were pressured into joining. At the outbreak of the **Korean War** in June 1950, many of its 350,000 members disappeared. Two television programs broadcast by Munhwa Broadcasting Corporation (MBC) in 2001 claimed that some 200,000 had been massacred on Rhee's orders by members of **Kim Chang-ryong**'s Counter Intelligence Corps early in the war. MBC claimed to have found the remains of many of those killed in a variety of mass graves.

NATIONAL SECURITY LAWS. The first National Security Law was enacted by the Constituent Assembly in November 1948, making it a crime to betray the **Constitution** by posing as a government or "in collusion with a betrayer" to seek to consolidate or group together with the purpose of disturbing the tranquility of the state. The second National Security Law was promulgated on 26 December 1958. It was aimed at punishing those individuals, associations, groups, or organizations "which seek to overthrow the state in violation of the national constitution and the activities for the realization of their objectives." The law declared that anyone who detected or gathered "national secrets" or aided and abetted such acts for the purpose of "benefiting the enemy" would be punished by the death penalty or penal servitude for life.

Article 22 of the new National Security Law stated that "anyone who had openly impaired the prestige of a constitutional organ by holding a meeting or by publishing documents, tape-recorded materials, drawings and other materials of expression . . . shall be punished by penal servitude for not more than ten years." The constitutional organs listed in Article 22 included the president, the speaker of the **National Assembly**, and the chief justice of the Supreme Court. The law provided that military intelligence agencies may conduct investigations of civilians who were suspected of having violated the National Security Law.

The National Security Law was enhanced when, at 3 A.M. on 28 December 1971, the ruling party rammed through the National Assembly the "Special Measures Law for National Security and Defense" (*Kokka Powipop*). In addition to imposing economic controls, the law empowered the president to curtail the freedom of the press, to issue national mobilization decrees, to prohibit outdoor assemblies and demonstrations, to restrict labor union activities, and to alter the national budget, when necessary to cope with emergency conditions.

In December 1980, the **Anti-Communism Law** was consolidated with the National Security Law. It was widely expected that there would be a far-reaching examination of the laws following the inauguration of the former political dissident, **Kim Dae-jung**, as president in February 1998. However, conservative opposition to such a move remained strong, as did fear of **North Korea**, and the National Security Laws remained in place, though with some modifications. From 1998, those who had been charged under these laws no longer had to renounce their beliefs before their cases could be reviewed. This allowed Kim to release a large number of "unconverted prisoners," who had been charged as North Korean spies and who had been held, in some cases, since the end of the **Korean War**. Some of these were allowed to return to North Korea in 2000. There was also a steady decline in the number of those charged under the laws. Although President **Roh Moo-hyun**, who came to power in 2003, had a reputation as a radical lawyer, he too showed no disposition to reform the National Security laws.

NATIONAL TEACHERS' UNION (*Chon'guk Kyowon Chopha*, or *Chon'gyojo*). The first teachers' unions were formed after the fall of the First Republic in 1960, and the Korean Federation of Teachers'

Labor Unions of primary and secondary school teachers emerged in May of that year. However, the government declared that the unions and the federation were illegal organizations, and they were dissolved following the **Military Revolution of 16 May 1961**.

Riding the new tide of democratization that developed in 1987 and the growing **labor movement**, and despite the law against the formation of unions by educators, in May 1989 radical teachers reestablished the National Teachers' Union, which soon reached a membership of 14,000. The Ministry of Education refused to recognize its legitimacy, and dismissed thousands of teachers who joined the organization. The struggle for recognition continued however, and in 1999, the Ministry of Education finally agreed to recognize the teachers' union. *See also* EDUCATIONAL DEVELOPMENT; FEDERATION OF KOREAN EDUCATION ASSOCIATIONS.

NATIONAL YOUTH CORPS. *See* KOREAN NATIONAL YOUTH CORPS.

NEUTRAL NATIONS SUPERVISORY COMMISSION (NNSC). This organization was created by the **Korean Armistice Agreement** signed in July 1953, and was established immediately after the signing of the agreement. It consisted of Swedish, Swiss, Czechoslovak, and Polish representatives. Its primary function was to supervise the observation of the armistice agreement by the signatories, and to bar any new arms build-up in either South or **North Korea**. South Korean President **Syngman Rhee** objected to it, and the Czechoslovak and Polish contingents were soon prevented from working in South Korea. North Korea took an equally hostile line toward the Swiss and the Swedes.

Following the breakup of Czechoslovakia in 1993, the North Koreans would not accept the Czech Republic as the successor state on the NNSC, and by 1995, the North Koreans refused to accept the Polish members. Although the NNSC still meets from time to time, it is now totally unable to carry out any of its original functions.

NEW COMMUNITY MOVEMENT (*Saemaul undong*). President **Park Chung-hee** launched the New Community Movement in 1972. The movement started as a rural modernization program intended to galvanize the tradition-bound and poverty-stricken rural society into participating actively in national development. To this end, three main goals were adopted: improvement of the living environment; spiritual enlightenment; and income enhancement. The three methods adopted to achieve these aims were the fostering of a spirit of self-help, development of diligent habits, and promotion of mutual cooperation. In the initial stage of the movement, the main emphasis was placed on environmental improvement with projects such as the cleanup of villages, sanitation works, housing renovation, and reconstruction of roads and waterways. After 1973, the emphasis was shifted to the promotion of income-generating enterprises.

In 1974, the movement spread nationwide to include the urban sector and schools in a comprehensive national regeneration reform movement. Between 1972 and 1984 an aggregate of 24 million persons from 36,000 villages took part in a total of 18,600 projects. By the end of 1987 some 4,350 miles (7,000 kilometers) of rural roads were rebuilt or repaired and 800 miles (1,287 kilometers) of canals, irrigation dykes, and other waterways were reconstructed.

Under President **Chun Doo-hwan**, whose younger brother, Chun Kyong-hwan, became the Saemaul secretary-general, the aims of the movement became less focused, and it was increasingly seen as a means of drumming up support for the government in rural areas. It suffered from its association with the younger Chun, who was widely seen as a corrupt. In 1984, "Saemaul for foreigners" was launched, so that other countries could benefit from the Korean experience. As a result, many foreign community leaders have been trained in South Korea over the years.

A "second phase" of the movement was formally launched in December 1998. The aims of *Saemaul Undong* were redefined to revitalize the country, construct a sound society, provide a good environment, prepare for reunification, and to work for international cooperation. It continues to exist, but with the steady decline of the rural population, and many other outlets for Koreans, it is far less important than it once was.

NEW DEMOCRATIC PARTY (*Shinmindang*). There have been three political parties with this name. The first was formed in February 1961 by the "old faction" members of the **Democratic Party** under the leadership of Kim To-yon. Its aim was "to promote liberal democracy." However, it was dissolved following the **Military Revolution of 16 May 1961**.

The second New Democratic Party was organized in February 1967 when the **Masses Party** and the **New Korea Party** merged. The new party, under the leadership of **Yu Chin-o**, advocated progressive reforms. It was at this juncture that younger leaders such as **Kim Dae-jung**, **Kim Young-sam**, and Yi Ch'ol-sung rose within the party. In 1967, its presidential candidate, **Yun Po-son**, ran but failed, and in the 1971 presidential election Kim Dae-jung lost by a narrow margin to the incumbent president, **Park Chung-hee**. In 1973, Kim Young-sam became president of the party, which was then the major opposition party.

The third New Democratic Party emerged in the aftermath of the defeat suffered by Kim Dae-jung's **Party of Peace and Democracy** (PPD) in the March 1991 local council elections. In April 1991, Kim effected a merger between the PPD and the **New Democratic United Party** of Yi Wu-jong to form the New Democratic Party. It was a centralist reformist party with the collective leadership of Kim and Yi, with Kim as its president. In September 1991, it merged with the Democratic Party.

NEW DEMOCRATIC REPUBLICAN PARTY (*Shin Minju Konghwadang*). In October 1987, **Kim Jong-p'il** reconstituted the **Democratic Republican Party**, the ruling party under President **Park Chung-hee**, which had become defunct in 1980 following Park's **assassination**, naming it the New Democratic Republican Party. Kim became its president and it won 35 seats in the 1988 **National Assembly** elections, becoming the third opposition party. In February 1990, the party merged with the ruling **Democratic Justice Party** and **Kim Young-sam**'s **Reunification Democratic Party** to form the **Democratic Liberal Party**.

NEW DEMOCRATIC UNITED PARTY (*Shin-minju Yonhap*). A party established in February 1990, following the merger of the **Reunification Democratic Party**, the ruling **Democratic Justice Party**, and **Kim Jong-p'il**'s **New Democratic Republican Party** to form the **Democratic Liberal Party**. Its leaders included Yi Wu-jong, a female professor turned politician, and others who objected to the cynical way in which ruling and opposition groups had come together. In April 1991, it merged with **Kim Dae-jung**'s **Party of Peace and Democracy**, to form the **New Democratic Party**.

NEW KOREA DEMOCRATIC PARTY (*Shin Han'guk Minjudang,* NKDP). A party was formed in January 1985 by politicians who regained their civil rights removed following the **December 1979 coup**. In November 1984, all but 19 former political leaders were freed from the political blacklist, and they immediately launched a new party movement in order to promote democracy. Yi Min-woo was named its president, and among its key leaders were **Kim Young-sam** and Yi Ch'ol-sung. **Kim Dae-jung**, who returned from exile in the **United States** in February 1985 did not join the party immediately, but he agreed to serve as adviser to the president of the party.

The New Korea Democratic Party quickly became the main opposition party, struggling against the **Democratic Justice Party** and the government of President **Chun Doo-hwan**. In 1986, it launched a nationwide movement for constitutional revision. However, it suffered badly when, in May 1987, Kim Young-sam broke away to form his own **Reunification Democratic Party** (RDP). Kim Dae-jung joined this new party in August. The NKPD then steadily dissolved as members left it, either to join the RDP, or the new **Party for Peace and Democracy** that Kim Dae-jung formed in November 1987.

NEW KOREA PARTY (*Shinhandang*). In May 1966, **Yun Po-son** formed this party, but in February 1967 it and the **Masses Party** were united, forming the **New Democratic Party**.

NEW KOREA PARTY (*Saehandang*). A short-lived party formed in January 1992 by Professor Kim Tong-gil of Yonsei University. A long-time critic of then existing parties, as well as the government since the late 1960s, Kim had set up a group known as the Asia-Pacific-Era Committee, promoting "new politics," and the New Korea Party emerged from this organization. Shortly after its formation, in February 1992 it merged first with the **New Democratic Party**, and then with **Chung Ju-yung**'s **Unification National Party**. Kim later joined the **United Liberal Democrats**.

NEW KOREA PARTY OF HOPE (NKPH, *Huimangui shinhankuk tang*). Small conservative party that contested the 2000 elections, and won one seat.

NEW PARTY FOR THE PEOPLE (NPP, *Kukmin shindang*). Short-lived party that emerged in 1997 as **Rhee In-je**'s vehicle for the presidential election. The party failed to survive Rhee's defeat, and its members generally drifted back to the **National Congress for New Politics**, as did Rhee himself. Its name was sometimes given in En- glish as the **New People's Party**.

NEW PEOPLE'S PARTY. *See* NEW PARTY FOR THE PEOPLE.

NOGUN-RI MASSACRE. In October 1999, newly declassified U.S. documents appeared to confirm rumors that **United States troops in South Korea** had carried out a massacre of South Koreans at a vil- lage called Nogun-ri in South Kyongsang Province in late July 1950 during the early stages of the **Korean War**. Former U.S. soldiers who came forward to testify appeared to provide further evidence to the alleged massacre, though subsequently some of this testimony was shown to be inaccurate. The Nogun-ri material led to many other sim- ilar allegations about the conduct of both the South Korean and the U.S. forces, and both launched enquiries. *See also* HAMP'YONG– KOCH'ANG INCIDENTS.

NORDPOLITIK. The concept of "Nordpolitik," or Northern Policy, was first advanced in June 1973 by then President **Park Chung-hee** when he announced that his government was willing to establish ties with countries having ideological and political systems different from South Korea's. It was hoped that this new **foreign policy** approach would allow South Korea to escape from the Cold War era and es- tablish relations with all of its neighbors, regardless of ideology.

South Korea had been obliged to rely on the west for international support, and was cut off completely from **China**, the **Soviet Union/Russia**, and other socialist countries. Park's other aim was to weaken the ties between **North Korea** and the Soviet Union and its allies by establishing diplomatic and commercial ties with as many socialist nations as possible. He also wanted South Korea to join the **United Nations**. However, under Park and his immediate successors, the policy made little progress, and it was not until the Sixth Repub- lic that an effective Northern Policy was implemented.

Less than a week after taking office, President **Roh Tae-woo** indi- cated on 1 March 1988 that his government would actively seek the es- tablishment of **diplomatic relations** with China, the Soviet Union, and other socialist countries. Accordingly, on 7 July 1988, he announced the adoption of the policy known as Nordpolitik, or "Northern Diplomacy."

Roh's approach was inspired by West Germany's Ostpolitik ("Eastern Policy") launched by former Chancellor Willy Brandt to improve his country's relations with the Soviet Union and Eastern European countries, as well as with East Germany. In his July declaration, Roh also indicated that his government would work for the establishment of amicable relations between North and South Korea. This strand of Nordpolitik would eventually lead to the 1991 **Agreement on Reconciliation, Nonaggression and Exchanges and Cooperation between the South and the North**, and related agreements.

The other strand was more successful. Taking advantage of the 1988 **Olympic Games** in **Seoul**, cultural exchanges began with Hungary, Poland, and the Soviet Union before the Olympics. The participation of sports teams from the Soviet Union, and other socialist countries (except Albania, Cuba, and North Korea) in the Seoul Olympics paved the way for commercial relations as well. Hungary moved even before the Olympics, and exchanged trade offices with South Korea in June 1988. Bulgaria, Poland, and Yugoslavia followed also in 1988, and in 1989 Czechoslovakia and the Soviet Union did likewise.

Diplomatic relations then followed, with Hungary again leading the way in February 1989, despite strong opposition and retaliatory action from North Korea. Poland did likewise in November, followed by Yugoslavia in December 1989. In March 1990, the trend became a flood, as relations were established with Bulgaria, Czechoslovakia, Romania, and Mongolia. Meanwhile, once-hostile Third World countries also moved to normalize relations with South Korea. Algeria did so in January 1990, and South Yemen in May. In June, South Korea restored its diplomatic relations with the Congo, which had been severed in 1965 when the Congo had recognized North Korea.

The main aim, however, was the establishment of full diplomatic relations with the Soviet Union and China, seen as the key to enhancing South Korea's security and paving the way to United Nations' membership. The Seoul government had made various gestures on several occasions to Moscow and Beijing, but there was little response either until the adoption by Soviet Union President Mikhail Gorbachev of the policies of *glasnost* and *perestroika*.

Taking advantage of Gorbachev's new domestic and foreign policy, Roh took positive steps to achieve his foreign policy objectives with new overtures to the Soviet Union. The results were positive. In September 1988, Gorbachev clearly indicated the possibility of opening the way to economic relations with South Korea. In addition to official contacts, Roh also encouraged nongovernmental contacts. In January 1989, **Chung Ju-yung**, head of the **Hyundai** Group visited Moscow, where he concluded agreements with the Soviet Union's Chamber of Commerce and Industry to set up South Korea–Soviet Union joint ventures in the timber, fishery, and shipbuilding industries. Chung returned in August, taking a 31-man study team with him to explore the possibilities for other joint ventures.

Meanwhile, in June 1989, **Kim Young-sam**, president of the opposition **Reunification Democratic Party**, visited Moscow and talked on various matters, including the conclusion of a diplomatic treaty between South Korea and the Soviet Union. Following this, two key members of the Soviet government visited South Korea in September 1989, and in October the new director of the Institute of World Economics and International Relations, Vladlen A. Martynov, himself visited Seoul, bringing a 12-man delegation with him. Such contacts led to the establishment of consular relations in December 1989, as well as the beginning of South Korean–Russian joint ventures in April 1990.

In 1990, South Korea–Soviet Union relations took a dramatic turn following the Moscow visit of Kim Young-sam, now executive chairman of the newly formed ruling **Democratic Liberal Party**. In March he led a delegation composed of high-level party and government officials to Moscow, and negotiated with the Soviet leaders as President Roh's personal envoy. Anatoly Dobrynin, former Soviet ambassador to the **United States**, flew to Seoul in May 1990. He met President Roh, and discussed a possible meeting between Roh and Gorbachev while the latter was on a state visit to the U.S. in June. Meanwhile, direct air services between Seoul and Moscow officially opened in April.

Roh and Gorbachev met in San Francisco on 4–5 June 1990. Although no official statements were made on the subject, it was now unmistakably clear that the establishment of full diplomatic relations was only a matter of time. In September 1990, Soviet Foreign Minister Eduard Shevardnadze visited **P'yongyang** and informed the North Korean government that the Soviet Union would establish diplomatic relations with South Korea, and in New York on 30 September, She-vardnadze and his South Korean counterpart, Ch'oe Ho-jung, an-nounced the establishment of full diplomatic relations. In mid-December 1990, President Roh made a state visit to the Soviet Union, consolidating the ties with that nation.

Relations with China moved in parallel with these developments, but more slowly. Despite occasional setbacks, from the early 1980s, Sino–South Korean trade had begun to expand, although its extent was not always openly admitted by either side. South Korean manu-factured goods found a ready market in China, while Chinese raw materials and traditional products such as medicines were welcomed in South Korea. Cultural and sporting links were also on the increase. Despite North Korean protests, PRC athletes attended the Asian Games in Seoul in 1986, and also the 1988 Olympic Games.

Relations with China were more complicated than relations with the Soviet Union, because of South Korea's long standing relationship with, and diplomatic recognition of, the "Republic of China" on Taiwan. As in negotiations with other countries, the Chinese made it clear that these relations would have to be broken if South Korea wanted diplomatic re-lations with the People's Republic. Finally, in 1992, and despite strong protests from Taiwan, South Korea and the PRC established full diplo-matic relations. The North Koreans made clear their opposition to this move by their closest ally, but such protests were now far more muted than when Hungary had began the process in 1988.

By the time South Korea and China established relations in 1992, both Koreas had already entered the United Nations, thus meeting an-other target of Nordpolitik. *See also* CROSS-RECOGNITION; DIPLOMATIC RECOGNITION.

NORTH KOREA (Democratic People's Republic of Korea, DPRK). The state that has occupied the northern half of the Korean Peninsula since 1948, North Korea is, at some 47,225 square miles (122,313 square kilometers), slightly larger than South Korea in area. A popu-lation in 1945 of about seven million, had reached 14,700,000 by 1973, and was estimated at about 24 million in 2003, or about 50 per-cent of that of the South. Until 1972, its official capital was **Seoul**, the capital of unified Korea since 1392, with **P'yongyang** designated the temporary capital. The Constitution adopted in 1972 no longer referred to Seoul, however, and since then the North Koreans have made much of P'yongyang's historical role as one of Korea's ancient cities.

North Korea emerged from the division of the Korean Peninsula in 1945 in order to take the Japanese surrender. The **Soviet Union/Russia** may not have intended to establish a state in Korea, but the administration it established in its zone of occupation soon began to take on the characteristics of a separate entity. These tendencies were increased with the onset of the Cold War.

Since its establishment in 1948, North Korea has remained a one-party state, under the rule of the Communist Party, whose official title is the Korean Workers' Party (KWP), led first by **Kim Il-sung** and since his death in 1994, by his son, **Kim Jong-il**. Having failed to reunify the peninsula during the 1950–1953 **Korean War**, Kim Il-sung concentrated on building up North Korea and his own position, so that by the mid-1960s, all known opposition had been eliminated. From about then, Kim also apparently began grooming his son as his successor.

Aided by the Soviet Union, **China**, and East European countries, North Korea had become an industrialized country by the early 1960s, with a higher standard of living than South Korea. However, this position began to slip in the 1970s, when an ambitious program of modernizing industry collapsed leaving a string of bad debts. At the same time, fearful of what it felt was the threat from the **United States**, North Korean military expenditure began to rise steadily, a trend that has continued ever since. This has distorted the economy, as did a heavy dependence on the Soviet Union. When the latter collapsed in 1991, so did the North Korean economy. Together with the problems inherent in a command economy, and a series of natural disasters in the mid-1990s, the end of Soviet support led to famine and great distress for much of the 1990s.

North Korea survived both the disasters of the 1990s and the death of Kim Il-sung in July 1994. Although Kim Jong-il was slow to take over his father's role, by 2000 when he met the South Korean president, **Kim Dae-jung**, at the **June 2000 Inter-Korean Summit**, he appeared fully in control.

North Korea–South Korea relations have been marked by hostility and suspicion, an inevitable legacy of the original circumstances in which the two states emerged and of the Korean War.

While there was some relaxation during the 1990s, each side remains wary of the other.

NORTH KOREA–SOUTH KOREA RELATIONS. The division of the Korean Peninsula in 1945 by the **Soviet Union/Russia** and the **United States** led eventually to the creation of two states, the Democratic People's Republic of Korea (**North Korea**) in the northern half of the peninsula, and the Republic of Korea (South Korea) in the south. Each state was backed by its erstwhile liberator, and both claimed to be the legitimate government of a united Korea. Some on both sides of the divide tried to bring about reconciliation, and the wartime allies devised a formula in the 1945 **Moscow Agreement** for the eventual reunification of the peninsula, but by 1948, the division was fixed.

In 1950, having put forward proposals for discussions on the division, North Korea under **Kim Il-sung** attempted to reunify the peninsula by force in the **Korean War**. The attempt was thwarted by **United Nations** intervention, and the war ended with the 1953 **Korean Armistice Agreement**, which perpetuated the division. Despite strong unification rhetoric from each side, after 1953 they each concentrated on postwar reconstruction, and there were no official contacts between them. Occasional military clashes and exchanges of fire along the **demilitarized zone** served as reminders of the underlying tension, but the presence of U.S./**United Nations forces** in South Korea and Chinese forces in the North prevented any escalation of these incidents.

The late 1960s saw developments that would eventually lead the two Koreas to the negotiating table. U.S.–Soviet détente was one such factor; the U.S.–**China** rapprochement of 1971 was another. Each Korea saw that its supporters had other interests that would be likely to prevail over their interest in Korea. It was in this context that the first links between North and South Korea were set up in 1971, with the 1971 **North–South Red Cross talks**, in which both governments took a strong interest. The Red Cross channel would continue to be used from time to time thereafter, but in 1972, formal governmental-level talks led to the **July 1972 statement on Korean unification.**

The talks seemed to indicate some common ground, but eventually fizzled out in mutual recrimination. South Korea's President **Park**

Chung-hee used the alleged communist threat posed by growing North–South contacts to introduce his **Yushin rule**, while the North broke off contacts after the alleged kidnapping by South Korean agents of the South Korean opposition politician, **Kim Dae-jung**.

There were no moves from the North at the time of Park's assassination in October 1979, or when General **Chun Doo-hwan** staged the **December 1979 coup**. Chun made some proposals to the North about resuming talks after he became president in August 1980 but the North rejected them. But in October 1980, Kim Il-sung put forward a revised version of a 1960 proposal for solving the problem of reunification by establishing a "Democratic Confederal Republic of Koryo," which has remained the essential basis of the North Korean position ever since. Instead of talking, the North appears to have tried terror, with the 1983 **Rangoon bomb attack** on Chun and his party during a state visit to Burma. Despite this, the Chun government reacted positively in 1984 to a North Korean offer of flood assistance, and North Korean goods flowed south. But there was no follow-up.

North Korea protested at the holding of the 1986 Asian Games in **Seoul**, while the bombing of **Korean Air Flight KA 858** by North Korean agents in 1987 aimed to discourage visitors to the 1988 **Olympic Games**. However, the U.S. successfully intervened to persuade the North Koreans against any such further acts, and there was no disruption of the games.

By that stage, Chun's successor, **Roh Tae-woo**, had begun his policy of **Nordpolitik**, which was at first directed toward the North Koreans as much as toward the other communist states. A series of high-level talks eventually led to the 1991 **Agreement on Reconciliation, Nonaggression and Exchanges and Cooperation between the South and the North**, and a number of other agreements. These represented the most comprehensive agreements ever reached between North and South. Although they have hardly been implemented, both sides continue to use them as a benchmark in relations.

The early 1990s were dominated by the possible consequences for North Korea of the collapse of the Soviet Union, and by growing international concern over the **North Korean nuclear program**. The fall of the Soviet Union and the end of communism throughout Eastern Europe led many in South Korea (and elsewhere) to predict that the North Korean political and economic system would also soon disappear.

While this in the short-term led to a certain degree of triumphalism, the nuclear issue showed that North Korea was still a force on the peninsula. As the crisis deepened in 1994, South Korea felt increasingly marginalized in the face of U.S.–North Korean negotiations. But contacts continued, and an agreement was reached for the first ever summit meeting between the leaders of North and South Korea in July 1994.

At this point, Kim Il-sung died. The South Korean president, **Kim Young-sam**, though he had been prepared to meet Kim a few days earlier, refused to express condolences. Expressions of mourning that took place on some university campuses were firmly suppressed by the **police**. Relations cooled, and were not improved when a North Korean submarine, apparently engaged in an infiltration attempt, went aground on South Korea's east coast in 1996. The North eventually apologized for the incident, which it claimed was the result of engine failure, and the cremated remains of the crew were returned on 30 December 1996 at **P'anmunjom**.

When the long-term opposition leader, **Kim Dae-jung**, became president in 1998, he announced a new policy toward the North, usually described as the **"sunshine policy."** Rather than confrontation, Kim said that while any attack or intrusion would be firmly dealt with, he assured the North that there would be no attempt at takeover and the South would be ready to provide assistance both to help the North feed its people and rebuild its economy. This policy has continued, despite periodic upsets. These included a further submarine incident in 1998, occasional tension in the **demilitarized zone**, and regular naval clashes in the West Sea during the May–June crab fishing season.

Despite such incidents, Kim Dae-jung and the North Korean leader **Kim Jong-il** were able to meet in **P'yongyang** for the **June 2000 Inter-Korean Summit**. Other links have been forged by private efforts such as that of the **Hyundai** Group, and a host of South Korean nongovernmental organizations. Whereas in the past, few if any South Koreans saw more of North Korea than the view across the demilitarized zone, since 1980, thousands have visited the North either as tourists on the **Mount Kumgang tours**, or in other capacities.

Such developments have not proved popular with all South Koreans. Many older people remain suspicious of the North and its motives. Others are concerned that most of the benefits from the new relationship lie with the North, which seems happy to take the South's money and assistance and to give little in return. Even in official circles, there has been a reluctance to accept North Korea's legitimacy. Displays of the North Korean flag and other state symbols are not normally allowed. The armed forces still officially view North Korea as their principal enemy. Despite the recent progress, full reconciliation is a long way off.

NORTH KOREAN NUCLEAR PROGRAM. North Korea began a civilian nuclear energy program in the 1950s, with assistance from the **Soviet Union/Russia**. Given the relative lack of other energy resources and the presence of graphite and uranium, this made sense. The Soviet Union provided training, and also an experimental reactor, which was built at Yonbyon in 1965. At Soviet insistence, this reactor was registered with the International Atomic Energy Authority (IAEA) in 1977, and subject to IAEA inspection. In 1987, again at Soviet insistence, North Korea joined the Non-proliferation Treaty (NPT), although it did not sign the required safeguards agreement or submit a full list of its nuclear facilities to the IAEA until 1992. Meanwhile, following a South Korean declaration that there were no nuclear weapons in South Korea, the two Koreas signed a nonnuclear declaration in December 1991. Like the **Agreement on Reconciliation, Nonaggression and Exchanges and Cooperation between the South and the North** signed at the same time, this has remained largely a dead letter.

By 1991, however, there was growing international concern that North Korea might be developing a nuclear weapons' program. Satellite photographs showed that there were more facilities at Yongbyon than the Soviet reactor. This was confirmed by the North Korean list supplied to the IAEA. What the North Koreans described as a radiochemical laboratory appeared to be a spent nuclear fuel reprocessing plant. This would allow the extraction of plutonium, necessary for nuclear weapons. IAEA attempts to inspect these facilities led the North Koreans to announce in March 1993 that they were withdrawing from the NPT.

This move threatened to put the whole international nonproliferation regime into jeopardy. Great pressure was put on North Korea, including the threat of **United Nations** sanctions, not to withdraw. It also emerged later that the **United States** government under President Bill

Clinton even considered military action, although this line was not pursued. The pressure on the North Koreans eventually worked, and they agreed to suspend their withdrawal from the NPT.

Following a visit to North Korea by former United States president, **Jimmy Carter**, in June 1994, negotiations began between North Korea and the U.S. that led to the signing of an "Agreed Framework" at Geneva in October 1994. Under this agreement, North Korea agreed to freeze all its activities at Yongbyon, while a consortium, to be known as the **Korean Peninsula Energy Development Organization** (KEDO), would supply two light-water reactors (LWRs) to North Korea, to meet its energy needs. In addition, it was agreed to supply heavy fuel oil to North Korea until the LWRs became operational, while the U.S. undertook to lift sanctions and to move toward diplomatic relations with North Korea. Only when the new LWRs were about to become operational would the IAEA fully investigate North Korea's past nuclear history. The groundbreaking ceremony for the LWRs took place in 1997, and the first concrete pouring for the reactors themselves in August 2002.

By then, there were new concerns. One was whether or not North Korea would fulfill its part of the 1994 agreement. The other, made public after the visit of a senior U.S. official to North Korea in October 2002, was whether North Korea had embarked on a separate road to a nuclear weapons' program using enriched uranium. The Americans claimed that the North Koreans had admitted such a program. The North denied this, but claimed that it had the right to do so, since the U.S. continued to target it with nuclear weapons. As the allegations flew, North Korea expelled the IAEA inspectors from Yongbyon, claimed to have restarted its program there, and formally withdrew from the NPT, the first state ever to do so. Once again, there was much international activity, eventually leading to talks involving the two Koreas, **China**, **Japan**, Russia and the U.S. in August 2003.

NORTH–SOUTH POLITICAL COORDINATING COMMITTEE. This committee, established after the **July 1972 statement on Korean unification**, held its preliminary meeting at **P'anmunjom** in August 1972. A total of six rounds of the full-dress meetings were held in **Seoul** and **P'yongyang** between October 1972 and July 1973. The meetings were designed to discuss and settle various procedural steps necessary for the achievement of peaceful reunification of the country in accordance with the 4 July statement. However, in August 1973, P'yongyang unilaterally suspended the dialogue in the wake of the kidnapping of **Kim Dae-jung** from Tokyo to Seoul.

NORTH–SOUTH RED CROSS TALKS. On 12 August 1971, the president of the South Korean Red Cross Society proposed to the Red Cross of **North Korea** that the two societies should begin talks to discuss ways to ease the sufferings of dispersed families in both the North and the South and ultimately arrange their reunion. Specifically, he proposed that both Red Cross societies launch a movement to search for separated family members, arrange an exchange of letters between them, and bring about their reunion. The North Korean Red Cross promptly accepted the proposal on 14 August, and talks began in September, but without satisfactory results. The only two memorable events that they brought about were the exchange of a 151-member group comprising hometown visitors and folk art troupes in late September 1982, and the offering of relief goods (food and clothing) by the North Korean Red Cross Society to the flood victims in the south in September 1984, which the South Korean Red Cross promptly accepted. Working-level meetings of the representatives were held in 1989 to arrange another exchange of hometown visitors and performing art troupes, but they failed to reach an agreement on that occasion.

Both sides continue to use the Red Cross as a channel when direct government-to-government contacts are difficult for whatever reason, and each has made sure that its own Red Cross is staffed by high-quality personnel. The two Red Cross organizations have continued to be involved with the issue of family exchanges, for example, leading to the introduction of a regular program of such contacts.

– O –

OLYMPIC GAMES. After hosting the Asian Games for the first time in 1986, South Korea held the Olympic Games in the capital, **Seoul,** in 1988. The games proved to be a great success, despite concerns that they might be disrupted by **North Korea** or by radical members of the **student movement**. Although North Korea did not participate, and tried to prevent its allies from attending, most of the other communist countries ignored the North and attended. At one time, the idea of a shared North–South Games was mooted, but this came to nothing. In domestic terms, the need for a trouble-free Olympics was one of the factors that led President **Chun Doo-hwan** to allow constitutional reform in 1987. *See also* WORLD CUP 2002.

ONGJIN PENINSULA. A peninsula to the northwest of the Han River estuary, south of the **38th parallel**. Haeju is the principle city. The division of the peninsula in 1945 left the peninsula on the southern side, but without land access to the rest of South Korea. It was the scene of a number of clashes between North and South forces in 1949–1950. The **United States Military Advisory Group** advised that it was dangerous to leave too many troops in such an exposed position, and by June 1950, there was only a single South Korean regiment on the peninsula. This came under heavy attack with the outbreak of the **Korean War**, and the surviving troops were evacuated by boat on 25–26 June. The end of the war left the whole peninsula in North Korean hands.

OVERSEAS KOREANS. Until the 1880s, Koreans were officially forbidden to leave Korea. In practice, numbers did drift into **China** and **Soviet Union/Russia**, where sizable Korean communities were established by 1900. After the annexation of Korea by **Japan** in 1910, large numbers of Koreans moved to the Japanese mainland and to other parts of the Japanese empire. In the 1930s, more Koreans were taken to Japan as forced labor to help the war effort. There was also emigration to Hawaii, where Korean laborers worked on the sugar plantations. These overseas communities played a role in the anti-Japanese resistance, either as a base for political groups, or, especially in northeastern China, as a source of guerrilla bands. In the Soviet Union, Stalin's fear that the Koreans might be a Fifth Column for the Japanese led to a massive resettlement of the community away from the Soviet–Korean border to parts of Soviet Central Asia, especially Uzbekistan and Kazakhstan. Although still thinking of themselves as Koreans, and often with recognizable Korean names, few of these now speak or understand Korean.

The end of the Pacific War in 1945 led to the repatriation of large numbers of Koreans from the Japanese empire, while the emergence of two states on the peninsula in 1945 divided the loyalties of the remaining overseas Korean communities. Both Korean states would claim the loyalty of all overseas Koreans, but until the 1980s, South Korea had little contact with or influence among Korean communities in China or the Soviet Union. **North Korea**, while maintaining strong links with the Korean community in Japan, which was an important source of economic assistance, had few links with the fast-growing communities in the **United States** and in newer destinations such as **Australia**. The Korean community in China provided many of the "Chinese People's Volunteers" who fought in the **Korean War**. In general, the Koreans in China fared better than their counterparts in the Soviet Union. They were well integrated into Chinese society, and usually were encouraged to keep their language and culture. However, like other minorities, they suffered badly both during the antirightist campaign of the late 1950s and even more during the Cultural Revolution between 1966–1976.

By the end of the 20th century, the number of overseas Koreans was estimated at about 5.6 million, compared with about 66 million people on the Korean Peninsula. There were just over 2 million in China, mostly in the **Yanbian Korean Autonomous Region**, and a similar number in the United States, compared to 660,000 in Japan, and just under half a million in the former Soviet Union. Canada and Australia were also popular destinations, and there were large numbers in Germany and **Great Britain**. Both Koreas continued to compete for their loyalty, but the old strict divisions began to break down in the 1980s. Even the pro–North Korean community in Japan began to move away from its previous close links with North Korea. Increasingly, other communities were becoming integrated in their new societies and less interested in their Korean homeland, despite vigorous attempts to maintain such links.

– P –

PAIK SUN-YUP (1920–). Paik Sun-yup was educated at the Manzhouguo Military Academy and served in **Japan**'s armed forces during World War II. He returned to Korea in 1945 and joined the newly formed Korean Constabulary and then the South Korean army.

When the **Korean War** began in June 1950, he was in command of the 1st Division, one of the four South Korean divisions on duty on the **38th parallel**. Despite many of his men being on leave, Paik's division fought well, and only retreated across the Han River after the fall of **Seoul** on 28 June. The 1st Division was quickly reformed, and following the September 1950 landing at **Inch'on**, Paik led the **United Nations forces** across the 38th parallel and into **North Korea**, taking **P'yongyang**, the North Korean capital, on 19 October.

Paik's next major role was at the armistice negotiations from July–October 1951. He then led "Task Force Paik," a combined military and **police** unit that conducted "Operation Ratkiller" against North Korean guerrilla forces in the southwest from December 1951–April 1952. It was deemed a success, but there have been accusations that Paik's force used great brutality in pacifying this region. President **Syngman Rhee** then appointed Paik army chief of staff, a post he held until 1954. He also became South Korea's first four-star general, aged 33. He again served as army chief of staff from 1957–1959, and in 1959, he became chairman of the chiefs of staff. However, he soon resigned, following allegations of corruption from younger officers. Following the **Military Revolution of 16 May 1961**, Paik served as an ambassador on several occasions, and was briefly minister of transport in 1969–1970. He later became a successful businessman. In 1992, he published his autobiography, *From Pusan to Panmunjom*, which carefully avoided some of the more controversial issues in his life, such as the question of wartime atrocities.

PAK SUN-CHON (1898–1983). Born in Tongnae, South Kyongsang Province, she received a modern education, and became a teacher in Masan. In 1919, she was imprisoned in connection with her direct involvement in the independence movement in that city. Released from prison, she went to Tokyo in **Japan** to study, graduating from Nihon Women's College in 1926. Returning to Korea, she became an educator and a leader in the nationalist **women's movement**, and in 1940 she established the private Kyongsong Academy. Elected to the **National Assembly** in 1950, she became one of the most influential politicians and a leading opposition member in the National Assembly until 1971. In 1960, she formed her own **Masses Party**, but in 1967 she and **Yun Po-son** formed the **New Democratic Party**, which became the main opposition party. After retiring from politics in 1972, she became head of a girls' school, and served as a member of the State Advisory Council from 1980.

P'ANMUNJOM. This hamlet, located some 25 miles (40 kilometers) north of Seoul on the **38th parallel**, was totally destroyed in the early stages of the **Korean War**. However, the site was declared a neutral area and became the second meeting place for the armistice talks between the **United Nations Command** and the North Korean–Chinese forces in September 1951. Here the **Korean Armistice Agreement** was signed in July 1953, and it was through P'anmunjom that exchanges of prisoners of war took place in April and August–September 1953. The headquarters of the **Neutral Nations Supervisory Commission** is located there and the **Military Armistice Commission** holds its meetings there. It is a joint security area under the United Nations Command and North Korean guards, with the **military demarcation line** running through the middle. There have been occasional North–South meetings at P'anmunjom, and until 2002, it remained the only recognized land crossing point between the two Koreas.

P'ANMUNJOM INCIDENT (Ax murders). On 18 August 1976, soldiers from **North Korea** attacked two **United States** Army officers and nine other ranks in the joint security area (JSA) at **P'anmunjom**. The American soldiers were involved in an operation to trim a poplar tree that obstructed vision from a **United Nations Command** (UNC) observation point. Earlier attempts to trim the tree had led to North Korean protests. On this occasion, the North Koreans demanded a halt to the trimming until the issue could be discussed at a security officers meeting. When the U.S. officer in command, Captain Bonifas, refused, North Korean Lieutenant Pak Chul seized one of the axes and struck Bonifas, who was then kicked to death. His fellow officer was also killed, and others on both sides sustained injuries. The UNC protested, and both sides raised their level of alert. On August 21, a UNC work group cut down the tree, and on 6 September the **Military Armistice Commission** negotiated the removal of North Korean observation posts from the south side of the **military demarcation line**. It was also agreed that only MAC personnel and

Neutral Nations Supervisory Commission staff would move freely in the JSA; others would keep to their own side.

PARK CHUNG-HEE (1917–1979). Born the youngest of seven children in a poor farm family in Sonsan, North Kyongsang Province, Park Chung-hee graduated from Normal School in **Taegu** and became a primary school teacher in 1937. After a fight with a Japanese teacher, he resigned from the school and went to the Japanese puppet state of Manzhouguo (Manchukuo), established in 1932 in northeast **China**, where he enrolled at the Manzhouguo Military Academy in 1942. After completing a two-year course there, in 1944, he enrolled at the Japanese Military Academy. Upon graduation from this school, he was commissioned as a second lieutenant in the Imperial Army of **Japan** and was assigned to the Kanto Army in Manzhouguo.

When the Pacific War ended, Park returned to Korea, and in 1946 he enrolled at the military academy established by the **United States Army Military Government in Korea**. After completing a short (three months) training course, Park was commissioned as a captain in the Korean Constabulary. When the South Korean **national defense forces** were formed, he remained in the military. He was implicated in the 1948 **Yosu–Sunch'on Rebellion**, and sentenced to death, but was reprieved. Restored to the military, Park fought in the **Korean War**, and rose to the rank of brigadier general in 1953. After studying at the War College in 1957, he was promoted to the rank of major general in 1958. In 1960, at the time he first formulated a plan for a military coup, he was commander of the Logistic Base Command in **Pusan**.

In 1961, Park brought about the **Military Revolution of 16 May 1961**, overthrowing the Second Republic and becoming the vice-chairman of the **Military Revolutionary Committee**. He served as chairman of the **Supreme Council for National Reconstruction** from July 1961, and upon the resignation of President **Yun Po-son** in March 1962, Park became acting president. He retired from the army as lieutenant general in 1963.

Elected in October 1963 as the president of the Third Republic, he was reelected in 1967, 1971, 1972, and 1978. During his presidency, he carried out a series of five-year **national development plans**, which laid the foundation of the modern South Korean **economic de-**

velopment, instituted the **Yushin rule**, launched the **New Community Movement**, and contributed to the modernization and industrialization of South Korea. However, he grew steadily more authoritarian as the years passed, especially after the death of his wife in a failed **assassination** attempt against him in 1974. By 1978, there was widespread opposition to his rule. Following disagreement among Park and his advisers on the handling of this opposition, he was shot to death by the then director of the Korean Central Intelligence Agency (later the **National Intelligence Service**) at a dinner party on 26 October 1979.

Park's political legacy lived on under President **Chun Doo-hwan** until 1987, and to a lesser extent under Chun's successor **Roh Tae-woo**. Even today, politicians of various groups trace their line back to Park, while **North Korea**'s leader, **Kim Jong-il**, is said to admire both his political methods and his results. His daughter, **Park Geun-hye**, has, to some extent, inherited his political mantle.

PARK GEUN-HYE (1952–   ). The daughter of former dictator **Park Chung-hee**, Park Geun-hye graduated from the Department of Electronic Engineering at Sogang University in 1974. After her father's **assassination** in 1979, she avoided politics and publicity, instead involving herself with various educational organizations. In 1995, however, she became an adviser to the then ruling **Grand National Party** (GNP), and entered the **National Assembly** in 1998 on the GNP ticket. Park became a vice president of the GNP during the 16th National Assembly session (2000 onward), but left the party in 2002, accusing its president, **Lee Hoi-chang**, of "imperialistic leadership." She then founded her own party, the **Korean Coalition for the Future** (KCTF), which she represented in the National Assembly. She was also nominated as the party's candidate in the 2002 presidential election. However, by the end of 2002, she had rejoined the GNP, and acted as campaign manager for Lee Hoi-chang in his failed second bid for the presidency. Park visited **North Korea** in March 2002, and met **Kim Jong-il**, who apparently expressed much respect for her late father.

PARTY FOR NEW POLITICAL REFORM (*Shinjongdang*). When the **New Korea Party** of Kim Tong-gil merged with the **Unification**

National Party in 1992, those former members of the New Korea Party who opposed the merger formed their own party named the Party for New Political Reform in late February 1992 under the leadership of Pak Ch'an-jong. It did not survive long.

PARTY FOR PEACE AND DEMOCRACY (*P'yonghwa minjudang or P'yongmindang*). A political party formed in November 1987 by **Kim Dae-jung**, who became its president as well as its presidential candidate in the 1987 election. Kim Dae-jung resigned the party presidency in March 1988, bowing to mounting public criticism of his continuing rivalry with **Kim Young-sam** and his failure to unite with Kim to present a single candidate in the 16 December 1987 presidential election. However, he returned to the presidency in May 1988, following the **National Assembly** elections held in April in which his party became the first opposition party by winning the second largest number of seats. *See also* REUNIFICATION DEMOCRATIC PARTY.

PEACE DAM. A dam constructed in Yanggu County, Kangwon Province, for the purpose of neutralizing an alleged possible water offensive from **North Korea**. The construction of the dam began in 1986 and was completed in 1988. It was designed to contain a large amount of water that might have been released by the North Koreans from a dam of their own suspected of having been built for military purposes. There were widespread suspicions about government corruption in the whole project.

PEACE LINE. *See* RHEE LINE.

PEACEFUL UNIFICATION FOREIGN POLICY. One of many policies enunciated by the South Korean government on the question of reunification. This one was set out in 1973 by President **Park Chung-hee** in his "26 June Declaration." The seven-point statement included the following:

1. The peaceful unification of Korea is the supreme task of the Korean people, and South Korea will continue to exert every effort to accomplish this task.
2. The South and the North should neither interfere with each other's internal affairs, nor commit aggression against each other.

3. South Korea would continue to make efforts with sincerity and patience to secure concrete results from the North–South dialogue based on the **July 1972 statement on Korean unification**.
4. South Korea would not oppose **North Korea**'s participation with it in international organizations.
5. South Korea would not object to its admittance into the **United Nations** together with North Korea.
6. South Korea would open its doors to all the nations of the world, and it urged those countries whose ideologies and social institutions were different from it to open their doors to South Korea.

7. Peace and good-neighborliness were the firm basis of the foreign policy of South Korea. *See also* CROSS-RECOGNITION; NORDPOLITIK; NORTH–SOUTH KOREA RELATIONS.

PEOPLE'S REPUBLIC OF CHINA. *See* CHINA.

PEOPLE'S REVOLUTIONARY PARTY CASE. In August 1964, the Korean Central Intelligence Agency (KCIA, now the **National Intelligence Service**) announced the arrest of what it described as a large espionage group of the "People's Revolutionary Party." The party may have been entirely fictional, though later in the 1960s, a People's Revolutionary Party, supposedly based in South Korea, was established by **North Korea**. Those arrested included radical college professors, students, newspaper reporters, and workers. The group was allegedly involved in an organized revolutionary movement to overthrow the Republic in collusion with the North Korean communists. In 1965, fourteen of them were given prison terms under the **Anti-Communism Law**, but because the prosecution bungled the case, many of those charged were not convicted.

Ten years later, however, the KCIA returned to the case, rearresting 21 of those detained in 1964. They were now charged with being a North Korean cell, stirring up student discontent. The aim of the arrests was apparently to justify the harsh repression of those opposed to **Yushin rule**. This action, and the torture of those detained, led to an active campaign against the arrests by Christian groups. These including the Urban Industrial Mission and two of its American advisers. In the end, the government prevailed. Eight of the accused were executed and the two Americans were deported. The case was a powerful factor in strengthening opposition to **Park Chung-hee**'s increasingly authoritarian rule.

POLICE. The first postliberation police force in South Korea was organized in 1945 by the **United States Military Government in Korea**. Following the establishment of the Republic of Korea in 1948, this became the Korean National Police (KNP). Although separate **national defense forces** were also established in 1948, the police retained a paramilitary role and its members were employed in military roles during the 1950–1953 **Korean War**.

Because many of its early recruits had served in the police under the Japanese **Government-General in Korea**, and because it was seen as a poorly qualified force, the KNP faced many difficulties in its early years. These were compounded by the force's use for political purposes by the **Syngman Rhee** regime, a tradition that would continue well into the 1980s. At the same time, however, the KNP began to develop into a more professional force, using increasingly modern crime detection processes. From 1975, the head of the KNP was of vice-ministerial rank, reporting directly to the minister of home affairs.

In addition to normal police functions, the KNP was also responsible for riot control, and various measures designed to protect the country from infiltration from **North Korea**. This led to a considerable overlap between the role of the police and other agencies, including the **National Intelligence Service**. One of its main functions in combating alleged threats to the state was the administration of the Combat, or riot, Police, established in 1967. This group, although theoretically under the Ministry of National Defense, was administered on a day-to-day basis by the KNP, and was often the police front line against activists in the **student movement** and the **labor movement**.

The KNP has been regularly accused of heavy-handed tactics and brutality against political opponents of the South Korean government. There have also been allegations that suspects held in police custody were particularly vulnerable to torture. Despite such complaints, few police officers were ever brought before the courts.

POLITICAL ACTIVITIES PURIFICATION LAW. Enacted on 16 March 1962 by the **Supreme Council for National Reconstruction**, it banished, until August 1968, "old and corrupt politicians" and others, including the members of the **Liberal Party**, the **Democratic Party**, the **New Democratic Party**, and leaders of progressive organizations. Under the law, a Political Purification Committee was established to screen those individuals to be banned. Some 4,369 were put on the purge list; of these, 1,336 were cleared. President **Yun Po-son** resigned on 22 March 1962, protesting against the law.

POLITICAL FRATERNAL SOCIETY FOR REVITALIZING RE-FORM (*Yushin jong'uhoe* or *Yujonghoe*). A political society that was formed in March 1973 mostly by those who had been connected with the **Military Revolution of 16 May 1961**. It was a sister political organization of the ruling **Democratic Republican Party**, and 73 of its members were appointed to the **National Assembly**, becoming a built-in progovernment group, supporting President **Park Chung-hee**'s **Yushin rule**. It was abolished in 1980.

POLITICAL PARTY LAWS. Laws that allowed the revival of political activity, after periods when political activity were banned. The first was promulgated on 26 December 1962, reviving organized political activities of politicians and bringing about the formation of four political parties. The law was promulgated in order to restore a civilian government. The second political party law was promulgated on 30 December 1972 for the purpose of reviving political party activities that had been curtailed in October. In similar manner as with the first law, this one also saw the rise of new political parties.

POLITICAL REFORM COMMITTEE. A committee established by the **Special Committee for National Security Measures** in November 1980 to screen and purge undesirable politicians. It put 835 former politicians on a blacklist, barring them from playing any political role.

PRESIDENTIAL ELECTIONS. *See* APPENDIX C.

PRESIDENTIAL ELECTORAL COLLEGE. Under the revised **Constitution** approved in the national referendum on 22 October

1980, a new presidential electoral college composed of "no less than 5,000 popularly elected delegates" was created, replacing the **National Conference for Unification**. On 11 February 1981, elections were held to choose 5,278 members of the electoral college. When the constitution was again revised following a national referendum on 27 October 1987, the electoral college was abolished, restoring the system of popular election of the president.

PRESS CODE OF ETHICS. In April 1957 the Korean Newspaper Editors Association was established. This adopted the press code of ethics primarily to protect national security and strengthen an anticommunist stand. The self-imposed **censorship** of the press remained in force until 1988. *See also* "MASSACRES OF THE MASS MEDIA."

PROGRESSIVE PARTY (*Chinbodang*). A party formed in November 1956 by **Cho Pong-am**, a progressive socialist who had served as the minister of agriculture and forestry under President **Syngman Rhee** from August 1948 to February 1949 and ran for the presidency in the 1952 presidential election. When Cho was executed for his alleged antistate activity in July 1959, his party collapsed.

PROTESTANTISM. *See* CHRISTIANITY; RELIGIONS.

PU-MA DISTURBANCES. This refers to antigovernment student demonstrations that took place in the **Pusan** and **Masan** area, accompanied by bloody clashes between the demonstrators and the riot **police** in October 1979. These violent demonstrations brought about the declaration of garrison law, and eventually led to the fall of the Fourth Republic. The news from Pusan and Masan led students in Seoul and elsewhere to prepare for large antigovernment demonstrations similar to those of April 1960. *See also* STUDENT MOVEMENT.

PUSAN. South Korea's major port and an industrial city in the southeast of the peninsula, Pusan is also the home of former president **Kim Young-sam**. It developed originally in the early Yi dynasty as the harbor for nearby Tonghae, which was an important point of contact with **Japan**, and where Japanese merchants were allowed to reside. After the 1876 Kangwha Treaty, the Japanese presence increased rapidly. A railway from **Seoul** to Pusan was begun in 1904; this was later extended to the border with **China** and connected to the trans-Siberian railway.

The city developed as the main port for Korean–Japan trade under the Japanese **Government-General of Korea**, and was the center of anti-Japanese strikes in 1921. Retreating South Korean and **United States troops**, and the South Korean government, arrived in the city in August 1950 during the **Korean War**. It remained the seat of government until 1954. Its population (2003) is about four million.

Pusan is the site of the **United Nations** Cemetery, established in 1951, and named the United Nations Memorial Cemetery in 1955. In 1960, the UN assumed charge of the land. At the end of the war, the cemetery held some 11,000 bodies, but many were repatriated in subsequent years, and today there are 2,299 soldiers of 11 nationalities, four unknown soldiers, and 11 nonbelligerents buried there. In 2002, Pusan hosted the Asian Games, the second South Korean city to do so.

PUSAN POLITICAL DISTURBANCE (*Pusan chongch'i p'adong*). This event took place in the latter part of May 1952 in connection with the controversy surrounding the constitutional revision proposed by the administration. When the opposition lawmakers refused to pass the constitutional revision bill and Prime Minister **Chang Myon**, the opposition leader, resigned in mid-April, President **Syngman Rhee** appointed a new prime minister and declared martial law on 25 May in the **Pusan** area. The military **police** arrested some 50 lawmakers from the **National Assembly** building, charged some of them with having received political funds from "international Communist organizations," and finally forced the National Assembly to pass the bill at midnight on 4 July revising the **constitution** so as to institute the direct, popular election of the president and vice president.

P'YONGYANG. P'yongyang was the "temporary capital" of **North Korea** from its establishment in 1948 until 1972; **Seoul**, the capital of Korea from 1392, was listed as the capital. After 1972, P'yongyang became the permanent capital of North Korea. The city, which occupies an important strategic position on the Taedong River, was probably the site of the Koguryo capital. It suffered heavily in the 1894–1895 Sino–Japanese and the 1904–1905 Russo–Japanese Wars. Under the Japanese **Government-General of Korea**, it began to develop as a modernized industrial center, with important railway connections. It was also a major center of **Christianity**.

During the 1950–1953 **Korean War**, the **United Nations Command** forces briefly occupied P'yongyang in the autumn of 1950. After their retreat, the city was subjected to heavy bombing, which left little standing. The government and the remaining inhabitants were forced to live underground. A massive reconstruction program, with help from many Eastern European countries and **China**, saw a new city arise in the 1950s. P'yongyang remains the political, educational, and economic center of North Korea, though it has not escaped the economic problems that have beset the North since the mid-1990s. Its population is estimated at 2.2 million. P'yongyang has been the scene for most meetings in North Korea between the North and the South, including the **June 2000 Inter-Korean Summit** meeting between **Kim Dae-jung** and **Kim Jong-il**. In September 2003, the first ever tour group from South Korea visited P'yongyang.

– R –

RADIO. *See* BROADCASTING.

RANGOON BOMBING. On 9 October 1983, a bomb explosion at the Aung Sun Mausoleum in Rangoon, Burma, killed four Burmese officials and sixteen leading officials of the government of South Korea, including the deputy prime minister, Suh Sook-joon, the minister for foreign affairs, **Yi Pom-suk**, and the minister for commerce and industry, Kim Dong-whie. The bomb was intended for the South Korean president, **Chun Doo-hwan**, who was on an official visit to Burma. Chun escaped because bombers thought that the South Korean ambassador's car was that of the president. Suspicions immediately fell on **North Korea**. The Burmese captured two of those involved, and a third committed suicide. Burma withdrew **diplomatic recognition** of North Korea and broke off diplomatic relations, as did a number of other countries.

REBELLION ON CHEJU ISLAND. *See* CHEJU REBELLION.

RELIGIONS. The traditional native religion of the Koreans was animistic **Shamanism**, which may have been brought in by the Neolithic people. It was joined by **Buddhism**, which was introduced to Korea in the 4th-century A.D. from **China** and eventually became a state religion in Paekche and Shilla, flourishing after the unification of Korea by Shilla and especially during the during the Koryo period (918–1392). Buddhism, which was rejected by the ruling class and the government of the Yi dynasty (1932–1910), became the religion of the rural population, but after 1900 it began to attract wider attention as religious toleration was practiced. Although **Confucianism** is sometimes described as a religion, it is more a set of precepts on moral behavior.

Christianity became a major religion in Korea, from its introduction, in the form of Roman Catholicism, from China in the 17th century. Its impact was much enhanced with the arrival of Protestantism in the late 19th century.

There are also a number of native religions. **Taejonggyo** is another religion with a deity named Hanul (Heaven), a trinity of creator, teacher, and temporal king who took the form of the person of Tan'-gun, the mythical founder of the Korean nation. This religion became virtually extinct in the 15th century, but it revived with the resurgence of Korean nationalism and spirit of independence in the late 19th and early 20th centuries.

Tonghak ("Eastern Learning") was founded in 1860. It grew strong among the oppressed and mistreated population, becoming an antiforeign force in the late 19th century. Its influence declined sharply after the failed "Tonghak Rebellion" of 1893–1894. In 1906, it was renamed **Ch'ondo-gyo** ("Teachings of the Heavenly Way"). It survives in both South and **North Korea**, though its numbers are now small. There were a half dozen other minor religions that were Confucian in ethics, Buddhist in rituals, and Taoist in beliefs.

After the liberation of Korea, both Buddhism and Christianity grew strong, while Ch'ondo-gyo and others maintained the status quo. Meanwhile, many new Christian sects emerged, one of the most successful being the **T'ongilgyo**, or the "Unification Church." Dozens of similar quasi-religious bodies also emerged, attracting ignorant people by quaint doctrines and methods.

Islam was introduced only in 1950, supposedly by Turkish troops during the **Korean War**. Its followers formed the Federation of Korean Islamic Churches in 1966.

By the mid-1980s, 12 million, or 30 percent of the population, claimed to be Christians—this figure included a number of indigenous Korean churches—9 million, representing some 21 percent, Buddhists, while Ch'ondo-gyo had around 53,000 followers. Ten years later, the figure was around 50 percent of the population, or 23 million, claimed to be Christian. Churches and temples increased to match these figures. In 1962, it was reported that there were about 2,500 registered Buddhist temples; by 1993, there were 10,632. Protestant churches had increased from 6,785 to 42,598, while Roman Catholic churches had gone from 313 to over 800 in a similar period. One church alone, the Yoido Full Gospel Church, claimed over 700,000 adherents.

REPRESENTATIVE DEMOCRATIC COUNCIL (*Minju Uiwon*). A 50-member advisory council established on 14 February 1946 by General **John R. Hodge**, United States military commander in South Korea, with Dr. **Syngman Rhee** as its chairman. The **United States Army Military Government in Korea** appointed half of its members, and the rest were selected by various Korean organizations. However, the leading liberals, as well as the leftists refused to serve in it. It did not cooperate with the American occupation authorities and was replaced by the **South Korean Interim Legislative Assembly** in December 1946.

REUNIFICATION DEMOCRATIC PARTY (*T'ongil minjudang*). A party formed in May 1987 by the followers of **Kim Young-sam** who defected from the **New Korea Democratic Party**. Kim Young-sam became its president, and when **Kim Dae-jung** joined the party, it gained a considerable amount of strength as many lawmakers who defected from the New Korea Democratic Party joined its ranks. However, when Kim Dae-jung left the party and formed his own **Party for Peace and Democracy** in November 1987, it was badly damaged as many of its lawmakers followed Kim Dae-jung.

In the 1987 presidential election, the two parties failed to form a united front and present a single presidential candidate, thus allowing

Roh Tae-woo to become president. In the 1988 **National Assembly**, the Reunification Democratic Party became the second major opposition party by winning the third largest number in the National Assembly. In February 1990, it merged with the ruling **Democratic Justice Party** and the **New Democratic Republican Party** to form the **Democratic Liberal Party**.

REUNITING OF SCATTERED FAMILY MEMBERS. The **Korean War** led to the separation of many families. Large numbers took to the roads to avoid bombing and military clashes. Estimates vary for the total number of refugees. Estimates for those who moved from **North Korea** range from 450,000 to over one million, while some 286,000 moved from South Korea to the North. Estimates of the numbers displaced also vary enormously. The oft-quoted figure of 10 million separated family members in South Korea is more an expression of the importance of the problem than it is an accurate picture of the numbers involved. The South Korean government has estimated that the number of first generation separated is about 480,000; if second- and third- generation family members are added in, the total comes to about 7.5 million. In addition, many families in the South became separated in the wartime confusion.

The **Korean Armistice Agreement**, signed on 27 July 1953 authorized the establishment of a **Committee for Assisting the Return of Displaced Civilians**. This was aimed at civilians who had become displaced as a result of the fighting, and did not cover civilians detained during the war. The latter were handled under the armistice arrangements for prisoners of war. None in North Korea applied to go to South Korea, and only 37 from the South eventually went North early in 1954. Thereafter, there were no mail or telephone contacts between North and South, and those separated where unable to trace their relatives. In the years following the war, the International Committee of the Red Cross tried without success to arrange exchanges of lists of missing persons between North and South.

For many years, no attempts were made by the South Korean government to reunite even those family members in South Korea who were separated during the war. From 1971 onward, the issue of separated families featured in the periodic **North–South Red Cross talks**, but without much progress before the talks were broken off in

1973. From that same year, the South Korean government allowed its citizens to correspond with Koreans in communist countries, except North Korea, and some reunions were eventually arranged in **China**.

In the 1970s, the South Korean media took up the issue of those living in South Korea who were separated, which at first evoked little interest. But it was a telethon launched by the state-run Korean Broadcasting System between 30 June and 14 November 1983 that brought about the reuniting of some 10,189 family members who had been separated and whose whereabouts had hitherto been unknown.

When the Red Cross talks resumed in 1985, agreement was reached on the first ever North–South family reunions. In September 1985, 50 individuals from each side crossed the **demilitarized zone**, but only 65 contacts were made. Further talks in 1989–1990, and in 1992, failed to reach agreement. At the **June 2000 Inter-Korean Summit**, the two leaders agreed on further exchanges. These began on Liberation Day (15 August) 2000 and have continued sporadically since then. In January 2003, the two sides reached agreement on the establishment of a permanent reunion site, in North Korea's Diamond (Kumgang) Mountains.

RHEE IN-JE (1948–). Rhee graduated in law from Seoul National University in 1972. He then became an attorney, and eventually a judge of the **Taejon** district court from 1981–1983, when he returned to his law practice. In 1987, he entered the **National Assembly** as a member of **Kim Young-sam**'s **Reunification Democratic Party**. When the party merged to form the **Democratic Liberal Party**, Rhee, too, switched. Following Kim Young-sam's election as president, Rhee became minister of labor from 1993–1994, and then governor of Kyonggi Province from 1995–1997. In 1997, he left what had then become the **New Korea Party** to stand as presidential candidate for the newly formed **New Party for the People**. He failed, but split the vote, allowing **Kim Dae-jung** to become president. Following this, Rhee eventually became a senior member of Kim Dae-jung's **Millennium Democratic Party** (MDP). However, he failed to win the party's nomination for the December 2002 presidential elections, and when **Roh Moo-hyun** was selected, Rhee left the party to join the **United Liberal Democrats**. In September 2003, he published a book alleging that his failure to win the MDP nomination was a conspiracy because he knew too much about how the **June 2000 Inter-Korean Summit** had been agreed.

RHEE (PEACE) LINE. A maritime demarcation line, running on an average up to 60 miles (97 kilometers) from the Korean shores but 170 miles (274 kilometers) at its farthest point in the **East Sea/Sea of Japan**, originally imposed by General **Douglas MacArthur** during the occupation of **Japan** as a means of keeping Japan closely within his jurisdiction and avoiding clashes between Japanese and Korean fishermen. General **Mark Clark**, then head of the **United Nations Command** reaffirmed it during the **Korean War** to restrict possible infiltrations from **North Korea**.

During the negotiations on the normalization of relations with **Japan** after the **Korean Armistice Agreement** of 1953, South Korean President **Syngman Rhee** reintroduced the line, now renamed the Rhee, or Peace Line, in order to conserve Korean fisheries' resources in the East Sea/Sea of Japan. The line, and South Korean efforts to enforce the prohibition of Japanese fishing in what the Japanese regarded as the high seas, became a bone of contention between South Korea and Japan. The dispute continued until the 1965 agreement on normalization of relations, in which the South Koreans agreed to a 12-mile (19-kilometer) fishing limit. In April 1978, the South Korean government proclaimed a 12-mile (19-kilometer) territorial waters limit.

RHEE SYNGMAN (1875–1965). Born Yi Sung-man in P'yongsan, Hwanghae Province, now in **North Korea**, he became a student activist as a member of a student society named *Hyopsonghoe* at a mission school (Paejae) in **Seoul**. He was an advocate of nationalism and cultural reform, joined the Independence Club when it was founded in 1896, and was imprisoned in 1898 for an alleged plot to overthrow the monarchy and establish a republic.

Released from prison in 1904, Rhee traveled to the **United States** to study, earning a doctoral degree in political science in 1910 from Princeton University. He returned to Korea, now annexed by **Japan**, but in 1912 he was forced by the Japanese to leave. Returning to the United States, he formed a nationalist society of the Koreans named *Tongjihoe* (Comrades Society), and in 1919 he was named premier of the **Korean Provisional Government**, which was established by the Korean nationalists in Shanghai. Dr. Rhee served the Provisional Government as its president when its administrative structure was revised, remaining in that capacity until 1931. While in the United States, he fought for Korea's freedom in a variety of ways, always seeking the official recognition of the Provisional Government as a legitimate government of the Koreans in exile by the American government and others.

Returning to Korea in October 1945 following liberation, Rhee became the leader of a rightist **National Council for the Rapid Realization of Korean Independence**, which included some 50 political and social organizations. After serving as chairman of the **Representative Democratic Council**, which the **United States Army Military Government in Korea** established in 1946, he was elected to the Constituent Assembly in May 1948, and in turn was elected by the Constituent Assembly as the first president of the Republic of Korea. He was reelected in 1952, 1956, and 1960, becoming more and more autocratic. During the **Korean War**, Rhee argued against any compromise with North Korea or **China**. He opposed the **Korean Armistice Agreement**, which he tried to jeopardize, even though he eventually agreed to abide by its terms.

Following the **April 1960 student uprising**, brought about by his supporter's heavy-handed rigging of the 1960 presidential election, Rhee was forced to resign from the presidency on 26 April 1960, marking the end of the First Republic. In late May, he left Korea in exile for Hawaii, where he died in 1965. His body was brought back to South Korea and buried at the National Cemetery. In 2000, it was decided to erect a statue to his memory in the **National Assembly**.

RIDGWAY, MATTHEW BUNKER (1895–1993). An American general, who ended World War II as the deputy supreme allied commander in the Mediterranean, Ridgway became commander of the 8th United States Army in Korea in December 1950, during one of the bleakest phases of the **Korean War**. **United Nations forces**, which in October 1950 had reached the Yalu River border with **China**, had been thrown back by Chinese and North Korean forces, which captured the South Korean capital, **Seoul**, for the second time in January 1951. Ridgway abandoned Seoul and regrouped his forces south of the capital on the Han River, from where he began a counterattack.

This was successful. Seoul was retaken in March 1951 and the UN forces pushed the enemy back to the region of the **38th parallel**, where the fighting had begun in June 1950. Ridgway resisted pressure from General **Douglas MacArthur** to take the war across the parallel again, and when United States President Harry S. Truman dismissed MacArthur in April 1951, Ridgway succeeded him as commander in chief of the **United Nations Command** (UNC). In this role, Ridgway continued to be cautious until General **Mark Clark** replaced him in May 1952.

In later life, Ridgway drew on his experiences in Korea to criticize the Vietnam War. He wrote a personal account of the Korean War, which appeared in 1967.

ROH MOO-HYUN (1946–). Roh was born in a farming village in South Kyongsang Province. He attended **Pusan** Commercial School, graduating in 1966. After military service, he studied for the bar, becoming a lawyer in 1975. In 1977, be became a district court judge in **Taejon**, but opened his own law office in 1978. During the protests against President **Chun Doo-hwan**, he began to work defending student activists. This led him to an active role in the June 1987 demonstrations that followed Chun's nomination of **Roh Tae-woo** as his successor. As a result, Roh Moo-hyun was imprisoned for a short period for helping striking workers.

In 1988, he entered the **National Assembly** as a member of the opposition **Reunification Democratic Party** (RDP), serving in a variety of roles. In 1990 he broke with the RDP over its decision to amalgamate with the ruling party and helped to form a new **Democratic Party**. That same year he resigned his National Assembly seat in protest of the forced passing of a **broadcasting** bill. In 1992, he ran the unsuccessful presidential campaign for the opposition candidate, **Kim Dae-jung**, and also failed to be reelected to the National Assembly. He also ran unsuccessfully as mayor of Pusan in 1995, and for the Chongno (central **Seoul)** National Assembly seat in 1996. In 1997, Roh ran Kim Dae-jung's successful campaign for the presidency as the candidate of the **National Congress for New Politics** (NCNP), and in 1998, he won the Chongno seat for the NCNP in a by-election. He gave up this seat in 2000, but failed to be elected for Pusan.

In 2000–2001, he was the minister for maritime affairs and fisheries, and he also served as an advisor and senior member of the central committee of the ruling **Millennium Democratic Party** (MDP). In 2002, the MDP chose him as its presidential candidate. In the elections, Roh, campaigning on the continuation of Kim Dae-jung's policies on North Korea, scored an unexpected victory over the opposition **Grand National Party**'s **Lee Hoi-chang**, to become the sixteenth president of the Republic of Korea. His election was widely seen as representing the final end of the political era of the "three Kims": **Kim Jong-p'il**, **Kim Young-sam**, and **Kim Dae-jung**.

However, Roh did not have an easy time as president. More conservative South Koreans viewed his radical background with suspicion. He was also seen as anti-American, and there were differences between him and the U.S. administration of President George W. Bush on how to handle the question of the **North Korean nuclear program**. He seemed unable to cope with the economic and political problems that beset the country, and by summer 2003, his popularity had plunged. The MDP split, leaving him with only a small supporting group in the National Assembly. Roh then quit the party, casting doubts on its future viability. Faced by mounting problems, Roh announced in October 2003 that he had lost confidence in his own ability as president, and suggested that there should be a referendum early in 2004 on whether or not he should continue.

ROH TAE-WOO (1932–). Born in a middle-class farm family in Talsong, North Kyongsang Province, Roh first attended **Taegu** Technical Middle School in 1945, and then transferred to Kyongbok Middle School, graduating in 1950. He joined the army, and in 1951 he entered the Korean Military Academy for training as a career military officer.

After graduating from the military academy in 1955, Roh served in various positions in the army. In 1959, he studied at the Special Warfare School in the **United States**, and in 1968 he graduated from the Korean Army War College. As he rose in rank, he served as commander of the 9th Special Forces Brigade (1974–1979), commander of the 9th Infantry Division (1979), commander of Capital Security Command (1979), and, after taking part in the **December 1979 coup** engineered by Gen. **Chun Doo-hwan**, he became commander of the **Defense Security Command** in August 1980.

When the **Democratic Justice Party** (DJP) was inaugurated, Roh joined it, and after retiring from the army as a four-star general in July

1981, he served as minister of state for political and security affairs (1981–1983), minister of sports (1982), and minister of home affairs (1982–1983). After the decision of the International Olympic Committee to award the 1988 **Olympic Games** to **Seoul**, he was named president of the Seoul Olympic Organizing Committee in July 1983, becoming president of the Korean Olympic Committee in October 1984.

Elected as a member of the **National Assembly** in 1985, Roh served as chairman of the ruling **Democratic Justice Party** (DJP). On 10 June 1987, the DJP nominated him as its presidential candidate for the 1987 presidential election. But following an outburst of anti-government demonstrations, Roh made the stunning **June 29th democratization declaration**, demanding that Chun introduce reforms and address political grievances.

When Chun accepted this, it defused the political crisis and on 5 August 1987, Roh replaced President Chun as president of the ruling DJP. In the 16 December 1987 presidential election, he won the election as the 13th president by 36.6 percent of the popular vote, defeating four other candidates. On 25 February 1988, Roh became president, inaugurating the Sixth Republic.

His presidency was notable for the successful Seoul Olympic Games in 1988, and for his policy of **Nordpolitik**, or rapprochement with the **Soviet Union** and the People's Republic of **China**. The same policy led to a series of agreements with **North Korea** in 1991–1992, but these remained largely unimplemented. The beginning of the **North Korean nuclear crisis** overshadowed the end of his presidency. In 1990 he concluded a political alliance with the veteran opposition leader, **Kim Young-sam**, who succeeded him as president in 1993.

After he left office, Roh, like his predecessor, **Chun Doo-hwan**, was under constant attack for his role in the 1979 coup and the 1980 **Kwangju uprising**, leading eventually to his arrest, together with Chun, in 1995 on charges of bribery and corruption. Later, charges of treason and mutiny were added. Sentenced to 22 years imprisonment and a fine in 1996, he was released, as was Chun, in 1997, although in theory the fine still remained.

ROYAL ASIATIC SOCIETY KOREA BRANCH (RAS). Founded by Western residents in Korea in June 1900, the RAS is loosely associated with the London-based Royal Asiatic Society. It is the oldest association in Korea, and had a membership of some 1,500 at home and overseas at the end of 2002. Its *Transactions*, which have appeared regularly since 1900, with the exception of the Pacific and **Korean War** years, provide a unique collection of scholarly articles on all aspects of Korean history, art, and culture.

RUSSIA. *See* SOVIET UNION/RUSSIA.

– S –

SAENARA DATSUN AUTOMOBILE SCANDAL. In February 1964, opposition party lawmakers brought charges of illegal stock market manipulation and dubious financial dealings against members of the **Democratic Republican Party** (DRP) in connection with importation of Saenara Datsun automobiles from the Datsun Company of **Japan** in 1963. These cases, plus two other scandalous financial and business dealings of ruling DRP members, constituted the so-called "four great economic scandals."

SAKHALIN KOREANS' RETURN. Under a joint government program between **Japan** and South Korea begun in 1997, some 1,000 Koreans from southern Sakhalin in **Soviet Union/Russia**, which had been Japanese territory until 1945, returned to South Korea and were resettled in **Seoul**. Only Koreans born before August 1945 and holding South Korean citizenship were eligible to relocate to South Korea. The South Korean government constructed a purpose-built apartment complex some 40 miles (60 kilometers) south of the capital, Seoul, to accommodate them, the Japanese government providing the funds for the building. In early 2000, some 40,000 Koreans and their families remained in Sakhalin. Since then, there has been a steady trickle of Koreans from Sakhalin to South Korea; not all have settled.

SEOUL. Capital of Korea from 1394 to 1945, and capital of South Korea since 1945, Seoul lies on the Han River, some 25 miles (40 kilometers) from the port of **Inch'on**. From 1948 until 1972, Seoul was also formally listed as the capital of **North Korea**. Seoul began to develop as a modern city in the last years of the Yi dynasty

(1392–1910) at the end of the 19th century. Under the Japanese **Government–General of Korea**, there was much new building, some of which, such as the City Hall, the main railway station, and the **Bank of Korea** survive. However, the main symbol of the Japanese colonial period, the **Capitol Building**, was demolished in the 1990s. The population grew steadily under the Japanese, and reached the million mark in 1944.

Seoul saw heavy fighting in the **Korean War** and suffered much destruction. It also suffered a dramatic drop in population, though this recovered when the government moved back from **Pusan** in 1954. Seoul today is a huge modern city, with a registered Korean population of 10,263,336 and an additional 67,908 foreigners in December 2001. It is the political, economic, educational, and social center of the country, with numerous **universities** and colleges. Most Korean companies have their headquarters in Seoul. Some attempt has been made to preserve a few of the city's older quarters but new wealth has brought new constructions to most parts of the city. It was the site of the Asian Games in 1986, the **Olympic Games** in 1988, and for some of the **World Cup 2002** football features.

Periodic proposals to shift the capital from its present position, which is regarded as too close to North Korea and to the **demilitarized zone**, have come to nothing. There has been some move of government buildings and institutions south of the Han River, however.

SEVEN-POINT CONDITIONS FOR DEMOCRATIZATION. Proposed on 24 December 1986 by the **New Korea Democratic Party**, these included guarantee for freedom of speech, assembly, and the press; adoption of a new fair election law; inauguration of local self-rule; political neutrality of government officials; strengthening of party politics; release of political prisoners; and restoration of civil rights of all former political leaders. President **Chun Doo-hwan** ignored them at the time, but some were introduced in 1987. *See also* JUNE 29TH DEMOCRATIZATION DECLARATION.

SHAMANISM. One of the earliest **religions** of the inhabitants of the Korean Peninsula recognizing a myriad of spirits that affect the well being of the people directly or indirectly. According to this belief, these spirits must be pacified to avoid evil consequences and their favors solicited to ensure the safety and good fortune of both individuals and village communities. Shaman priests and priestesses, commonly called *mudang*, perform a variety of religious rituals to exorcise evil spirits. There are no specific temples or shrines for the spirits, as in the case of **Buddhism** and **Confucianism**, but Korean villages used to have their shaman shrines (usually huts) called *songhwangdang* in remote locations near the villages. Regarded as superstition by the educated and often frowned upon by the state, Shamanism was practiced mostly by the uneducated population, particularly by women. Under President **Park Chung-hee**, Shamanism was officially banned, but it survived in remote areas. In recent years its popularity has increased, and it is now seen as an important part of traditional Korean culture. *See also* ZO ZA-YANG.

SHIN IK-HUI (1892–1956). Born in Kwangju, Kyonggi Province, Shin became a champion of Korean freedom while studying at Waseda University in **Japan**. After graduating from Waseda in 1913, he returned to Korea and taught first at secondary school, and then at Posong College for Commerce and Law. In 1918, Shin became involved in the independence movement. In the spring of 1919, he fled to Shanghai where he participated in the establishment of the **Korean Provisional Government** in exile there, becoming vice-chairman of its legislative council in 1922. He served in various positions in the Provisional Government until he returned to Korea in 1945.

On his return, Shin founded Kungmin University in **Seoul** and served as a member of the **South Korean Interim Legislative Assembly** in 1947 when he and Chi Ch'ong-ch'on of the **Taedong Youth Corps** united their organizations into the **Korean Nationalist Party**. He was elected to the Constituent Assembly in May 1948, serving as its vice-chairman first, and then chairman, replacing Dr. **Syngman Rhee** who was elected president of the Republic. In 1949, Shin's party and the **Korean (Han'guk) Democratic Party** merged into the **Democratic Nationalist Party**. Elected to the **National Assembly** in 1950, Shin expanded his party into the **Democratic Party** in 1955, becoming its president. Although nominated by his party as a presidential candidate in the 1956 presidential election, he died of a stroke during his heated campaign.

SIX PLEDGES OF THE MILITARY REVOLUTIONARY COMMITTEE. After the **Military Revolution of 16 May 1961**, the **Military Revolutionary Committee** announced on 18 May the following pledges to win the support of the people:

1. Positive, uncompromising opposition to communism is the basis of our policy.
2. We shall respect and observe the **United Nations** Charter, and strengthen our relations with the United States and other Free World Nations.
3. We shall eliminate corruption, and eradicate other social evils that have become prevalent in our country; we shall inculcate fresh and wholesome moral and mental attitudes among the people.
4. We shall provide relief for poverty-stricken and hungry people, and devote our entire energies toward the development of a self-sustaining economy.
5. We shall strengthen our military power and determination to combat communism, looking forward to the eventual achievement of our unchangeable goal of national unification.
6. As soldiers, after we have completed our mission, we shall restore the government to honest and conscientious civilians, and return to our proper military duties. As citizens, we shall devote ourselves without reservation to the accomplishment of these tasks, and to the construction of a solid foundation for a new and truly democratic republic.

16 NATIONS DECLARATION ON KOREA. On 27 July 1953, when the **Korean Armistice Agreement** was signed, the 16 nations whose troops composed the **United Nations forces** and fought in the **Korean War** issued a "Joint Policy Declaration Concerning the Korean Armistice," pledging that they would again unite to resist any renewed communist aggression. On 15 July 1954 at Geneva, these 16 nations also declared that further consideration and examination of the Korean question should be transferred to the **United Nations**. Since then, there have been no further declarations by this group. *See also* GENEVA POLITICAL CONFERENCE.

SOCIAL AND CULTURAL DEVELOPMENTS. The most significant social change in South Korean society since 1948 has been the rise of the middle class. After the country's annexation by **Japan** in 1910, colonial rule modernized the traditional social structure of Korea somewhat by reducing the power and privileges of the upper class (*yangban*) and created new conditions that allowed the rise of the commoners.

However, it was South Korea's rapid **economic development** from the late 1960s that increased the number of professional and skilled people, turning them into a solid and growing middle class. Since the mid-1980s, polls have regularly indicated that some 65 percent of the population regarded themselves as "middle class." As the economic structure changed, migration of the rural population into urban areas and new industrial centers took place. The urban population grew at an annual average rate of 5 percent after 1955, while the population in rural areas showed a commensurate decrease. The migration of the rural population grew faster from the mid-1960s. The number of people engaged in **agriculture**, forestry, and fisheries declined from 9.1 million in 1966 to 3.6 million in 1985 while the number of industrial workers grew from 1.1 million in 1966 to 4.6 million, and the number of those who were engaged in the social services sector grew from 2.5 million in 1966 to 8.2 million in 1987. According to the 1985 census, the urban population stood at 26.5 million, or 66 percent of the total population of 40.5 million, and the rural population was 14 million, or 34 per cent of the total population.

The population of **Seoul** grew from about one million in 1948 to 10 million by 1987, that of **Pusan** from 500,000 to 3.5 million, that of **Taegu** from 250,000 to 2.0 million, and those of **Inch'on**, **Taejon**, and **Kwangju** grew to a just over one million each. These figures have remained constant into the 21st century, indicating that the great wave of urbanization that began in the 1960s is now over.

With the improvement in living standards, the death rate and the rate of birth decreased. The percentage of the annual rate of birth declined from 3.0 percent in the 1950s to 1.3 percent in the 1980s, but the population grew from 21.5 million in 1955 to 42 million in 1987, and to 49.7 million in 1997. This was due to the fact that the average life expectancy increased from 51.1 years for men and 53.7 years for women in 1960, to 69.5 for men, 73.3 for women in 1987, and to 70.6 years for men and

78.1 years for women by the end of the century. The average Korean woman had 6.1 children in 1960, but this dropped to 4.2 in 1970, 2.8 in 1980, 2.3 in 1987, and to 1.42 in 1999. By 1997, 6.3 percent of the population was over 65; this had risen to 7.1 percent by July 2000. The rate of population growth between 1960–1966 was 2.7 percent, but it dropped to 2.3 percent in the 1966–1970 period, 1.9 percent in the 1972–1975 period, and in 1987 it was 1.37 percent. By the mid 1990s, it had fallen below 1 percent, reaching 0.71 percent in 2000.

The disappearance of the traditional social class structure, along with the rise of a new middle class and a new elite business community, contributed to the growth of social equality. Individual ability and educational background, rather than birthright, became the means by which to rise in social status. Although many political leaders came from a formerly high social class, such as *yangban*, a majority of the new Korean business leaders were from the commoner class. The economic development that affected the rural economy also closed the gap between the living standards of the urban population and the rural areas in conjunction with the **New Community Movement**.

Another important social change was the rise in the social status of women. A growing number of women with higher education became professionals, and along with the increasing number of women wage earners they brought about a growing social equality with men, although there are many areas where considerable disparity still exists. Many traditional attitudes toward family and society have altered with the increase in nuclear families and the commensurate decrease in extended families.

As the educated population grew, the number of newspapers increased to 31 by 1987. Of these, five were national papers, the rest local papers. There were also two English-language dailies. The total circulation of daily newspapers surpassed the 15 million mark in 1987; subsequently, newspaper readership has declined as new media, especially the **Internet**, have appeared. Meanwhile, meeting the growing demands for more reading materials, hundreds of magazines and journals were published and the number of book titles published reached nearly 29,000 in 1998, though it has declined since.

From the 1950s onward, radio **broadcasting** and later television spread throughout South Korea. By the mid-1980s, no part of the country was out of reach of the electronic media, nearly all Korean homes had radio and television sets, thanks to electrification of the rural areas. Although reviving traditional national culture, especially music, dance, and painting, South Korea at the same time promoted modern culture, importing international culture, particularly in the area of music and art. Meanwhile, the traditional **religions** (**Buddhism** and **Shamanism**) remained strong while **Christianity** became the major religion. **Confucianism** is still practiced by a vast number of people as they maintain Confucian morality and ethics, rituals, and social values. The Confucian shrine in Seoul observes semiannual rituals in honor of the Chinese sage. *See also* EDUCATIONAL DEVELOPMENT; "MASSACRE OF THE MASS MEDIA"; TRANSPORTATION AND COMMUNICATIONS; WOMEN'S MOVEMENT.

SONG CHIN-U (1889–1945). Born to a well-to-do family in Tamyang, South Cholla Province, he received both traditional and modern education in Korea as a child, followed by secondary education in **Japan**. While studying at Meiji University from 1911, be became a student activist in the Korean students' nationalist movement. Graduating from Meiji University in 1915, he returned to Korea and became the principal of the private Chung'ang School that his friend, **Kim Song-su**, had established in **Seoul**. There he promoted ethnic consciousness and patriotism among students.

Arrested for his nationalistic activity in connection with the March First Movement of 1919, he was imprisoned for 18 months. In 1920, when the *Tong-a Ilbo* newspaper was established, he was made its president, playing an important role as a nationalist leader during the Japanese colonial period.

At the time of the Japanese surrender in 1945, Song, **An Chaehong**, and **Yo Un-hyong** were asked by the Japanese Governor General Abe Nobuyaki to superintend the transition period before the arrival of United States forces. Together they formed the **Committee for the Preparation of National Reconstruction**. Later, with his childhood friends, such as Kim Song-su, he formed the **Korean (Han'guk) Democratic Party**, which represented a conservative, nationalist, propertied class, and became one of its key leaders. Although he opposed left-wing groups, his views regarding the Allied plan to impose a trusteeship in Korea as set out in the **Moscow Agreement** of 1945 alienated him from other right-wing leaders, for he was in support of such steps for Korean independence for practical reasons. Two days after his statement regarding his support for the trusteeship plan on 28 December 1945 was made public, he was assassinated by an ultra right-wing youth. *See also* ASSASSINATION AND ASSASSINATION ATTEMPTS.

SONG DU-YUL (1944–). Song studied at Seoul National University, and then moved to West Germany. After further studies at the Universities of Heidelberg and Frankfort-on-Maine, he became a German citizen and professor of sociology at the University of Münster. He has published on a wide range of subjects, including the question of relations between South and **North Korea**. There have been persistent claims in South Korea that he is a North Korean supporter, especially after he visited the North in 1991. In 1999, the North Korean defector, **Hwang Jang-yop**, claimed that Song was a member of the North Korean ruling party's Political Bureau, using the name of Kim Chul-Su. Song denied the charge, and sued Hwang for defamation in the South Korean courts, winning the case in 2001.

In 2002, Song planned to return at the invitation of the Korean Democracy League, but when the **National Intelligence Service** announced that it wished to interview him about his alleged links with North Korea, the League withdrew the invitation. However, it was reissued in 2003, and Song returned to **Seoul** in September 2003. Song has been the subject of South Korean film, called *Border City*, which was shown at the 53rd Berlin Film Festival and the 2002 **Pusan** Film Festival. *See also* EAST BERLIN CASE; YUN I-SANG.

SOUTH KOREA–JAPAN NORMALIZATION TREATY. Several series of talks to establish normal relations between South Korea and **Japan**, which were held between the representatives of the two governments and eventually led to the signing of this treaty on 22 June 1965 in Tokyo, settling several thorny issues which the two countries had faced. The main features of the Normalization Treaty included the establishment of diplomatic and commercial relations between the two countries, nullification of all treaties that had been signed prior to 22 August 1910 between Korea and Japan, and Japan's affirmation that the government of the Republic of Korea was the only lawful government in the Korean peninsula. With the conclusion of this treaty, Japan recognized the legitimacy of the **Rhee (Peace) Line**, made property compensation (reparation) of $300 million, and agreed to make government and commercial loans to South Korea amounting to an additional $300 million. Difficult issues, such as the status of Koreans residing in Japan and the ownership of **Tokto** (Takeshima in Japanese), an uninhabited island group in the **East Sea/Sea of Japan**, were left unsettled.

The long series of talks leading to the treaty began in October 1951, but full meetings of the representatives of both governments were not held until 15–21 April 1952, after the coming into force of the Japanese Peace Treaty. The second full meeting was held between 15 April and 23 July 1953, and the third full meeting began on 6 October 1953. However, the talks were broken off on 21 October when Japan's chief delegate, Kuboda Kan'ichiro, made a statement regarding "beneficial Japanese rule in Korea," inflaming anti-Japanese sentiment in South Korea.

Only after Kuboda withdrew his statement were the talks resumed in April 1958, but the **April 1960 Student Uprising** interrupted them in 1960. After some preliminary meetings, the fifth full meeting began on 25 October 1960, but it, too, was cut short by the **Military Revolution of 16 May 1961**. Those who came to power then were anxious to solve the pending problems between South Korea and Japan in order to secure Japanese financial and technical assistance for South Korea's economic reconstruction. Therefore, in October 1961 the military junta took the initiative in reopening the talks. During the period of the sixth series of talks, the leader of the military coup, General **Park Chung-hee**, met Japanese Prime Minister Ikeda Hayato on 12 November 1961 in Tokyo on his way to the **United States**. As a result, special meetings of the foreign ministers of South Korea and Japan were held in March 1962 and March 1963, followed by an exclusive meeting between **Kim Jong-p'il** and Japanese Foreign Minister Ohira Masayoshi in Tokyo from 20 October to 12 November 1962, which led to the Kim–Ohira Memorandum. These top-level special meetings resulted in the culmination of the long drawn out negotiations, and the seventh round of talks that began on 3 December 1964 saw the initialing on 20 February 1965 of the Normalization Treaty in Seoul. The treaty was officially concluded in Tokyo on 22 June.

SOUTH KOREA–UNITED STATES MUTUAL DEFENSE TREATY. Recognizing that "an armed attack in the Pacific Area on either of the Parties . . . would be dangerous to its own peace and safety . . ." the Republic of Korea and the **United States** signed a mutual defense treaty on 1 October 1953. Under the treaty, the United States provided defense assistance to South Korea and maintained its troops there as a deterrent to a possible renewed attack from **North Korea**. Although nothing was said officially, the treaty was also designed to restrain South Korean President **Syngman Rhee** from attempting to reopen the **Korean War**.

SOUTH KOREAN INTERIM GOVERNMENT (SKIG, *Namchosun kwado chongbu*). With the appointment of **An Chae-hong** as Civil Administrator in February 1947, the Korean element of the **United States Army Military Government in Korea** that actually handled administration was named the South Korean Interim Government. However, the American military government was not abolished, and South Korea continued to be ruled by an American military governor. The SKIG had no independent power, and ceased to exist with the establishment of the Republic of Korea in 1948.

SOUTH KOREAN INTERIM LEGISLATIVE ASSEMBLY (SKILA, *Namchosun kwado ippop uiwon*). Following an announcement on 3 October 1946 by General **John R. Hodge**, commander of **United States troops in South Korea**, the South Korean Interim Legislative Assembly was established as a branch of the **South Korean Interim Government** (SKIG), replacing the **Representative Democratic Council**. It had 90 members; 45 of them were appointed by the American military government, while the others were popularly elected. More than half were right-wing nationalists, 16 were moderates, and 14 were leftists. However, the Assembly legislated no laws as such for the SKIG; only certain laws requested by the U.S. **Army Military Government in Korea** (USAMGIK) were passed.

SOUTH KOREAN NUCLEAR PROGRAM. South Korea has a major energy problem because of lack of resources. Before 1945, much of the electricity for the southern half of the peninsula came from the north, but this ceased after the division of the country.

Under President **Park Chung-hee**, the need for energy increased as the country embarked on a massive industrialization program as part of its **economic development**. Under the circumstances, it seemed natural to turn to nuclear power supplies, and South Korea began to build civilian nuclear power stations in the 1960s. The first of these came on line in 1978, and the program has continued to expand ever since. By 1995, there were eight light-water reactors in operation, producing 11 percent of the country's energy needs. This program operated under full International Atomic Energy Authority (IAEA) safeguards.

The existence of a civilian nuclear program led many to speculate that South Korea might be tempted into a military program. Nuclear weapons, held by **United States troops in Korea**, had been present on the peninsula since at least the end of the **Korean War** in 1953, and South Korea seemed content with this nuclear umbrella. However, increasing contacts between the **Soviet Union/Russia** and the **United States** in the 1960s, the beginnings of U.S. contacts with **China**, and the withdrawal of some U.S. forces from Korea, appears to have led President **Park Chung-hee** to look at the possibility of developing South Korea's own nuclear weapons, even though South Korea had signed the Nuclear Non-proliferation Treaty (NPT) in 1975.

There was no open admission of such a program, but there was clearly some concern in the U.S. about South Korean policies. The U.S. brought pressure to bear on third countries not to supply South Korea with material that could have weapons potential. In addition, the U.S. halted troop withdrawals and renewed the nuclear umbrella pledge. These moves were successful, in that South Korea ratified the NPT in 1975, and any weapons program appears to have stopped. In 1991, the U.S. withdrew its tactical nuclear weapons worldwide, which allowed the then South Korean President, **Roh Tae-woo**, to announce that there were no nuclear weapons in South Korea, clearing the way for the **Joint Declaration of the Non-nuclearization of the Korean Peninsula** at the end of the year.

The emergence of the **North Korean nuclear program**, however, has led some in South Korea to argue that the country needs nuclear weapons to counter a possible threat from **North Korea**, but formally, South Korea remains bound by the NPT.

SOUTH KOREAN WORKERS' PARTY. *See* KOREAN COMMU-
NIST PARTY.

**SOVIET UNION/RUSSIAN RELATIONS WITH SOUTH KO-
REA.** From the establishment of the Republic of Korea (South Korea) in September 1948 until the early 1970s, there was no contact between South Korea and the Union of Soviet Socialist Republics
(USSR/Soviet Union). South Korea, dominated politically by right-
wing groups that looked to the **United States** for support, feared
communism and blamed the Soviet Union for perpetuating the 1945
temporary division of the peninsula. When the **Korean War** began in
June 1950, South Korea saw it as part of a Soviet plot, and thus felt
even less inclined to make any attempt to develop relations. Soviet
support for **North Korea** confirmed the South Korean belief that the
Soviet Union was an enemy.

Changes in U.S. policies toward the USSR and the People's Republic of **China** in the 1960s led President **Park Chung-hee** to re-
consider South Korea's anticommunist policies. In 1973, Park announced that South Korea would not oppose contacts with
"nonhostile communist states." There was at first little response. In
public, the USSR continued to support North Korea and to attack
the South as a U.S. puppet regime, but some tentative contacts began. A South Korean journalist visited Moscow in 1973. That same
year, the first South Korean athletes were allowed to take part in
the Universiad Athletic Competition, held in Moscow. Gradually,
South Koreans applying for visas for international conferences in
the Soviet Union found that they were no longer automatically rejected. In 1978, the then health minister, Shin Hyun-hwak, became
the first South Korean minister to visit the Soviet Union when he
attended a World Health Organization Conference at Alma-Alta. In
another first, the Soviet media used the official name of the Republic of Korea in reporting Shin's speech to the conference.

Visits by Soviet officials to South Korea were slower in coming,
but eventually they too began. South Korean **economic development**
also attracted Soviet interest, and soon there was a small-scale bilateral trade. By 1981, two-way trade amounted to more than U.S.$30
million, and was growing.

Relations then suffered a setback, following the shooting down by Soviet fighter planes of **Korean Air Lines Flight KE 007** on 31 August/1 September 1983. For a time, relations seemed likely to return to Cold War levels, especially as the USSR began to increase contacts with North Korea. As time passed however, both sides made moves to renew links, a process crowned by the Soviet decision to attend the 1988 **Olympic Games** held in the South Korean capital, **Seoul**. The new direction in Soviet foreign policy under Mikhail Gorbachev from the mid-1980s, and President **Roh Tae-woo**'s policy of **Nordpolitik**, further helped to improve relations. Trade increased, reaching nearly $600 million by 1990. After a determined South Korean campaign, including promises of economic assistance to the Soviet Union, Roh and Gorbachev met in San Francisco on 4 June 1990. This was followed by an exchange of consular and trade officials, and then by full diplomatic relations in September 1990, much to the fury of North Korea.

Gorbachev's fall and the collapse of the Soviet Union in 1991, however, led many in South Korea to argue that their country had paid too high a price for winning over the Soviet Union. Since 1991, relations between South Korea and Russia have developed normally, but have been much affected by the economic and political problems that have affected Russia. Relations are less important than they were in the days of the Soviet Union, and are overshadowed by relations with China. However, continued Russian involvement with North Korea, especially over the issue of the **North Korean nuclear program**, means that South Korea still needs to engage with Russia. *See also* CROSS-RECOGNITION; DIPLOMATIC RECOGNITION; FOREIGN POLICY.

SPECIAL COMMITTEE FOR NATIONAL SECURITY MEASURES (SCNSM). On 31 May 1980, in the wake of the **Kwangju uprising**, the government established this committee, granting it extraordinary power. General **Chun Doo-hwan**, commander of the **Defense Security Command**, was named by president **Ch'oe Kyu-ha** as head of the Standing Committee of the SCNSM. Composed of some 30 high-ranking army officers, the SCNSM replaced the **National Assembly** and decreed many laws. In addition, it adopted several **constitutional amendments**, dissolved all existing political parties, and it put a total of 835 persons on a political blacklist, depriving them of any rights to engage in political activity. The SCNSM was abolished in October 1981 following the establishment of the Fifth Republic in March.

SPECIAL COMMITTEE FOR THE INVESTIGATION OF ILLEGAL ACTIVITIES OF THE FIFTH REPUBLIC. A special committee of the **National Assembly** formed in June 1988 to investigate alleged wrongdoings of the ex-president **Chun Doo-hwan** and top leaders of the Fifth Republic. Although former President **Ch'oe Kyu-ha** refused to testify before the National Assembly, the committee was able to make Chun do so in December 1989. While the Special Committee failed to expose most of the serious wrongdoings of the Chun administration, in February 1989, the Prosecutor-General's Office arrested some 47 persons, most of whom had been high government officials and close relatives of ex-president Chun.

SPECIAL COMMITTEE ON CONSTITUTIONAL AMENDMENT. This ad hoc 24-member committee of the **National Assembly** was established in November 1979 for the purpose of drafting a new **constitution**, abolishing that introduced during the period of **Yushin rule**.

SPECIAL MEASURES LAW FOR NATIONAL SECURITY AND DEFENSE. On 26 December 1971, following the proclamation of a state of national emergency by President **Park Chung-hee** on 6 December, the **National Assembly** passed this law in the absence of the opposition party lawmakers. The law empowered the president to exercise, whenever the need arose, the same power that he would otherwise be able to invoke only under martial law. The law, which was immediately proclaimed, authorized the president to curb press freedom, freeze wages and prices, restrict outdoor meetings and demonstrations, and forbid labor strikes. *See also* LABOR MOVEMENT; NATIONAL SECURITY LAWS.

SPECIAL PARLIAMENTARY COUNCIL ON REUNIFICATION ISSUES. A committee of the **National Assembly** set up in June 1988 to deal with all matters related to the reunification of Korea.

Other organizations and institutions gradually took over its work during President **Roh Tae-woo**'s pursuit of **Nordpolitik**.

STATE AFFAIRS COUNCIL. The cabinet of the Republic of Korea was known as the State Council until 1962. Up to August 1960, it was a consultative administrative council of ministers controlled by the president. During the Second Republic period (August 1960–May 1961), it was a cabinet responsible to the **National Assembly**. After the fall of the Second Republic, the State Council was renamed the State Affairs Council, becoming a consultative body to the president. The president appointed the prime minister, while the prime minister appointed all cabinet ministers with the approval of the president.

STUDENT MOVEMENT. Korean students had been politically active during the time of the Japanese **Government-General in Korea**, engaged in various anti-Japanese activities and campaigning for national independence as well as cultural and social movements. This legacy passed to students of the postliberation period, and from time to time they demonstrated against both the **American Army Military Government in Korea**, and after 1948, against the autocratic rule of President **Syngman Rhee** and the corrupt political practices of his administration and the **Liberal Party**. This culminated in the **April 1960 Student Uprising** that overthrew Rhee and the First Republic.

After the **Military Revolution 16 May of 1961**, the student movement continued to grow in strength as students increased their demand for democracy. Students also demonstrated in 1964 against the conclusion of a "humiliating treaty" with **Japan** and the dispatch of South Korean troops to **Vietnam**, which led to the declaration of a state of emergency in the **Seoul** area in June 1964. When President Park imposed his **Yushin rule** in October 1972, students became the most active protesters, critics, and advocates for the revision of the **constitution** and the restoration of democracy.

In these years, students set up many groups and alliances, which formed and reformed, with much frequency and many changes of name. They included the "Student League for the Protection of People's Rights" (*Mingwon suho haksaeng yonmaeng*) at Seoul National University in 1971, and the broader based "Federation of Democratic

Youth and Students" (*Chonguk minju chongnyo haksaeng yonmaeng minchong hangnyon*) in 1974, but there were many other groups as well. Student protests and government repression eventually led to serious riots in **Pusan** and **Masan** in October 1979. These spread to Seoul and were the cause of the quarrel within the leadership that led to the **assassination** of President Park. Along with demands for more democracy, students were also protesting against compulsory student military training, progovernment professors, and economic and social injustices. Following the death of President Park, the student movement was directed toward the adoption of a new constitution to replace the Yushin Constitution, the lifting of Emergency Martial Law issued on 27 October 1979, and the establishment of campus autonomy. The movement steadily escalated into more violent and frequent on-campus demonstrations.

Following the **December 1979 coup** and the appointment of General **Chun Doo-hwan** as acting director of the Korean Central Intelligence Agency (KCIA—now the **National Intelligence Service**) in April 1980, "a great march for democracy" of the students began, accompanied by widespread street demonstrations and violence in May. On 17 May, some 90 representatives of the student associations in Seoul met and discussed their plans of action.

When the **Kwangju uprising** broke out on 18 May 1980, hundreds of students in that city led the citizens in a bloody confrontation with troops, resulting in the "Kwangju massacre." There was a growing anti-American sentiment among the students, because of **United States**' support for Chun, as well as a desire for early Korean unification. There were many violent clashes with the riot **police** and deaths among the students. Some 2,900, or 85.2 percent of 3,400 political prisoners were students as of December 1986. Between 1980 and 1987, a total of 124,600 students were expelled from colleges and **universities**.

During the struggle against President Chun, students put their efforts into broadening the basis of their movement by pursuing intercampus cooperation and a variety of forms of solidarity movements with the working people. At the same time, the movement expanded into a force of 2,000 students who were radicalized and imbued with a militant political ideology. Thus, in April 1985 radical students from 23 colleges and universities formed a new "National Federation of Student Associations" (*Chonhakyon*), and its political arm called the "Committee for the Three People's Struggle" (*Sammint'uwi*). These claimed to have three basic goals: the liberation of the masses (*minjung haebang*); the attainment of democracy (*minju chaengch'wi*); and the unification of the Korean people (*minzok t'ongiul*). The leadership of the "Committee for the Three People's Struggle" disintegrated with the arrest of its leaders, but in the spring of 1986 two more militant, antistate organizations called "People's Struggle for Democracy" (*Minmint'u*) and "Self-oriented Struggle for Democracy" (*Chamint'u*).

Some members of these radical groups left their schools, securing employment at various industrial establishments disguised as laborers and arousing a new social awareness among the workers as they organized them for the labor struggle. The "People's Struggle for Democracy" group held that the current problems of South Korean society were created by internal forces, its class structure, and its inherent contradictions, and believed that by overthrowing the "military fascist regime" it was possible to eliminate the influence of foreign powers, achieve people's democracy, and bring about the unification of the country. The followers of the "Self-oriented Struggle for Democracy" group argued that the existing contradictions of Korean society developed because of the external forces that influenced the internal workings of Korean society. They saw South Korea as a neocolonial society and advocated following the so-called *juche* (self-oriented) ideology of **North Korea**'s **Kim Il-sung**. Known as the *jusap'a* (the *juche* faction), this group focused its efforts on the elimination of foreign imperialist influences, pursuing antiforeignism, anti-imperialism, and antineocolonialism. On the whole, the "People's Struggle for Democracy" group sought to bring about "anti-imperialist people's democratic revolution," while the "Self-oriented Struggle for Democracy" group pursued the goal of bringing about a "national liberation people's democratic revolution."

In June 1988, following the crackdown on radical groups, the national liberation movement of the "Self-oriented Struggle for Democracy" (*Chamint'u*) formed the "National Council of University Student Representatives" (*Chondachyop*) of some 115 colleges, pursuing three goals of democratization with socialism, the anti-U.S. reunification movement, and North-South student tasks, which sent a coed to North

Korea's World Youth Festival held in **P'yongyang** in July 1989. Radical student activism resulted in a number of serious clashes, as well as violent demonstrations on campuses and in the streets in 1988 and 1989. The participation in the P'yongyang festival, and the disclosure of the killing by torture of a student in October 1989, allegedly a spy for the intelligence agencies, by members of the "National Council of University Student Representatives," led to a split between the radical faction, advocating national liberation with the *chuch'e* ideology, and the moderate faction, preaching "people's democracy" without such an ideology. The latter group formed a separate "National Federation of Students for People's Democracy" (*Chonminhakyon*).

In fact, the growing radicalism of the student political groups and the successful transition of power from Chun Doo-hwan to **Roh Tae-woo** in 1988, which was widely seen as a victory for those, including students, who took to the streets in 1986, began to have an impact on the student movement. Numbers involved in political activism started to fall, and while student demonstrations did not disappear, they were more likely to be on campus than on the streets. This trend would continue as democratization progressed in the 1990s, and many of those who had once been activists gravitated toward more conventional politics.

There were still issues that could bring the students onto the streets, however. Protests against the U.S. or Japan were not uncommon during the 1990s. Students ostentatiously mourned North Korea's Kim Il-sung in July 1994, provoking **police** intervention on a number of campuses. Seoul's Yonsei University saw massive on-campus demonstrations in favor of reunification in August 1996, which were eventually broken up by the police. Autumn 1999 saw protests about the alleged **Nogun-ri massacre**, while the killing of two girls by American soldiers in a road accident in June 2002 provoked a massive outpouring of anti-American sentiment. But in all cases, while student organizations such as the "Federation of Korean Student Councils" (*Hanchongryon*) took part although officially outlawed, they were far less in evidence than in the past.

STUDENT NATIONAL DEFENSE CORPS. Established in March 1949, the corps was aimed at providing spiritual and military training to college students, as well as enhancing national security. All college students were required to take a certain number of hours in military training. When the **Korean War** broke out, in July 1950, student volunteer units were organized and they were sent to the battlefields to augment the regular army. The corps and compulsory military training were abolished in 1988.

"SUNSHINE POLICY." When **Kim Dae-jung** became South Korean president in 1998, he announced that his government would follow a new, "sunshine policy" toward **North Korea**. The origins of the term can be found in a Korean folk tale, in which the wind and the sun contend in trying to persuade a traveler to take off his overcoat. The wind blows and buffets the traveler as hard as possible, without success, but the sun, by shining steadily, succeeds.

In essence, the policy was one of engagement with, and assistance to, the North, with certain clear rules laid down if the North behaved in hostile fashion toward the South. The idea of such a policy of engagement was not new, but unlike his predecessors, Kim stuck to it. The policy appeared to have worked when Kim and the North Korean leader, **Kim Jong-il**, met in the North's capital, **P'yongyang**, at the **June 2000 Inter-Korean Summit**, but there were always critics who claimed that South Korea was giving away too much for too little. When toward the end of Kim Dae-jung's term in office, it began to emerge that the summit had been brought about by payments to the North, the criticism increased. However, Kim's successor, President **Roh Moo-hyun**, announced in 2003 that he would continue the policy, albeit with a somewhat different title. *See also* NORTH KOREA–SOUTH KOREA RELATIONS.

SUPREME COUNCIL FOR NATIONAL RECONSTRUCTION. The military junta that carried out the **Military Revolution of 16 May 1961** established a **Military Revolutionary Committee** (MRC) consisting of five generals, to exercise executive, legislative, and judicial functions. Its first three decrees froze all bank assets, closed airports and harbors, placed publications under strict **censorship**, and forbade assembly. The committee, headed by Lieutenant General **Chang To-yong**, issued six revolutionary pledges on 18 May 1961. On 20 May, the committee was renamed the **Supreme Council for National Reconstruction** (SCNR) following the proclamation of the **Law Concerning Extraordinary Measures for National Reconstruction** on 19 May. It became the supreme organ of the state, consisting of 30 councilors and two advisers. Three councilors were Marine Corps generals, one each came from the air force and the navy, and the rest from the army. The two advisers were retired military officers. Of the 30 members, 19 were generals, and about a third of them were lieutenant colonels and colonels.

Chang served as its chairman until July, when Maj. Gen. **Park Chung-hee** replaced him. Its chairman was the head of the cabinet, or the prime minister. The Supreme Council adopted the following: the Law Concerning Temporary Measures aimed at the Settlement of Critical Situations; the Revolutionary Court and Prosecution Law; the **Political Activities Purification Law**; the **Political Party Law**; and **the Anti-Communism Law**. In June 1961 it established the Korean Central Intelligence Agency (later the **National Intelligence Service**). With the restoration of a civilian government in December 1963, the Supreme Council completed its task and went out of existence. *See also* NATIONAL DEFENSE FORCES.

– T –

TAEDOK INDUSTRIAL RESEARCH TOWN. A new science town established in 1977 by the government on the outskirts of **Taejon**, South Ch'ungch'ong Province, to ensure cooperative research among the various fields of science and joint utilization of facilities and equipment by bringing various research institutes together in one area. Among some of the major research institutes that were relocated at Taedok are the Korea Research Institute of Ships and Oceanography, the Korea Standard Research Institute, the Nuclear Fuel Development Institute, the Korea Research Institute of Geosciences and Mineral Resources, the Korea Telecommunications Institute, and the Korea Chemical Research Institute.

TAEDONG YOUTH CORPS. An ultra right-wing youth organization established in September 1947 by General Chi Ch'ong-ch'on, a military leader who returned to Korea from **China** in 1945, and who was noted for his racist views. With Dr. **Syngman Rhee** as its president, it combated left-wing groups, particularly the communists. In the 1948 general elections for the **Constituent Assembly**, its members won 12 seats. It gave strong support to President Rhee after 1948. At one point, it had more than a million members.

TAEGU. The capital of North Kyongsang Province in the southeastern part of South Korea, Taegu is an important agricultural and industrial city, with a tradition of political activism. In 1946, local workers rioted in support of left-wing activists threatened with arrest. In 1948–1949, it was a major center of guerrilla activity. During the first phase of the **Korean War**, it was the temporary capital for a few days as President **Syngman Rhee** fled south in front of the communist forces. Taegu then became the center point of the Pusan perimeter, the line along which **North Korea**'s advance was stopped in August–September 1950. For the **United States** and South Korea, it became a symbol of their determination to prevent any further communist gains. After the breakout from the Pusan perimeter in September 1950, Taegu ceased to play an active role in the war.

Taegu students joined in the nationwide protests that led to the overthrow the Syngman Rhee regime. Presidents **Park Chung-hee**, **Chun Doo-hwan**, and **Roh Tae-woo** all came from the area and attended school in Taegu, which led to a widespread belief in the 1980s and early 1990s that the "T-K (Taegu-Kyongsang) faction" of former classmates played a dominant role in South Korean politics.

TAEHAN YOUTH CORPS. *See* KOREAN NATIONAL YOUTH CORPS.

TAEJON. An important industrial and education center, and the capital of South Ch'ungch'ong Province, Taejon lies 100 miles (160 kilometers) south of South Korea's capital, **Seoul**, and about 130 miles (210 kilometers) northwest of the port of **Pusan**. Before **Japan** annexed Korea in 1910, it was a small and poor village, but later developed into an important railway centre. During the **Korean War**, it served briefly as the national capital from 28 June–16 July 1950 after the fall of Seoul, but was abandoned as the North Korean forces swept south. It also served as the main center for South Korean and

United States forces in early July 1950, and the Taejon Agreement, placing South Korean forces under U.S. operational command was signed there on 12 July. On 19 July 1950, a full-scale battle began for control of the city, which eventually fell to North Korean forces. The city suffered much destruction in the war, but was rebuilt in the 1950s.

TAEJONGGYO. One of South Korea's new **religions**, whose followers regard a divinity called Hanul as the supreme god. Hanul is a trinity: creator, teacher, and temporal king, who took human form in the person of Tan'gun, and as father, teacher, and king of the Korean people, founded the first Korean nation in 2333 B.C. Whatever the claimed origins, the indigenous cult of Tan'gun had long since disappeared when Na Ch'ol reinvented it in 1910. Na committed suicide in 1916 and his followers moved to northeast **China**. After 1945, they returned to South Korea, and the religion has enjoyed a modest following ever since, being especially associated with Korean nationalism. On 3 October each year, they celebrate the founding of the Korean nation by Tan'gun. With the growth of **Christianity** in South Korea, much opposition to the cult of Tan'gun has come from fundamentalist Christian groups.

TAEKWONDO. This Korean form of martial art has in theory a long history, dating back to the Koguryo period. In reality, what is now known as Taekwondo probably only dates from a post-1945 attempt to give a Korean heritage to the Japanese martial art, karate. Under President **Park Chung-hee**, the various "schools" of Taekwondo were brought together in the 1960s *Kukki taekwondo*, or National Taekwondo. Since then, Taekwondo has developed in quite a different fashion from karate, and has come to be regarded as a different sport. In 1994, Taekwondo became an official **Olympic Games** sport, and it has a widespread international following. *See also* CHOI HONG-HI.

TEAM SPIRIT. A joint **United States**–South Korean military exercise, first staged in 1976, Team Spirit was particularly concerned with coordination of the two armed forces in time of war. It was not the first joint service exercise, but it was the most comprehensive, testing all aspects of army, navy, marine, and air force cooperation, with troops airlifted from the U.S. to supplement those already in South Korea. It was held annually until 1991. **North Korea** always protested at the exercise, and went onto an enhanced state of military preparedness while the exercise was in progress on the grounds that it could be used to cover a real attack. Following the 1991 North–South **Agreement on Reconciliation, Non-aggression and Cooperation**, Team Spirit was canceled in 1992, but it was reinstated in 1993. Despite tension because of the **North Korean nuclear program** in 1994, Team Spirit was again canceled, and it has not subsequently been reinstated. Other joint exercises, such as Ulchi Lens and Foal Eagle, have continued, despite North Korean protests, and seem to cover much of the same ground as Team Spirit.

TELEVISION. *See* BROADCASTING.

38th PARALLEL. The parallel 38° N cuts through the center of the Korean Peninsula, bisecting farms, villages, and long-existing administrative units for 150 miles (240 kilometers). When **Soviet/Russian** troops moved down swiftly southward following their invasion of Korea that began on 10 August 1945, (two days after the Soviet Union declared war on **Japan**), there was concern in the **United States** that the entire Korean Peninsula might be occupied by Soviet troops before the arrival of American forces. Therefore on 13 August 1945, the U.S. government proposed that Korea be divided into two military operational zones along this parallel line. Although this proposal put the capital, **Seoul**, under U.S. control, Stalin accepted the 38th parallel without objection, though he asked for minor changes in other matters.

The line of demarcation was "intended to be temporary and only to fix responsibility" between the two sides for carrying out the Japanese surrender, but the parallel eventually became the boundary between North and South Korea in 1948. It lost its significance at the end of the **Korean War** in 1953 when the **Korean Armistice Agreement** created the **demilitarized zone** and the **military demarcation line** (MDL). The latter marked the line of actual control at the end of the fighting. Since 1953, the MDL has remained the dividing line between the two Koreas, neither of which regards it as a national boundary.

TOKTO DISPUTE. The Tok Islands, known as Takeshima in Japanese, are a small group of barren rocks east of the Korean Peninsula and northwest of **Japan**. Older Western maps show them as the Liancourt Rocks, after a French ship of that name, which called there in 1849. The Korean name means Solitary Island, the Japanese, Bamboo Island. The former is more accurate since there is very little vegetation on the islands, and no natural water. The seas around are good fishing grounds. The group has been claimed by both South Korea and Japan since 1952, and **North Korea** also claims them as Korean territory. No other country has taken a position on the status of the islands. The intensity of the dispute over Tokto tends to wax and wane depending on the broader state of Japan–South Korean relations. From 1953 onward, a small group of South Korean **police** has occupied the islands.

TONGHAK. *See* CH'ONDO-GYO.

T'ONGILGYO. *See* UNIFICATION CHURCH.

TOURISM. Although South Korea has many fine scenic spots, and a number of world-class historic sites, unlike its neighbors, China (the Great Wall) and **Japan** (Mount Fuji), the country lacks any obvious tourist symbol. It was also far less well known in the West before 1945. During the 1950s and 1960s, as the era of mass tourist travel began, Korea continued to suffer from the negative images of the **Korean War**, the continued security threat from **North Korea**, and the student violence that brought down President **Syngman Rhee**. Continued student protests and the authoritarian regime of **President Park Chung-hee** helped to perpetuate this somewhat bleak picture of Korea during the 1970s and into the 1980s.

Even under Park Chung-hee, however, South Korea was determined to increase tourism. The government established the Korea National Tourist Organization (KNTO) in 1963, to promote a more positive image of the country and to attract more visitors. But a general lack of tourist infrastructure did not help, and the total of visitors remained low. In 1970, for example, about 160,000 out of some 480,000 claimed to be visiting as tourists rather than on business. About one third of the total were from the **United States**, and many may have been connected with the military in Korea. The second largest group was Japanese, mostly men. Tourist figures remained low during the 1970s and into the 1980s, despite a number of campaigns to bring people to Korea, and a steady relaxation in border controls. The KNTO opened more overseas offices, and if there was perhaps a mismatch between what it was offering and what tourists came for, the numbers began to climb. The **Seoul 1988 Olympic Games** were a big attraction, and helped to create a more positive image of South Korea. It also led the government to do more to make Korea an attractive destination, with improved hotel, restaurant, and toilet facilities. By 1992, well over half those visiting South Korea claimed to be doing so for tourism.

By 1999, tourist numbers had climbed to over four and a half million, bringing in receipts of U.S.$6,801.9 million. By 2001, the figures were over five million tourists, and estimated revenues of $6,282.5 million. The make-up of those arriving had also changed. Japanese tourists were by far the largest group, at over two million annually and rising. Americans had by 2001 been pushed into third place, after those from **China**. Tourists were also staying longer. By 2002, the average stay in South Korea was 11 days, whereas in the 1970s, it had been two or three days. These figures would be further boosted by the **World Cup 2002** competition, which brought a much wider selection of tourists to South Korea. The country might still lack an obvious tourist symbol, but it had arrived on the world tourism map.

Until the 1980s, South Koreans could not easily travel abroad, except for education or business. Tourism was discouraged because it was seen as a drain on the country's resources. The rules have been steadily relaxed, even though events such as the 1997 economic crisis did lead to a temporary revival of old attitudes. South Koreans now travel the world, increasingly as solo rather than group travelers. Thus South Koreans going abroad as tourists totaled a mere 2,000 in 1985. By 1990, the figure had reached 590,000, and by 2001, some 2,647,000 were traveling. That year, tourism accounted for 43.5 percent of all departures.

Domestic tourism has also grown steadily, especially since the mid-1980s, as has the increase in ownership of private automobiles. South Koreans have tended not to take long holidays, but this, too, may be changing. Since the late 1990s, a new development in domestic tourism has been the **Hyundai** group's **Mount Kumgang tours** to North Korea. From September 2003, these have been supplemented by direct tourist flights to the North Korean capital, **P'yongyang**. Should these continue, the North could become an important destination for South Koreans. *See also* TRANSPORTATION AND COMMUNICATIONS.

TRADE. *See* ECONOMIC DEVELOPMENT.

TRANSPORTATION AND COMMUNICATIONS. South Korea's modern transportation system was begun during the last years of the Yi dynasty (1392–1910), with the introduction of railways. The first line, which was constructed between 1896 and 1900, ran from Chemulp'o (**Inch'on**) to **Seoul.** Long distance routes followed. Other developments before the Japanese colonial period included tramways in Seoul and new harbors. After **Japan**'s annexation of Korea in 1910, the Japanese **Government-General of Korea** modernized the railway system. From the 1920s, road transport became increasingly motorized, although there were few paved roads outside the major cities.

Since 1945, railway mileage has expanded from 2,318 miles (3,730 kilometers) in 1945 to 4,089 miles (6,580 kilometers) by 1997. Of this, 560 miles (901 kilometers) are double-track railways while 411 miles (661 kilometers) are electrified. All railways are nationally owned. Plans to build a high-speed line from Seoul to **Pusan**, modeled on the French TGV system, received a setback following the 1997 economic crisis.

The highway mileage also increased as four-lane expressways were constructed and highway projects were launched in the 1960s. The Seoul–Inch'on Expressway was opened in 1960, followed in 1970 by the 270-mile (435 kilometer) Seoul–Pusan Expressway. The latter runs the whole length of the country from Seoul, passing through such industrial and urban centers as Suwon, **Taejon**, and **Taegu.** Following the completion of these projects, additional expressways were built, bringing the total mileage of expressways close to 1,200 miles (1,931 kilometers). By 2004, the length of expressways is expected to reach 2,175 miles (3,500 kilometers). Meanwhile, a subway system completed between 1974 and the late 1990s reduced traffic problems in the capital city, and there were also subways in Pusan and Taegu by the end of 1997.

The government-owned and operated **Korean Air Lines** (now **Korean Air**) was turned over to a private company in 1963, while another Korean airline company, **Asiana**, received a charter in 1988, for both domestic and foreign air traffic. By the late 1990s, South Korea had civil air agreements with 73 countries, and the two Korean airlines served 116 international air routes, covering 80 cities in 33 countries. There were also 33 domestic air routes.

The communication system was also modernized with the introduction of a new telegraph and telephone system. By 1997, the number of telephone subscribers had reached 20.4 million; there were also 5.7 million cellular phone subscribers. By 2001, these had become 24 million landline subscribers and 28 million cellular phone users. Use of the **Internet** has also increased substantially; over 26 million South Koreans were on e-mail by 2002.

– U –

ULSAN. A major port and industrial city situated in South Kyongsang Province, some 40 miles (60 kilometers) north of **Pusan**, with a population of about 680,000. Ulsan was an important garrison town in the Yi dynasty (1392–1910), and one of the places where the Japanese were allowed to trade before the 1870s. Links with **Japan** continued to be important during the colonial period, when it was a stage for flights from Japan to **China**. Since the early 1960s, Ulsan's importance has rested on its industrial development, beginning with steel, which in turn led to the establishment of the **Hyundai** shipbuilding yards and automobile factories, as well as oil refineries and chemical plants. By the end of 1998, it was responsible for over 11 percent of the country's industrial output, and had bypassed both Pusan and **Inch'on** as a cargo port. The town is also the home of the University of Ulsan, which began as South Korea's first Institute of Technology. Ulsan became a city in 1962 and a metropolitan, or self-governing, city in 1997.

UNDERWOOD FAMILY. One of the major missionary families in Korea, which has been closely involved with the religious, educational, and political development of Korea since Horace Grant Underwood (1859–1916) arrived in **Seoul** as a missionary for the American Presbyterian Church in 1885 and remained there until his death. One of the orphans for whom he cared was the nationalist leader **Kim Kyu-shik**, who also acted as his secretary for a time. Horace Grant Underwood's brother, John, who founded the Underwood Typewriter Company, gave a donation of $50,000 that formed the original endowment of Chosun Christian College, which later became Yonsei University, and supported the college with additional funds later.

Horace's son, Horace H. Underwood, was also a missionary, and taught for many years at Chosun Christian College, where he was principal from 1934–1941. He was then imprisoned by the Japanese, and repatriated to the **United States** in 1942. Among his contacts was Pak Hon-yong (1900–1955), later a communist leader and vice-premier and foreign minister in **North Korea.** These contacts with Underwood were used in 1955 by **Kim Il-sung** to discredit and execute Pak. Horace H. Underwood returned to Korea after 1945, and resumed teaching at Chosun Christian College. He also acted as an advisor to the **United States Army Military Government in Korea**. He died in 1951. His wife, Ethel Van Wagoner Underwood, whom he married in 1916, also taught at Chosun Christian College. In 1949, she was **assassinated** at their house on the campus by suspected communist guerillas.

Three of their sons played prominent roles in Korea. The eldest, Horace G. Underwood II, taught at Chosun Christian College before World War II. He returned in 1945, and served as registrar for Seoul National University, and later as a Presbyterian missionary. During the **Korean War**, he acted as a guide for **United Nations forces** advancing on Seoul after the **Inch'on** landing, and was later chief interpreter for the **United Nations Command** (UNC) at the negotiations at **P'anmunjom** leading to the 1953 **Korean Armistice Agreement**. He then returned to academic and missionary work.

One brother John T. Underwood was a missionary in Korea from 1947 onward; he was also an army interpreter in the Korean War. A third brother Richard F. Underwood also served as an interpreter at Panmunjom, and later as a missionary. He was the head of the Seoul Foreign School for many years.

The Underwood family has been attacked in North Korean propaganda as American spymasters, and may have been the model for the hostile American missionaries portrayed in the novel, *Love*, published by the North Korean novelist Han Sor-ya in 1970. *See also* EDUCATION; RELIGIONS; UNIVERSITIES.

UNIFICATION CHURCH (*T'ongilgyo*). One of South Korea's successful new **religions**, which was established in **P'yongyang** by a former Presbyterian elder, **Moon Sun-myong**, shortly after Korea's liberation from **Japan**. Moon was arrested on several occasions in **North Korea**, but ended up in **Seoul** in 1953. There he reorganized his group as T'ongilgyo, or the "Holy Spirit Association for the Unification of World Christianity," known in English as the Unification Church or, more familiarly, as the "Moonies." Moon argued for his own divinity and that of his wife, and kept a tight control over his followers. When Moon fell foul of the authorities in South Korea in 1973, he relocated to the **United States**, expanding the activities of the sect, and preaching that salvation would come from Korea. Implicated in the 1970s **"Koreagate"** scandal and convicted of U.S. income tax fraud in 1982, Moon moved to Brazil. From there, he returned to South Korea in 1998. Although his followers are not large in numbers in South Korea, the Unification Church is relatively rich and operates on an international scale. In South Korea, it is particularly associated with the ginseng monopoly and with arms manufacturing. Since the early 1990s, there have been growing links between the church and **North Korea**, especially in the economic field.

UNIFICATION NATIONAL PARTY (*T'ongil kungmindang*). This party is also known as United People's Party. It was formed in January 1992 by **Chung Ju-yung**, founder and chairman of **Hyundai**. In February, it merged with the **New Korea Party** of Kim Tong-gil (formed in January 1992). A little over a month after its formation, its candidates won 24 district seats in the 14th **National Assembly** elections held in March 1992. When the new National Assembly was formed, the Unification National Party was allocated seven at-large seats, making it for a short time a viable opposition party.

UNIFICATION REVOLUTIONARY PARTY CASE. An underground "party" said to have been established in South Korea by **North Korea**. In August 1968, the Korean Central Intelligence Agency (KCIA, now the **National Intelligence Service**) arrested some 73 of its members as antistate, espionage terrorists, and imprisoned them.

UNITED LIBERAL DEMOCRATS (ULD, *Jayu minju yonmaeng*). Party created in 1995 by the veteran politician, **Kim Jong-p'il** after being forced out of the leadership of the **Democratic Liberal Party**. It claimed to be the only genuine conservative party in South Korea. It enjoyed modest electoral success, with 50 members elected in the 1996 **National Assembly** elections.

In a surprise move, the party joined with **Kim Dae-jung**'s **National Congress for New Politics** in 1997, in order to contest the presidential election. Despite their long years of hostility to each other, the two agreed that Kim Dae-jung would be the presidential candidate. After his narrow win in 1997, Kim Dae-jung made Kim Jong-p'il his prime minister. As prime minister, Kim Jong-p'il advocated a cabinet system of government, to replace the executive president system. Early in 2000, the coalition broke up, and Kim Jong-p'il resigned as prime minister, to contest the April 2000 general election as ULD leader. However, his party did badly in the election, and by May 2000, he was again in a coalition with Kim Dae-jung.

The election of **Roh Moo-hyun** as president in 2002, and the passing from the political scene of Kim Dae-jung in 2003, has left only Kim Jong-p'il from the era of the "three Kims," as the period since the early 1970s has come to be known. He continues to head the ULD, but it must be assumed that his days as a political leader are numbered. The ULD seems unlikely to survive his departure.

UNITED NATIONS (UN). The United Nations (UN), established in June 1945, has been involved in the Korean Peninsula since 1947, when the **United States**, unable to reach agreement with the **Soviet Union/Russia** on Korean reunification, referred the issue to the UN General Assembly. In November 1947, the General Assembly passed a resolution calling for a unified government in Korea through peninsula-wide general elections, and established the **United Nations**

Temporary Commission on Korea (UNTOK) to oversee these elections. The inability of UNTOK to operate in the northern part of the peninsula led to its disbandment in December 1948 and replacement by the **United Nations Commission for the Unification and Rehabilitation of Korea** (UNCURK), which survived until 1973.

UN involvement in Korea increased after the outbreak of the **Korean War** in June 1950. Although the U.S. was in many ways the driving force, it operated through the **United Nations Command** (UNC), and the forces that fought in Korea did so as **United Nations forces.** Even 50 years after the end of the Korean War, the UN flag still flies over certain military installations in South Korea, although the UNC is now a shadow of its former self.

In the years before 1950, both South and **North Korea** applied for UN membership but each application was blocked by the other side's supporters. After the Korean War, South Korea pursued an active policy of joining UN specialized agencies such as the UN Development Program (UNDP) and the World Health Organization. Although at first reluctant, North Korea eventually did the same. South Korea also regularly attempted to join the UN especially during the 1960s and 1970s, but was prevented by opposition from communist countries, and it was not until 1991 that its campaign was successful. By then, North Korea had reluctantly decided that it too should join, and both Koreas did so within days of each other. *See also* UNITED NATIONS KOREAN RECONSTRUCTION AGENCY; UNITED NATIONS RESOLUTIONS ON KOREA.

UNITED NATIONS CIVIL ASSISTANCE COMMAND. *See* CIVIL RELIEF IN KOREA.

UNITED NATIONS COMMAND (UNC). Following the outbreak of the Korea War in June 1950, the **United Nations** Security Council condemned **North Korea** as an aggressor and resolved in July 1950 to establish the **United Nations forces** and a United Nations Command headquarters. General **Douglas MacArthur**, supreme commander for the Allied powers in **Japan**, was named commander of the UNC, and its troops, contributed by 16 UN member nations and South Korea, countered the North Korean and the Chinese forces in the Korean War.

UNITED NATIONS COMMISSION FOR UNIFICATION AND REHABILITATION OF KOREA (UNCURK). In October 1950, the General Assembly of the **United Nations** (UN) established this commission, replacing the UN Temporary Commission on Korea. Two months later, UNCURK's rehabilitation work was taken over by the **United Nations Korean Reconstruction Agency** (UNKRA).

UNCURK remained formally in existence, however, charged with bringing about Korean reunification. This provided many countries with a legal reason for not recognizing **North Korea**, since UNCURK's remit was based on **United Nations resolutions** that recognized only one legal government on the Korean Peninsula, that of South Korea. Following contacts between the two Koreas in the early 1970s, and a modification in South Korea's own position, the UN made a consensus decision to end UNCURK on 21 November 1973. *See also* DIPLOMATIC RECOGNITION; UNITED NATIONS TEMPORARY COMMISSION ON KOREA.

UNITED NATIONS FORCES. Following the outbreak of the **Korean War** in June 1950, the **United Nations** Security Council, after condemning **North Korea** as an aggressor, on 27 June 1950 called upon UN member nations to provide troops to aid South Korea to repel the aggressors. A total of 16 nations provided ground forces, eight nations provided naval forces, and five nations air forces. On 10 July 1950, a **United Nations Command (UNC)** was established, with General **Douglas MacArthur** of the **United States** as its commander. Ground forces came from **Australia**, Belgium, Canada, Colombia, Cuba, Ethiopia, France, **Great Britain**, Greece, Luxembourg, the Netherlands, New Zealand, the Philippines, Thailand, Turkey, and the United States; naval forces from Australia, Canada, Colombia, France, the Netherlands, Thailand, and the United States; and air forces from Australia, Canada, the Union of South Africa, Great Britain, and the United States. Denmark, India, Italy, Norway, and Sweden provided medical services. Bolivia, the Chinese Nationalists on Taiwan, Costa Rica, El Salvador, and Panama also offered troops, but acceptance of their offer was deferred. All armed forces provided by these nations, plus those of South Korea, were put under the UNC.

UNITED NATIONS KOREAN RECONSTRUCTION AGENCY (UNKRA). Established in December 1950 to undertake long-run reconstruction projects at the end of the **Korean War**, a role it took over from the **United Nations Committee for Unification and Rehabilitation of Korea**, it actually provided only $150 million for the purpose up to June 1960.

UNITED NATIONS RESOLUTIONS ON KOREA. Following the failure of the **Joint United States–Soviet Union Commission on Trusteeship** to solve the question of Korean reunification, the **United States** Government laid the issue before the **United Nations**. On 14 November 1947, the United Nations General Assembly adopted a resolution to establish a unified government of Korea through general elections under UN supervision. This resolution was followed by others, especially once the **Korean War** began in June 1950. *See also* UNITED NATIONS COMMISSION FOR UNIFICATION AND REHABILITATION OF KOREA; UNITED NATIONS TEMPORARY COMMISSION ON KOREA.

UNITED NATIONS TEMPORARY COMMISSION ON KOREA (UNTCOK). After the adoption of the resolution on Korea on 14 November 1947, the General Assembly of the **United Nations** created a United Nations Temporary Commission on Korea, consisting of representatives of **Australia**, Canada, **China**, El Salvador, France, India, the Philippines, Syria, and the Ukrainian Socialist Soviet Republic, for the purpose of fulfilling the program outlined in the resolution, namely to establish a unified government through general elections. After conducting the 10 May 1948 general elections only in South Korea, the UN General Assembly, under a **United States** proposal, adopted a resolution on 12 December to replace UNTCOK with a new UN Commission on Korea, and authorized it to travel, consult, and observe throughout Korea for the purpose of fulfilling the original aims of the UN resolution of 14 November 1947. During the **Korean War**, it was replaced by other UN agencies. *See also* UN COMMISSION FOR UNIFICATION AND REHABILITATION OF KOREA; UN RESOLUTIONS ON KOREA.

UNITED PEOPLE'S PARTY. *See* UNIFICATION NATIONAL PARTY.

UNITED STATES, RELATIONS WITH. Since its establishment in 1948, South Korea has maintained extremely close links with the United States across the whole spectrum of relations. Many Koreans, indeed, look back to the U.S. role in the opening of Korea in the 19th century, and the centenary of diplomatic relations was celebrated with much ceremony in 1982. The long involvement of U.S. missionaries and educators is also remembered with affection; several missionary families, such as the **Underwood family**, are still either present in South Korea today or maintain close links with the country. A number of private **universities** and colleges are also closely linked with the U.S. Older Koreans tend to see the U.S. as the country that saved them from communism in 1945 and again during the **Korean War**. Although they acknowledge the role of the **United Nations**, they believe that if the U.S. had not rallied that body, then its help would not have been forthcoming.

The massive U.S. postwar aid, the continued U.S. military presence, and the educational, culture, and economic links that developed after the Korean War are also powerful factors in the U.S.–South Korean relationship. The U.S. has been the most consistent supporter of South Korea internationally, even when South Korean governments were being criticized for dictatorial methods. All South Korean presidents from **Syngman Rhee** onward have regularly visited the U.S., and have found a body of supporters in the U.S. prepared to overlook their faults. Many other South Koreans have lived, studied, and worked in the U.S., which increases the bond.

Inevitably, the relationship is not always easy. Some South Koreans blame the U.S. for the division of the peninsula in 1945, or for sending the wrong signals in 1950, which persuaded **North Korea** to launch the Korean War. Like other U.S. allies, South Koreans sometimes think that U.S. trade practices are not always fair. Over the years, as the U.S. has moved away from some of its rigid Cold War positions, there have been concerns in South Korea that Korean interests would be swamped in the U.S. desire to improve relations with the **Soviet Union/Russia**, **China**, or even, in the light of the **North Korean nuclear program**, with the country's greatest threat, North

Korea. On the other side of the political line, the **South Korean student movement** has consistently attacked the U.S. military presence and what it sees as U.S. dominance of the country. Problems from the past and the present, whether the allegations about the **Nogun-ri massacre** or the tensions created by the **United States–South Korea Status of Forces Agreement**, can quickly ignite student demonstrations.

Yet, despite all the problems, the U.S.–South Korean relationship is solid, and seems likely to remain so for the foreseeable future. *See also* OVERSEAS KOREANS.

UNITED STATES ARMY MILITARY GOVERNMENT IN KOREA (USAMGIK). General **John Reed Hodge** established USAMGIK on his arrival in Korea in 1948 as the political arm of the United States occupation forces with Major General A.V. Arnold as first military governor. Arnold, in effect, took over the Japanese **Government-General in Korea**, and for a short time even used Japanese officials. The USAMGIK ruled South Korea until 15 August 1948. Despite a formal commitment to establishing democracy in Korea, USAMIGK was distrustful of most Korean politicians and tried to keep real power in American hands.

UNITED STATES MILITARY ADVISORY GROUP. *See* UNITED STATES TROOPS IN KOREA.

UNITED STATES–SOUTH KOREA COMBINED FORCES. On 7 November 1978, the **United States** and the South Korean Combined Forces Command was formally activated for the purpose of strengthening South Korea's defense posture. Under the agreement, the commander of the U.S. Forces in Korea and of the **United Nations Command** (UNC) was to be commander of the Combined Forces with a Korean general as deputy commander. Under this system, nearly all South Korean combat troops were put under the control of the joint U.S.–South Korea Military Commission.

UNITED STATES–SOUTH KOREA MUTUAL DEFENSE TREATY. The Mutual Defense Treaty between the United States and the Republic of Korea was signed on 1 October 1953 in Washington D.C. The most crucial aspect of the six-article treaty is found in Article

III, which stated, "Each Party recognizes that an armed attack in the Pacific area on either of the Parties in territories now under their respective administrative control, or hereafter recognized by one of the Parties as lawfully brought under the administrative control of the other, would be dangerous to its own peace and safety and declares that it would act to meet the common danger in accordance with its constitutional processes." The U.S. Senate gave its advice and consent to the ratification of the treaty with the understanding "that neither party is obligated, under Article III of the [Treaty], to come to the aid of the other except in case of an external armed attack against such party; nor shall anything in the present Treaty be construed as requiring the United States to give assistance to Korea except in the event of an armed attack against territory which has been recognized by the United States . . ."

The treaty was for an indefinite period, and either party could terminate it one year after giving notice to the other party. *See also* KOREAN WAR.

UNITED STATES–SOUTH KOREA STATUS OF FORCES AGREEMENT (SOFA). An Agreement on the Status of American Forces in Korea (SOFA) was signed on 9 July 1966, with South Korea, as a supplementary agreement to Article IV of the **United States–South Korea Mutual Defense Treaty**. Until the signing of this agreement, the legal status of the **United States troops in South Korea** had been determined by individual *ad hoc* agreements that were initially agreed upon during the **Korean War**. Along with agreements on facilities and areas used by the U.S. armed forces, this agreement provides the means of resolving critical problems of legal jurisdiction when crimes are committed, property is damaged or destroyed, and/or local inhabitants are injured by the visiting forces. In 1990, the agreement was modified to give the Korean side more latitude in the arrest and prosecution of American military personnel charged with crimes in South Korea. The problem of crimes committed by U.S. forces in Korea continues to cause problems. See also KOREAN WAR.

UNITED STATES TROOPS IN SOUTH KOREA. The presence of United States troops in South Korea began with the arrival of an advance team of the XXIVth Corps on 4 September 1945, followed by the landing of 72,000 men of the Seventh, the Fortieth, and the Sixth infantry divisions of the XXIV Corps of the U.S. Eighth Army between 8 September and 8 October. The commander of the U.S. Forces in Korea was Lieutenant General **John R. Hodge**, who was assigned to accept the surrender of the Japanese governor-general in Korea, disarm Japanese troops and repatriate them, and maintain law and order. He was also instructed to establish an effective government along democratic lines and rebuild a sound economy as a basis for Korean independence, and train Koreans in handling their own affairs so as to prepare them to govern themselves as a free and independent nation. The American occupation forces established their headquarters in South Korea at **Yongsan military base** in Seoul, which had been the main military base of the Japanese in Korea. Hodge established his headquarters at the Bando Hotel in downtown **Seoul**, and after outlawing the **Korean People's Republic**, in mid-September, he established the **United States Army Military Government in Korea** (USAMGIK).

Following the establishment of the Republic of Korea in August 1948, the American occupation of Korea ended, and USAMGIK was abolished. The evacuation of U.S. troops began in September, and in January 1949, the Headquarters of the XXIV Corps itself left Korea, leaving behind the 7,500-man Fifth Regimental Combat Team and a U.S. Military Advisory Group of 500 officers and enlisted men to train South Korean troops. In May and June, the Fifth Regimental Combat Team also withdrew from South Korea, completing the evacuation of all U.S. troops on 29 June 1949.

The outbreak of the **Korean War** in June 1950 brought U.S. troops back to Korea, first from **Japan**, spearheaded by the Twenty-Fourth Infantry Division commanded by Major General William Dean, and then from the mainland United States. U.S. forces in South Korea during the war consisted of three army corps, one marine division, three naval groups, four air force groups and other supporting groups, totaling some 360,000 men at the end of the war. During the war, the headquarters of the **United Nations Command** (UNC) and that of the Eighth Army were relocated to **Seoul** from Tokyo. The war produced some 147,262 American casualties (33,625 dead, 105,785 wounded, and 7,852 missing). Following the signing of the **Korean Armistice Agreement** in July 1953, U.S. troop withdrawals began in March 1954. However, under the **United States–South Korea Mutual Defense Treaty**, signed in October 1953, more than 40,000 U.S. troops remained in Korea. Most were stationed along, or near, the **demilitarized zone** and in the vicinity of Seoul as a deterrent against renewed North Korean aggression. In July 1966, the **United States–South Korea Status of Forces Agreement** was signed, and the Headquarters of the UNC and that of the Eighth Army, which had moved back to Tokyo in November 1954, returned to Seoul in July 1967, making Yongsan their new home.

In 1970, 40,000 U.S. troops were still in South Korea. But, with the withdrawal of the Seventh Infantry Division from South Korea under President Richard Nixon's new Asian policy, the number of U.S. troops in Korea was reduced to about 30,000. U.S. President **Jimmy Carter** proposed to withdraw all U.S. ground troops from South Korea, but the plan, announced in March 1976, was not carried out. However, some 3,400 U.S. troops were withdrawn in December 1978. Meanwhile, in order to enhance mutual cooperation between U.S. and South Korean military establishments, in November 1978 the **United States–South Korean Combined Forces Command** was created, and the strength of the U.S. Air Force in South Korea was greatly increased.

In 1989, the U.S. and South Korea agreed to relocate the U.S. military base from Yongsan to near **Taejon**, the South Korean government defraying the cost. This has been a slow process, however, and many U.S. troops remained in the capital. As of 2003, there were some 37,000 American forces in South Korea, augmenting South Korea's national defense. These forces periodically train with South Korean forces, thus creating a more integrated military force.

UNIVERSITIES. The history of modern tertiary education is a major part of **educational development** in South Korea. It begins with a series of colleges begun by Western missionaries in the late 19th and early 20th centuries. These include Yonsei University, originally Chosun Christian College, still closely associated with the **Underwood family**, who helped found it; Korea University (Posung College), founded by **Kim Song-su**; and Ewha Women's University. Under the Japanese **Government-General of Korea**, none of these had university status; that was reserved for Keijo (**Seoul**) Imperial University, founded in 1924, and largely intended for Japanese residents in Korea.

After the division of the peninsula, the **United States Army Military Government in Korea** and other Americans, together with some Korean educationalists, reorganized the Imperial University as Seoul National University (SNU). There were then 19 institutes of higher education. SNU remained the only formal university until 1950, when it was decided to upgrade many existing colleges to university status, and to found new ones. The **Korean War** severely disrupted the development of higher education, but its development formed an important part of postwar reconstruction. By 1967, there were 211 higher education institutions, and the number reached over 600 in the next 25 years. About a fifth of the total were full four-year universities. By 2002, the number of four-year colleges was 206, with an additional 40 tertiary-level institutions also offering four-year specialized courses. There were also 184 junior colleges. In 2001, four-year students totaled 1.7 million. In addition to domestic colleges and universities, South Koreans have been enthusiastic seekers after foreign education, with large numbers studying in the **United States** in particular.

Despite this, and despite the fact that much American assistance has helped the development of modern Korean higher education, the universities have been major centers of anti-American and anti-government activity since the late 1950s. Every decade since the 1960s has witnessed radical activity by the **student movement**, a tradition that is now well established. Students believe that it was their predecessors' actions that brought down **Syngman Rhee** in 1960, led to the death of **Park Chung-hee** in 1979, and brought about the 1987 **June 29th democratization declaration**.

URBANIZATION. *See* SOCIAL AND CULTURAL DEVELOPMENTS.

USS *PUEBLO*, CAPTURE OF. On 23 January 1968, naval ships from **North Korea** seized a **United States** intelligence ship, the USS *Pueblo*, under Commander Lloyd M. Bucher and with a crew of 83 aboard, some 15 miles (24 kilometers) east of the North Korean east coast port of Wonsan. One crewmember was killed during the attack. The United States claimed that the ship was on the high seas at the time of its capture; the North Koreans said that it was within their territorial waters. After protracted negotiations in the **Military Armistice Commission** at **P'anmunjom**, and an American apology, Commander Bucher and 82 surviving crewmembers were returned to South Korea on 23 December 1968, but the ship was not. The U.S. promptly repudiated the apology once the crew had been released.

The *Pueblo* was periodically on display at Wonsan until about 1998, when it was moved to the Taedong River in **P'yongyang**, the North Korean capital.

– V –

VIETNAM. Vietnam has played an important role in modern South Korean history. Before 1975, South Korea and South Vietnam were naturally drawn together by their colonial pasts, by their common hostility toward communism, by what the two sides saw as their common experience of invasion in the claimed cause of national unification, and by their close links to the **United States**. These various links, but especially the last, led the government of **Park Chung-hee** to commit South Korean forces to the growing conflict in Vietnam from 1965 onward. Beginning with marine engineers and a marine artillery battery, the South Korean presence was augmented by additional marine forces and by two brigades from the Capital Division. From the latter's tiger badge, the Koreans took the name "Tiger Division." The Koreans totaled over 50,000 by September 1967, compared with 5,200 **Australians**, 2,000 Filipinos, 2,000 Thais, and 300 from New Zealand. The South Korean forces were theoretically all volunteers, who received U.S.$1.20 per day in addition to their normal pay. They acquired the reputation of tough fighters, and there were accusations of atrocities by Korean units from the beginning of their involvement in the conflict.

By 1972, the South Koreans were the only non-U.S. outside forces in Vietnam. But they had already begun to withdraw as early as April 1971, and by mid-1973, they had all gone. The Vietnam War provided important combat experience for South Korean forces; both the future presidents **Chun Doo-hwan** and **Roh Tae-woo** served there. More importantly, it gave a major boost to the South Korean economy, and greatly helped Park's push for **economic development**.

The eventual North Vietnamese victory in 1975 led to the severance of all contact between South Korea and Vietnam. Three South Korean diplomats who were trapped in Saigon were not released until 1980, while a South Korean businessman, also left behind, had to wait until 1987 for release. By that time, there were some signs that Vietnam wished to renew contact with South Korea. There was a growing, if formally unacknowledged, trading relationship, which became more open in February 1989 with an exchange of trade missions. In July 1989, a direct shipping line opened. In the early 1990s, sports and youth exchanges took place, to be followed by liaison offices in October 1992, and formal diplomatic relations in December 1992.

This opened the way for a closer South Korean involvement in Vietnam's development. Although the Vietnamese have not forgotten South Korea's role in the Vietnam War, they have clearly decided that there are more advantages in concentrating on the present than the past.

– W –

WAR MEMORIAL. The South Korean War Memorial, opened in **Seoul** in 1994, is an extensive museum, similar to the Australian War Memorial in Canberra. It was some three decades in the making, mainly because of problems raising the funds to build it. The museum, which replaced an earlier private one on Yoido Island in the heart of the city, is on the site of the former South Korean army headquarters. Although the **Korean War** features prominently, the museum goes well beyond that conflict, claiming to show all wars in which Koreans have been involved, including the struggle against **Japan** and the war in **Vietnam**. There is no mention, however, of the anti-Japanese activities of **Kim Il-sung** or other communist fighters.

In addition to the displays, the museum also contains extensive archives relating to conflicts involving Koreans and has a library and a research center. It also records the names of the 160,000 South Koreans killed since 1946, including members of the **police** force who died on duty. *See also* NATIONAL MUSEUM OF KOREA.

WHITE SKELETON CORPS (*Paekkoltan*). A terrorist youth group, established in 1952 in **Pusan**. It actively supported President **Syngman Rhee**, intimidating his opponents.

WOMEN'S LEAGUE FOR THE CONSTRUCTION OF THE NATION. *See* WOMEN'S MOVEMENT.

WOMEN'S MOVEMENT. Although in early times, there is evidence that Korea women enjoyed a relatively high degree of freedom, this became eroded as time passed. Under the Yi dynasty (1392–1910), the role of women was severely curtailed, especially among the upper classes. They were subject to **Confucianism**'s rules on subordination, and expected to be in turn dutiful daughters and wives and daughters-in-law. Even in old age, when women enjoyed more freedom, they still had to accept subordination to their sons. In the home, women were expected to manage the household without disputes and to produce a male heir.

With the opening of the country in the 19th century, new ideas about the role of women began to take root in Korea. Western missionaries had a more positive view of women, and in particular encouraged **educational development** for women. **Japan**'s encroachment on Korea after 1904 saw the emergence of a number of patriotic women's organizations. After the complete Japanese takeover in 1910, women continued to be active both in the cause of increased female participation in society and in the anti-Japanese movement. A relatively large number of women took part in the 1 March 1919 demonstrations. After the Japanese authorities relaxed their control over publications, a number of journals aimed at women appeared. However, there were strong pressures from men for women to accept masculine control of the nationalist movement. But in these years, the foundations were laid for many later debates about the status of women, the family and similar matters. There was also a growing division between those who believed that the stress should be on education and development of women, and those, especially on the left, who emphasized the political dimension.

A separate women's movement revived with the liberation of Korea in 1945. Two organizations emerged almost immediately. The first group was the left-wing Women's League for the Construction of the Nation (*Konguk puin tongmaeng*), established in August 1945. Its goals included the political, economic, and social liberation of Korean women; promotion of the solidarity of Korean women to contribute to the establishment of a completely independent nation; and development of a new consciousness among Korean women. The second women's organization was the right-wing Korean Women's Nationalist Society (*Taehan Yoja kungminhoe*), which was organized for the establishment of political, economic, and social rights of women, as well as for the elevation of their capacities. Its particular aims were to bring about the construction of a democratic society with women's strength, improve the standard of living, construct a healthy economy, and promote national culture.

Among other women's organizations formed in 1945 were the Korean Patriotic Women's Society (*Taehan Aeguk Puinhoe*), a revival of an earlier title, the Patriotic Women's Society for the Rapid Realization of Independence (*Tongnip Ch'oksong Aeguk Puinhoe*), and the League for the Protection of Women's Rights (*Yogwon Poho Tongmaeng*). The movement remained split along ideological lines, with the rightists following the lead of the newly emerged National Federation of Women's Organizations (*Chonguk Yosong Tanch'e Ch'ongyonmaeng*), and the General League of Korean Women (*Chosun Punyo Ch'ongdonemaeng*) leading the left-wing faction. However, these women's national organizations and the Young Women's Christian Association (YMCA), campaigned for social reform. They launched a movement to abolish public prostitution and the so-called "*kisaeng* house" (large Korean-style restaurants called *yojong*, where female entertainers entertained men guests). Their campaign persuaded the **United States Military Government in Korea** to issue Ordinance No. 70 of 17 May 1946, which banned the sale of women. At the same time, the two opposing camps were engaged in a bitter struggle in connection with the **Moscow Agreement** and the Allies' plan to impose trusteeship in Korea.

Shortly after the establishment of the **South Korean Interim Legislative Assembly** (SKILA) in late 1946, to which four women were appointed, these women's organizations and the newly emerged moderate left-wing Democratic Women's League (*Minju Yosong Tongmaeng*), presented a petition to SKILA for the enactment of a law guaranteeing equality of the sexes in political, economic, social, and cultural fields. Specifically, they sought equal voting rights, equal educational opportunity, equality in marriage and divorce, and equality in property inheritance, and the abolition of public prostitution. This last campaign was successful, leading to the promulgation of a law abolishing public prostitution by the American military government on 14 February 1948. The Korean women gained their voting rights without any struggle as these were granted by the **United Nations Temporary Commission on Korea** (UNTOK), and guaranteed in the **Constitution** of 1948. However, the struggle for equal rights had to be continued because, although the 1948 Constitution established democratic principles and equality of the sexes, there were many laws and social traditions that undermined these principles. Meanwhile, the left-wing women's movement declined after the fall of 1947 as many communist leaders escaped to the North.

In July 1948, several right-wing organizations merged to form the Korean Women's Society (*Taehan Puinhoe*). This became an ally to the autocratic **Syngman Rhee** administration first, and then of his **Liberal Party** after 1952. As a result, the development of the women's movement for social and economic equality suffered.

The **Korean War** had a decisive impact on the "inner revolution" of Korean women as they experienced an awakening of a new self in a tragic situation. Some 600,000 Korean women became war widows and breadwinners during and after the war, and, as heads of households, they took care of over one million war orphans. As the traditional dependency on men weakened, the desire for freedom from bondage of the old order grew stronger while traditional ethical values and morality deteriorated.

Although contributing to economic recovery and the restoration of social stability, the leaders of Korean women's associations, along with the Institute for the Study of Women's Problems, fought for the adoption by the government of a democratic civil code and a new **family law** that would establish equal rights for women in many areas.

Not satisfied with the new civil code and a family law of 1957 because it failed to allow women to be legal heads of households, prohibited marriages between men and women of the same clan origin, and did not establish women's property rights, the leaders launched a new struggle for the revision of these laws. In order to strengthen their campaign, in 1959, some 64 women's societies formed the National Council of Women's Organizations (NCWO).

In August 1962, the NCWO along with other women's societies petitioned the government to revise the family and inheritance laws, as well as to establish family courts. The government was favorably disposed to the latter, and in October 1963, the **Family Court** was created to handle civil matters involving family members. The government, however, was unwilling to take any steps to revise the civil code and the family law. Later, as part of their social reconstruction movement, Korean women leaders formed some 500 mother's clubs and launched a drive to popularize family planning in 1968. Their slogan was "Stop at Two and Raise Them Well." This movement gained momentum as women took steps to reduce the number of pregnancies.

In April 1972, the NCWO and the YWCA cosponsored a lecture series on the need for the revision of the family law. In June 1972, some 1,200 women, representing 61 women's associations, formed the Pan-Women's Association for the Acceleration of Revision of the Family Law. The Association adopted a 10-point resolution that demanded, among other things, the abolition of the system of male household head; the abolition of the law against marriage between men and women of the same clan origin; the establishment of equal rights of father and mother; a woman's right to property upon divorce; and the rationalization of the system of property inheritance. However, the government of **Park Chung-hee** remained very traditional in its attitude to the status of women. Conservative women leaders received government support and in 1974 established an institute called *Han'guk Yejiwon*, for the preservation of what they called Korea's "beautiful manners and good customs," a traditional Confucianist phrase to describe the ideal role for women.

Progressive reform-minded women did not give up their struggle in the face of growing conservative opposition led by followers of Confucianism. Holding a series of seminars on women at Christian Academy House in **Seoul** from 1973, Korean women leaders expressed a particular interest in promoting the status of women. In September 1974, as they prepared to celebrate 1975 as the start of the **United Nations** Decade of Women, some 2,000 representatives of 64 women's societies and 28 university women's groups held a national conference and adopted a resolution calling for the presidential declaration of 1975 as the Year of Women, the establishment of a presidential commission on promotion of the status of women, and the revision of the family law. Meanwhile, they proclaimed the "Women's Human Declaration," emphasizing the rights of women and their equality with men. In 1976, they formed the Council of Consumers as a lobbying organ of Korean women consumers. In the 1970s, Korean women of all groups joined the struggle to end the **Yushin rule** and establish a democratic and egalitarian society.

Academic institutions for women were actively involved in the promotion of women's studies, paying particular attention to legal, economic, and social problems. Thus the Research Center for Asian Women emerged at Sookmyung Women's University in 1960, followed by the Korean Women's Institute at Ewha Woman's University in 1977. Both had undergraduate and graduate programs in women's studies. The Korean Association of Women's Studies, which was established in October 1984, was joined by several other academically oriented women's societies, publishing journals and promoting new women's movements.

At the same time, there were new developments affecting women in both the countryside and the towns. In rural areas women enthusiastically participated in the **New Community Movement**, forming new community clubs of women of ages between 20 and 60. They did so because the movement stressed reforming the way of life of men as well as women, and it promoted new habits among rural people. These clubs encouraged family planning, the promotion of various money-making projects, and the increase of knowledge about how to improve living conditions, increase savings, and develop a cooperative spirit. Some three million women joined these clubs. Later, when the New Community Movement became discredited, rural women began to organize themselves in their own associations.

Another new development was the emergence of urban women workers as South Korea pursued **economic development**. From the late 1960s onward, an increasing number of Korean young women working in factories began to become politically active in the **labor movement** in the face of restrictions and discrimination in their workplaces. They campaigned for payment of back wages and improved living and working conditions, and were supported by student activists and others. The government treated all such movements as procommunist, and tried to suppress them, but the steady politicization of younger Korean women continued under **Chun Doo-hwan's** Fifth Republic. They were resolved also to establish equal employment opportunities and equal wages for women. Their efforts were partly rewarded when the government adopted a minimum wage system, and in early 1988, the **National Assembly** passed the Equality Law of Male and Female Employees. The late 1980s saw the establishment of local workingwomen's associations in most major cities. By 1992, these groups had come together as the Korean Women's Workers Associations United, a body that received official recognition from the

Department of Labor in June 1995. By 1998, there were some eight million workingwomen in South Korea, who accounted for 47 percent of the workforce.

Meanwhile, the struggle for more legal reforms in the status of women continued, gradually gaining new strength with the spread of democracy in the 1980s and 1990s. The family law was revised in 1977, but the result was disappointing since there was only a token concession to women's claims. Efforts therefore continued to bring about a complete change in the family law. To this end, in 1988, the representatives of 54 women's societies formed the Korean National Council of Women (KNCW) of 1.7 million members. Another major development was the establishment under government auspices of the **Korean Women's Development Institute** (KWDI) in 1982.

The late 1980s saw the process of change for women accelerating. In 1988, President **Roh Tae-woo** appointed a minister for public affairs II, to handle women's affairs; this post would later be subsumed in that of the president of the Presidential Commission on Women's Affairs in 1998, under President **Kim Dae-jung**.

Women's issues also featured in the **National Development Plans**. A "Basic Law on the Development of Women" was passed in 1995. In 1997, a "Comprehensive Women's Development Plan," was integrated into the "Five Year Economic and Social Development Plan," which covered the years 1998–2002. Laws also improved women's entitlement to maternity leave and support, and provided for assistance to women establishing businesses. In 1999 came the "Gender Non-Discrimination and Relief Act," and in 2001, the various organizations dealing with women and family matters were brought together in the Ministry of Gender Equality.

Formally, therefore, Korean women have achieved something approaching full equality. In practice, as elsewhere, the situation is often better on paper than it is in reality. Few women reach the top positions, a problem that it is hoped will be overcome by setting targets. By 1998, women held three cabinet rank positions, including that of president of the Presidential Commission on Women's Affairs. The first female ambassador was only appointed in 1996, and the first female general in 2001, when Army Colonel Yang Sung-sook became a brigadier-general on being appointed head of the military nursing academy. President Kim Dae-jung appointed the first female prime minister, Chang Sang, in July 2002, but the **National Assembly** refused to confirm the appointment. *See also* SOCIAL AND CULTURAL DEVELOPMENTS.

WORKING PEOPLE'S PARTY (*Kullo inmindang*). A short-lived party, originally called the Socialist Labor Party (*Sahoe Nodong-dang*) created by **Yo Un-hyong** in May 1947. It was formed from the union of three moderate left-wing parties.

WORLD CUP 2002. Soon after the successful 1988 **Olympic Games** in **Seoul**, South Korea made a bid to hold the International Football Association Federation (known as FIFA from the initials of the French version of its title) 2002 World Cup. The other main contender was **Japan**. In 1996, FIFA made the unprecedented decision to award the 2002 competition jointly to both countries. In South Korea, this decision prompted a major program to build stadia for the competition, which continued even after the onset of the **IMF crisis** in 1997–1998. New buildings were constructed in most major cities, including Seoul, **Inch'on**, **Taegu**, and several others.

Given the past history of Korean–Japanese relations, and continued tensions over matters such as textbooks and visits by Japanese ministers to the Yasukuni shrine, associated with war criminals, there was concern that the competition would be marred by hostility. In any case, the 2002 World Cup was a great success, with no untoward incidents. Japan was knocked out early on, but South Korea made it to the quarterfinals, a cause of great pride. The games brought South Korea to a wide audience worldwide, including even **North Korea**, where highlights of the competition were shown on domestic television.

– Y –

YANBIAN KOREAN AUTONOMOUS REGION. Situated on the Chinese border with **North Korea**, this region has the largest concentration of ethnic Koreans in **China**. Although there are Korean claims that this is historically part of Korea, in modern times, Koreans settled the region from the late 19th century onward. The total Korean population of

China is about 1.2 million, with a majority living in the Yanbian (Yong-byong in Korean) area. The region has always had strong links with North Korea, but since the late 1980s, ties have also developed with South Korea. Many South Korean businesses have established factories in the area, and there are close links between South Korean educational institutes and those in Yanbian. *See also* OVERSEAS KOREANS.

YI CH'ONG CH'ON. *See* CHI CH'ONG-CH'ON.

YI KI-PUNG (1896–1960). Born in **Seoul**, he studied in the **United States**. While in New York, he participated in the Korean nationalist movement as one of the publishers of a Korean-language newspaper, *Samil Shinmun*. He returned to Korea in 1934. In 1945, he became secretary to Dr. **Syngman Rhee**, and in 1949 he was appointed mayor of Seoul. While serving as the minister of defense in 1951, he and others founded the **Liberal Party**, becoming one of its key leading members. Elected to the **National Assembly** in 1954, he became the speaker, closely allied with Dr. Rhee.

Yi ran as the vice presidential candidate of the Liberal Party in 1956, but was defeated. He ran again in the March 1960 presidential election, and was elected vice president. However, when the **April 1960 Student Uprising** overthrew the First Republic, Yi, his wife, and son all committed suicide.

YI KU (1931–). The only son of the last crown prince of the Yi dynasty, which ruled Korea from 1392–1910, Yi Ku was born in **Japan** in 1931. His father, Yi Un (1897–1970), married the minor Japanese princess, Nashimoto Masako (1901–1989), who was known in Korea as Yi Pangja. She became much respected for her interest in social issues and the arts.

Yi Ku qualified as an architect at the Massachusetts Institute of Technology, and practiced in Japan, South Korea, and the **United States**. Yi Ku married an American, Julia Mullock in 1959. They had no children and subsequently divorced. Yi retired to **Seoul** in 1996. He has shown no interest in reviving a claim to the Korean throne.

YI POM-SUK (1900–1972). Born in **Seoul**, he fled to **China** in 1915. After graduating from a Chinese military school in 1919, he joined the Korean army in Manchuria, participating in the anti-Japanese Ch'ongsan-ri battle of 1920. In 1933, he became commander of the Korean military unit at the Chinese Nationalists' Loyang Military Academy, and in 1941, he became chief of staff of the Korean Restoration Army in China, engaged in the war against **Japan** on the side of the Chinese Nationalists.

Yi returned to Korea in August 1945. In October 1946, he formed the **National Youth Corps**. In 1948, he became the first prime minister and concurrently the minister of defense of the newly established Republic of Korea. After serving as ambassador to Nationalist China in 1950, Yi became vice president of the **Liberal Party** and was named the minister of home affairs in April 1952. He was nominated by the Liberal Party as its vice presidential candidate, but failed to get elected. He tried again in 1954, but was again defeated. When the **House of Councilors** was established in 1960, he ran for office and was elected. In 1963, he formed the Party of the People, but thereafter played only a minor role in politics.

YI POM-SUK (1922–1983). Better known to foreigners as Lee Bum Suk, he was foreign minister of the Republic of Korea (ROK) from May 1982 until his death in the 1983 **Rangoon bombing incident**. He was born in **P'yongyang**, and graduated from Posung College, the forerunner of Korea University in 1936. He later studied at the University of Maryland and at George Washington University in Washington D.C. He served in the military during the **Korean War**, and later joined the Foreign Ministry. He was vice president of the (Republic of) Korea Red Cross in 1972, and in this role he was the senior South Korean delegate to the **North–South Red Cross Talks** from 1972 to 1976. In 1976, he became ambassador to India. When **Chun Doohwan** became president in 1980, Yi was appointed minister of national unification, but achieved little before becoming foreign minister.

YI SI-YONG (1868–1953). Yi was a former high-ranking official in the government of the Yi dynasty. In 1910, at the time of **Japan**'s annexation of Korea, he fled to Manchuria, where he established a military school to train young Koreans. After serving as the minister of justice and the minister of finance in the **Korean Provisional Government** in **China** from 1919, in 1930 he and **Kim Ku** formed the

Korean Independence Party. On returning to Korea in 1945, he played a leading role in the **National Council for Rapid Realization of Korean Independence** as its chairman. He was elected vice president of the Republic of Korea in 1948, but in 1951 he resigned the vice presidency in protest against the undemocratic rule of Dr. **Syngman Rhee**. In 1952, he ran unsuccessfully for the presidency in opposition to Rhee.

YI SUNG-MAN. See RHEE, SYNGMAN.

YO UN-HYONG (1885–1947). Born in Yanp'yong, Kyonggi Province, he founded private schools in 1907 and 1908. Following the annexation of Korea by **Japan** in 1910, his schools were closed. Yo converted to Christianity and entered the Presbyterian Theological Seminary in **P'yongyang**. In 1914, however, he went to **China** to fight for Korea's liberation. In 1918, after attending a college in Nanjing for a brief period, he organized the New Korean Youth Party in China.

When the **Korean Provisional Government** in exile was established in Shanghai, Yo became a member of its legislative assembly. In 1919, he attended the meeting of the Korean Youth Independence Association in Tokyo that drafted the Declaration of Independence. It is not clear whether he joined the **Korean Communist Party**, established in China in 1919, but he did attend the Conference of Oppressed Peoples of the Far East held in Moscow in 1921. Returning to Korea some time in late 1920s, he was imprisoned for three years by the Japanese.

In 1933, when he was released from prison, he became president of the *Chung'ang Ilbo* newspaper until the Japanese closed it down in 1936. In 1944, he organized a secret society named the Alliance for Restoration of the Korean Nation, but he was again imprisoned. Released from prison in August 1945, he organized the **Committee for the Preparation of National Reconstruction**, and in September he helped establish the **Korean People's Republic**, becoming its vice-chairman. When the **United States Military Government in Korea** outlawed the Korean People's Republic, he established the **Korean People's Party** (*Chosun Inmindang*) in November 1945, and in February 1946 his party joined the left-wing Korean National Demo-

cratic Front (*Chosun Minjujuui Minjok Chonson*, or *Minjon*), supporting the implementation of the Allies' **Moscow Agreement**.
Yo collaborated with radical communists of the Korean Communist Party for a while, but in September 1946, he severed his ties with them, and joined the moderate right-wing nationalists in forming the **Coalition Committee for Cooperation between the Rightists and the Leftists** for the purpose of establishing "a democratic transitional government" of Korea in cooperation with the Allies under the Moscow Agreement. Meanwhile, he helped unify three other moderate leftist parties, forming a new party named Socialist Labor Party (*Sahoe Nodongdang*), which was renamed as the Working People's Party (*Kullo Inmindang*) in May 1947. For unknown reasons, Yo left the Coalition Committee for Co-operation between the Rightists and Leftists in December 1946, but did not withdraw his support for its aims. Yo's opposition to the rightists and the radical leftists made him the target of bitter criticism and attack by both groups. In the end, having endeavored in vain to unite the middle groups for the solution of the Korean question, he was **assassinated** on 19 July 1947 by a right-wing nationalist youth. *See also* COMMITTEE FOR THE PREPARATION OF NATIONAL RECONSTRUCTION; KOREAN NATIONAL DEMOCRATIC FRONT.

YONGSAN MILITARY BASE. Situated in what is now the heart of **Seoul**, the Yongsan military base was originally the headquarters of **Japan**'s military forces in Korea during the colonial period. During the **Korean War**, it became the headquarters of the **United States** Eighth Army, which it remains. In 1994, following an agreement signed in 1989, however, the U.S. military authorities gave up some of the land of the base to the Seoul Municipal Government, which turned the area into a park. The continued occupation of the rest of the base area remains a matter of contention, though in 2003, the U.S. government announced its intention to move all its forces in Korea, except for a small number attached to the **United Nations Command** and the **Combined Forces Command**, to bases south of Seoul.

YONHAP NEWS AGENCY. Up to 1980, South Korea had two general news agencies, the Hapdong News Agency, which dated from 1945, and the more recently established Orient Press. In the course of the "massacres of the mass media" that took place following the **December 1979 coup**, these were forced to amalgamate into the Yonhap News Agency. Yonhap was nominally independent of the government, but in reality until **Roh Tae-woo**'s government relaxed press controls in 1987, it normally followed the government line on domestic stories, while suppressing international news deemed to be unfavorable. It continued to be subordinate to the government even under President **Kim Dae-jung**. Yonhap has a large staff in **Seoul**, and has some 19 correspondents worldwide. It is noted for technical innovations. It has published the *Korea Annual*, formerly published by Hapdong, since 1981. See also NAEWOE NEWS AGENCY.

YOSU–SUNCH'ON REBELLION. In the autumn of 1948, following the **Cheju Rebellion** in April 1948, the newly formed government of **Syngman Rhee** took rigorous moves to suppress it. But the communist-infiltrated 14th Regiment of the Army, based in Yosu in South Cholla Province, on 19 October 1948 refused to go to **Cheju Island** as ordered. When the military insurrection began, communists and communist sympathizers in the Yosu and Sunch'on areas joined in, resulting in a large-scale rebellion. At this juncture, the communist-infiltrated 4th Regiment, based in **Kwangju**, also carried out an abortive rebellion.

The rebels in the Yosu–Sunch'on area seized government buildings, **police** stations, and set up people's committees and tribunals that tried local officials and civilian leaders, killing some 1,200 local officials, police, and their family members, and destroyed several hundreds of homes and public buildings. In the wake of the rebellion, the government proclaimed martial law in the area and arrested some 23,000 rebels and civilian collaborators, over 80 percent of whom were found guilty and several hundreds of them were executed. The rebellion was crushed by early November, but many rebels fled into mountainous areas, especially in the Mount Chiri area, in the southern regions of the country, and harassed the local officials and inhabitants, leading to events, such as the **Hamp'yong–Koch'ang incidents**. During and after the Yosu–Sunch'on Rebellion, some troops of the 6th Regiment stationed at **Taegu**, who had been members of the underground South Korean Workers' Party, attempted to take over the regiment in November and December 1948.

YU CHIN-O (1906–1988). A graduate of Keijo (**Seoul**) Imperial University in 1929, Yu joined a nationalist society named *Suyang Tong'uhoe* that was formed in 1922. Becoming one of its active members, he edited its publication, *Tonggwang* (The Eastern Light) from 1932 until **Japan**'s colonial government abolished the society in 1939. Under Japanese pressure, Yu joined the Korean Society of Literary Persons established in 1939.

In 1946, Yu became professor of law at Korea University, and then served as director of the Office of Government Legislative Affairs from August 1948 to June 1949. After being elected as a member of the National Academy of Science in 1954, he served as president of Korea University until 1966. He became a key member of the new **Masses (Minjung) Party** formed in May 1965, and was elected to the **National Assembly** in 1966. He was nominated by his party to run in the 1967 presidential race, but he brought about the merger of his party with the **New Democratic Party** (NDP) of **Yun Po-son** in February 1967, making Yun the sole presidential candidate of the major opposition party. Following the establishment of the Fourth Republic in 1972, Yu retired from politics, playing the role of an elder statesman and adviser to the NDP (1970–1979) and the National Unification Board (1980–1984).

YUJONGHOE. *See* POLITICAL FRATERNAL SOCIETY FOR REVITALIZING REFORM.

YUN I-SANG (1917–1995). Yun was perhaps the most famous Korean composer of the 20th century, but for most of his life, he was more honored in **North Korea** than in the South. He was born in Tongyong, in South Kyongsang Province, and studied in **Japan**, where he was active in Korean revolutionary groups. He returned to Korea and, in 1955, he won a major award from the **Seoul** city government, which allowed him to study music in West Germany. There he acquired an international reputation, but in 1967, he and his wife, along with other South Koreans in Germany, were kidnapped by the then Korean Central Intelligence Agency (KCIA, now the **National Intelligence Service**) and brought back to South Korea, accused of spying for the North. Yun was sentenced to life imprisonment, but following an international outcry, he was released after two years and allowed to return to Germany.

Thereafter, Yun's music became more political. He visited North Korea several times, but never returned to the South, where his music was banned. After his death, however, the changed political climate in the South led to increased interest in his music, which is now regularly performed in the South. He also remains popular in the North. **P'yongyang's** main concert hall is dedicated to his memory, there is an annual series of concerts in his name, and a Yun I-sang music festival was held in North Korea in 1998. *See also* EAST BERLIN CASE; SONG DU-YUL.

YUN PO-SON (1897–1990). Born into a former *yangban* family, Yun graduated from Edinburgh University in Scotland in 1930. He played no political role before 1945, but in November 1945, he joined the **Korean Independence Party,** which had returned from **China.** He was appointed mayor of **Seoul** in 1948, and served as the minister of trade and industry (1949–1950). Elected to the **National Assembly** in 1954, he gained political importance as the chief representative of the opposition.

In August 1960, when the First Republic fell, Yun was elected by the National Assembly as the president of the Second Republic, and was thus president at the time of the **Military Revolution of 16 May 1961.** He remained in the office until March 1962. He then resigned the presidency in protest at the Political Purification Law and the activities of the Political Purification Committee. Yun ran for the presidency twice thereafter: first in 1963 as the candidate of the **Civil Rule Party,** and the second time in 1967 as the candidate of the **New Democratic Party** (NDP). He was founder of the Civil Rule Party (1963), the **New Korea Party** (1966), and helped found the NDP (1967). On leaving party politics in the mid-1980s, after serving as adviser to the president of the NDP, he played the role of an elder statesman.

YUSHIN RULE. Shortly after his reelection for the third time in April 1971 under the revised **Constitution** of 1969, and his inauguration on 1 July, President **Park Chung-hee** proceeded to tighten the control of the government over the nation in view of the rapidly changing domestic and international situations, particularly in view of new developments in relations with **North Korea.** Then on 17 October 1972, Park proclaimed nationwide martial law, suspending some provisions of the Constitution, dissolving the **National Assembly,** and banning all political activities. This action became known as known as the "October Yushin" ("Revitalizing Reform"), ending the Third Republic and preparing for the coming of the Fourth Republic. Park claimed that his reasons for this action were "to have unity in order to have a dialogue with the North," and to deal with the "great changes" that occurred on the international scene. Yushin was designed to remove politics from the vagaries of the politicians and electorate and at the same time, to completely centralize policymaking and the execution of functions in the hands of the president. In effect, Park staged a *coup d'etat* against himself.

Under the Yushin program, the government proposed a series of **constitutional amendments**, and on 21 November, the amended constitution was approved in a national referendum. With this, the new electoral college, named the **National Conference for Unification**, was established, with 2,359 members being elected by popular vote on 15 December 1972. The new electoral college elected the incumbent president as the president of the Fourth Republic, without the limit of the term of office. The Yushin Constitution was proclaimed on 12 December 1972 as President Park took the oath of office as the eighth president. His death in October 1979 led to the formal end of the Yushin system, although elements of it lingered on under Presidents **Chun Doo-hwan** and **Roh Tae-woo**. *See also* POLITICAL FRATERNAL SOCIETY FOR REVITALIZING REFORM.

– Z –

ZO ZAYANG (1926–2000). Korean folklorist, who tried to preserve the traditions of Shamanism in the face of the relentless modernization of South Korea. He studied architecture and engineering at Harvard University, where he took a Ph.D., and practiced architecture for a time. From the 1970s onward, however, his focus was on the preservation of traditional folk paintings, especially those of tigers and the "Old Man of the Mountains." To this end he established the Emille Museum in 1968. His efforts met government opposition, especially under **Park Chung-hee**, but in his later years, he found a more appreciative audience both officially and privately.

Bibliography

INTRODUCTION

Only after Korea's liberation from Japanese rule in 1945 did Korean studies begin to emerge as a distinct discipline in the West. Until then, the study of Korea had been very limited, with many seeing Korea politically and culturally as a part of the Chinese world up to 1894, and after that date as under Japanese domination, and eventually a Japanese colony.

The first book written by a Westerner on Korea was Hendrick Hamel's *An Account of the Ship Wreck of a Dutch Vessel on the Coast of the Isle of Quelpart, Together with a Description of the Kingdom of Corea*, published in Amsterdam and Rotterdam in 1668. In 1704, an English version of Hamel's book, edited by John Churchill, was published in London, but generally Korea remained a *terra incognita* for most Western people.

At the end of the 18th century appeared *A Voyage of Discovery to the North Pacific Ocean*, etc., by the British naval explorer William Broughton, which gave an account of his visit to Korea in 1797. It was followed by two books recording an 1816 visit to Korea by other British ships: Basil Hall's *Voyage to Corea and the Island of Loo-choo* (London: 1817) and John M'Leod's *Narrative of a Voyage in His Majesty's Late Ship* Alceste, etc., (London 1817). Other books of exploration followed. Charles Dallet published his important work, *Histoire de l'église de Corée*, etc., in Paris in 1874, partly based on French missionary letters from Korea. It was followed by Leon de Rosny's *Les Coréens, aperçu ethnologique et historique* (Paris: 1886) and Ernest Oppert's *A Forbidden Land: Voyages to the Corea* (London: 1880). Some of these works appeared in the United States, but the first properly American work on Korea was William Elliot Griffis' *Corea: The Hermit Nation* (New York: 1882), followed by Percival Lowell's *Choson, The Land of Morning Calm: A Sketch of Korea* (Boston: 1888). In the late 1890s and early

1900s, British (including Canadians and other members of the British Empire) and American missionaries and diplomats published more books about Korea, thus increasing knowledge about Korea in the West.

After the Japanese annexation of Korea in 1910, Western books about Korea were comparatively rare. On the other hand, the Japanese government, as well as the Japanese colonial Government-General in Korea, published numerous English-language publications. Many of these were for propaganda purposes, designed to create a positive view of Japanese rule in Korea. Since 1945, the division of the peninsula, the Korean War, South Korea's economic development, and the continued tension in the Korean peninsula, as well as a widespread interest in Korean art, have all contributed to a growing interest in Korean studies. Like other new fields of studies, Korean studies sometimes lacked balance in their development and were accompanied by certain weaknesses. However, Korean studies in the West, particularly in the United States, have developed rapidly in recent decades, filling the gap that used to exist in certain areas, making available more English-language books and articles that are included in this bibliography.

The purpose of this bibliography is to assist further research and reading. Only English-language materials are included. When books are unavailable, journal articles and doctoral dissertations have been substituted.

Readers should also be aware of the huge amount of material on both Koreas that is now available on the Internet. Most Korean newspapers have their own websites, and several are available in English versions. The South Korean government provides much information online, as do a number of South Korean embassies; the website of the embassy in Washington D.C. is particularly good. Many educational institutions maintain websites, making available bibliographies and other useful sources of information. A selection of such sites, covering all fields, appears as the final section of this bibliography. However, even government websites have a habit of changing and altering, so this list should be regarded only as a guide. A good search engine will often produce additional information. A few CD-ROMs are also listed.

In updating the bibliography for the second edition, I have kept most of what Professor Nahm included, even if some of the material may seem relatively obscure. But he knew the literature rather better than I do, and it seems sensible to continue to draw on his scholarly knowledge.

The following four bibliographies provide further information on source materials in Korean studies. They are as follows:

1. Institute of Asian Studies, Seoul National University, *Korean Studies Today: Development and State of the Field*. Seoul: 1970. This English-language publication offers bibliographical essays on ancient arts, dramatic arts, classical literature, modern literature, customs and folklore, history, economy, science, sociology, traditional music, traditional political and legal systems, religion, linguistics, and philosophy. Each section has its own bibliography that mainly includes works by Korean and Japanese authors.
2. Korean National Committee of Historical Science. *Historical Studies in Korea: Recent Trends and Bibliography (1945–1973)*. Seoul: National History Compilation Committee, Ministry of Education, Republic of Korea, 1975. This English-language guide covers works by Koreans living in Korea. It provides authors' names and titles of books in Chinese. It is divided into three parts: Korean history, Eastern history, and Western history.
3. Han-kyo Kim, ed. *Studies on Korea: A Scholar's Guide*. Honolulu: University Press of Hawaii, 1980. This important guide includes English, French, German, and other European-language materials such as books, journal articles, doctoral dissertations, and master's theses. It is divided into the following sections: bibliographies, handbooks, journals, and other publications; archaeology; history (up to 1945, including the history of science); philosophy and religion; language and linguistics; literature and folklore; art, music, and dance; education; geography and natural environment; people, family, and society; the economic system; government and politics; the legal system; international relations and national reunification; North Korea; and Russian-language materials. Each section, edited by one or more editors, has a brief bibliographical essay.
4. Hoffman, Frank, Matthew J. Christensen, and Kirk W. Lansen, compilers. *The Harvard Korean Studies Bibliography: 80,000 References on Korea*. Cambridge, Mass.: Harvard University Korea Institute, 1999. CD-ROM. A collection that provides a vast amount of material, covering all aspects of Korea as reflected in Western languages from the first publications in the 18th century to 1997. About one quarter of the material, mostly journal articles, is annotated.

Readers should also consult the *Bibliography of Asian Studies* (Ann Arbor, Michigan: Association for Asian Studies), which has been produced by the American Association for Asian Studies since 1941, and which lists book-length studies of Asia. The main emphasis is on history, politics, and economics.

Most areas of Korean studies now have a reasonably up-to-date body of works for the reader to consult. As well as those noted below, most useful is the Yonhap News Agency's *Korea Annual*, whose subtitle "A Comprehensive Handbook on Korea" has become more accurate in recent years since it now includes a relatively dispassionate section on North Korea. It is usually available from late August in the year carried on the cover, and contains information up to the early part of that year. It is a descriptive handbook, a directory of organizations, and a biographical dictionary in one.

Looking at more specialist works, perhaps the one area where there is a real lack is geography. Here it is still necessary to consult books such as Patricia Bartz's *South Korea* (1962) or even the much older work by Hermann Lautensach originally published in German in the 1940s, but reissued in an English translation in 1988. Occasional articles supplement such works but it is surprising that there has not been more published, given the huge changes that have taken place in the South Korean landscape.

New guidebooks appear all the time. The only recommendation, given the rapid pace of change in South Korea, is to use the latest available. One positive development is the appearance of local guides to cities such as Taegu and Pusan; up until recently only Seoul tended to have such a luxury. L. Robert Kohls' *Learning to Think Korean: A Guide to Living and Working in Korea* (2001) will answer many questions for the newcomer.

Among recent books on art, Jane Portal's *Korea: Art and Archaeology* (2000) marks the opening of a Korean Gallery in London's British Museum, while Robert Moes' *Auspicious Spirits: Korean Folk Painting and Related Objects* (1983), covers a subject often neglected.

South Korea's economic development has produced many studies. Much useful information is available from government publications, including annual statistics. These are also available on CD-ROM and from the (South) Korean Government Statistical Office website. A popular account of how South Korea did it can be found in Robert P. Kearney's *The Warrior Worker: The History and Challenge of South Korea's Economic Miracle* (1991). One growing area is the study of women in South Korea's economic development. Here *Gender Division of Labor in Korea* (1994), edited by Cho Hyoung and Chang Pil-wha, is helpful. The 1997–1998 economic crisis still waits for a good general account, but for those who can get hold of it *Korea Rebuilds: From Crisis to Opportunity*, published by the East Asia Analytical Unit of the Australian Department of Foreign Affairs and Trade in 1999, is a good start.

A number of general histories have appeared in recent years. The most readable is probably Bruce Cumings' *Korea's Place in the Sun* (1997). Cumings is often seen as a controversial historian but in this elegant work, he provides a good general history in a pleasing style. To get a feel for Korean source material, the reader should turn to the two volumes edited by Yongho Ch'oe, William Theodore de Bary, and Peter H. Lee, *Sources of Korean Tradition*, published by Columbia University Press in 1997 and 2000. *Korea: A Historical and Cultural Dictionary* (1999), by Keith Pratt and Richard Rutt, with additional material by James Hoare, is a useful handbook to accompany all these volumes.

Work on the Korean War has produced a huge literature, especially but not exclusively, on the diplomatic context. Accessible to most readers will be James E. Hoare and Susan Pares' *Conflict in Korea: An Encyclopedia* (1999), which also covers the relationship between the two Koreas since the war, and *Encyclopedia of the Korean War: A Political, Social, and Military History* (2000) edited by Spencer C. Tucker. In 2003, Scarecrow Press produced the equally accessible *The Korean War: A Historical Dictionary,* edited by Paul M. Edwards. For a South Korean perspective on the war, there is the massive three-volume *The Korean War*, edited by the Korea Institute of Military History (1997–1999).

South Korean politics are well covered, though often in conference-derived volumes. John Oh's two books *Democracy on Trial* (1968) and *Korean Politics: The Quest for Democratization and Development* (1999) explain the political landscape with much detail and a sure touch. Yang Sung Chul, appointed ambassador to Washington, D.C. by President Kim Dae-jung, shows the parallels and the divergences between the two Koreas in his *The North and South Korean Political Systems: A Comparative Analysis* (1994). *Understanding Korean Politics: An Introduction* (2001), edited by Soong Hoom Kil and Chung-in Moon, is a set of essays that also looks at both Koreas' political development.

For scholars who wish to go further, extensive English-language archive materials are available in the United States, Great Britain, and a number of other countries. In most cases, government-generated archives are open to researchers after 30 years, so that material relating to the early 1970s is now accessible at the National Archives in Washington, D.C. or at the British Public Record Office at Kew near London. In the United States, the Freedom of Information Act has meant that more recent documents can sometimes be made available, but there is no guarantee that any particular paper will be opened. Even when such documents are made available, certain parts are often excluded.

The most extensive use of archive material so far has probably been in relation to the origins of the Korean War, and to the diplomatic maneuvers that marked the conflict's progress. However, older material should not be ignored. In the 19th and early 20th centuries, diplomats often traveled all over the Korean Peninsula, and their reports provide many insights into Korean life and culture. As well as written reports, there are also unpublished maps and photographs to be found in archival material. Although much archival material has been made available in published form, such publications rarely include maps or photographs.

Missionary archives are another useful source of information on Korea of the past. Most missionaries came from the United States, and their archives will be found there, but the Australian Presbyterians were also important, and even the British Anglican (Episcopalian) mission has left surprisingly detailed records. Again, most missionary archives operate some form of time restriction on access, even to bona fide researchers, varying from 30–50 years. Although much of the material is inevitably concerned with mission details, other subjects such as the relationship between Koreans and the Japanese colonial authorities are also likely to be featured.

The organization of the present bibliography is as follows:

1. Bibliographies and Korean Studies Guides
2. Periodicals and Newspapers
3. General
   A. Travel/Guide Books
   B. Map Collection
   C. Handbooks/Statistical Abstracts

4. Culture
   A. General
   B. Archeology
   C. Architecture
   D. Arts
   E. Drama/Theater
   F. Language/Linguistics
   G. Literature
   H. Music/Dance
   I. Philosophy/Religion
   J. Press
5. Economy
   A. General
   B. Agriculture
   C. Development
   D. Finance
   E. Trade
   F. Industry
   G. Labor
   H. Transportation/Communications
6. History
   A. Autobiography/Biography
   B. General
   C. Ancient/Pre-Modern
   D. Colonial Period
   E. Post-Independence Period
   F. The Korean War
   G. Diplomatic History/Foreign Relations
7. Politics
   A. General
   B. Government
   C. Law
   D. Political Parties
8. Science
   A. Geography/Geology
   B. Public Health/Medicine
   C. Science/Technology

1. BIBLIOGRAPHIES AND KOREAN STUDIES GUIDES

Academy of Korean Studies, comp. *Selected Bibliography of Korean Studies*. Seoul: Korea Foundation, 1995.

Asiatic Research Center, Korea University. *Bibliography of Korean Studies: A Bibliographical Guide to Korean Publications on Korean Studies Appearing from 1945 to 1958*. Seoul: Asiatic Research Center, Korea University, 1961.

Blanchard, Carroll H. *Korean War Bibliography and Maps of Korea*. Albany, New York: Korean Conflict Research Foundation, 1964.

Chung, Yong Sun. *Korea: A Selected Bibliography, 1959–1963*. Kalamazoo, Mich.: Korea Research and Publications, 1965.

Edwards, Paul M. *The Korean War: An Annotated Bibliography*. Westport, Conn.: Greenwood Press, 1998.

Elrod, James McRee. *An Index to English Language Periodical Literature published in Korea 1890–1940*. Seoul: Yonsei University, 1960.

———. *An Index to English Language Newspapers published in Korea 1896–1937*. Seoul: National Assembly Library, 1966.

Gompertz, G. St. G. M. "The First Section of a Revised and Annotated Bibliography of Western Literature on Korea from the Earliest Times until 1950 based on Horace G. Underwood's 'Partial Bibliography of Occidental Literature on Korea.'" *Transactions of Korea Branch of the Royal Asiatic Society* 40 (1963), 1–263.

Henthorn, William E. *A Guide to Reference and Research Materials on Korean History: An Annotated Bibliography*. Honolulu: East–West Center, 1968.

Hoare, J. E., with the assistance of Susan Pares. *Korea*. (World Bibliographical Series Vol. 204.) Santa Barbara, Calif.: Clio Press, 1997.

Hoffman, Frank, Matthew J. Christensen, and Kirk W. Lansen, compilers. *The Harvard Korean Studies Bibliography: 80,000 references on Korea*. Cambridge, Mass.: Harvard University Korea Institute, 1999. CD-ROM.

Institute of Asian Studies, Seoul National University. *Korean Studies Today: Development and State of the Field*. Seoul: Institute of Asian Studies, 1970.

Jones, Helen D., and Robin L. Winkler, comp. *Korea: An Annotated Bibliography of Publications in Western Languages*. Washington, D.C.: Library of Congress, 1950.

Kang, Kil-su. *A Short Bibliography in the English Language Material on Korea and Its Evaluation*. Pittsburgh, Penn: IDEP, University of Pittsburgh, 1968.

Kang, Sangwoon. *List of Articles on Korea in the Western Languages, 1800–1964*. Seoul: Tangudang, 1967.

Kenz, Eugene, and Chang-su Swanson. *A Selected and Annotated Bibliography of Korean Anthropology*. Seoul: National Library of the Republic of Korea, 1968.

Kim, Han-kyo, ed. *Studies on Korea. A Scholar's Guide*. Honolulu: University of Hawaii Press, 1980.

Koh, Hesung Chun. *Korea: An Analytical Guide to Bibliographies*. New Haven, Conn.: Human Relations Area Files, 1971.

———. *Social Science Resources on Korea: A Preliminary Computerized Bibliography*. New Haven, Conn.: Human Relations Area Files, 1968.

Korean National Committee for Historical Science. *Historical Studies in Korea: Recent Trends and Bibliography (1946–1973)*. Seoul: National History Compilation Committee, Ministry of Education, Republic of Korea, 1975.

McFarland, Keith D. *The Korean War: An Annotated Bibliography*. New York: Garland, 1986.

Marcus, Richard, ed. *Korean Studies Guide*. Compiled by Benjamin H. Hazard Jr. and others. Berkeley: University of California Press, 1954.

Nahm, Andrew C., comp. *Japanese Penetration of Korea, 1894–1910: A Checklist of Archives in the Hoover Institution*. Stanford, Calif.: Hoover Institution, 1959.

National Assembly Library, comp. *An Index to English Language Periodical Literature published in Korea 1941–1968*. Seoul: National Assembly Library, 1969.

Park Hong-kyu. *The Korean War: An Annotated Bibliography*. Marshall, Tex.: Demmer Co. Inc., 1971.

Shulman, Frank J. *Doctoral Dissertations on Asia: An Annotated Bibliographical Journal of Current International Research*. Vol. I. Ann Arbor, Mich.: Xerox University Microfilms, 1975; Vol. II, Nos. 1 & 2, 1988.

———. *Doctoral Dissertations on Japan and Korea, 1969–1974. A Classified Bibliographical Listing of International Research*. Ann Arbor, Mich.: University Microfilms International, 1976.

———. *Japan and Korea. An Annotated Bibliography of Doctoral Dissertations in Western Languages, 1877–1969*. Chicago: American Library Association, 1970.

Silberman, Bernard S. *Japan and Korea: A Critical Bibliography*. Tucson: University of Arizona Press, 1962.

Underwood, Horace H. "Korean Literature in English: A Critical Bibliography." *Transactions of Korea Branch of the Royal Asiatic Society* 50 (1976), 65–115.

2. PERIODICALS AND NEWSPAPERS

Acta Koreana. Biannual. Taegu. Academia Koreana, Keimyung University, 1996–.
Business Korea. Monthly. Seoul. Business Korea Ltd., later Hanwool International Company Ltd. 1983–.
Journal of Korean Affairs. Silver Spring, Md.: The Research Institute on Korean Affairs. Quarterly. 1971–76.
Journal of Korean Studies. Seattle: Society for Korean Studies, later Los Angeles, Center for Korean Studies, UCLA. Annual. 1979–.
Journal of Modern Korean Studies. Fredericksburg, Va.: Mary Washington College. Annual. 1984–.
Journal of Social Science and Humanities. (Formerly *Bulletin of the Korean Research Center*). Seoul: The Korean Research Center. Semi-annual. 1960–.
Korea and World Affairs: A Quarterly Review. Seoul: Research Center for Peace and Unification. 1977–.
Korea Focus on Current Topics. Seoul: Korea Foundation. Bimonthly, 1993–.
Korea Herald. Daily. Seoul. 1953–. Also available on line.
Korea Journal. Seoul: Korean National Commission for UNESCO. Monthly. 1961–.
Korea Now (originally *Korea Newsreview*). Seoul: International Cultural Society of Korea. Weekly. 1961–2000. Biweekly. 2000–.
Korea Observer. Seoul: Academy of Korean Studies. Quarterly. 1968–.
Korea Review. Philadelphia. Monthly. 1919–1922.
Korea Review. Seoul: Methodist Publishing House. Monthly. 1901–06.
Korea Times. Seoul. Daily, 1950–. Also available online.
Korean Culture. Los Angeles: Korean Cultural Society. Quarterly, 1979–.
Korean Quarterly. Seoul: International Research Center, 1974–.
Korean Repository. Seoul: Trilingual Press. Monthly. 1892, 1895–1898.
Korean Social Science Journal. Seoul: Korean Social Science Research Council, Korean National Commission for UNESCO. Annual. 1981–.
Korean Studies. Honolulu: Center for Korean Studies, University of Hawaii. Annual. 1976–.
Korean Survey. Washington, D.C.: Korean Pacific Press. Bimonthly, 1952–1961.
Papers of the British Association for Korean Studies. London, later Sheffield, England. Annual. 1991–.
Review of Korean Studies. Seoul: Academy of Korean Studies. Biannual, 1998–.
Seoul: The Monthly Magazine of Korea Illustrated. Seoul: HEK Communications, 1985–.
Social Science Journal. Seoul: Korean National Commission for UNESCO. Annual. 1973–1980.
Transactions of the Korea Branch of the Royal Asiatic Society. Annual. 1900–1941, 1948–.
Voice of Korea. Washington, D.C. Korean Affairs Institute. Bimonthly. 1943–1961.

3. GENERAL

A. Travel/Guide Books

Adams, Edward B. *Korea Guide*. Seoul: Taewon, 1976.

———. *Kyongju Guide. Cultural Spirit of Silla in Korea*. Seoul: Seoul International Tourist Company, 1979.

———. *Through Gates of Seoul*. Seoul: Seoul International Tourist Co., 2 vols., 1971.

———. *Palaces of Seoul*. Seoul: Taewon, 1982.

Chung, Kyung Cho et al. *The Korea Guidebook*. Boston, Mass.: Houghton Mifflin, 1988.

Clark, Allen D., and Donald N. Clark. *Seoul: Past and Present: A Guide to Yi T'aejo's Capital*. Seoul: Royal Asiatic Society, Korea Branch, 1969.

Fodor's Korea. New York: Fodor's Travel Publications, 1993.

Grayson, James H., and Donald N. Clark. *Discovering Seoul. A Historical Guide*. Seoul: Royal Asiatic Society, Korea Branch, 1986.

Han, Suzanne C. *Korea: A Pictorial Guide Book*. Seoul: Hollym, 1988.

Hoare, James, and Susan Pares. *The Simple Guide to Customs and Etiquette in Korea*. Folkestone, England: Global Books, 2000.

Hoefer, H. et al. *Insight Guides: Korea*. Hong Kong: APA Publications, 2003.

Hollym. *Compact Guide to Korea*. Seoul: Hollym, 1988.

———. *Seoul: A Pictorial Guide Book*. Seoul: Hollym, 1985.

Kirkbride, Wayne A. *Panmunjom: Facts About the Korean DMZ*. Seoul: Hollym, 1988.

Kohls, L. Robert. *Learning to Think Korean: A Guide to Living and Working in Korea*. Yarmouth, Maine: Intercontinental Press, 2001.

Middleton, Dorothy and William D. *Some Korean Journeys*. Seoul: Royal Asiatic Society, Korea Branch, 1975.

Popham, Peter. *The Insider's Guide to Korea*. Seoul: Seoul International Publishing House, 1987.

Price, David. *Between Two Seas: A Journey Into South Korea*. Seoul: Seoul International Publishing House, 1988.

Rucci, Richard B., ed. *Living in Korea*. Seoul: Seoul International Tourist Co., 1984.

Saccone, Richard. *Travel Korea Your Way*. Seoul, Elizabeth N.J.: Hollym, 1994.

Seoul City Hall, ed. *A Budget Traveler's Guide to Seoul*. Seoul: Seoul City Hall, 2000.

Storey, Robert, and Geoffrey Crowther. *Korea: A Travel Survival Kit*. Oakland Calif.: Lonely Planet, 2001.

———. *Seoul*. Oakland Calif.: Lonely Planet, 1999.

B. Map Collection

Korea, Republic of, Ministry of Education. *Korean Gazetteer*. Seoul, 1972.
———. Office of Rural Development. Institute of Plant Environment. Korean Soil Survey. *Reconnaissance Soil Map of Korea*. 9 vols. Seoul: 1971.
Lee, Ch'an. *Korean Old World Maps*. Seoul: Seoul National University Press, 1971.
———. *Old Maps of Korea*. Seoul: Korean Library Science Research Institute, 1977.
National Construction Research Institute. *The History of Mapping in Korea*. Seoul: 1972.
National Geographic Institute. *Maps of Korea (Past, Present and Future)*. Seoul: Korean Geography Research Society, 2000.
Nelles Maps. *Korea*. Munich: Nelles Verlag, 1999.
Park, Yonghan. *Atlas of Korea*. Seoul: Moonwhasa, 2000.
U.S. Army Map Service. *Far East. Korea*. AMS Series L 551, 651, 751, and 1052. Washington, D.C.: 1952–76.

C. Handbooks/Statistical Abstracts

American University. Foreign Areas Studies Division. *U.S. Army Handbook for Korea*. Washington, D.C.: Government Printing Office, 1964.
Bank of Korea. *Economic Statistics Yearbook*. Seoul: 1960–.
———. *Monthly Economic Statistics*. Seoul, 1960–.
Clare, Kenneth D., et al. *Area Handbook for the Republic of Korea*. Washington, D.C.: Government Printing Office, 1970.
Hapdong News Agency, Korea. *Korea Annual*. Seoul: 1962–80.
Hakwon-sa. *Korea. Its Land, People and Culture of All Ages*. Seoul: 1963.
Korea, Republic of, Ministry of Agriculture and Fisheries. *Yearbook of Agriculture and Fisheries Statistics*. Seoul: 1963–.
———. Ministry of Health and Social Welfare. Office of Labor Affairs. *Yearbook of Labor Statistics*. 1953–.
———. Overseas Information Service. Ministry of Culture and Information. *Facts About Korea*. Seoul: 1960–.
———. *A Handbook of Korea*. Seoul: 1978–.
Korean National Commission for UNESCO. *Review of Educational Statistics in Korea*. Annual. Seoul: 1972–.
Nilsen, Robert. *South Korea Handbook*. Chico, Calif.: Moon Publishing, 1997.
Savada, Andres M., and William Shaw. *South Korea: A Country Study*, Washington, D.C.: Government Printing Office, 1992.

Vreeland, Nena et al. *Area Handbook for South Korea*. Washington, D.C.: Government Printing Office, 1975.
Yonhap News Agency, Korea. *Korea Annual*. Seoul: 1981–.

4. CULTURE

A. General

Covell, Jon C. *Korea's Cultural Roots*. Seoul: Hollym, 1981.
Ch'oe, Yongho, William Theodore de Bary, and Peter H. Lee, editors. *Sources of Korean Tradition*. 2 vols. New York: Columbia University Press, 1997, 2000.
Ha, Tae-hung. *Folk Culture and Family Life*. Seoul: Korean International Society, 1958.
——. *Guide to Korean Culture*. Seoul: Yonsei University Press, 1979.
——. *Korean Culture Series*. 12 vols. Seoul: Yonsei University Press, 1978.
International Cultural Foundation. *Buddhist Culture of Korea*. Korean Culture Series, No. 3. Seoul: 1960.
——. *Folk Culture in Korea*. Korean Culture Series, No. 4. Seoul: 1974.
——. *Thought and Culture in Korea*. Korean Culture Series, No. 10. Seoul: 1979.
——. *Upper-class Culture in Yi-dynasty Korea*. Korean Culture Series, No. 2. Seoul: 1973.
Jeon, Kyu-tae. *Korean Heritage*. Seoul: Jeong Eum Sa, 1975.
Kang, Hugh W., ed. *The Traditional Culture and Society of Korea: Thought and Institutions*. Occasional Paper, No. 5. Center for Korean Studies, University of Hawaii, 1975.
Koo, John H., and Andrew C. Nahm, eds. *Introduction to Korean Culture*. Seoul: Hollym International, 1997.
Korean Overseas Information Service, comp. *Korean Cultural Heritage*. Seoul: Korean Overseas Information Service, 1997.
Lee, Hugh W., ed. *The Traditional Culture and Society of Korea: Art and Literature*. Occasional Paper, No. 4. Center for Korean Studies, University of Hawaii, 1975.
Morse, Ronald A. *Wild Asters: Explorations in Korean Thought, Culture and Society*. Lanham, Md.: University Press of America, 1987.
Pearson, Richard J., ed. *The Traditional Culture and Society of Korea: Prehistory*. Occasional Paper, No. 3. Center for Korean Studies, University of Hawaii, 1975.
Yang, Sunny. *Hanbok: the Art of Korean Clothing*. Seoul: Hollym, 1998.

Yu, Eui-young, and Earl H. Phillips. *Traditional Thoughts and Practices in Korea*. Los Angeles: Center for Korean-American and Korean Studies. California State University, Los Angeles, 1983.

B. Archeology

Barnes, Gina L. *The Rise of Civilization in East Asia: The Archaeology of Chin, Korea and Japan*. London: Thames and Hudson, 1999.
Gardiner, J. H. H. *The Early History of Korea: The Historical Development of the Peninsula up to the Introduction of Buddhism in the Fourth Century A.D.* Honolulu: University of Hawaii Press, 1969.
Ham, Pyong-sam. "Neolithic Culture of Korea," *Korea Journal*, 14:4 (April 1974), 12–17.
Kim, Chewon, and Moo-byong Young. *Studies of Dolmens in Korea*. 6 vols. Seoul: National Museum of Korea, 1967.
Kim, Jeong-hak. *The Prehistory of Korea*. Trans. Richard J. Pearson and Kazue Pearson. Honolulu: University of Hawaii Press, 1979.
Kim, Won-yong. *Art and Archeology of Ancient Korea*. Seoul: Taegwang, 1986.
Pearson, Richard J. "Archeology in Korea," *Antiquity*, 46:183 (1972), 227–30.
Pai, Hyung Il. *Constructing "Korean" Origins: A Critical Review of Archaeology, Historiography and Racial Myth in Korean State: Formation Theories*. Cambrdige, Mass: Harvard University Asia Center, 2000.
Portal, Jane. *Korea: Art and Archaeology*. London: British Museum Press, 2000.
Sohn Pow-key. "Palaeolithic Culture of Korea," *Korea Journal*, 14:4 (April 1974), 4–12.
——. *The Upper Palaeolithic Habitation Soichang-ni, Korea: A Summary Report*. Seoul: Yonsei University Press, 1973.

C. Architecture

Adams, Edward B. *Palaces of Seoul*. Seoul: Taewon, 1972.
Bacon, Wilbur. "Tombs of the Yi Dynasty Kings and Queens," *Transactions of the Korea Branch of the Royal Asiatic Society* 33 (1957), 1–40.
Chapin, Helen B. "A Little Known Temple in South Korea and Its Treasures," *Artibus Asiae*, 11:3 (1948), 189–195.
——. "Kyongju, Ancient Capital of Silla," *Transactions of the Korea Branch of the Royal Asiatic Society* 32 (1951), 55–72.
——. "Palaces in Seoul," *Transactions of the Korean Branch of the Royal Asiatic Society* 32 (1951), 3–50.
Chong, In-kook. "Two Styles of Korean Wooden Architecture," *Korea Journal*, 15:2 (Feb. 1975), 4–15.

Korea Institute of Architecture. *Architectural Guide to Seoul*. Seoul: Bal-Eon, 1995.

Kwang Jang Press. *Korean Architecture Series*. Seoul: 1984.

Lee, Kyu. "Aspects of Korean Architecture," *Apollo*, No. 88 (Aug. 1968), 94–107.

Park, Sam Y. *An Introduction to Korean Architecture: Vol. I. In the Land of Morning Calm: Vol. II. A Cultural Treasure to Cherish.* Seoul: Jungwoo-sa, 1992.

Pratt, Keith. *Old Seoul*. New York: Oxford University Press, 2002.

D. Arts

Adams, Edward B. *Art Treasures of Seoul With Walking Tour*. Seoul: International Tourist Publishing, 1980.

——. *Korean Folk Art and Craft*. Seoul: International Publishing House, 1987.

——. *Korea's Pottery Heritage*. Seoul: International Publishing House, 1986.

Barinka, J. *The Art of Ancient Korea*. Translated from German by Iris Urwin. London: Peter Nevill, 1962.

Covell, Alan Carter. *Folk Art and Magic: Shamanism in Korea*. Seoul: Hollym, 1988.

——. *Shamanistic Folk Paintings: Korean Eternal Spirits*. Seoul: Hollym, 1984.

Eckardt, P. Andreas. *A History of Korean Art*. Translated from German by J. M. Kindersley. London: E. Goldston, 1929.

The Folkist Society. *Folkism*. 2 vols. Seoul: Emille Museum, 1972–73.

Goepper, Roger, and Roderick Whitfield. *Treasures from Korea*. London: British Museum, 1984.

Gompertz, G. St. G. M. *Korean Celadon and Other Wares of the Koryo Period*. London: Faber and Faber, 1963.

——. *Korean Pottery and Porcelain of the Yi Period*. London: Faber and Faber, 1968 and New York: Praeger, 1968.

Hak Dang Publishing. *Cultural Treasures of Korea*. 8 vols. Seoul: Hak Dang Publishing, 1986.

Honey, William B. *Corean Pottery*. London: Faber and Faber, 1947.

Huh, Dong-hwa. *Crafts of the Inner Court: The Artistry of Korean Women*. Seoul: Museum of Korean Embroidery, 1987.

Hyung-mi Publishing, *Korean Folk Painting*. Seoul: Hyung-mi Publishing, 1980.

Janata, Alfred. *Korean Painting*. Translated by M. Shenfield. New York: Crown, 1964.

Kim, Chewon, and G. St. G. M. Gompertz. *The Ceramic Art of Korea*. London: Faber and Faber, 1961.

Kim, Chewon, and Lena Kim Lee. *Arts of Korea*. Tokyo: Kodansha International, 1974.

Kim, Chewon, and Won-Yong Kim. *Treasures of Korean Art: 2000 Years of Ceramics, Sculpture and Jeweled Arts*. New York: Abrams, 1966.

Kim, Won-yong. *The Art and Archaeology of Ancient Korea*. Seoul: Taegwang, 1986.

Kim, Won-yong et al, eds. *The Arts of Korea*. 6 vols. Seoul: Tong Hwa, 1986.

Kim, Yong-joon. *Dan Won: Kim Hong-do*. P'yongyang: Foreign Language Publishing House, 1956.

Korea, Republic of, Ministry of Culture and Information. *The Ancient Arts of Korea*. Seoul: 1975.

———. *Survey of Korean Art*. 2 vols. Seoul: 1972.

———. National Academy of Fine Arts. *Survey of Korean Arts: Fine Arts*. 2 vols. Seoul: 1974.

Korean National Commission for UNESCO. *Modern Korean Painting*. Seoul: 1971.

Kyemyong-sa. *The Folk Crafts of Korea*. Seoul: 1980.

McCune, Evelyn G. *The Arts of Korea: An Illustrated History*. Rutland, Vt.: Tuttle, 1962.

———. *The Inner Art: Korean Screens*. New York: Asian Humanities Press, 1983.

Moes, Robert. *Auspicious Spirits: Korean Folk Painting and Related Objects*. New York: International Exhibitions' Foundation, 1983.

Portal, Jane. *Korea: Art and Archaeology*. London: British Museum Press, 2000.

Si-sa-yong-o-sa. *Traditional Korean Art*. Seoul: Si-sa-yong-o-sa, 1984.

Smith, Judith G., ed. *Arts of Korea*. New York: Metropolitan Museum of Art, 1998.

Soper, Alexander. *Chinese, Korean and Japanese Bronzes*. Series Orientale Roma, No. 35. Rome: ISMEO, 1966.

Swan, Peter. *Art in China, Korea and Japan*. New York: Praeger, 1965.

Togchun Publishing. *Masterpieces of 500 Years of Korean Painting*. Seoul: Togchun Publishing, 1978.

Yi, Sumg-mi. *Korean Costume and Textiles*. Seoul: IBM Korea, 1992.

Yoo, Yushin. *Korea the Beautiful: Treasures of the Hermit Kingdom*. New York: Condall Publishers, 1987.

Zo, Zayong, ed. *The Humor of Korean Tiger*. Seoul: Emille Museum, 1970.

———. *Introduction to Korean Folk Painting*. Seoul: Emille Museum, 1977.

———. *The Flavor of Korean Folk Painting*. Seoul: Emille Museum, 1981.

E. Drama/Theater

Cho, Oh-kon, translator. *Traditional Korean Theatre*. Seoul: Asian Humanities Press, 1988.

Choe, Sang-su. *A Study of a Korean Puppet Play*. Seoul: Korea Book Publishing, 1960.

———. *A Study of a Mask Play of Hahoe*. Seoul: Korea Book Publishing, 1959.

Kardose, John. *An Outline History of Korean Drama*. Greenville, N.Y.: Long Island University Press, 1966.

Korea, Republic of, National Academy of Arts. *Survey of Korea Arts: Folk Arts*. Seoul: National Academy of Arts, 1974.

Korean National Commission for UNESCO, *Traditional Performing Arts of Korea*. Seoul: 1975.

Shin, Chong-ok, "The Reception of British–American Drama and Its Influence on Modern Korean Theater." *Korea Journal*, vol. 28, no. 4 (April 1988), 20–33.

F. Language/Linguistics

Chang, Namgui, and Yong-chol Kim. *Functional Korean: A Communicative Approach*. Seoul: Hollym, 1988.

Chang, Suk-jin. *A Generative Study of Discourse: Pragmatic Aspects of Korea with Reference to English*. Seoul: Language Research Institute, Seoul National University, 1973.

Cho, S. B. *A Phonological Study of Korea*. Acta Universitatis Upsaliensis. Uppsala: Almqvist & Wiksells, 1967.

De Mente, Boyé Lafayette. *NTC's Dictionary of Korea's Key Business and Cultural Code Words*. Chicago: NTC, 1998.

Gale, James S. *Korean Grammatical Forms*. Seoul: Trilingual Press, 1894.

Grant, Bruce K. *A Guide to Korean Characters: Reading and Writing Hangul and Hanja*. Seoul: Hollym, 1988.

Kanazawa, Shosaburo. *The Common Origin of the Japanese and Korean Languages*. Tokyo: 1910.

Kim-Renaud, Young-Key. *The Korean Alphabet: Its History and Structure*. Honolulu: University of Hawaii Press, 1997.

Kim, Soon-ham Park. *A Transformational Analysis of Negation in Korean*. Seoul: Paekhap Publishing, 1967.

Lee, Chung-min. *Abstract Syntax and Korea with Reference to English*. Seoul: Pan Korea, 1974.

Lee, Jeong-ho. *Explanation and Translation of Huminchong'um*. Seoul: Korean Library Science Research Institute, 1973.

Lee, Ki-moon, and Kim Wan-jin. *Language Atlas of Korea*. Seoul: Korean National Academy of Sciences, 1993.

Lee, Sang-baek. *The Origins of the Korean Alphabet Hangul According to New Historical Evidence*. Seoul: National Museum, 1957.

Martin, Samuel E. *Korean Morphophonemics*. Baltimore, Md.: Linguistics Society of America, 1954.

——. *A Reference Grammar of Korean: A Complete Guide to the Grammar and History of the Korean Language.* Tokyo; Rutland, Vt.: Tuttle, 1992.

Park, Byung-soo. *Complement Structure in Korean: A Systematic Study of the Verb "ha."* Seoul: Kwangmun-sa, 1974.

Phil, Marshall R. Jr. *A Study on Non-conclusives in Modern Korean.* Seoul: T'ongmungwan, 1965.

Ramsteedt, G. J. *Studies in Korean Etymology.* Helsinki: Suomalais Ugrilainen Senra, 1949–1953.

Rogers, M. C. *Outline of Korean Grammar.* Berkeley: University of California Press, 1953.

Sohn, Ho-min, ed. "The Korean Language: Its Structure and Social Projection." *Occasional Papers*, no. 6. Honolulu. Center for Korean Studies, University of Hawaii, 1975.

Song, Ki-joong. *Basic Glossary of Korean Studies.* Seoul: Korea Foundation, 1993.

——. *Korean.* London: Routledge, 1994.

Song, Seok Choong. *Explorations in Korean Syntax and Semantics.* Berkeley: Institute of East Asian Studies, University of California, 1988.

Sunoo, Hag-won. *A Korean Grammar.* Prague: Statni pedagoicke nakladateristivi, 1952.

Yang, In-seok. *A Korean Syntax: Case Markers, Delimiters, Complementation, and Relativization.* Seoul: Paekhap-sa, 1972.

G. Literature

Buck, Pearl S. *The Living Reed: A Novel of Korea.* New York: John Day, 1963.

Carpenter, Frances. *Tales of a Korean Grandmother.* Garden City, N.J.: Doubleday, 1947.

Chang, Tok-sun, comp. *The Folk Treasury of Korea: Sources of Myth, Legend and Folktale.* Trans. Tae-wung Kim. Seoul: Society for Korean Oral Literature, 1970.

Griffis, William E. *The Unmannerly Tiger and Other Korean Tales.* New York: Crowell, 1918.

Hong, Myong-hee, trans. *Korean Short Stories.* Seoul: Ilchi-sa, 1975.

International Cultural Foundation. *Humour in Korean Literature.* Korean Culture Series, No. 1, Seoul: 1977.

——. *Korean Folk Tales.* Korean Culture Series, No. 7. Seoul: 1979.

Kim, Chong-un, trans. *Postwar Korean Short Stories.* Seoul: Seoul National University Press, 1974.

——, and Bruce Fulton, eds. and trans. *A Ready-made Life: Early Masters of Modern Korean Fiction.* Honolulu: University of Hawaii Press, 1998.

Kim Hunggyu. *Understanding Korean Literature*, trans. Robert J. Fouser. Armonk, N.Y.: M. E. Sharpe, 1997.

Kim, Jaihiun. *The Immortal Voice: An Anthology of Modern Korean Poetry*. Seoul: Inmun, 1974.

Kim, So-an. *The Story Bag*. Rutland, Vt.: Tuttle, 1957.

Ko, Won, comp. and trans. *Contemporary Korean Poetry*. Iowa City: University of Iowa Press, 1970.

Koh, Chang-woo. *Anthology of Contemporary Korean Poetry*. Seoul: International Publishing House, 1987.

Korean Culture and Arts Foundation, comp. *Who's Who in Korean Literature*. Seoul: Hollym, 1996.

Korean National Commission for UNESCO. *Modern Korean Short Stories: 109 Best Korean Short Stories*. Seoul: Si-sa-yong-o-sa, 1983.

———. *Synopses of Korean Novels. Reader's Guide to Korean Literature*. Seoul: 1972.

Lee, Peter H. *Anthology of Korean Literature From Early Times to the Nineteenth Century*. Honolulu: University of Hawaii Press, 1981.

———. *Anthology of Korean Poetry From the Earliest Era to the Present*. New York: John Day, 1964.

———, ed. *Flowers of Fire. Twentieth Century Korean Stories*. Honolulu: University of Hawaii Press, 1974.

———. *Korean Literature: Topic and Themes*. Tucson: University of Arizona Press, 1965.

———. trans. *A Korean Storyteller's Miscellany: The P'aegwan chapki of O Sukkwon*. Princeton, N.J.: Princeton University Press, 1989.

———. trans. with an Introduction. *Pine River and Lone Peak: An Anthology of Three Choson Dynasty Poets*. Honolulu: University of Hawaii Press, 1991.

———. *Studies in the Saenaenorae: Old Korean Poetry*. Rome: Istituto Italian per il Medio ed Estremo Oriente, 1959.

McCann, David R. *Form and Freedom in Korean Poetry*. Leiden: E.J. Brill, 1988.

Metzger, Berta. *Tales Told in Korea*. New York: Frederick S. Stokes, 1932.

Midang So Chong-ju. *Poems of a Wanderer*, trans. Kevin O'Rourke. Dublin: Dedalus, 1995.

O'Rourke, Kevin. *Ten Korean Short Stories*. Seoul: Yonsei University Press, 1973.

Phil, Marshall R. *Listening to Korea: A Korean Anthology*. New York: Praeger, 1973.

Rutt, Richard. *An Anthology of Korean Sijo*. Taejon: Ch'ongja Sijo Society, 1970.

———. *The Bamboo Grove: An Introduction to Sijo*. Berkeley: University of California Press, 1971.

———, and Chong-un Kim, trans. *Virtuous Women: Three Masterpieces of Traditional Korean Fiction*. Seoul: Korean National Commission for UNESCO, 1974.

Skillend, W. E. *Kodae Sosol: A Survey of Traditional Korean Style Popular Novels*. London: School of Oriental and African Studies, University of London, 1968.

Stout, Mira. *One Thousand Chestnut Trees: A Novel of Korea*. New York: Riverhead Books, 1998.

Sym, Myung-ho. *The Making of Modern Poetry: Foreign Influence and Native Creativity*. Seoul: Seoul National University Press, 1982.

Yi Mun-yol. *The Poet*, trans. Chong-wha Chung and Brother Anthony of Taizé. London: Harvill Press, 1995.

Zong, In-sob. *Folk Tales from Korea*. London: Routledge and Kegan Paul, 1952.

———. *A Guide to Korean Literature*. Seoul: Hollym, 1986.

Yun, Miya. *House of the Winds*. New York: Interlink, 1998.

H. Music/Dance

Chang, Sa-hun. *Glossary of Korean Music*. Seoul: Korean Musicological Society, 1972.

Cho, Won-kyung. *Dances of Korea*. New York: Norman J. Seaman, 1962.

Heyman, Alan. *Dances of the Three Thousand Leagues Land*. Seoul: Myungju University, 1966.

Howard, Keith. *Bands, Songs and Shamanistic Rituals*. Seoul: Royal Asiatic Society, Korea Branch, 1989.

Lee, Hey-ku. *An Introduction to Korean Music and Dance*. Seoul: Royal Asiatic Society, Korea Branch, 1977.

———. *Essays on Korean Traditional Music*, trans. Robert C. Provine, Seoul: Royal Asiatic Society, Korea Branch, 1980.

Pratt, Keith. *Korean Music: Its History and Its Performance*. Seoul: Jeong Eum Sa, 1987.

Si-sa-yong-o-sa. *Traditional Korean Music*. Seoul: Si-sa-yong-o-sa, 1984.

Song, Bang-song. *Source Readings in Korean Music*. Seoul: Korean National Commission for UNESCO, 1980.

I. Philosophy/Religion

Ahn, In-sik. *Ri Yul-kok, His Life and Works*. Seoul: Sungkyungwan University, 1958.

Buswell, Robert E. Jr. *The Formation of Ch'an Ideology in China and Korea: The Vajrasamadhi-Sutra, A Buddhist Apocraphon*. Princeton, N.J.: Princeton University Press, 1989.

———, trans. *The Korean Approach to Zen: The Collected Works of Chinul*. Honolulu: University of Hawaii Press, 1983.

Choi, Min-hong. *A Modern History of Korean Philosophy*. Seoul: Songmunsa, 1980.

Chon, Sin-yong, ed. *Buddhistic Culture in Korea*. Korean Culture Series, No. 3. Seoul: International Cultural Foundation, 1974.

Clark, Allen D. *History of the Korean Church*. Seoul: Christian Literature Society, 1961.

Clark, Charles A. *Religions of Old Korea*. New York: Revell, 1932, and Seoul: Christian Literature Society of Korea, 1961.

Clark, Donald N. *Christianity in Modern Korea*. Lanham, Md.: University Press of America, 1986.

Covell, Alan C. *Folk Art and Magic: Shamanism in Korea*. Seoul: Hollym, 1986.

de Bary, William T., and Jahyun Kim Haboush. *The Rise of Neo-Confucianism in Korea*. New York: Columbia University Press, 1985.

Grayson, J. H. *Early Buddhism and Christianity in Korea: A History in the Emplantation of Religion*. Leiden: E. J. Brill, 1985.

———. *Korea: A Religious History*. Oxford: Clarendon Press, 1989.

———. "The Myth of Tan'gun: A Dramatic Structural Analysis of a Korean Foundation Myth." *Korea Journal*, vol. 37, no.1 (Spring 1997), 35–52.

Howard, Keith, ed. *Korean Shamanism: Revivals, survivals and change*. Seoul: Royal Asiatic Society Korea Branch, 1998.

Huhm, Halla Pai. *Kut: Korean Shamanist Rituals*. Seoul: Hollym, 1980.

Hunt, Everett H. *Protestant Pioneers in Korea*. New York: Orbis Books, 1980.

Janelli, Roger. *Ancestor Worship in Korean Society*. Stanford, Calif.: Stanford University Press, 1982.

Kang, Wi Jo. *Religion and Politics in Korea Under the Japanese Rule*. Lewiston, N.Y.: Edwin Mellen Press, 1988.

Kendall, Laurel. *The Life and Hard Times of a Korean Shaman: Of Tales and the Telling of Tales*. Honolulu: University of Hawaii Press, 1988.

———. *Shamans, Housewives and Other Restless Spirits*. Honolulu: University of Hawaii Press, 1985.

Kendall, Laurel, and Griffin Dix. *Religion and Ritual in Korean Society*. Berkeley: Institute of East Asian Studies, University of California, 1987.

Kim, Hai-jin. *Buddhism and Korean Culture*. New Delhi: The International Academy of Indian Culture, 1958.

Kim, Yong-choon. *The Ch'ondogyo Concepts of Man: An Essence of Korean Thought*. Seoul: Pan Korea, 1978.

Kusan Sunim. *The Way of Korean Zen*. New York: John Weatherhill, 1985.

Lankaster, Lewis R., Kikun Suh, and Chai-shin Yu, eds. *Buddhism in Koryo: A Royal Religion*. Berkeley, Calif.: Institute of East Asian Studies University of California, 1996.

———, and Chai-shin Yu, eds. *Buddhism in the Early Choson: Suppression and Transformation*. Berkeley, Calif.: Institute of East Asian Studies University of California, 1996.

———, and Richard K. Payne, eds. *Religion and society in contemporary Korea*. Berkeley, Calif.: Institute of East Asian Studies University of California, 1997.

Lee, Jung Young, ed. *Ancestor Worship and Christianity in Korea*. Lewiston, N.Y.: Edwin Mellen Press, 1988.

Paik, L. George. *The History of Protestant Mission in Korea (1832–1910)*. P'yongyang: Union Christian College Press, 1929. Reprinted Seoul: Yonsei University Press, 1971.

Palmer, Spencer J. *Confucian Rituals in Korea*. New York: Asian Humanities Press, 1984.

———. *Korea and Christianity: The Problems of Identification with Tradition*. Seoul: Hollym, n.d.

Phillips, Earl H., and Eui-young Yu, ed. *Religions in Korea: Beliefs and Cultural Values*. Los Angeles: Center for Korean–American and Korean Studies, California State University, Los Angeles, 1982.

Ruiz de Medina, Juan. *The Catholic Church in Korea: Its Origins*, trans. John Bridges. Seoul: Royal Asiatic Society, Korea Branch, 1991.

Setton, Mark. *Chang Yagyong: Korea's Challenge to Orthodox Neo-Confucianism*. Albany, N.Y.: State University of New York Press, 1997.

Starr, Frederick. *Korean Buddhism*. Boston, Mass.: Marshall Jones, 1918.

Tian, Valeri. "Form and Philosophy in Korean Buddhist Temple Landscape and Architecture." *Transactions of the Royal Asiatic Society Korea Branch* 71 (1996), 55–95.

Weems, Benjamin. *Reform, Rebellion and the Heavenly Way*. Tucson: University Press of Arizona, 1964.

Wells, Kenneth M. *New God, New Nation: Protestants and Self-Reconstruction Nationalism in Korea 1896–1937*. Sydney: Allen & Unwin, 1990.

Yang, Key P., and Gregory Henderson. "An Outline History of Korean Confucianism," *Journal of Asian Studies*, 17:11 (1958), 81–101 and 18:2 (1959), 259–276.

Ye, Yun Ho. *A New Cult in Postwar Korea*. Princeton: Princeton Theological Seminary, 1959.

Yu, Chai-shin, and R. Guisso, eds. *Shamanism: The Spirit World of Korea*. New York: Asian Humanities Press, 1988.

J. Press

Chang, Won Ho. "*Yonhap* News Agency: Gatekeeper of International News in Korea," *Korean Studies* 9 (1985), 14–37.

Choi, Won-Young. "Freedom of the Press and Its Impact on the Second Republic of Korea." Ph.D. thesis, University of Newcastle, 1997.

Chong, Chin-sok. "The South Korean Press," in *Korea Briefing 1992*, ed. Donald C. Clark. Boulder, Colo.: Westview Press in conjunction with the Asia Society, 1992, 117–39.

Halvorsen, David E. *Confucianism Defies the Computer: The Conflict within the Korean Press.* Honolulu: East–West Center, 1992.

Kang, Hyeon-dew. *Media Culture in Korea.* Seoul: Seoul National University Press, 1991.

Kim, Bong-gi. *Brief History of the Korean Press.* Seoul: Korean Information Service, 1963.

Kotch, John Barry. "The Chosun Ilbo vs. JoongAng Ilbo: Historiographical Warfare in the Post-Cold War South Korean Press," *Korea Journal*, vol. 30, no. 3 (Fall, 1999), 443–66.

Oh, In-Hwan, and George Won. "Journalism in Korea: A Short History of the Korean Press." *Transactions of the Korea Branch of the Royal Asiatic Society* 51 (1976), 1–55.

Wade, James, ed. "Mass Communications in a Developing Korea." *Transactions of the Korea Branch of the Royal Asiatic Society* 45 (1969), 1–129.

Youm, Kyu-ho. *Press Law in South Korea.* Ames, Iowa: Iowa State University Press, 1996.

5. ECONOMY

A. General

Cho, Lee-jay, and Yoon Hyung Kim, eds. *Economic Development in the Republic of Korea.* Honolulu: East West Center, 1991.

Choi, Ho-chin. *The Economic History of Korea: From the Earliest Times to 1945.* Seoul: Freedom Library, 1971.

Chung, Kae H., and Hak Chong Lee, eds. *Korean Managerial Dynamics.* Westport, Conn.: Praeger, 1989.

Eckert, Carter Jr. *Offspring of Empire: The Koch'ang Kims and the Colonial Origins of Korean Capitalism, 1867–1945.* Seattle, Washington: University of Washington Press, 1991.

Gills, Barry K., and Dong-sook S. Gills. "South Korea and Globalization: The Rise to Globalization." *Asian Perspectives* (Seoul), vol. 23, no. 4, 199–228.

Hansan, Paryez. *Korea: Problems and Issues in a Rapidly Growing Economy.* Baltimore, Md.: Johns Hopkins University Press, 1976.

International Cultural Foundation. *Economic Life in Korea.* Korean Culture Series, No. 8. Seoul: 1978.

Keon, Michael. *Korean Phoenix: A Nation from the Ashes*. Englewood Cliffs, N.J.: Michael Keon, 1977.

Kim, Choong Soon. *A Korean Nationalist Entrepreneur: A Life History of Kim Songsu, 1891–1955*. Albany: State University of New York, 1998.

Kim, Samuel S., ed. *Korea's Globalization*. New York: Cambridge University Press, 2000.

Kirk, Donald. *Korean Crisis: Unraveling of the Miracle in the IMF Era*. New York: St. Martin's Press, 2000.

Korea Development Institute. *Korea's Economy: Past and Present*. Seoul: KDI, 1975.

Kwon, Jene J., ed. *Korean Economic Development*. New York: Greenwood Press, 1990.

Lee, Yeon-ho. *The State, Society and Big Business in South Korea*. London: Routledge, 1997.

Lee, You-il. *The Political Economy of Korean Crisis: A Turning Point or the End of the Miracle*. Aldershot, England: Ashgate, 2000.

Lie, John. *Han Unbound: The Political Economy of South Korea*. Stanford, Calif.: Stanford University Press, 1998.

Lindauer, David L., Jong-Gie Kim, Joung-Woo Lee, Hy-sop Lim, Jae-Young Son, and Ezra Vogel. *The Strains of Economic Growth: Labor Unrest and Social Dissatisfaction in Korea*. Cambridge, Mass.: Harvard University Press for the Harvard Institute for International Development, 1997.

Kearney, Robert P. *The Warrior Worker: The History and Challenge of South Korea's Economic Miracle*. New York. Henry Holt, 1991.

Sorensen, Clark. *Over the Mountains Are Mountains*. Seattle: University of Washington Press, 1983.

Steers, Richard. *Made in Korea: Chung Ju Yung and the Rise of Hyundai*. London: Routledge, 1999.

Suh, Sang-chul. *Growth and Structural Changes in the Korean Economy, 1910–1940*. Cambridge, Mass.: Council on East Asian Studies, Harvard University, 1978.

Various. "The First Look at the Korean Economic Crisis." *Korea Journal*, vol. 38, no. 2 (Summer 1998), 5–65.

Woronoff, Jon. *Asia's "Miracle" Economies*. Armonk, N.Y.: M. E. Sharpe, 1986.

———. *Korea's Economy: Man-made Miracle*. Seoul: Si-sa-yongo-sa, 1983.

B. Agriculture

Chang, Oh-hyun. *Land Reform in Korea: A Historical Review*. Madison: University of Wisconsin Press, 1973.

Korea Land Economics Research Center. *A Study of Land Tenure System of Korea*. Seoul: 1966.

Korea University College of Agriculture. *A Study of the Regional Characteristics of Korean Agriculture*. Seoul: 1967.

Lee, Hoon Koo. *Land Utilization and Rural Economy in Korea*. Chicago: University of Chicago Press, 1936.

Pitts, Forrest R. *Mechanization of Agriculture in the Republic of Korea*. n.p., 1960.

Ramchandran, Vijaya. "Does Agriculture Really Matter? The Case of Korea 1910–1970," *Journal of Asian Economies*, vol. 6, no. 3 (Fall 1995), 367–84.

———, and Kenneth Kang. "Economic Transformation in Korea: Rapid Growth without an Agricultural Revolution?" *Economic Development and Cultural Change*, vol. 47. no. 4 (July 1999), 783–801.

United Nations Food and Agricultural Organization. *Agricultural Survey and Demonstration in Selected Watersheds: Republic of Korea*. New York: 1969.

———. *Rehabilitation and Development of Agriculture, Forestry and Fisheries in South Korea*. New York: Columbia University Press, 1954.

Wade, Robert. *Irrigation and Agricultural Politics in South Korea*. Boulder, Colo.: Westview Press, 1982.

C. Development

Adelman, Irma, ed. *Practical Approaches to Development Planning in Korea: Second Five-Year Plan*. Baltimore, Md.: Johns Hopkins University Press, 1969.

Brown, Gilbert T. *Korean Price Policies and Economic Development in the 1960s*. Baltimore, Md.: Johns Hopkins University Press, 1973.

Burmeister, Larry L. *Research, Realpolitik and Development in Korea: The State of the Green Revolution*. Boulder, Colo.: Westview Press, 1988.

Cho, Lee-jay, and Yoon Hyung Kim, eds. *Economic Development in the Republic of Korea: A Policy Perspective*. Boulder, Colo.: Westview Press, 1990.

Chung, Joseph S. H., ed. *Patterns of Economic Development: Korea*. Kalamazoo, Mich.: Korea Research and Publications, 1966.

Cole, Davis C., and Princeton N. Lyman. *Korean Development: The Interplay of Politics and Economics*. Cambridge, Mass.: Harvard University Press, 1971.

East Asia Analytical Unit Department of Foreign Affairs and Trade. *Korea Rebuilds: From Crisis to Opportunity*. Canberra ACT: Commonwealth of Australia, 1999.

Huer, Jon. *Marching Orders. The Role of the Military in South Korea's Economic Miracle, 1961–1971*. Westport, Conn.: Greenwood Press, 1989.

Kim, Kyong-dong, ed. *Dependency Issues in Korean Development*. Korean Studies Series of the Institute of Social Science, Seoul National University, No. 11. Seoul: 1987.

Kim, Seung-hee. "Economic Development of South Korea." In *Government and Politics of Korea*, Se-jin Kim and Chang-gyun Cho, ed. Silver Spring, Md.: Research Institute on Korean Affairs, 1972.

Korea, Republic of, Economic Planning Board. *The Korean Economy: Present and Future*. Seoul: 1973.

———. *Major Economic Indicators of the Korean Economy, 1953–61*. Seoul: 1977.

———. *Major Indicators of the Korean Economy, 1962–73*. Seoul: 1973.

———. *Major Indicators of the Korean Economy, 1974–79*. Seoul: 1979.

———. *A Summary of the First Five-Year Economic Plan, 1962–66*. Seoul: 1962.

———. *A Summary of the Second Five-Year Economic Plan, 1967–71*. Seoul: 1966.

———. *A Summary of the Third Five-Year Economic Plan, 1972–76*. Seoul: 1971.

———. *A Summary of the Fourth Five-Year Economic and Social Development Plan, 1977–81*. Seoul: 1981.

Kuznets, Paul W. *Economic Growth and Structure in the Republic of Korea*. New Haven, Conn.: Yale University Press, 1977.

Lewis, J. P. *Reconstruction and Development in South Korea*. Washington, D.C.: National Planning Association, 1955.

Mason, Edward et al. *The Economic and Social Modernization of the Republic of Korea: Studies in the Modernization of the Republic of Korea, 1945–1975*. Cambridge, Mass.: Harvard University Press, 1980.

Steinberg, David I. *The Republic of Korea: Economic Transformation and Social Change*. Boulder, Colo.: Westview Press, 1988.

Wang, In-keun. *Rural Development Studies*. Cambridge, Mass: Harvard University Press, 1986.

Whang, In-jong. *Management of Rural Change in Korea. The Saemaul Undong*. Seoul: Seoul National University Press, 1981.

D. Finance

Ahn, Seung Chul. "A Monetary Analysis of the Korean Economy, 1953–1966, on the Basis of Demand and Supply Functions of Money." Ph.D. Dissertation, University of California, Berkeley, 1968.

Gurley, John G. et al. *The Financial Structure of Korea*. Seoul: Bank of Korea, 1965.

Kim, Jung-sae. "The Evaluation of the Financial Structure for Industrialization." ILCORK *Working Paper*, 13. Seoul: 1971.

Kim, Seung-hee. *Foreign Capital for Economic Development. A Korean Case*. New York: Praeger, 1970.

Kim, Young-chin, and Jane K. Kwon. *Capital Utilization in Korean Manufacturing, 1962–1971. Its Level, Trend and Structure*. Seoul: Korean Industrial Development Research Institute, 1973.

Korea, Republic of, Ministry of Finance. *An Introduction to Korean Taxation*. Seoul: 1968.

——. *Outline of Banking System and Policy of Korea*. Seoul: 1966.

Kwak, Yoon Chick et al. *Credit and Security in Korea: The Legal Problems of Development Finance*. Manila: Asian Development Bank, 1973.

Lee, Seung Yun, and Byong Kuk Kim. *Determinants of Money Supply and the Scope of Monetary Policy, 1954–64*. Seoul: Research Institute for Economic and Business, Sogang University, 1968.

Lyong, Gene. *Military Policy and Economic Aid: The Korean Case*. Columbus: Ohio State University Press, 1961.

Park, Chin Keun. "The Role of the Exchange Rate in a Developing Economy: A Case Study of Korea," Ph.D. Dissertation, University of California, Los Angeles, 1972.

U.S. Comptroller General of the United States. *U.S. Assistance for the Economic Development of the Republic of Korea*. Series B 164264. Washington, D.C.: General Accounting Office, 1973.

E. Trade

Amsden, Alice H. "Trade Policy and Performance in South Korea." In *Trade and Growth: New Dilemmas in Trade Policy*, Agosin, Manuel R. and Diana Tussie, ed. New York: St. Martin's Press, 1993.

Hong, Wontack. *Trade and Growth: A Korean Perspective*. Seoul: Kudara International, 1994.

Lee, Dae Sung. "International Trade and the Economic Development of the Korean Economy." Ph.D. Dissertation, University of Massachusetts, 1970.

Lee, Hy Sang. "International Trade of South Korea." In *Foreign Policies of Korea*, Young C. Kim, ed. Washington, D.C.: Institute for Asian Studies, George Washington University, 1973.

Luedde-Neurath, Richard. *Import Controls and Export-Oriented Development. A Reassessment of the South Korean Case*. Boulder, Colo.: Westview Press, 1986.

Most, Amicus. *Expanding Exporters: A Case Study of the Korean Experience*. Washington, D.C.: U.S. Agency for International Development, 1969.

Park, Seong Ho. "Export Expansion and Import Substitution in the Economic Development of Korea, 1955–1965." Ph.D. Dissertation, American University, 1969.

Rubens, Edwin P. "Commodity Trade, Export Taxes and Economic Development: The Korean Experience," *Political Science Quarterly* 7 (March 1965), 55–62.

Sanford, Dan C. *South Korea and the Socialist Countries: The Role of Trade.* New York: St. Martin's Press, 1990.

Voivodas, Constantin. "Exports, Foreign Capital Inflow, and South Korean Economic Growth," *Economic Development and Cultural Change* (April 1974), 480–84.

F. Industry

Amsden, Alice H. *Asia's Next Giant: South Korea and Late Industrialization.* New York: Oxford University Press, 1989.

Byun, Hyung-yoon. "Industrial Structure in Korea with Reference to Secondary Industry," *Seoul National University Economic Review*, No.1 (December 1967), 31–69.

Hamilton, Clive. *Capitalist Industrialization in Korea.* Boulder, Colo.: Westview Press, 1986.

Janelli, Roger L., with Dawnhee Kim. *Making Capitalism: The Social and Cultural Construction of a South Korean Conglomerate.* Stanford, Calif.: Stanford University Press, 1993.

Jonsson, Gabriel. *Shipbuilding in South Korea: A Comparative Study.* Stockholm: Stockholm University Institute of Oriental Languages, 1995.

Kim, Choong Soon. *The Culture of Korean Industry: An Ethnography of Poongsan Corporation.* Tucson: University of Arizona Press, 1992.

Kirk, Donald. *Korean Dynasty: Hyundai and Chung Ju Yung.* Armonk, N.J.: M. E. Sharpe, 1994.

Korea, Republic of, Heavy and Chemical Industry Promotion Council. *Heavy and Chemical Industry Development Plan.* Seoul: 1973.

———. *Heavy and Chemical Industry Development Policy of Korea.* Seoul: 1973.

Korea Development Bank. *Industry in Korea.* Seoul: 1976.

Kuznets, Paul W. "Korea's Emerging Industrial Structure." ILCORK *Working Paper*, No. 6, Seoul: 1971.

Lim, Youngil. Gains and Costs of Postwar Industrialization in South Korea. Occasional Paper, No. 2. Center for Korean Studies University of Hawaii, 1973.

McNamara, Dennis L. "State and Concentration in Korea's First Republic." *Modern Asian Studies*, vol. 26, no. 4 (1992), 701–18.

Medium Industry Bank of Korea. *An Introduction to Small Industries in Korea.* Seoul: 1966.

Ogle, George Ewing, with introduction by Ray Marshall and Bruce Cumings. *South Korea: Dissent within the Economic Miracle.* London: Zed Books, in association with International Labor Rights Education and Research Fund, Washington, D.C., 1990.

Rhee, Jong-chan. *The State and Industry in South Korea: The Limits of the Authoritarian State*. London: Routledge, 1994.

Steers, Richard M. *Made in Korea: Chung Ju Yung and the Rise of Hyundai*. London: Routledge, 1999.

U.S. Department of the Interior, Bureau of Mines. *The Mineral Industry of the Republic of Korea*. Washington, D.C.: Government Printing Office, 1974.

G. Labor

Cho, Yong Sam. *Disguised Unemployment in Underdeveloped Areas with Special Reference to South Korean Agriculture*. Berkeley: University of California Press, 1963.

Choe, Ehn-hyun. *Population Distribution and Internal Migration in Korea*. 1960 Census Monograph Series. Seoul: Bureau of Statistics, Economic Planning Board, Republic of Korea, 1966.

Cho, Hyoung, and Chang Pil-wha, eds. *Gender Division of Labor in Korea*. Seoul: Korean Women's Institute Series, Ewha Women's University Press, 1994.

Kim, Kyong-dong. "Industrialization and Industrialism: A Comparative Perspective in Values of Korean Workers and Managers." ILCORK *Working Paper*.

Kim, Seung-kyung. *Class Struggle or Family Struggle? The Lives of Women Factory Workers in South Korea*. Cambridge, England: Cambridge University Press, 1997.

Koo, Hagen. "The Dilemmas of Empowered Labor in Korea: Korean Workers in the Face of Global Capitalism." *Asian Survey*, vol. 40, no. 2 (March/April 2000), 227–50.

McVoy, Edgar C. *Manpower Development and Utilization in Korea*. Washington, D.C.: U.S. Department of Labor, 1965.

U.S. Department of Labor. *Labor Law and Practices in the Republic of Korea*. BLS Series No. 361. Washington, D.C.: Government Printing Office, 1969.

Watanabe, Susumu. "Exports and Employment: The Case of the Republic of Korea," *International Labor Review* (Geneva), 106:6 (December 1972), 445–526.

H. Transportation/Communications

Hahn, Dae-ho. *Communications Policies in the Republic of Korea*. Paris: UNESCO, 1978.

Owen, Wilfred. *Transportation Factors in Korea's Long-range Development*. Seoul: Korean Development Institute, 1977.

Korea, Republic of, Ministry of Communications. *The Direction of Korean Telecommunications Policy*. Seoul: 1989.

Wade, James. *Mass Communications in Developing Korea*. Seoul: Royal Asiatic Society, Korea Branch, 1969.

6. HISTORY

A. Autobiography/Biography

Allen, Richard C. *Korea's Syngman Rhee: An Unauthorized Portrait*. Rutland, Vt.: Tuttle, 1960.

Chong, Key Ray. "Ch'oe Che-u's Tonghak Doctrine: Its Sources and Meanings," *Journal of Korean Studies*, 1:2 (1971), 71–84.

Clark, Donald N. "Yun Ch'i-ho (1864–1945): Portrait of a Korean Intellectual in an Era of Transition." *Occasional Papers on Korea*, No. 4 (Sept. 1975), 36–76. Seattle: Society for Korean Studies.

Cook, Harold, "Pak Yong-hyo: Background and Early Years," *Journal of Social Science and Humanities*, The Korean Research Center, No. 31 (Dec. 1965), 1–24.

Finch, Michael. *Min Yong-hwan: A Political Biography*. Honolulu: University of Hawaii Press, 2002.

Hyegyong, Lady. *The Memoirs of Lady Hyegyong: The Autobiographical Writings of a Crown Princess of Eighteenth-century Korea*. Translated with an introduction and notes by JaHyun Kim Haboush. Berkeley: University of California Press, 1996.

Jaisohn, Muriel. "Philip Jaisohn, B.S., M.D. (1869–1951)," *Medical Annals of the District of Columbia*, 21 (1952), 250–353.

Jho, Sung-do. *Yi Sun-shin: A National Hero of Korea*. Chinhae: Choongmukong Society, 1970.

Kang, Young-hill. *The Grass Roof*. New York: Scribner's, 1931.

Kim, Agnes Davis. *I Married a Korean, with Sketches of the Author*. New York: John Day, 1953; reprinted, with an extra chapter, Seoul: Royal Asiatic Society Korea Branch, 1979.

Kim, Richard G. *Lost Names: Scenes from a Korean Boyhood*. New York: Praeger, 1970.

Kim, Yong-dok. "A Life and Thought of Pak Che-ga," *Korea Journal,* 12:7 (July 1972), 40–43.

King Seijong Memorial Society. *King Seijong the Great: A Biography of Korea's Most Famous King*. Seoul: King Seijong Memorial Society, 1970.

Ko, Byung-ik. "Chung Yak-yong's Version of Progress as Expressed in His Kiye-ron (Essays on Art and Technique)," *Journal of Social Science and Humanities*, 23 (1965), 29–36.

Lee, Peter H., Trans. *Lives of Eminent Korean Monks: The "Haedong kosung chon."* Harvard-Yenching Institute Studies, No. 25. Cambridge, Mass.: Harvard University Press, 1969.

Li, Mirok. *The Yalu Flows: A Korean Childhood.* Trans. H.A. Hammelmann. East Lansing: Michigan State University, 1956.

New, Ilhan. *When I Was a Boy in Korea.* Boston: Lothrop, Lee and Shepard, 1928.

Oliver, Robert T. *Syngman Rhee: The Man Behind the Myth.* New York: Dodd Mead, 1954.

Pahk, Induk. *September Monkey.* New York: Harper, 1954.

Pak, No-ch'un. "Pak Chi-won, Satirist of the Aristocratic Society," *Korea Journal,* 13:3 (March 1973), 48–53.

Song, Chu-yong. "Yu Hyung-won," *Korea Journal,* 13:7 (July 1, 1972), 33–39.

Yi, Pangja. *The World is One: Princess Yi Pangja's Autobiography.* Seoul: Taewan, 1973.

Yi Sun-sin. *"Imjin changch'o": Admiral Yi Sun-sin's Memorials to Court.* Translated by Ha Tae-hung and Lee Chang-young. Seoul: Yonsei University Press, 1981.

———. *"Nanjung ilgi": War Diary of Admiral Yi Sun-sin.* Translated by Ha Tae-hung, edited by Sohn Pow-key. Seoul: Yonsei University Press, 1977.

Yim, Louise. *My Forty Years Fight for Korea.* Seoul: International Cultural Research Center, Chungang University, 1951.

B. General

Allen, Horace, N. *Korea, Fact and Fancy.* Seoul: Methodist Publishing House, 1904.

———. *Things Korean: A Collection of Sketches and Anecdotes, Missionary and Diplomatic.* New York: Revell, 1908.

Center for East Asian Cultural Studies, comp. and revised. *A Short History of Korea.* Tokyo, 1963. (Originally published as *Korean History Handbook* by the Government-General of Korea in 1937).

Choy, Bong-youn. *Korea. A History.* Rutland, Vt.: Tuttle, 1971.

Chung, Kyung Cho. *New Korea: New Land of the Morning Calm.* New York: Macmillan, 1962.

Cumings, Bruce. *Korea's Place in the Sun: A Modern History.* London and New York: W. W. Norton, 1997.

Eckert, Carter J. et al. *Korea Old and New: A History.* Seoul: Ilchokak for Harvard University Press, 1990.

Gale, James S. *The History of the Korean People.* Seoul: Christian Literature Society, 1927.

Grayson, James Huntley. *Korea: A Religious History.* Oxford: Clarendon Press, 1989.

Ha, Tae Hung. *Korea: Forty Three Centuries*. Korean Cultural Series, 1. Seoul: Yonsei University Press, 1962.

Han, Woo-keun. *The History of Korea*. Trans. and ed. by Kyun-shik Lee and Grafton K. Mintz. Seoul: Eul-yoo Publishing Company, 1969.

Hatada, Takashi. *A History of Korea*. Trans. Warren S. Smith, Jr. and Benjamin H. Hazard. Santa Barbara, Calif.: CLIO, 1969.

Henderson, George. "Chong Ta-san: A Study of Korea's Intellectual History," *Journal of Asian Studies* 16 (May 1957), 377–86.

Henthorn, William E. *A History of Korea*. New York: Free Press, 1971.

History Research Institute. Academy of Social Science, Democratic People's Republic of Korea, comp. *The Outline of Korean History*. P'yongyang: Foreign Languages Publishing House, 1977.

Hoare, J. E., and Susan Pares. *Korea: An Introduction*. London: KPI, 1988.

Hong, Sung-gi. "Trends in Western Historiography on Korea," *Korea Journal*, vol. 39, no. 3 (Autumn 1999), 338–77.

Hulbert, Homer B. *The History of Korea*. Seoul: Methodist Publishing House, 1905. New edition, edited by Clarence Norwood Weems, New York: Hillary House Publications, 2 vols., 1962.

——. *The Passing of Korea*. New York: Doubleday, 1916.

Ilyon. "*Samguk yusa*": *Legends and History of the Three Kingdoms of Ancient Korea*. Trans. Tae Hung Ha and Grafton K. Mintz. Seoul: Yonsei University Press, 1972.

Ireland, Alleyne. *The New Korea*. New York: E. P. Dutton, 1929.

Joe, Wanne J. *Traditional Korea: A Cultural History*. Seoul: Chungang University Press, 1972.

Kleiner, Juergen. *Korea: A Century of Change*. River Edge, New Jersey: World Scientific, 2001.

Korea, Republic of, Korean Overseas Information Service. *Korea: Its History and Culture*. Seoul, 1994.

——, Korean Overseas Information Service. *Korean Cultural Heritage*. Seoul, 1997.

——, Office of Public Information. *Korea: Her History and Culture*. Seoul: 1954.

Lee, Ki-baek. *A New History of Korea*. Trans. and expanded by Edward W. Wagner and Edward J. Schultz. Cambridge, Mass.: Harvard University Press, 1984.

Longford, Joseph, H. *The Story of Korea*. New York: C. Scribner's, 1911.

Lowell, Percival. *Choson: The Land of the Morning Calm: A Sketch of Korea*. Boston: Ticknor, 1888.

MacDonald, Donald S. *The Koreans: Contemporary Politics and Society.* Boulder, Colo.: Westview, 1988. Third edition, edited and revised by Donald N. Clark, 1996.

Nahm, Andrew C. *A Panorama of 5000 Years: Korean History*. Seoul: Hollym, 1983.

——. *Korea: Tradition and Transformation: A History of the Korean People*. Seoul and Elizabeth, N.J.: Hollym International, 1987.

Ross, John. *History of Corea, Ancient and Modern: With Description of Manners, Customs, Language and Geography*. London: Elliot Stock, 1891.

Rutt, Richard. *James Scrath Gale and His History of the Korean People*. Seoul: Royal Asiatic Society, Korea Branch, 1972.

Sohn, Pow-key et al. *The History of Korea*. Seoul: Korean National Commission for UNESCO, 1970.

Tennant, Roger. *A History of Korea*. London: Kegan Paul International, 1996.

Wagner, Ellasue. *Korea: The Old and the New*. New York: Revell, 1931.

Weems, Clarence Norwood, ed. *Hulbert's History of Korea*. New York: Hillary House, 2 vols. 1962.

C. Ancient/Pre-Modern

Choe, Chin-young. *The Rule of the Taewon'gun, 1864–1873: Reconstruction in Yi Korea*. Cambridge, Mass.: East Asian Research Center, Harvard University, 1972.

Choi, Woon Sang. *The Fall of the Hermit Kingdom*. Dobbs Ferry, New York: Oceana Publications, 1963.

Conroy, Hillary. *The Japanese Seizure of Korea, 1868–1910: A Study of Realism and Idealism in International Relations*. Philadelphia, Pa.: University of Pennsylvania Press, 1960.

Cook, Harold F. *Korea's 1884 Incident: Its Background and Kim Ok-kyun's Elusive Dream*. Seoul: Royal Asiatic Society, Korea Branch, 1972.

Deuchler, Martina. *The Confucian Transformation of Korea: A Study of Society and Ideology*. Cambridge, Mass.: Council of East Asian Studies, Harvard University, 1992.

Duus, Peter. *The Abacus and the Sword: The Japanese Penetration of Korea, 1895–1910*. Berkeley, Calif.: University of California Press, 1995.

Gale, James S. *Korea in Transition*. New York: Eaton and Maines, 1909.

Gardiner, K. J. H. *The Early History of Korea. The Historical Development of the Peninsula Up to the Introduction of Buddhism in the Fourth Century A.D.* Honolulu: University of Hawaii Press, 1969.

Haboush, JaHyun Kim. *A Heritage of Kings: One Man's Monarchy in the Confucian World*. New York: College University Press, 1988.

——, and Martin Deuchler, eds. *Culture and State in Late Chosôn Korea*. Cambridge Mass.: Harvard University Asia Center, 1999.

Hamel, Hendrik. *Hamel's Journal and a Description of the Kingdom of Korea, 1653–66*. Translated from the Dutch manuscript by Jean-Paul Buys. Seoul: Royal Asiatic Society, 1994.

Henthorn, William F. *Korea: The Mongol Invasions*. Leiden: Brill, 1963.

Jo, Yung-hwan, ed. *Korea's Response to the West*. Kalamazoo, Mich.: Korea Research and Publications, 1971.

Kim, C. I. Eugene, and Han-kyo Kim. *Korea and the Politics of Imperialism, 1876–1910*. Berkeley, Calif.: University of California Press, 1967.

Ledyard, Gari. *The Dutch Come to Korea: An Account of the Life of the First Westerners in Korea (1653–1666)*. Seoul: Royal Asiatic Society, Korea Branch, 1971.

Lee, Chang-soo. *Modernization of Korea and the Impact of the West*. Los Angeles: East Asian Studies Center, University of Southern California, 1981.

McCune, Shannon. *Korea: The Land of Broken Calm*. New York: Van Nostrand, 1961.

McGrane, George A. *Korea's Tragic Hours: The Closing Years of the Yi Dynasty*. Ed. Harold F. Cook and Alan M. MacDougall. Seoul: Taewon, 1973.

McKenzie, Frederick A. *The Tragedy of Korea*. London: Hodder and Stoughton, 1908. Reprinted Seoul: Yonsei University Press, 1969.

Oh, Se Eung. *Dr. Philip Jaisohn's Reform Movement, 1896–1898: A Critical Appraisal of the Independence Club*. Lanham, Md.: University Press of America, 1995.

Oppert, Ernest. *A Forbidden Land: Voyages to the Corea*. London: Sampson, Low, Marston, Searle and Revington, 1880.

Palais, James B. *Politics and Policy in Traditional Korea*. Harvard East Asian Series, No. 82. Cambridge, Mass.: Harvard University Press, 1974.

Pearson, Richard J. "The Traditional Culture and Society of Korea: Prehistory." *Occasional Paper* No. 3. Honolulu: Center for Korean Studies, University of Hawaii, 1975.

Wagner, Edward W. *The Literati Purges: Political Conflict in Early Yi Korea*. Cambridge, Mass.: East Asian Research Center, Harvard University, 1974.

Weems, Benjamin B. *Reform, Rebellion, and the Heavenly Way*. Tucson: University of Arizona Press, 1964.

Wilkinson, W. H. *The Corean Government: Constitutional Change, July 1894–October 1895, with an Appendix on Subsequent Enactment to June 3rd 1896*. Shanghai: Statistical Department of Inspectorate General of Customs, 1897.

Yi, Kyu-tae. *Modern Transformation of Korea*. Trans. Sung Tongmahn et al. Seoul: Sejong, 1970.

D. Colonial Period

Bennett, Terry. *Korea: Caught in Time*. Reading, England: Garnett, 1997.

Bishop, Isabella L. B. *Korea and Her Neighbors: A Narrative of Travel with an Account of the Recent Vicissitudes and Present Condition.* 2 vols. London: John Murray, 1897. Single-volume edition, London: KPI, 1985.

Chung, Henry. *The Case of Korea: A Collection of Evidence on the Japanese Domination of Korea, and On the Development of the Korean Independence Movement.* New York: Revell, 1921.

Clark, Donald N. *Living Dangerously in Korea: The Western Experience, 1900–1950.* Norwalk, Conn.: EastBridge, 2003.

Curzon, George N. *Problems of the Far East: Japan–Korea–China.* London: Longmans, Green, 1894.

Dennet, Tyler. *Americans in East Asia: A Critical Study of the Policy of the United States with Reference to China, Japan and Korea in the Nineteenth Century.* New York: Macmillan, 1922.

Denny, Owen N. *China and Korea.* Shanghai: Kelly and Walsh, 1888.

Deuchler, Martina. *Confucian Gentlemen and Barbarian Envoys: The Opening of Korea, 1875–1885.* Seattle: University of Washington Press, 1983.

Eckert, Carter J. *Offspring of Empire: The Koch'ang Kims and the Colonial Origins of Korean Capitalism.* Seattle: University of Seattle Press, 1991.

Drake, H. B. *Korea of the Japanese.* London: John Lane/ Bodley Head, 1930.

Frazer, Everett. *Korea and Her Relations with China, Japan and the United States.* Orange, N.J.: Chronicle Books, 1884.

Grageert, Edwin H. *Landownership under Colonial Rule: Korea's Japan Experience, 1900–35.* Honolulu: University of Hawaii Press, 1994.

Grajdanzev, Andrew J. *Korea Looks Ahead.* IPR Pamphlet 15. New York: American Council, Institute of Pacific Relations, 1944.

———. *Modern Korea.* New York: Institute of Pacific Relations, 1944; reprinted Seoul: Kyung-in Publishing Company for the Royal Asiatic Society, Korea Branch, 1975.

Harrington, Fred H. *God, Mammon and the Japanese: Dr. Horace N. Allen and Korean–American Relations, 1884–1905.* Madison: University of Wisconsin Press, 1944.

Hicks, George. *The Comfort Women: Sex Slaves of the Japanese Imperial Army.* London: Souvenir Press, 1995.

Howard, Keith, editor, translations by Lee Young Joo. *True Stories of the Korean Comfort Women: Testimonies compiled by the Korean Council for Women Drafted for Military Sexual Slavery by Japan and the Research Association on the Women Drafted for Sexual Military Slavery by Japan.* London: Cassell, 1995.

Ireland, Alleyne. *The New Korea.* New York: E. P. Dutton, 1926; reprinted Seoul: Kyung-in Publishing Company for the Royal Asiatic Society, Korea Branch, 1975.

Japan. Government-General of Korea. *Annual Report on Administration of Chosen.* Keijo (Seoul), 1907–1937.

——. *Thriving Chosen: A Survey of Twenty-five Years' Administration.* Keijo (Seoul): 1935.

Kim, C. I. Eugene, and Doretha E. Mortimore, eds. *Korea's Response to Japan: The Colonial Period, 1910–1945.* Kalamazoo: Center for Korean Studies, Western Michigan University, 1975.

Ku, Dae-Yeol. *Korea Under Colonialism: The March First Movement and Anglo-Japanese Relations.* Seoul: Royal Asiatic Society Korea Branch, 1985.

Ladd, George T. *In Korea with Marquis Ito.* New York: C. Scribner's, 1908.

Lee, Chong-sik. *The Politics of Korean Nationalism.* Berkeley: University of California Press, 1965.

McKenzie, Frederick A. *Korea's Fight for Freedom.* New York: Revell, 1920. Reprinted Seoul: Yonsei University Press, 1969.

McNamara, Dennis L. *The Colonial Origins of Korean Enterprise 1910–45.* Cambridge, England: Cambridge University Press, 1990.

Nahm, Andrew C., ed. *Korea Under Japanese Colonial Rule: Studies of the Policy and Techniques of Japanese Colonialism.* Kalamazoo: Center for Korean Studies, Western Michigan University, 1973.

Oliver, Robert. *Korea: Forgotten Nation.* Washington, D.C., Public Affairs Press, 1944.

Park, Soon Woon. *Colonial Industrialization and Labor in Korea: The Onoda Cement Factory.* Cambridge Mass.: Harvard University Press, 1999.

Rhee, Syngman. *Japan Inside Out: The Challenge of Today.* New York: Revell, 1941.

Robinson, Michael Edwin. *Cultural Nationalism in Colonial Korea, 1920–1925.* Seattle: University of Washington Press, 1988.

——, and Gi-Wook Shin, editors. *Colonial Modernity in Korea.* Cambridge Mass.: Harvard University Press, 1999.

Scalapino, Robert A., and Chong-sik Lee. *Communism in Korea.* 2 vols. Berkeley: University of California Press, 1972.

Suh, Dae-sook. *The Korean Communist Movement, 1918–1948.* Princeton, N.J.: Princeton University Press, 1967.

Suh, Sang-Chul. *Growth and Structural Change in the Korean Economy, 1910–1940.* Cambridge, Mass: Council on East Asian Studies, Harvard University, 1978.

E. Post-Independence Period

Caldwell, John C. *The Korea Story.* New York: Henry Regnery, 1952.

Cho, Soon-sung. *Korea in World Politics, 1940–1950: An Evaluation of American Responsibility.* Berkeley: University of California Press, 1967.

Chung, Henry. *The Russians Came to Korea*. Seoul: Korean Pacific Press, 1947.

Chung, Kyung Cho. *Korea: The Third Republic*. New York: Macmillan, 1971.

Clark, Donald N., ed. *The Kwangju Uprising: Shadow Over the Regime in South Korea*. Boulder, Colo.: Westview, 1987.

Clough, Ralph N. *Balancing Act: The Republic of Korea Approaches 1988*. FPI Policy Brief 5. Lanham, Md.: University Press of America, 1987.

Cumings, Bruce. *The Origins of the Korean War: I. Liberation and the Emergence of Separate Regimes, 1945–1947*. Princeton, N.J.: Princeton University Press, 1981.

——, *The Origins of the Korean War: II. The Roaring of the Cataract, 1947–1950*. Princeton, N.J.: Princeton University Press, 1990.

Gleysteen, William H. *Massive Entanglement, Marginal Influence: Carter and Korea in Crisis*. Washington D. C.: Brookings Institution Press, 1999.

Goodrich, Leland M. *Korea: A Story of U.S. Policy in the United Nations*. New York: Council on Foreign Relations, 1956.

Han, Sungjoo. *The Failure of Democracy in South Korea*. Berkeley.: University of California Press, 1974.

Hurst, E. Cameron, III. *Korea 1988: A Nation at the Crossroad*. Lanham, Md.: University Press of America, 1988.

Kim, Se-jin. *The Politics of Military Revolution in Korea*. Chapel Hill: University of North Carolina Press, 1971.

Korea, Republic of, Supreme Council for National Reconstruction. *The Military Revolution in Korea*. Seoul: 1961.

Lee, Jai Eui. *Kwangju Diary: Beyond Death, Beyond the Darkness of the Age*. Los Angeles, Calif.: Center for Pacific Rim Studies, 1999.

Lewis, Linda S. *Laying Claim to the Memory of May: A Look Back at the 1980 Kwangju Uprising*. Honolulu: University of Hawaii Press, 2002.

Mason, Edward S. et al. *The Economic and Social Modernization of the Republic of Korea: Studies in the Modernization of the Republic of Korea, 1945–1975*. Cambridge, Mass.: Harvard University Press, 1980.

McCune, George M., and Arthur Grey Jr. *Korea Today*. Cambridge, Mass.: Harvard University Press, 1951.

Meade, Grant. *American Military Government in Korea*. New York: Columbia University Press, 1951.

Nahm, Andrew C., ed. *Korea and the New Order in East Asia*. Kalamazoo: Center for Korean Studies, Western Michigan University, 1975.

——, ed. *Studies in the Developmental Aspects of Korea*. Kalamazoo: Graduate College and Institute of International and Area Studies, Western Michigan University, 1969.

Oh, John K. C. *Korea: Democracy on Trial*. Ithaca, N.Y.: Cornell University Press, 1968.

——, *Korean Politics.* Ithaca, New York: Cornell University Press, 1999.
Reeve, W. D. *The Republic of Korea: A Political and Economic History.* London: Oxford University Press, 1963.
Sawyer, Robert. *Military Advisors in Korea. KMAG in Peace and War.* Washington, D.C.: Office of the Chief of Military History, 1962.
Scott-Stokes, Henry, and Jai Eui Lee, editors. *The Kwangju Uprising: Accounts of Korea's Tiananmen.* Armonk, New York: M. E. Sharpe, 2000.
Shin, Doh C. *Mass Politics and Culture in Democratizing Korea.* Cambridge, England: Cambridge University Press, 1999.
Wickham, John A. *Korea on the Brink: From the "12/12 Incident" to the Kwangju Uprising.* Washington D.C.: National Defense University, 1999.

F. The Korean War

Berger, Carl. *The Korean Knot: A Military-Political History.* Philadelphia: University of Pennsylvania Press, 1957.
Clark, Mark W. *From the Danube to the Yalu.* New York: Harper, 1954.
Foot, Rosemary. *The Wrong War: American Policy and the Dimensions of the Korean Conflict, 1950–1953.* Ithaca, N.Y.: Cornell University Press, 1985.
——. *A Substitute for Victory: The Politics of Peacemaking at the Korean Armistice Talks.* Ithaca, N.Y.: Cornell University Press, 1990.
Gardner, Lloyd C., ed. *The Korean War.* New York: Quadrangle Books, 1977.
Hastings, Max. *The Korean War.* New York: Simon & Schuster, 1987.
Heinl, Robert Debs. *Victory at High Tide: The Inchon–Seoul Campaign.* New York: Lippincott, 1968.
Hickey, Michael. *The Korean War.* London: John Murray, 2000.
Highsmith, Carol M., and Ted Landphair. *Forgotten No More: The Korean War Veterans Memorial Story.* Washington, D.C.: Chelsea Publishing, 1995.
Kaufman, Burton I. *The Korean War: Challenge in Crisis, Credibility and Command.* New York: Alfred A. Knopf, 1986.
Kim, Chun-kon. *The Korean War, 1950–53.* Seoul: Kwangmyong, 1973.
Lowe, Peter. *The Origins of the Korean War.* London: Longman, 1986; third edition 2000.
McCann, David R., and Barry S. Strauss. *War and Democracy: A comparative Study of the Korean War and the Peloponnesian War.* Armonk, New York: M. E. Sharpe, 2000.
Merrill, John. *Korea: The Peninsular Origins of the War.* Newark: University of Delaware Press, 1989.
Noble, Harold J. *Embassy at War.* Edited with an introduction by Frank Baldwin. Seattle: University of Washington Press, 1975.
Oliver, Robert T. *Verdict in Korea.* State College, Pa.: Bald Eagle Press, 1952.

Paige, Glenn D. *The Korean Decision: June 24–30*. New York: The Free Press, 1968.

Ra, J. Y. "The Politics of Conference: The Political Conference on Korea in Geneva, 26 April–15 June 1954," *Journal of Contemporary History*, vol. 34, no. 3 (July 1999), 399–416.

Reese, David. *Korea: The Limited War*. New York: St. Martin's Press, 1964.

Ridgway, Matthew B. *The Korean War*. New York: Popular Library, 1967.

Riley, John W., and Wilbur Schramm. *The Reds Take a City: The Communist Occupation of Seoul, with Eyewitness Accounts*. New Brunswick, N.J.: Rutgers University Press, 1954.

Spur, Russell. *Enter the Dragon: China at War in Korea*. New York: Newmarket Press, 1988.

Stone, Isidor F. *The Hidden History of the Korean War*. New York: Monthly Review Press, 1952.

Stueck, William W. *The Korean War: An International History*. Princeton, N.J.: Princeton University Press, 1995.

Summers, Harry G. *Korean War Almanac*. New York: Facts on File Inc., 1990.

Tucker, Spencer C., ed. *Encyclopedia of the Korean War: A Political, Social and Military History*. 3 vols. Santa Barbara, Calif.: ABC–CLIO, 2000.

Vatcher, William H. *Panmunjom: The Story of the Korean Military Armistice Negotiations*. New York: Praeger, 1958.

West, Philip, and Suh Ji-Moon. *Remembering the "Forgotten War": The Korean War Through Literature and Art*. Armonk, New York: M. E. Sharpe, 2000.

Whiting, Allen A. *China Crosses the Yalu: The Decision to Enter the Korean War*. New York: Macmillan, 1960.

Williams, William J., ed. *A Revolutionary War: Korea and the Transformation of the Postwar World*. Chicago: Imprint Publications, 1993.

G. Diplomatic History/Foreign Relations

Baldwin, Frank, ed. *Without Parallel. The American–Korean Relationship Since 1945*. New York: Pantheon Books, 1974.

Baynard, Thomas O., and Soo-gil Young, ed. *Economic Relations Between the United States and Korea: Conflict or Cooperation?* Washington, D.C.: Institute for International Economics, 1989.

Bergsten, C. Fred and SaKong Il, eds. *Korea–United States Cooperation in the New World Order*. Washington, D.C.: Institute for International Economics, 1996.

Burnett, Scott, S., ed. *Korean–American Relations: Documents Pertaining to the Far Eastern Diplomacy of the United States. Vol. III: The Period of Diminishing Influence, 1896–1905*. Honolulu: University of Hawaii Press, 1989.

Buss, Claude A. *The United States and the Republic of Korea. Background for Policy*. Stanford, Calif.: Hoover Institution Press, 1982.

Chien, Frederick Foo. *The Opening of Korea: A Study of Chinese Diplomacy, 1876–1885*. Hamden, Conn.: Shoe String Press, 1967.

Choi, Woon Sang. *The Fall of the Hermit Kingdom*. Dobbs Ferry, N. Y.: Oceana Publications, 1967.

Chung, Chong-wha, and J. E. Hoare, eds. *Korean–British Relations: Yesterday, Today, and Tomorrow*. Cho'ongju: Ch'ongju University, 1984.

Clough, Ralph N. *Embattled Korea: The Rivalry for International Support*. Boulder, Colo.: Westview, 1987.

Coleman, Craig S. *American Images of Korea: Korea and Koreans as Portrayed in Books, Magazines, Television, News Media and Film*. Seoul: Hollym, 1998.

Cumings, Bruce, ed. *Child of Conflict: The Korean–American Relationship, 1943–1953*. Seattle: University of Washington Press, 1983.

———. *Parallax Visions: Making Sense of American–East Asian Relations at the End of the Century*. Durham, N.C.: Duke University Press, 1999.

Dong, Wonmo, ed., *The Two Koreas and the United States: Issues of Peace, Security and Economic Co-operation*. Armonk, N.Y.: M. E. Sharpe, 1999.

Foley, James. *Korea's Divided Families: Fifty Years of Separation*. London: Routledge Curzon, 2003.

Gills, B. K. *Korea versus Korea: A Case of Contested Legitimacy*. London: Routledge, 1996.

Gregor, A. James. *Land of the Morning Calm: Korea and American Security*. Washington, D.C.: Ethics and Public Policy Center, 1990

Grinker, Rory Richard. *Korea and Its Futures: Unification and the Unfinished War*. London: Macmillan 1998.

Han, Sung-joo, ed. *U.S.–Korea Security Cooperation: Retrospects and Prospects*. ARC Foreign Policy Studies No. 4. Seoul: Asiatic Research Center, Korea University 1983.

Harris, Stuart, and James Cotton, eds. *The End of the Cold War in Northeast Asia*. Melbourne, Australia: Longman Cheshire, 1991.

Hoare, James Edward. *Embassies in the East: The Story of the British and Their Embassies in China, Japan and Korea from 1859 to the Present*. Richmond, Surrey: Curzon Press, 1999.

Kim, Ilpyong. *Historical Dictionary of North Korea*. Lanham, Md.: Scarecrow Press, 2003.

Kim, Young C., ed. *Foreign Policies of Korea*. Washington, D.C.: Institute for Asian Studies, George Washington University, 1973.

———. *Major Powers and Korea*. Silver Spring, Md.: Research Institute on Korean Affairs, 1973.

Koo, Young-nok, and Suh, Dae-sook, eds. *Korea and the United States: A Century of Cooperation*. Honolulu: University of Hawaii Press, 1984.

Koo, Young-nok, and Han, Sung-joo, eds. *The Foreign Policy of the Republic of Korea*. New York: Columbia University Press, 1985.

Kwak, Tae-hwan et al, eds. *The Two Koreas in World Politics*. Seoul: Institute for Far Eastern Studies, Kyungnam University, 1983.

———. *U.S.–Korean Relations, 1882–1982*. Boulder, Colo.: Westview, 1983.

Lee, Chae-jin. *China and Korea: Dynamic Relations*. Stanford, Calif.: Hoover Institute Press, 1996.

Lee, Manwoo et al, eds. *Alliance Under Tension: The Evolution of South Korean–U.S. Relations*. Boulder Colo.: Westview, 1989.

Lee, Yur-bok. *Diplomatic Relations Between the United States and Korea, 1866–1887*. New York: Humanities Press, 1970.

———. *West Goes East: Paul Georg von Mollendorff and Great Power Imperialism in Late Yi Korea*. Honolulu: University of Hawaii Press, 1988.

Lee, Yur-bok, and Wayne Patterson, eds. *One Hundred Years of Korean–American Relations, 1882–1982*. Tuscaloosa: University of Alabama Press, 1986.

Mazarr, Michael J. et al, eds. *Korea 1991: The Road to Peace*. Boulder, Colo.: Westview, 1991.

McCune, George M. "The Exchange of Envoys Between Korea and Japan During the Tokugawa Period," *Far Eastern Quarterly* 5 (May 1946), 308–25.

McCune, George M., and John A. Harrison, eds. *Korean–American Relations: Documents Pertaining to the Far Eastern Diplomacy of the United States. Vol. 1: The Initial Period, 1883–1886*. Berkeley, Calif.: University of California Press, 1951.

Moon, Katherine H. S. *Sex among Allies: Military Prostitution in US–Korea Relations*. New York: Columbia University Press, 1997.

Morse, Ronald, ed. *Reflections on a Century of United States–Korean Relations*. Lanham, Md.: University Press of America, 1983.

Nahm, Andrew C., ed. *Korea and the New Order in East Asia*. Kalamazoo: Center for Korean Studies, Western Michigan University, 1975.

———, ed. *The United States and Korea: American–Korean Relations, 1866–1976*. Kalamazoo: Center for Korean Studies, Western Michigan University, 1979.

Nelson, Melvin F. *Korea and the Old Order in Eastern Asia*. Baton Rouge: Louisiana State University, 1945. Reprinted New York: Russel and Russel, 1967.

Noble, Harold J. *Embassy at War*. Edited with an introduction by Frank Baldwin. Seattle: University of Washington Press, 1975.

Oh, John K. C., and Bonnie Bongwon Cho Oh. *The Korean Embassy in America*. Seoul: Hollym, 2003.

Oliver, Robert T. *Syngman Rhee and American Involvement in Korea, 1942–1960: A Personal Narrative*. Seoul: Panmun, 1978.

Olsen, Edward A. *U.S. Policy and the Two Koreas*. Boulder, Colo.: Westview, 1988.

———. *Towards Normalizing U.S.–Korean Relations: In Due Course?* Boulder, Colo.: Lynne Rienner, 2002.

Palmer, Spencer J. *Korean–American Relations: Documents Pertaining to the Far Eastern Diplomacy of the United States. Vol. II: The Period of Growing Influence, 1887–1895*. Berkeley, Calif.: University of California Press, 1963.

Park, Tong Whan, editor. *The U.S. and the Two Koreas: A New Triangle*. Boulder, Colo.: Lynne Rienner, 1998.

Rockhill, William. *China's Intercourse with Korea from the XVth Century to 1895*. London: Luzac, 1950.

Sands, William J. *Undiplomatic Memoirs: The Far East, 1896–1905*. New York: McGraw-Hill, 1930.

Sanford, Dan C. *South Korea and the Socialist Countries: The Politics of Trade*. New York: St. Martin's Press, 1990.

Steinberg, David I. *Korea: Nexus of East Asia*. New York: American–Asian Educational Exchange, 1970.

Swartout, Robert R. J. *Mandarins, Gunboats, and Power Politics: Owen Nickerson Denny and the International Rivalries in Korea*. Honolulu: University of Hawaii Press, 1980.

Taylor, William J. Jr. et al, eds. *The Future of South Korean–U.S. Security Relations*. Boulder, Colo.: Westview, 1989.

White, Nathan N. *U.S. Policy Toward Korea: Analysis, Alternatives, and Recommendations*. Boulder, Colo.: Westview, 1978.

7. POLITICS

A. General

Cole, David G., and Princeton N. Lyman. *Korean Development: The Interplay of Politics and Economics*. Cambridge, Mass.: Harvard University Press, 1971.

Diamond, Larry, and Byong-kook Kim, eds. *Consolidating Democracy in South Korea*. Boulder, Colo.: Lynne Rienner, 2000.

Han, Sungjoo. *The Failure of Democracy in South Korea*. Berkeley: University of California Press, 1974.

Henderson, Gregory. *The Politics of the Vortex*. Cambridge, Mass.: Harvard University Press, 1968.

Hoare, James Edward, and Susan Pares. *Conflict in Korea: An Encyclopedia*. Santa Barbara, Calif.: ABC–CLIO, 1999.

Kihl, Young Whan. *Politics and Policies in Divided Korea: Regimes in Contest*. Boulder, Colo.: Westview Press, 1984.

Kil, Soong Hoom, and Chung-in Moon, eds. *Understanding Korean Politics: An Introduction*. Albany: State University of New York, 2001.

Kim, C. I. Eugene, ed. *A Pattern of Political Development. Korea*. Kalamazoo, Mich.: Korea Research and Publications, 1964.

Kim, Ilpyung, and Young Whan Kihl, eds. *Political Change in South Korea*. New York: Korean PWPA, 1988.

Kim, Joungwon Alexander. *Divided Korea: The Politics of Development, 1945–1972*. Cambridge, Mass.: East Asia Research Center, Harvard University, 1975.

Lee, Chong-sik. *Japan and Korea: The Political Dimension*. Stanford, Calif.: Hoover Institution, 1985.

Lee, Manwoo. *The Odyssey of Korean Democracy: Korean Politics, 1987–1990*. New York: Praeger, 1990.

Nam, Koon Woo. *South Korean Politics: The Search for Political Consensus and Stability*. Lanham, Md.: University Press of America, 1989.

Oh, John K. C. *Democracy on Trial*. Ithaca, N.Y.: Cornell University Press, 1968.

———. *Korean Politics: The Quest for Democratization and Development*. Ithaca, N.Y.: Cornell University Press, 1999.

Oh, Katy, editor. *Korea Briefing, 1997–1999: Challenges and Change at the Turn of the Century*. Armonk, N.Y.: M. E. Sharpe, 2000.

Pak, Chi-young. *Political Opposition in Korea, 1945–1963. The Institute of Social Science*. Korean Studies Series, No. 2. Honolulu: University of Hawaii Press, 1980.

Palais, James B. *Politics and Policy in Traditional Korea*. Cambridge, Mass: Harvard University Press, 1975.

Shin, Doh C. *Mass Politics and Culture in Democratizing Korea*. Cambridge, England: Cambridge University Press, 1999.

Sohn, Hak-kyu. *Authoritarianism and Opposition in South Korea*. London: Routledge, 1989.

Soh, Chunghee Sarah. *Women in Korean Politics*. Boulder, Colo.: Westview, 1993.

Suh, Dae-sook, and Chae-jin Lee, eds. *Political Leadership in Korea*. Seattle: University of Washington Press, 1975.

Tewksburg, Donald G., comp. *Source Materials on Korean Politics and Ideologies*. New York: Institute of Pacific Relations, 1950.

Wells, Kenneth M. *South Korea's Minjung Movement: The Culture and Politics of Dissidence*. Honolulu: University of Hawaii Press, 1995.

Wright, Edward, ed. *Korean Politics in Transition*. Seoul: Royal Asiatic Society, Korea Branch, 1974.

Yang, Sung Chul. *Korea and Two Regimes: Kim Il Sung and Park Chung Hee*. Cambridge, Mass: Schenkman, 1981.

———. *The North and South Korean Political Systems: A Comparative Analysis*. Seoul: Seoul Press, 1994.

Yoon, Woo-kon. "Korean Bureaucrats' Behavior": An Analysis of Personality and Its Effect," *Korea Journal*, 14:7 (July 1974), 22–29.

B. Government

Ch'oe, Young-ho. *The Civil Examinations and the Social Structure in Early Yi Dynasty Korea, 1392–1600*. Seoul: Korean Research Center, 1987.

Haboush, JaHyun Kim. *A Heritage of Kings: One Man's Monarchy in the Confucian World*. New York: Columbia University Press, 1988.

Kihl, Young Whan. *Local Elections, Power Structure and the Legislative Process in Korea*. Occasional Paper, No. 8. Comparative Legislative Research Center, Iowa University, 1975.

Kim, Bum-woong, and Joon Rho, eds. *Korean Public Bureaucracy*. Seoul: Kyobo Publishing, 1982.

Kim, Kwan Bong. *The Korean–Japanese Treaty Crisis and the Instability of the Korean Political System*. New York: Praeger, 1971.

Kim, Se-jin, and Chang-hyun Cho, eds. *Government and Politics of Korea*. Silver Spring, Md.: Research Institute on Korean Affairs, 1972.

Koh, Byung Chul, ed. *Aspects of Administrative Development in South Korea*. Kalamazoo, Mich.: Korea Research and Publications, 1967.

Lee, Hahn-been. *Korea: Time, Change, and Administration*. Honolulu: East–West Center Press, 1968.

Oh, Chung Hwan. "The Civil Service of the Republic of Korea." Ph.D. Dissertation, New York University, 1961.

Paik, Wanki. "Modernization of Korean Bureaucracy," Ph.D. Dissertation, Florida State University, 1972.

Rhee, Yong-pil. *The Breakdown of Authority Structure in Korea in 1960*. Honolulu: University of Hawaii Press, 1982.

Wagner, Edward W. *The Literati Purges: Political Conflict in Early Yi Korea*. Cambridge, Mass.: East Asian Research Center, Harvard University, 1974.

Yoo, Hoon. "Social Background of Higher Civil Servants in Korea," *Korea Quarterly*, 10:1 (1968), 35–55.

C. Law

Chun, Bong Duck. "The Commercial Laws in Korea," *Digest of Commercial Laws of the World*, vol. 2. Dodds Ferry, N.Y.: Oceana Publications, 1966.

Dull, Paul S. "South Korean Constitution." *Far Eastern Survey*, 17:17 (Sept. 1948), 205–207.

Hahm, Pyong-choon. *The Korean Political Tradition and Law: Essays in Korean Law and Legal History*. Seoul: Royal Asiatic Society, Korea Branch, 1967.

International Cultural Foundation. *Legal System of Korea*. Korean Culture Series, No. 5. Seoul: 1975.

Korea, Republic of, Central Election Management Committee. *Korean Constitution, Election and Political Party Law*. Seoul: 1964 and 1987.

——, Office of Labor Affairs. *Labor Law of Korea*. Seoul: 1969.

Korean Legal Center. *Laws of the Republic of Korea*. Seoul: 1975.

Kwack, Yoon Chick. "The Korean New Civil Code," *Bulletin of the Korean Research Center*, 17 (1962), 11–23.

Pak, C. Y. "Third Republic (Constitution of Korea)," *Western Political Quarterly* 21 (March 1968), 110–22.

Park, Byong Ho. "Characteristics of Traditional Korean Law," *Korea Journal*, 16:7 (July 1970), 4–16.

Ryu, Paul Kichyon. *The Korean Criminal Code*. American Series of Foreign Penal Code No. 2. South Hackensack, N.J.: Fred B. Rothmann, 1960.

Shaw, William. "Traditional Korea Law: A New Look," *Korea Journal*, 13:9 (Sept. 1973), 40–53.

——, ed. *Human Rights in Korea: Historical and Policy Perspectives*. Cambridge, Mass.: East Asia Studies Program of the Harvard Law School and Council on East Asian Studies Harvard University, 1991.

U. S. Department of Labor. *Labor Law and Practices in the Republic of Korea*. BLS Series No. 361. Washington, D.C. Government Printing Office, 1969.

World Peace Through Law Center. *Law and Judicial Systems of Nations. Korea*. Washington, D.C., 1968.

Yoon, Dae-kyu. *Law and Political Authority in South Korea*. Boulder Colo.: Westview Press and Masan: Kyungnam University Press, 1990.

D. Political Parties

Chu, Shao-hsien. "Past and Present of the Political Parties in the Republic of Korea," *Issues and Studies*, 1:10 (July 1965), 20–30.

Kim, Hyun-woo. "Elections, Electoral Behavior and Political Parties in Korea 1981–1992: A Logit Approach to Ecological Analysis and Inference." Ph.D. Dissertation, University of Hawaii, 1992.

Han, Ki-shik. "Development of Parties and Politics in Korea," *Korea Journal*, 14:9 (Sept. 1974), 37–49.

Han, Tae-soo. "A Review of Political Party Activities in Korea (1945–1954)," *Korean Affairs* 1 (1962), 413–27.

Han, Y. C. "Political Parties and Political Development in South Korea," *Pacific Affairs*, 42.4 (Winter 1969–1970), 444–64.

Kihl, Young Whan. "Research on Party Politics in Korea: An Analytical Scheme," *Korean Political Science Review* 6 (June 1972), 279–96.

Kim, C. I. Eugene, and Young Whan Kihl, eds. *Party Politics and Elections in Korea.* Silver Spring, Md.: Research Institute on Korean Affairs, 1976.

Kim, Chulsu, "Parties and Factions in Korean Politics." Ph.D. Dissertation, University of Massachusetts, 1973.

Kong, Tat Yan. "Power Alternation in South Korea," *Government and Opposition*, vol. 35, no. 3 (Summer 2000), 370–91.

Park, Hoon Tark. "The Decline of Mass Democracy in south Korea: Personalized Politics, State Nationalism, Poliitcal Regionalism, and Mass Democracy." Ph.D. dissertation, University of Georgia, 1993.

8. SCIENCE

A. Geography/Geology

Bartz, Patricia M. *South Korea.* Oxford, England: Clarendon Press, 1972.

Canada. Dept. of Mines and Technical Survey. *Korea: A Geographical Appreciation.* Foreign Geography Information Series, No. 4. Ottawa: 1951.

Cavendish, Alfred E., and Henry E. Goold-Adams. *Korea and the Sacred Mountain.* London: G. Philip, 1894.

Chen, Cheng-siang. *Agricultural Geography of Korea.* Research Report No. 31. Hong Kong: University of Hong Kong, 1970.

Choe, Suh Myun. "Tokdo in Old Maps," *Korea Observer*, vol. 29, no. 1 (Spring 1998), 187–203.

Chi, Chang-jo. "*P'ungsu*: The Korean Traditional Geographic Thought." *Korea Journal*, vol. 26, no. 5 (May 1986), 35–45.

Hall, Basil. *Account of Voyage of Discovery to the West Coast of Corea and the Great Loo-choo Island.* London: John Murray, 1818.

Korea, Republic of. *Geological Survey of Korea: An Outline of the Geology of Korea.* Seoul: 1956.

——. *Geological Survey of Korea: Hydrogeologic Maps of Korea: Anseong River Basin.* Seoul: 1961.

Landor, Henry Savage. *Corea: Or Chosen, the Land of the Morning Calm.* London: Heinemann, 1895.

Lautensach, Hermann, trans. from the German and edited by Kathering Dege and Eckart Dege. *Korea: A Geography based on the Author's Travels and Literature.* Berlin: Springer-Verlag, 1988.

Lee, Dai-sung, ed. *Geology of Korea.* Seoul: Kyohak-sa, 1988.

McCune, Shannon. *Korea's Heritage: A Regional and Social Geography.* Rutland, Vt.: Tuttle, 1956.

———. *Views of the Geography of Korea, 1935–1960.* Seoul: Korean Research Center, 1980.

Paek, Ryong-jun, ed. *Geology of Korea.* P'yongyang: Foreign Languages Book Publishing, 1996.

Reedman, Anthony J., and Sangho Um. *The Geology of Korea: An Account of the Geological Development of the Republic of Korea.* Seoul: Geological and Mineral Institute of Korea, 1975.

Zaichikov, V. T. *Geography of Korea.* Translated from the Russian by Albert Parry with an introduction by Shannon McCune. New York: Institute of Pacific Relations, 1952.

B. Public Health/Medicine

Bowman, Newton H. "The History of Korean Medicine," *Transactions of the Korea Branch of the Royal Asiatic Society* 6 (1915), 1–34.

Lee, Sun Ju. *Korean Folk Medicine.* Seoul: Seoul National University Press, 1966.

National Economy Research Associates, eds. *The Health Care System in Korea.* London: National Economy Research Associates, 1994.

No, Chong-u. "Chinese Medicine in Korea," *Korea Journal,* 11:2 (February 1971), 24–29.

Yang, Chae-mo. *Review of the Primary Health Care Program of Korea with Policy Recommendations.* Seoul: Institution of Population and Health Services Research, Yonsei University, 1983.

Yeon, Ha–cheong. *Primary Health Care in Korea. An Approach to Evaluation.* Honolulu: University of Hawaii Press, 1981.

C. Science/Technology

Cheon, Sang-woon. *Science and Technology in Korea: Traditional Instruments and Techniques.* Cambridge: MIT Press, 1974.

———. *A History of Science in Korea.* Seoul: Jinmoondang, 1998.

Needham, Joseph et al. *The Hall of Heavenly Records: Korean Astronomical Instruments and Clocks, 1380–1780.* London: Cambridge University Press, 1959. Reprinted 1986.

Park, Seong-rae. "Introduction of Western Science into Korea, 1876–1910," *Korea Journal,* vol. 21, no. 5 (May 1981), 29–38.

———. "Korea–Japan Relations and the History of Science and Techology," *Korea Journal,* vol. 32, no. 4 (Winter 1992), 80–86.

Sohn, Pow-key. *Early Korean Typography.* Seoul: Korean Library Science Research Institute, 1971.

Underwood, Horace H. *Korean Boats and Ships*. Seoul: Yonsei University Press, 1979.

9. SOCIETY

A. Anthropology

Allen, Horace N. *Things Korean: A Collection of Sketches and Anecdotes, Missionary and Diplomatic*. New York: Revell, 1908.

Bergman, Stan. *In Korean Wilds and Villages*. Trans. Frederick Whyte. London: Travel Book Club, 1938.

Brandt, Vincent S. R. *A Korean Village Between Farm and Sea*. Cambridge, Mass.: Harvard University Press, 1971.

Carles, William R. *Life in Corea*. London: Macmillan, 1888.

Choe, Sang-u. *Annual Customs of Korea*. Seoul: Seomun Dang, 1983.

Chun, Kyung-soo. *Reciprocity and Korean Society: An Ethnography of Hasami*. Seoul: Seoul National University Press, 1985.

Dallet, Charles. *Traditional Korea*. New Haven, Conn.: Human Relations Area Files, 1964.

Gale, James S. *Korean Sketches*. Nashville, Tenn.: Publishing House of the Methodist Episcopal Church South, 1898.

Gifford, Daniel L. *Every-day Life in Korea: A Collection of Studies and Stories*. New York: Revell, 1898.

Lee, Ou Young. *In This Earth and in This Wind: This Is Korea*. Seoul: Hollym, 1967.

Lett, Denise Potrzeba. *In Pursuit of Status: The Making of South Korea's "New" Urban Middle Class*. Cambridge Mass.: Harvard University Press for the Harvard University Asia Center, 1998.

Lowell, Percival. *Choson: The Land of the Morning Calm: A Sketch of Korea*. Boston, Mass.: Ticknor and Co., 1885.

Moose, J. Robert. *Village Life in Korea*. Nashville: Publishing House of the Methodist Episcopal Church South, 1911.

Nelson, Laura C. *Measured Excess: Status, Gender, and Consumer Nationalism in South Korea*. New York: Columbia University Press, 2000.

Pak, Ki-hyuk and Sidney D. Gamble. *The Changing Korean Village*. Seoul: Royal Asiatic Society, Korea Branch, 1975.

Pares, Susan. *Crosscurrents: Korean Western Culture in Contrast*. Seoul: Seoul International Publishing House, 1985.

Rutt, Richard. *Korean Works and Days: Notes from the Diary of a Country Priest*. Seoul: Royal Asiatic Society, Korea Branch, 1964.

Underwood, Lillian H. *Fifteen Years Among the Top-Knots, or Life in Korea*. New York: American Tract Society, 1908.

B. Education

Adams, Donald K. "Education in Korea 1945–1955." Ph.D. Dissertation, University of Connecticut, 1955.

Choo, Young-ha. *The Education in the Yi Dynasty.* Seoul: Soodo Women's Teachers College, 1961.

Dodge, Herbert W. "A History of the U.S. Assistance to Korean Education: 1953–1966." Ph.D. Dissertation, George Washington University, 1971.

Edman, Marion L. *Primary Teachers of Korea Look at Themselves.* Seoul: Central Educational Research Institute, 1962.

Fisher, James W. *Democracy and Mission Education in Korea.* New York: Columbia University Press, 1928. Reprinted Seoul: Yonsei University Press, 1970.

Kim, Chong-chol. "Higher Education in the Republic of Korea," *Bulletin of the UNESCO Regional Office of Education in Asia,* 7:1 (Sept. 1972), 89–99.

Kim, Helen Kiteuk. *Rural Education for the Regeneration of Korea.* New York: Columbia University Press, 1931.

Kim, Hyun-chul. "History of Education in Korea." Ph.D. Dissertation, American University, 1931.

Korea, Republic of, Ministry of Education. *Education in Korea.* Annual. Seoul: 1961–.

Korea, Republic of, Presidential Commission for Educational Reform. *Korean Educational Reform: Towards the 21st Century.* Seoul: Presidential Commission for Educational Reform, 1987.

———. *Higher Educational Reform in the Republic of Korea.* Seoul: 1963.

———. *Summary of Education in Korea.* Annual. Seoul: 1963–.

Korean National Commission for UNESCO. *Review of Educational Studies in Korea.* Seoul: 1972.

Lee, Kyu-hwan. *The Equalization Policy of Middle Schools in the Republic of Korea.* Seoul: Ewha Woman's University, 1972.

Lee, Yung Dug. *Educational Innovations in the Republic of Korea.* Geneva: International Bureau of Education, 1974.

McGinn, N. J. et al. *Educational Development in Korea.* Cambridge: Harvard University Press, 1980.

Meineske, Charlotte. *Education in Korea.* Seoul: Ministry of Education, Republic of Korea, 1958.

Morgan, Robert, and C. B. Chadwick. *System Analysis for Educational Change: The Republic of Korea.* Tallahassee: Florida State University, 1971.

Nam, Byung-hun. "Educational Reorganization in South Korea under the United States Army Military Government, 1945–48." Ph.D. Dissertation, University of Pittsburgh, 1962.

Pai, Hyung Il, and Timothy R. Tangerherlini. *Nationalism and the Construction of Korean Identity*. Berkeley, Calif.: Institute of East Asian Studies University of California, 1998.

Underwood, Horace H. *Modern Education in Korea*. New York: International Press, 1926.

UNESCO. "Republic of Korea," *World Survey of Education*. Vol. 2. Primary Education. Paris: 1958.

———. "Republic of Korea," *World Survey of Education*. Vol. 3. Secondary Education. Paris: 1961.

———. "Republic of Korea," *World Survey of Education*. Vol. 4. Higher Education. Paris: 1965.

———. "Republic of Korea," *World Survey of Education*. Vol. 5. Educational Policy, Legislation and Administration. Paris: 1971.

UNESCO. Regional Advisory Team for Educational Planning in Asia. *Long-Term Projections for Education in the Republic of Korea*. Bangkok: 1965.

Werk, Richard. "Educational Development under the South Korean Interim Government," *School and Society*, 69 (April 20, 1949), 305–309.

World Bank, comp. *Republic of Korea: Transition to a Knowledge-Based Economy*. N.p.: World Bank, 2000.

You, In-jong. "The Impact of the American Protestant Missions on Korean Education from 1885–1932." Ph.D. Dissertation, University of North Carolina, 1967.

Yu, Hyung-jin. "Educational Developments in the Republic of Korea: 1957–1967," *Bulletin of UNESCO Regional Office of Education in Asia*, 2:1 (Sept. 1967), 37–43.

C. Sociology

Aqua, Ronald. *Local Institutions and Rural Development in South Korea*. Ithaca, N.Y.: Cornell University Press, 1974.

Ban, Sung Hwan. *The New Community Movement in Korea*. Seoul: Korean Development Institute, 1975.

Barringer, Herbert R. "Social Stratification and Industrialization in Korea." *ILCORK Working Paper*, No. 11. Seoul: 1971.

Brunner, Edward de S. *Rural Korea*. New York: International Missionary Council, 1942.

Chung, Sei-wha, ed., Shin Chang-hyun et al trans. *Challenge for Women: Women's Studies in Korea*. Seoul: Ewha Woman's University Press, 1986.

Crane, Paul. *Korean Patterns*. Seoul: Hollym, 1967.

Gilmore, George W. *Korea from Its Capital with a Chapter on Missions*. Philadelphia: Presbyterian Board of Publication, 1892.

Hong, Sawon. *Community Development and Human Reproductive Behavior*. Seoul: Korea Development Institute, 1979.

International Cultural Foundation. *Korean Society*. Korean Culture Series, No. 6. Seoul: 1976.

Kendall, Laural, and Mark Peterson, eds. *Korean Women: Views from the Inner Room*. New Haven, Conn.: East Rock Press, 1983.

Kim, Agnes Davis. *I Married a Korean*. New York: The John Day Company, 1953. Reprinted, with an additional chapter, Seoul: Royal Asiatic Society, Korea Branch, 1979.

Kim, C. I. Eugene, and Changboh Chee. *Aspects of Social Change in Korea*. Kalamazoo, Mich.: Korea Research and Publications, 1963.

Kim, Yung-chung, ed. *Women of Korea: A History from Ancient Times to 1945*. Seoul: Ewha Woman's University Press, 1977.

Kwon, Tae Hwan. *Demography of Korea*. Seoul: Seoul National University, 1973.

Kwon, Tae Hwan et al. *The Population of Korea*. Seoul: Population and Development Studies Center, 1975.

Lee, Han Soon. *A Study on Korean Internal Migration in the 1960s*. Seoul: Kyunghee University, 1973.

Lee, Hyo-jae. "Changing Family in Korea," *Bulletin of the Korean Research Center*, 29 (Dec. 1968), 87–89.

———. "Industrialization and the Family in Korea." *ILCORK Working Paper*. Honolulu: University of Hawaii, 1971.

Lee, Man Gap. *The Social Structure in a Korean Village and Its Change*. Seoul: Seoul National University, 1973.

———. *Sociology and Social Change in Korea*. Seoul: Korea Development Institute, 1982.

Lee, Man Gap, and Herbert R. Barringer, eds. *A City in Transition: Urbanization in Taegu, Korea*. Seoul: Hollym, 1971.

MacDonald, Donald S. *The Koreans: Contemporary Politics and Society*. Third edition, revised and ed. Donald Clark. Boulder, Colo.: Westview, 1996.

Mason, Edward S. et al. *The Economic and Social Modernization of the Republic of Korea: Studies in the Modernization of the Republic of Korea, 1945–1975*. Cambridge, Mass.: Harvard University Press, 1980.

Mattielli, Sandra, ed. *Virtues in Conflict: Tradition and the Korean Women Today*. Seoul: Royal Asiatic Society, Korea Branch, 1977.

Morse, Ronald, ed. *Wild Asters: Explorations in Korean Thoughts, Culture and Society*. Lanham, Md.: University Press of America, 1987.

Oppert, Ernest. *A Forbidden Land: Voyages to the Corea*. London: Sampson Low, Marston, Searle and Rivington, 1880.

Pak, Ki-hyuk, and Seung Yun Lee. *Three Clan Villages in Korea*. Seoul: Yonsei University Press, 1963.

Pak, Ki-hyuk, and Sidney D. Gamble. *The Changing Korean Village.* Seoul: Royal Asiatic Society, Korea Branch, 1975.

Park, Chong Keel. *Social Security in Korea: An Approach to Socio-Economic Development.* Seoul: Korea Development Institute, 1979.

Park, Chung Hee. *Saemaul: Korea's New Community Movement.* Seoul: Korea Textbook Co., 1979.

Research Center for Korean Women, Sookmyung Women's University. *Women of the Yi Dynasty.* Studies on Korean Women Series, No. 1. Seoul: 1986.

Steinberg, David I. *The Republic of Korea. Economic Transformation and Social Change.* Boulder, Colo.: Westview, 1988.

Struyk, Raymond J., and Margery Austin Turner. *Finance and Housing Quality in Two Developing Countries: Korea and the Philippines.* Lanham, Md.: University Press of America, 1986.

Trewartha, Glen T., and Wilbur Zelinsky. "Population Distribution and Change in Korea, 1925–1949," *Geographical Review,* 45:1 (January 1955), 1–26.

Wagner, Edward W. "The Korean Chokpo as a Historical Source." In *Studies in Asian Genealogy,* Spencer J. Palmer, ed. Provo, Utah: Brigham Young University Press, 1972.

——. "The Ladder of Success in Yi Dynasty Korea," *Occasional Papers on Korea* 1 (April 1974), 1–8. Seattle: Korean Studies Society.

——. "Social Structure in Seventeenth Century Korea: Some Observations from a 1663 Census Register," *Occasional Papers on Korea* 1 (April 1974), 36–54. Seattle: The Korean Studies Society.

Yoon, Jong-joo. *A Study on Rural Population.* Seoul: Seoul Women's College, 1974.

10. WEBSITES AND CD-ROMS

A. CD-ROMS

Consumer Price Index 1965–2000. Seoul: Korean National Statistical Office, 2001. Mainly Korean, but main information also in English.

Exploring Korea's Culture. Seoul: Korean National Tourism Organization, 1996.

Hoffman, Frank, Matthew J Christensen, and Kirk W. Lansen, compilers. *The Harvard Korean Studies Bibliography: 80,000 References on Korea.* Cambridge Mass.: Harvard University Korea Institute, 1999.

P'yongyang Computer Center. *Samchonri.* P'yongyang. 2001. An excellent interactive atlas of the whole of the Korean Peninsula, with accurate and up to date information on towns, provinces, and other features.

A Window on Korea. Seoul: Korean Overseas Information Service, 1994, 2000.

B. Websites

Websites come and go, but a link on one will often take you to another, or to one that appears to be missing. The following small selection is not exhaustive but will lead to others.

www.cia.gov/publications/factbook/geos/ks.html Takes you to the U.S. Central Intelligence Agency's factbook on South Korea.

www.dur.ac.uk/BAKS Website of the British Association for Korean Studies; some links.

www.hankuki.com/times *Korea Times* web page.

www.hawaii.edu/korea/bibliography A vast bibliography.

www.kimsoft.com A very useful site, with many links.

www.korea.army.mil U.S. Army in Korea site.

www.korea.net Straight to the South Korean Government home page, with links to all ministries, organizations, etc.

www.koreaherald.co.kr *Korea Herald* home page.

www.koreanhistoryproject.org A Korean War veterans site that has expanded much beyond its original purpose.

www.koreafm.com Korean Broadcasting System (KBS) site.

www.koreasociety.org New York–based Korea Society site with very useful links.

www.lifeinkorea.com Mainly for expatriates but again, useful links.

www.yonhapnews.co.kr/Engnews South Korea's News Agency.

Appendix A
Government Structure of the Republic of Korea
(September 2003)

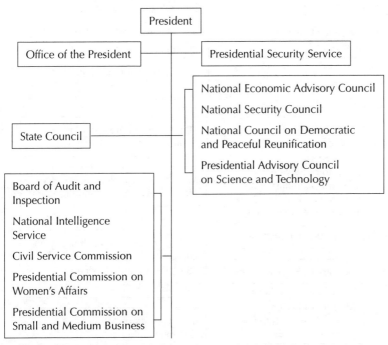

President

Office of the President

Presidential Security Service

State Council

National Economic Advisory Council

National Security Council

National Council on Democratic and Peaceful Reunification

Presidential Advisory Council on Science and Technology

Board of Audit and Inspection

National Intelligence Service

Civil Service Commission

Presidential Commission on Women's Affairs

Presidential Commission on Small and Medium Business

A: Independent Organs: Central Election Management Committee; Constitution Court; Courts

```
                          ┌─────────────────┐
                          │ Prime Minister  │
                          └────────┬────────┘
                                   │
```

Prime Minister's Secretariat	Ministry of Planning and Budget
	Government Legislative Agency
Office for Government Policy Coordination	Government Information Agency
	Fair Trade Commission
	Patriots' and Veterans' Administration Agency
Emergency Planning Commission	Financial Services Commission
	Ombudsman
	Commission on Youth Protection

Ministry of Trade & Economy Tax Service Customs Service Supply Administration National Statistics Office	Ministry of Culture and Tourism Culture Properties Administration
	Ministry of Agriculture & Forestry Rural Development Administration Forest Services
Ministry of Unification	
Ministry of Foreign Affairs	Ministry of Commerce, Industry and Energy Small & Medium Business Administration
Ministry of Justice Public Prosecutor's Office	Ministry of Information & Communication
Ministry of National Defense Ministry Manpower Administration	Ministry of Health & Welfare Food & Drug Administration

B: Independent Organs: Central Election Management Committee; Constitution Court; Courts

Ministry of Government Administraton & Home Affairs National Police Agency	Ministry of Environment
Ministry of Education & Human Resources Development	Ministry of Labor

Ministry of Science & Technology
  Meteorological Administration
	Ministry of Construction & Transportation
	  National Railroad Administration

Ministry of Maritime Affairs & Fisheries National Maritime Police Agency	

B: Independent Organs: Central Election Management Committee; Constitution Court; Courts (continued)

Appendix B
Presidents, Vice Presidents, and Prime Ministers

PRESIDENTS

Syngman Rhee   August 1948–April 1960
Ho Chong (Acting)   April–June 1960
Kwak Sang-hun (Acting)   June 1960
Ho Chong (Acting)   June–August 1960
Yun Po-Son   August 1960–March 1962
Park Chung-hee (Acting)   March 1962–December 1963
Park Chung-hee   December 1963–October 1979
Ch'oe Kyu-ha (Acting)   October 1979
Ch'oe Kyu-ha   October 1979–August 1980
Park Choong-hoon (Acting)   August 1980
Chun Doo-hwan   September 1980–March 1981
Chun Doo-hwan   March 1981–February 1988
Roh Tae-woo   February 1988–February 1993
Kim Young-sam   February 1993–February 1998
Kim Dae-jung   February 1998–February 2003
Roh Moo-hyun   February 2003–

VICE PRESIDENTS
(This office was abolished in June 1960)

Yi Si-Yong   August 1948–May 1951
Kim Song-su   May 1951–May 1952
Ham Tae-yong   August 1952–August 1956
Change Myon   August 1956–April 1960

PRIME MINISTERS
(There was no premiership between November 1954 and August 1960)

Lee Pom-sok   August 1948–April 1950
Shin Song-mo (Acting)   April–November 1950
Chang Myon   November 1950–April 1951
Ho Chong (Acting)   November 1951–April 1952
Lee Yun-yong (Acting)   April–May 1952
Chang T'aek-sang   May–October 1952
Paik Too-chin (Acting)   October 1952–April 1953
Paik Too-chin   April 1953–June 1954
Pyon Yong-t'ae   June–November 1954
Chang Myon   August 1960–May 1961
Chang To-yong   May–July 1961
Song Yo-ch'an   July 1961–June 1962
Kim Hyun-chul   June 1962–December 1963
Ch'oe Tu-son   December 1963–May 1964
Chong Il-kwon   May 1964–December 1970
Paik Too-chin   December 1970–June 1971
Kim Jong-p'il   June 1971–December 1975
Ch'oe Kyu-ha (Acting)   December 1975–March 1976
Ch'oe Kyu-ha   March 1976–December 1979
Shin Hyun-hwak   December 1979–May 1980
Park Choong-hoon (Acting)   May–September 1980
Nam Duck-woo (Acting)   September 1980
Nam Duck-woo   September 1980–January 1982
Yoo Chang-soon (Acting)   January 1982
Yoo Chang-soon   January–June 1982
Kim Sang-hyop (Acting)   June–September 1982
Kim Sang-hyop   June 1982–October 1983
Chin Iee-chong (Acting)   October 1983
Chin Iee-chong   October 1983–February 1985
Lho Shin-yong (Acting)   February–May 1985
Lho Shin-yong   May 1985–May 1987
Lee Han-key (Acting)   May–June 1987
Kim Chung-yul (Acting)   July–August 1987
Kim Chung-yul   August 1987–February 1988

Lee Hyun-jae (Acting)   February–March 1988
Lee Hyun-jae   March–December 1988
Kang Young-hoon   December 1988–December 1990
Ro Jae-bong   December 1990–May 1991
Chung Won-shik   May 1991–October 1992
Hyun Soong-jong   October 1992–February 1993
Hwang In-sung   February 1993–December 1993
Lee Hoi-chang   December 1993–April 1994
Lee Yong-duk   April 1994–December 1994
Lee Hong-koo   December 1994–December 1995
Lee Soo-sung   December 1995–March 1997
Goh Kun   March 1997–March 1998
Kim Jong-p'il (Acting)   March–August 1998
Kim Jong-p'il   August 1998–January 2000
Park Tae-jong   January–May 2000
Lee Hun-jai (Acting)   May 2000
Lee Han-dong (Acting)   May–June 2000
Lee Han-dong   June 2000–July 2002
Chang Sang (f) (Acting)   July 2002
Jeon Yun-churl (Acting)   July–August 2002
Chang Dae-whan (Acting)   August–September 2002
Kim Suk-soo (Acting)   September–October 2002
Kim Suk-soo   October 2002–February 2003
Goh Kun   February 2003–

Spelling of the names according to official records.

Appendix C
Presidential Elections

A total of 16* presidential elections were held between 20 July 1948 and 19 December 2002. The dates, number of candidates, number of eligible voters, number of votes cast, and methods of elections were as follows:

No.	Date	Cands.	Poss. Voters	Cast	Elected by
1st	20 July 1948	4	198	196	National Assembly
2nd	5 Aug. 1952	4	8,259,428	7,275,883	Popular vote
3rd	15 May 1956	3	9,606,870	9,067,063	Popular vote
	(15 Mar. 1960*)	2	11,196,490	10,862,272	Popular vote
4th	12 Aug. 1960	12	263	258	National Assembly
5th	15 Oct. 1963	5	12,985,015	11,036,075	Popular vote
6th	3 May 1967	6	13,035,093	11,645,215	Popular vote
7th	27 Apr. 1971	7	15,552,236	12,147,824	Popular vote
8th	23 Dec. 1972	1	2,359	2,359	National Conference for Unification**
9th	6 July 1978	1	2,578	2,578	National Conference for Unification
10th	6 Dec. 1979	1	2,560	2,549	National Conference for Unification
11th	27 Aug. 1980	1	2,540	2,525	National Conference for Unification
12th	25 Feb. 1981	4	5,277	5,274	Presidential Electoral College***

(continued)

No.	Date	Cands.	Poss. Voters	Cast	Elected by
13th	16 Dec. 1987	5	25,873,624	23,070,748	Popular vote
14th	18 Dec. 1992	3	29,22,658	24,096,643	Popular vote
15th	18 Dec. 1997	3	32,290416	25,642,438	Popular vote
16th	19 Dec. 2002	2	35,000,000#	24,562,290	Popular vote

*The results of the 15 March 1960 presidential and vice presidential elections were nullified as a result of the April Student Uprising, and it is not normally numerically listed.

**The National Conference for Unification was established as an electoral college under the Yushin Constitution.

***The new Presidential Electoral College replaced the National Conference for Unification as an electoral college.

Rounded.

Appendix D
National Assembly Elections

	Dates	Seats	Candidates	Eligible Votes Cast	Voters
1st	10 May 1948	300*	942	7,840,871	7,497,649
2nd	30 May 1950	210	2,227	8,434,737	7,752,076
3rd	20 May 1954	203	1,207	8,446,509	7,698,380
4th	2 May 1958	233	841	10,164,328	8,923,905
5th	29 July 1960**				
	Lower House	233	1,518	13,344,149	9,778,921
	Upper House	58	210	13,344,149	9,747,688
6th	26 Nov. 1963	175	976	13,344,149	9,622,183
7th	8 July 1967	175	821	14,717,354	11,203,317
8th	25 May 1971	204	696	16,616,258	11,430,202
9th	27 Feb. 1973	219+	339	15,690,130	11,196,484
10th	12 Dec. 1978	231++		19,489,490	15,029,387

In October 1980, the National Assembly was dissolved and replaced by the Legislative Council for National Security of 81 members.

	Dates	Seats	Candidates	Eligible Votes Cast	Voters
11th	25 Mar. 1981	276*+	634	20,909,210	15,403,151
12th	12 Feb. 1985	276*+	440	23,987,830	20,290,867

(continued)

	Dates	Seats	Candidates	Eligible Votes Cast	Voters
13th	26 Feb. 1988	299*+	1,045	26,198,205	19,853,890
14th	24 Mar. 1992	299*+	1,052	29,003,828	20,844,403
15th	11 April 1996	299*+	n/a	31,491,070	20,122,799
16th	13 April 2000	273*+	n/a	33,748,844	19,473,083

*When the National (Constituent) Assembly was established in May 1948, 100 seats of the 200-seat assembly were reserved for the representatives from the North.

**Under a revised constitution adopted in 1960, a bicameral legislative assembly of the 58-member House of Councilors (upper house) and the 233-member House of Representatives (lower house) was established.

+Only 146 members were elected, and according to the Yushin Constitution of 1972, one-third (73 seats) of the members of the National Assembly were filled by the members of the Yujonghoe, who were nominated by the president and elected by the National Conference for Unification.

++Only 154 members were elected by the popular vote in the 1978 National Assembly elections, and 77 seats were filled by the members of the Yujonghoe as was the case in 1973.

*+Under the revised constitution of 1980, a certain number of seats was allotted to major political parties as "representatives at large," according to the number of seats won by each party by the popular vote. Thus, in the National Assembly elections of 1981 and 1985, only 184 members were popularly elected and 92 seats were distributed according to the formula. In the 1988 National Assembly elections, 224 were popularly elected and 75 seats were likewise distributed. In the 1992 National Assembly elections, 237 were popularly elected and 62 seats were distributed under a revised formula. In the 1996 elections, 244 were popularly elected and 55 seats were distributed. In 2000, the number of seats was reduced to 273, with 227 elected and 46 distributed.

Appendix E
Text of the December 1991 Agreement on Reconciliation, Nonaggression and Exchanges and Cooperation between the South and the North

Preamble:

Whereas in keeping with the yearning of the entire people for the peaceful unification of the divided land, the South and the North reaffirm the unification principles enunciated in the 4 July (1972) South–North Joint Communique;

Whereas both parties are determined to resolve political and military confrontation and achieve national reconciliation; Whereas both desire to promote multi-faceted exchanges and cooperation to advance common national interests and prosperity;

Whereas both recognize that their relations constitute a special provisional relationship geared to unification; and Whereas both pledge to exert joint efforts to achieve peaceful unification;

Therefore, the parties hereto agree as follows:

SOUTH–NORTH RECONCILIATION

Article 1: The South and the North shall respect each other's political and social system.

Article 2: Both parties shall not interfere in each other's internal affairs.

Article 3: Both parties shall not slander and vilify each other.

Article 4: Both parties shall not attempt in any manner to sabotage and subvert the other.

Article 5: Both parties shall endeavor to transform the present armistice into a firm state of peace between the South and the North and

---

Note: Appendix E is an official translation of the Agreement by the South Korean government, as exchanged at the sixth round of the high-level (premiers) talks held in P'yongyang, 18–21 February 1992.

307

shall abide by the present Military Armistice Agreement (of 27 July 1953) until such time as such a state of peace has taken hold.

Article 6: Both parties shall cease confrontation on the international stage and shall cooperate and endeavor together to promote national interests and esteem.

Article 7: To ensure close consultation and liaison between both parties, a South–North liaison office shall be established at P'anmunjom within three months of the effective date of this Agreement.

Article 8: A South–North Political Subcommittee shall be established within the framework of the Inter-Korean High Level Talks within one month of the effective date of this Agreement with a view to discussing concrete measures to ensure the implementation and observance of the accords on South–North reconciliation.

SOUTH–NORTH NON-AGGRESSION

Article 9: Both parties shall not use armed force against each other and shall not make armed aggression against each other.

Article 10: Differences of opinion and disputes arising between the two parties shall be peacefully resolved through dialogue and negotiations.

Article 11: The South–North demarcation line for non-aggression shall be identical with the Military Demarcation Line specified in the Military Armistice Agreement of July 27, 1953, and the areas that have been under the jurisdiction of each party respectively thereunder until the present.

Article 12: To abide by and guarantee non-aggression, the two parties shall create a South–North Joint Military Committee within three months of the effective date of this Agreement. The said Committee shall discuss and carry out steps to build military confidence and realize arms reductions, including the mutual notification and control of major movements of military units and major military exercises, the peaceful utilization of the Demilitarized Zone (DMZ), exchanges of military personnel and information, phased reductions in armaments including the elimination of weapons of mass destruction and surprise attack capabilities, and verifications thereof.

Article 13: A telephone hotline shall be installed between the military authorities of both sides to prevent accidental armed clashes and other military emergencies and avoid their escalation.

Article 14: A South–North Military Subcommittee shall be established within the framework of the Inter-Korean High-Level Talks within one month of the effective date of this Agreement in order to discuss concrete measures to ensure the implementation and observance of accords on non-aggression and to resolve military confrontation.

SOUTH–NORTH EXCHANGES AND COOPERATION

Article 15: To promote an integrated and balanced development of the national economy and the welfare of the entire people, both parties shall conduct economic exchanges and cooperation, including joint development of resources, trade in goods as a kind of domestic commerce and joint investment in industrial projects.

Article 16: Both parties shall carry out exchanges and cooperation in diverse fields, including science, technology, education, literature, the arts, health, sports, the environment and publishing and journalism, including newspapers, radio, television and publications in general.

Article 17: Both parties shall guarantee residents of their respective areas free inter-Korean travel and contacts.

Article 18: Both parties shall permit free correspondence, reunions and visits between family members and other relatives dispersed South and North, shall promote the reconstitution of divided families on their own and shall take measures to resolve other humanitarian issues.

Article 19: Both sides shall reconnect railroads and roads that have been cut off and shall open South–North land, sea and air transport routes.

Article 20: Both parties shall establish and link facilities needed for South–North postal and telecommunications services and shall guarantee the confidentiality of inter-Korean mail and telecommunications.

Article 21: Both parties shall cooperate on the international stage in the economic, cultural and various other fields and carry out joint business undertakings abroad.

Article 22: To implement accords on exchanges and cooperation in the economic, cultural and various other fields, both parties shall establish joint committees for specific sectors, including a South–North Economic Exchanges and Cooperation Committee, within three months of the effective date of this Agreement.

Article 23: A South–North Exchanges and Cooperation Sub-committee shall be established within the framework of the Inter-Korean High-Level Talks within one month of the effective date of this Agreement with a view to discussing concrete measures to ensure the implementation and observance of the accords on South–North exchanges and cooperation.

AMENDMENTS AND EFFECTUATION

Article 24: This Agreement may be amended or supplemented by concurrence between both parties.

Article 25: This Agreement shall enter into force as of the day both parties exchange instruments of ratification following the completion of their respective procedures for bringing it into effect.

Appendix F
North–South Joint Declaration of 15 June 2000

True to the noble will of all the fellow countrymen for the peaceful re-unification of the country, Chairman Kim Jong-il of the National De-fense Commission of the Democratic People's Republic of Korea and President Kim Dae-jung of the Republic of Korea had a historic meet-ing and summit in Pyongyang from 13–15 June 2000.

The heads of the North and the South, considering that the recent meeting and summit—the first of their kind in history of the division—are events of weighty importance in promoting mutual understanding, developing inter-Korean relations, and achieving peaceful reunifica-tion, declare as follows:

1. The North and the South agreed to solve the question of the coun-try's reunification independently by the concerted efforts of the Korean nation responsible for it.
2. The North and the South, recognizing that a proposal for federa-tion of lower stage advanced by the North side and a proposal for confederation put forth by the South side for the reunification of the country have elements in common, agreed to work for the reunification in this direction in the future.
3. The North and the South agreed to settle humanitarian issues, in-cluding the exchange of visiting groups of separated families and relatives and the issue of unconverted long-term prisoners, as early as possible on the occasion of 15 August this year.
4. The North and the South agreed to promote the balanced develop-ment of the national economy through economic cooperation and build mutual confidence by activating cooperation and exchanges in all fields, social, cultural, athletic, public health, environmental and so on.

5. The North and the South agreed to hold dialogues between the authorities as soon as possible to implement the above-mentioned agreed-upon points in the near future.

President Kim Dae-jung cordially invited Chairman Kim Jong-il DPRK National Defense Commission to visit Seoul and Chairman Kim Jong-il agreed to visit Seoul at an appropriate time in the future.

15 June 2000
Kim Jong-il, Chairman of the National
Defense Commission, DPPRK
Kim Dae-jung, President of the Republic of Korea

About the Authors

Dr. Andrew C. Nahm arrived in the United States in 1948. He took his B.A. at Andrews University, an M.A. at Northwestern University, and a Ph.D. at Stanford University. From 1960, he taught at Western Michigan University, where he founded and directed the Center for Korean Studies. He later became professor of history emeritus and consultant to the Office of International Affairs of Western Michigan University, and concurrently adjunct professor of history at Kalamazoo College. Dr. Nahm published numerous articles in academic and professional journals. He edited *Korea Under Japanese Colonial Rule—Studies of the Policy and Techniques of Japanese Colonialism* and *The United States and Korea: American–Korean Relations, 1866–1976*. Other publications included *North Korea: Her Past, Reality and Impression*; *A Panorama of 5000 Years: Korean History*; *Korea: Tradition and Transformation—A History of the Korean People*; and *Introduction to Korean History and Culture*. Dr. Nahm died on 1 August 1995.

Dr. James E. Hoare served in the British Diplomatic Service from 1969 until his retirement in January 2003. He holds a B.A. and a Ph.D. from the University of London. He served in the British Embassies in Seoul (1981–1985) and Beijing (1988–1991), and was in charge of opening the embassy in P'yongyang (2001–2002). He is the editor/author of a number of works, including *Japan's Treaty Ports and Foreign Settlements 1859–1899: Uninvited Guests in Meiji Japan*; *Korea* (ABC–CLIO Bibliographies vol. 204); *Embassies in the East: The Story of the British and Their Embassies in China, Japan and Korea from 1859 to the Present*; and with his wife, Susan Pares, *Korea: An Introduction*; *Conflict in Korea: An Encyclopedia*; and *Beijing* (ABC–CLIO Bibliographies vol. 226). He lives in London.